# The
# Morningside
# Years

# The Morningside Years

PETER GZOWSKI

M&S

**Canadian Cataloguing in Publication Data**

Gzowski, Peter
The Morningside years

Accompanied by CD of theme music, interviews, etc.
ISBN 0-7710-3706-6

1. Morningside (Radio program).   I. Morningside (Radio program).
II. Title.

PN1991.3.C3G96   1997   791.44'72   C97-931601-4

The publishers acknowledge the support of the Canada Council for the Arts and the
Ontario Arts Council for their publishing program.

Selections from *The Moons of Jupiter* by Alice Munro © 1982; reprinted by
permission of Macmillan Canada.

"Mourning Dove" reprinted by permission of Emil Sher.

"Life with Jessie" used by permission of Nancy Huggett.

Caricatures of Margaret Atwood, Robertson Davies, Timothy Findley, Margaret
Laurence, W.O. Mitchell, and Alice Munro used by permission of Anthony Jenkins.

The Obituary by Robert Fulford first appeared in *Toronto Life* magazine, June 1997.
Reprinted by permission of Robert Fulford.

As always, every effort has been made to reach the authors of the various letters and
recipes in these pages. We couldn't track all of them down, but as we've said before,
we'd rather risk annoying them than leave them out.

Set in Janson by M&S, Toronto
Printed and bound in Canada

McClelland & Stewart Inc.
*The Canadian Publishers*
481 University Avenue
Toronto, Ontario
M5G 2E9

1 2 3 4 5    01 00 99 98 97

# CONTENTS

# FOREWORD

## by Dalton Camp

≈

*Forgive this shameless self-exposure, but I must confess that I have never actually listened to* Morningside. *Really. (Well, I did once, but it was an accident. The car radio was mysteriously tuned to* CBC *one mid-morning a few years ago, and suddenly the air was heavy with the sounds of Mr. Gzowski's ecstasy over Peter Appleyard's vibraphone. Worried about operating heavy machinery under this influence, I switched stations.)*

*The thing is, I'm not alone.*

— Janice Kennedy,
*The Ottawa Citizen*

I am a morning person, more productive, more energetic, able to write better, function better, in the morning. Most of the mischief and plain dumb things I have done, much that I wish could be undone, have been done at night. When the sun goes down, once darkness has settled over the land, I am good for a little light wine and conversation or, safe in a chair, suitable as an audience. Anything else is high risk.

When I say I'm a morning person, I'm talking about 10:00 a.m. or, in moments of crisis, 9:30. This seems a sensible arrangement for one's time and resources, allowing the maximum release of energy and zeal for one's work with a minimum of stress and exertion. As in any of the performing arts, including writing poetry or hang-gliding, four hours a day of honest exertion produces your best; after that, the yield and quality diminish.

In the fifteen years Peter Gzowski has been the host of *Morningside* — indeed, became *Morningside* — his day began at 4:00 a.m., which allowed time for ablutions, to dress, drive to the studio, read the morning papers and the mail, write his billboards, brief himself on the program's guests, drink a litre of coffee, smoke half a pack of cigarettes, then shuffle to the studio, settle in his chair, and invent a country for a million and a half Canadians.

To begin one's day this way every day, before dawn, before the sound of the dove, or rooster, or hum of traffic, suggests a hard, demanding life even before it begins. Obstetricians have similar lives but under better conditions. During the post-mortems conducted over the death of *Morningside*, journalists discussed the importance of Peter Gzowski; they left unremarked the lonely rigour of *being* Peter Gzowski. It is impressive that his writ ran as long as it did, the more so when one considers the hours.

*Economist William Watson, recently named editorial page editor of Conrad Black's Ottawa paper, wrote that the Reform party is so intimidated by Gzowski that they put privatization of CBC-TV in their platform, but not radio. With Gzowski gone, Watson said, they should gather their courage.*

— Rick Salutin,
*The Globe and Mail*

On the eve of his departure from morning radio, Gzowski received a distinguished Peabody Award for broadcast journalism. I suspected there would be trouble, and there was. You can, in this country, draw too much water, get too big for your boots: the certain harbinger of success is envy, which often becomes the critic's adrenaline. It was a surprise to some to know, as the switch was pulled on *Morningside*, that Gzowski had his detractors. Geoff Pevere's observation that his idea of hell would be *Morningside* twenty-four hours a day gained wide circulation in the print media.

The most intelligent criticism of Peter Gzowski's creation came from Salutin himself. No surprise. Salutin's complaint of *Morningside* was its softness, lack of edge, and the irrepressible civility of its host. No question about Gzowski: Don Imus he ain't. Howard Stern he ain't. He will never be mistaken for Mike Wallace.

I do not know Gzowski well enough to know if he has an edge. My own experience with him suggests there may be sharp, dark corners in the private persona, but as the host of *Morningside* he was incurably civil. There was wit without cynicism, chagrin without petulance, and sorrow without bathos, but most of all there was a thoroughly predictable decency. One felt comfortable in the presence of a rational, reasonable, responsible adult; the demeanour was not an act but an art.

Canadians are often goaded into representations of themselves — as alienated, resentful, cynical — to accommodate the media's troubled analysis of the national psyche. The truth is more likely we are among the most serene people on earth, with few complaints and nearly limitless indulgence. But we do occasionally act up, provoked by accusations we are a dull, uninspiring lot and of little account or interest. Gzowski's portrayal of Canada, with its bitchiness, charitableness, and neighbourliness, struck many of us as about the right mix for a peaceful, gentle country divided only by its politicians and publishers.

I suspect the popularity of *Morningside*'s weekly panel of political commentators — principally Eric Kierans, Stephen Lewis, and me — was a pain in the ass to many. The troika offended the CBC's gender requirements and more — we were all white males and over forty. All of us were, from time to time, rebuked by partisan listeners for not standing up for our presumed parties. The Liberals filed a formal complaint about the continued reluctance of Kierans to uphold Liberalism, and, according to Gzowski, people complained wherever he travelled about my inadequacies as a spokesperson for the proper Conservative view, nor did Lewis escape charges of lacking socialist fervour.

Kierans, Lewis, and Camp had a long run on *Morningside*. Parker Barss-Dunham wrote a piece on us for the *Reader's Digest*. In the piece, he quoted Kierans, who told him the reason the panel worked so well was because of Gzowski's role as catalyst and referee. (I had, in fact, told him the same thing.) Discerning friends believed I had reached the pinnacle of my career in radio when the article appeared.

KCL (Kierans, Camp, and Lewis) enjoyed its success on *Morningside* in part because of Gzowski's skill in framing the questions, letting each panellist have his say, allowing for the occasional digression while discouraging irrelevancy and discursiveness. But there were other reasons. Usually, we knew what we were talking about. Kierans's political career included membership in Jean Lesage's cabinet during the Quiet Revolution in Quebec and, later, as a minister in the Trudeau government in Ottawa. He was also an economist, and had served as president of the Montreal Stock Exchange. Lewis had been leader of the NDP in Ontario, Leader of the Opposition in the provincial legislature, and a member of a distinguished and gifted political family.

Verisimilitude, weighted with experience, is a powerful asset to a political panel. A wealth of memory and anecdote were also helpful, as well as the fact that while we were not intimates, we had a common political memory and, though we disagreed often enough, each of us respected the other's opinion. As we went along, we came to like one another, and the mutual affection, and mutual respect, showed. *Morningside*'s listeners enjoyed KCL for the civil tongue the panel kept in its head, or cheek, which effectively demonstrated what most Canadians believe, which is that politics can be argued with sincerity and passion but without heat and still shed light on the subject.

KCL worked because none of us felt obliged to represent a designated political view. Each said pretty well what he thought. The candour proved infectious. We were not obliged to be role-players, to provoke controversy for its own sake, or to feign outrage, injury, or piety. It was not *Crossfire*, but *Morningside*.

The trouble with putting a high value on riotous political discourse, in measuring the worth of political debate by decibels, is that it becomes a way of trivializing politics and demeaning those involved. Politics is not a search for confrontation but for reconciliation; those who seek to portray it otherwise are either actors looking for parts or producers seeking ratings.

KCL ended as Eric found himself drawn to world travel; Stephen, for the second time, left Canada for the United Nations; I was confronted by a serious health problem. The long run of KCL was over. It was flattering that so many expressed sorrow at our departure. Even today, I meet strangers who insist they still hear us each week on *Morningside*.

*If it takes Medicare, the CBC and cheap tuition to distinguish us from the Americans or the Mexicans, how in the world are we to explain the generations of self-confident Canadians who lived without any of those things?*

— David Frum,
*The Financial Post Magazine*

Sweden, Switzerland, the United Kingdom, Belgium, Japan, France, Australia, and Italy all contribute more funding, per capita, to public broadcasting than does Canada. But Canadians do spend more per capita ($32.19) supporting public broadcasting than does the United States ($3.92).

Successive Mulroney and Chrétien governments have cut the budget of the CBC by nearly $500 million. One-third of the total CBC staff of 11,700 has been dispatched. Following the "final" round of cuts, CBC funding on a per capita basis will have fallen to $19.11 — 47 per cent lower than when Peter Gzowski was beginning his marathon run on *Morningside*.

If *Morningside* had not been paid off, to use a navy term, she would have sunk anyway on the shoals of budget cuts. In the Fredericton CBC station where I often went for my appearances on *Morningside*, the original radio staff of twenty-one has since become ten; no one is under any illusion the quality and variety of news and public affairs coverage has not suffered.

On the departure of *Morningside*, the attacks on Gzowski — "hard-edged" and raising "tough" questions — were less personal than ideological, less directed at Gzowski than at the principle of public radio and television. The triumph of his departure lies in the expectation the corporation will be further weakened and vulnerable. One does not need to be an economist to see the possibilities.

The eclecticism of Gzowski's creation — *Morningside* — provoked those who are convinced Canadians suffer from lack of focus. *Morningside* was a community bulletin board, a public forum, and it was a distraction. It was "off message" and sometimes sentimental. There was a real world out there, goddamn it, and *Morningside* helped 1.5 million Canadians to escape it. It was, for some, counterculture.

A twenty-eight-year-old magazine editor I know says that when he thinks of *Morningside*, he thinks of Inuit throat-singers; the radio in his office is perpetually tuned to the CBC and he heard Gzowski's voice every day at work. "It was like sonic wallpaper," he told me.

The media wars, between the press and the CBC, are a natural catastrophe. It has become a life struggle for audience and for the ascendant power that bequeaths influence. The free press, in a curious twist of irony, is now committed to private interests — indeed, owned by them — while the CBC, perhaps for lack of choice, has cast its lot with the general public. But the luxury of not being owned by corporate interests, or by Conrad Black, is not without cost; while criticism of the CBC seethes with conflict of interest, the press nonetheless still exerts influence and leverage upon the politicians who have only recently emerged from the Stone Age to enter the Linear Age. The ease and speed with which the Corporation was downsized and restructured would do credit to the management style of "Chainsaw Al" Dunlop, the Sunbeam CEO and the inventor of employee firings for improved share values. Looking for friends, during the purge, the CBC found few in Ottawa. Being hard on the CBC proved a politician was not soft on privatization, a signal of accommodation, compliance, and resignation.

In this era of synthetics and virtual realities, there is nothing more representative than the establishment's belief in the public enthusiasm for privatization. Politicians, who often have a better idea of how the public feels, have been reluctant converts to the great cause, presenting themselves as merely gradualist enthusiasts. One initiative for gradually privatizing the CBC is already under way: Starve the sucker.

Another way is to insist the CBC do more "serious" drama — as well as "more meaningful" public affairs. Reading Lysiane Gagnon's review of contemporary French fiction recently, my heart raced. There is the new fiction of Lise Bissonnette, publisher of *Le Devoir*, a journalist of whom I remain a devoted reader. Ms Bissonnette writes, it is reported, of "women [who] drink sperm, which turns into cement in their stomachs; towers are built over them, symbols of male power; they rebel and start moving, causing cities to crumble. A young woman listens to a priest masturbating in an empty church. . . ."

Adapted for *Morningside*, this would almost certainly have harvested a fistful of awards, including one for seriousness. At the very least, it might be more riveting than Peter's mustard pickles.

The media-induced mania for privatization has accelerated the erosion of public space. *Morningside* has served as public space, something like Main Street before there was the abomination of the malls. A student at McGill, Patrick McDougall, has sent me his paper bearing on this subject in which he quotes Jürgen Habermas and the concept of the "public sphere." Habermas notes its "disintegration" under the pressures of commercialization and consumerism.

Where, originally, private individuals gathered to discuss public matters, public discussion now has become a "business" — this "interweaving of the public and private realms" leads to "a kind of refeudalization of the public sphere." In our space, what is left to the public, and where access is assured and all can participate in an unrestricted discussion of public affairs, is in the loci of the CBC.

Admittedly, there is not one public but many; people are free to listen, or not listen. What has seemed important is that the public(s) had space in which to exercise their options.

Canadians have not yet got it into their heads the importance of the CBC as part — a huge part — of this finite public space. *Morningside* became the longest Main Street in the country; the largest public domain in the national media, and despite its unilingualism, more representative of Canadian thought and opinion, more revealing of Canadian character, and more open and accessible to eccentrics, minorities, and the exceptional, than could be found anywhere else, outside the public libraries.

Its mandate was not to save the country — which always needs saving — or even to hold it together. Nor was it to entertain. But it did inform and enlighten and sometimes amuse, and often — in Harold Laski's vivid phrase — prick people into the insurgency of thought.

This is a lot to do, in the morning, while listeners are shaving, combing out their hair, driving to work, arriving at their offices, or at work. Yet, for all those in such various states and conditions of disarray, in bed, in transit, or in traction, *Morningside* became their meeting place, a public thoroughfare, a town hall, a continuing dialogue, and a movable feast of Canadiana, culture, controversy, and kitsch.

*I will lose a dear friend. A friend who has stirred my patriotism and introduced me to artists whose records and novels now fill my collections, and to average Canadians whose strength of character has inspired me. . . . I have laughed and cried with Peter Gzowski, and marvelled at his grace, compassion and gentle manner.*

— Marion M. Mitchell,
letter to the editor, *The Toronto Star*

Or, as a friend remarked the other day, about Gzowski, a guy with so many friends and so few enemies must have something wrong with him. But he did seem too good to be true, as did the country he discovered and portrayed.

It's trite to say, as some have said on his walking into *Morningside*'s last sunset, that we will never see his like again. It is true, to the extent that — like fingerprints and DNA — there is only one Peter Gzowski. Even so, there is more than one Gzowski in the one we have.

I had an affection for the old CBC radio building on Jarvis Street in Toronto. When in the city, I would do the KCL panel out of the old radio building, where I would see Peter. He had an interesting office: a guest area with strong coffee, the *Times*, and enough old newspapers piled about to set fire to a stone quarry. Peter, who would always emerge to say hello, worked in a back office, or in his smoking closet (the nicotine bans were in effect), where his lungs struggled to recycle the accumulated trapped debris of a one-man incinerator. The office had a cluttered, chaotic, but controlled air about it, which seemed to reflect the man in charge of it.

Waiting to go on air, or for a taxi afterwards, one met interesting people, including old friends, and old adversaries. (Again, the public space.) On one memorable occasion, I encountered Margaret Atwood as we passed in the darkened passage between the studio and the office; she stopped me, kissed my cheek, and moved quickly and wordlessly on. It might have been something in the coffee or, better, perhaps something I'd said.

Gzowski has won journalism awards for his skills as an interviewer. I think he also taught public manners; he was a marvellous listener. He was, as a result, instructive to the business.

In the fashionable school of Gotcha journalism, the interviewed is seen as victim. Some deserve their fate. But one learned from the master that the interview is meant for the listener, not for the trophy room.

Of course, civility doesn't always work; sometimes, nothing works. Much depends on who you're talking to: there's Margaret Visser, then there's Simon Reisman. (No one better understood Gzowski's unique problem with Reisman than I. On one occasion, I recall an attempt by the Clerk of the Privy Council to "interview" Simon about his experience as Canada's free-trade negotiator. Simon's responses were in character: blunt, unresponsive, and unprintable.)

But as I have testified before, what Gzowski did best was to remind all of us of the forgotten virtue of listening. We all prefer the sound of our own inner voice, which we carry about, like an invisible Walkman. While others talk, we listen to ourselves. We treat silences as opportunities to be heard. There is nothing wrong with the deference that commands silence, so we ourselves may hear.

This was, I think, part of Peter's appeal and of his art. It made *Morningside* a haven for listeners, a sanctuary for the finished thought, with answers as long as the questions (of significant meaning with Peter, who asked questions the way baseball pitchers get around to making their pitch, with elaborate introductory manoeuvre and circumlocution).

We are being assured, in the press, there will be life without Peter Gzowski, which is, of course, true. Happily, there will be more of life with Gzowski. But these querulous mock-assurances mask the more important question: What will life be without *Morningside*?

The public space is, if we are to believe what we hear, to be reconfigured to conform with recent polls. Snappier answers. Younger voices. Gender balance. More earnest humour. Regional origination to better reflect the nation. A mall, perhaps. (I'm making this up.)

When the invitations went out for the CBC Radio farewell party for *Morningside* — "The Finale" — the invitation to Gzowski from CBC Communications misspelled his name.

Enclosed, some of the best of Gzowski, suitable for framing. I conclude with a familiar signature:

Thanks for this, Peter.

1 July 1997,
Northwood, New Brunswick

# INTRODUCTION

*by Peter Gzowski*

⌒

By the spring of 1982, when I'd been away from daily radio for eight years, I had pretty well given up hope of ever getting back. I'd done a number of things since I left: hosted a late-night television show (which I'm now convinced wasn't quite as bad as everyone, including me, made out), tried my hand at a daily newspaper column, written a few books, and a lot of magazine articles, narrated a film or two—even taken a whack at reviving Nathan Cohen's old *Fighting Words* on TV. But none had come anywhere near matching the pleasure and the satisfaction of my three years as host of the CBC Radio program we called *This Country in the Morning*. I missed it, and, as time rolled on, I often wondered how things would have worked out if, in the autumn of 1974, I'd just kept chugging along.

Why did we walk away — for both Alex Frame, the executive producer and the real inventor of *This Country in the Morning*, and I left together? You know, at this point I'm not really sure, although I do remember making a lot of statements about wanting to go out like Ted Williams, who hit a home run in his last time at bat, tipped his hat to the crowd and disappeared into the dugout forever, and not like Willie Mays, who staggered for so long around the outfields he had once appeared to own that it was possible to forget his original skill and grace. And it's true Frame and I wanted to try some television that would follow some of *This Country*'s informality and its respect for its audience. But, hell (1) I'm not a baseball player (I'd be a lot richer if I were) and I had scarcely turned forty when we left; I doubt I was quite burned out, and (2) I wish young broadcasters — including me at the time — would realize that television is not radio gone big-time. It's a different medium, in many ways more visual than the one with the pictures, the screen of the imagination being unlimited — just read, for example, Emil Sher's splendid drama "Mourning Dove" in these pages, or follow our staging of a new trial, jury verdict and all, for Louis Riel. Radio values content over style. I remember noting in my late-night television days that people who'd seen you the night before commented almost solely on how people — including me — *looked*. On radio, if they've heard you, they talk about what people *said*. I've said many of these things before, but one more comment, if I may, before I move on. Radio listeners, in the television age, are almost always alone — in their cars, their kitchens, their bedrooms, or on their tractors. When families or friends gather, they do so in front of the TV screen, the way we used to, but no longer do, huddle round the radio for *L for Lanky* or *Lux Radio Theatre*. Radio is the most intimate medium there is, with the single possible exception of the phone.

Well, enough. I left. And once out the door it was as if I'd fallen out of CBC Radio's memory.

Two women I had known earlier were influential in my eventual return. One was Barbara Frum, who had started at *As It Happens* the same season we launched *This Country* but had stayed on for a full ten years before preparing for her vastly more successful career on television — vastly more successful than mine, I mean; her mastery of radio was unparalleled. We ran into each other at a social gathering when my radio days seemed to be long over. "What happened?" she asked. "I never hear you any more." "I don't know," I said. "The phone just doesn't ring. " Not many days later, it did. The producers of *As It Happens* wanted me to sit in for Barbara for a good chunk of the summer. I know whose suggestion it had been. Then others started offering me guest shots — at *Cross Country Check-Up*, among other places. And finally Nicole Bélanger asked if I'd substitute for Don Harron for a couple of weeks on the program that had now become *Morningside*.

I had a lot of trepidation. For one thing, the program had evolved a long way from the days of *This Country in the Morning* and I wasn't sure if I could keep up with the changes. For another (really part of the same evolution, I suppose), Don was — is — a very different broadcaster than I am; I'm not even sure if he would agree with all the suggestions I've tried to make here about what radio should be. He's an actor, a comedian, able to make written material — his own or someone else's — come alive. I'm not. While I remember W. O. Mitchell, bless his heart, snorting in derision when I insisted one evening that what I did on the radio wasn't a "performance" (he was right, of course, and he should know), the truth is I can't play a *role* to save my life. Don's so good he can take the list of questions his producers have prepared for him and practically read them cold, sounding as if he's making them up on the spot. I have to mull everything over, and wrestle with its intent, then try to phrase it in my own words.

He's also brilliant, as capable of chatting with Northrop Frye as with Gordie Tapp, and except for his obsessive punning and his sometimes tasteless Charlie Farquharson routines, he was — is — a hard act to follow.

Still, Nicole insisted. I think — know, actually — she'd had a hard time convincing some of her superiors to let me back on the morning airwaves, even temporarily. They thought, variously, that I was yesterday's man (I had some sympathy for Jean Chrétien later on) or that I'd made my bed when I'd left eight years earlier and had no right to come back now. She won her point. She wins a lot of her points. She's a soft-spoken, perfectly bilingual veteran radio and film producer with a youthful history of political commitment and activism, but, like a lot of old lefties, she's scrupulously fair to those she disagrees with and very capable of criticizing some of the movements she used to be a part of. I like her a lot, as you can no doubt tell, and will always be grateful to her for bringing me back to an institution I perhaps, as I say, shouldn't have left in the first place.

Her two-week experiment was a success. The audience response was warm and favourable. The staff and I got along splendidly. And when Don decided that the next season was his time to step aside, Nicole offered me the job. It took me about thirty seconds to accept.

This lovely book (or lovely to me) is about some of the ways we continued to evolve and change and grow for the fifteen years that followed that decision. It's not a history of Canada from 1982 to 1997. There's very little politics, for example, and very little economics, even though both those departments of our lives went through radical change as the century drew to a close, and even though *Morningside* covered and discussed those changes all the time.

People — not us — used to call *Morningside* "the rope (or sometimes the glue) that held the country together." We never saw ourselves as an adhesive. We were a radio program, part of the CBC's long tradition, a place where Canadians could get to know one another, and from which they could look out at the world.

I think that of all the ways the program changed during my time at its on-air helm, those I'm proudest of are the way we brought the written word back to radio, both through our conversations with authors and our now-famous letters from listeners, and the ways — including the reading of what we called our "listener credits" — we gave our audience a sense of ownership of their public radio network.

In the fifteen years I sat in the studio chair, Nicole Bélanger gave way to Gloria Bishop, Gloria to Hal Wake, Hal to Patsy Pehleman, Patsy to Susan Reisler, and Susan, for the last couple of years, to Gloria Bishop once again. All were marvellous bosses and all became cherished friends. I am more grateful than I can say for the feeling of collegial excitement we shared every day, with the scores and scores of producers and other colleagues who spent some time on our team, and for the feeling of support, affection, and proprietorship that came from the most important people of all, the listeners.

Sutton, Ontario,
Summer 1997

# CONVERSATIONS WITH WRITERS I: ALICE MUNRO

Anthony Jenkins, *The Globe and Mail*

*Alice Munro is the first important writer I ever tried to interview on the radio. That was in the early seventies, on* This Country in the Morning. *She was also the first important writer I talked to when I returned — this time on* Morningside *in 1982. So it's appropriate, don't you think, that one of our visits together is the first of six literary conversations in* The Morningside Years.

## PART ONE

PETER GZOWSKI You've said you can read your stories not quite from the inside out, but you compare the structure of your stories to that of a house in which you can come in at any room you say. Do you really think people can do that?

ALICE MUNRO I hope so. I go into a story that way because I don't go in to find out what happens. I would assume this is the way some people must read me. You go in to find yourself in a certain environment, a certain climate, whatever. What I want from a story is a kind of texture. A created world. What is happening in the story, the content — you say, this story is about this and this, but that isn't what I'm interested in. I'm interested in the world it creates for me, and I would think that a lot of readers read that way.

PG That's an interesting approach to what we're going to do through this week. You will read passages from some short stories and then we'll talk about whatever crosses our mind from those readings. So, can I inveigle you into beginning? You're going to pick out one of your stories and start in the middle, right? Start at the end? Here's Alice Munro reading backwards.

AM I'm going to start in the middle, because I'm starting at the beginning of the story called "The Stone in the Field," which is the second part of a linked story.

> My mother was not a person who spent all her time frosting the rims of glasses and fancying herself descended from the aristocracy. She was a businesswoman really, a trader and dealer. Our house was full of things that had not been paid for with money, but taken in some complicated trade, and that might not be ours to keep. For a while we could play a piano, consult an *Encyclopaedia Britannica*, eat off an oak table. But one day I would come home from school and find each of these things had moved on. A mirror off the wall could go as easily, a cruet stand, a horsehair love seat that had replaced a sofa that had replaced a daybed. We were living in a warehouse.
>
> My mother worked for, or with, a man name Poppy Cullender. He was a dealer in antiques. He did not have a shop. He too had

a house full of furniture. What we had was just his overflow. He had dressers back-to-back and bedsprings upended against the wall. He bought things — furniture, dishes, bedspreads, doorknobs, pump handles, churns, flatirons, anything — from people living on farms or from little villages in the country, then sold what he had bought to antique stores in Toronto. The heyday of antiques had not yet arrived. It was a time when people were covering old woodwork with white or pastel paint as fast as they were able, throwing out spool beds and putting in blond maple bedroom suites, covering patchwork quilts with chenille bedspreads. It was not hard to buy things, to pick them up for next to nothing, but it was a slow business selling them, which was why they might become part of our lives for a season. Just the same, Poppy and my mother were on the right track. If they had lasted, they might have become rich and justified. As it was, Poppy kept his head above water and my mother made next to nothing. And everybody thought them deluded.

They didn't last. My mother got sick. And Poppy went to jail, for making advances on a train.

There were farmhouses where Poppy was not a welcome sight. Children hooted him; wives bolted the door as he came toiling through the yard in his greasy black clothes, rolling his eyes in an uncontrollably lewd or silly way he had and calling in a soft, pleading voice, "Ith anybody h-home?" To add to his other problems he had both a lisp and a stammer. My father could imitate him very well. There were places where Poppy found doors barred and others, usually less respectable, where he was greeted, cheered and fed, just as if he had been a harmless weird bird dropped out of the sky, valued for its very oddity. When he had experienced no welcome he did not go back; instead, he sent my mother. He must have had in his head a map of the surrounding country with every house in it, and just as some maps have dots where the mineral resources are, or the places of historical interest, Poppy's map would have marked the location of every known or suspected rocking chair, pine sideboard, piece of milk glass, moustache cup. "Why don't you run out and take a look at it?" I would hear him say to my mother when they were huddled in the dining room looking at something like the maker's mark on an old pickle crock.

He didn't stammer when he talked to her, when he talked business. His voice though soft was not humble and indicated that he had his own satisfactions, maybe his own revenge. If I had a friend with me, coming in from school, she would say, "Is that Poppy *Cullender*?" She would be amazed to hear him talking like an ordinary person, amazed to find him inside somebody's house. I disliked his connection with us so much that I wanted to say no.

Not much was made, really, of Poppy's sexual tendencies. People may have thought that he didn't have any. When they said he was queer, they just meant queer: odd, freakish, disturbing. His stammer and his rolling eyes and his fat bum and his house full of throwaways were rolled up into that one word. I don't know if he was very courageous, trying to make a life for himself in a place like Dalgleish where random insults and misplaced pity would be what was always coming at him, or whether he was just not very realistic. Certainly it was not realistic to make such suggestions as he did to a couple of baseball players on the Stratford train.

I never knew what my mother made of his final disastrous luck, or what she knew about him. Years later she read in the paper that a teacher in the college I was going to had been arrested for fighting in a bar over a male companion. She asked me did they mean he was defending a friend, and, if so, why didn't they say so? *Male companion?*

And she said, "Poor Poppy. There were always those who were out to get him. He was very smart, in his way. Some people can't survive in a place like this. It's not permitted."

PG You know, the first time you and I met was also the first time we talked on the radio, and we mentioned we come from about the same time and about the same place, which is southern Ontario. If we never had that or any other conversation, it was just occurring to me, listening to you, that your vocabulary of things, as well as of words, is my vocabulary — moustache cups and mustard glasses, chenille and all of that.

AM Yes.

PG There was a Poppy Cullender where I grew up, too. He wasn't the same age, he wasn't close to me, I didn't know him, he wasn't friends with my mother, but I had one.

AM  Yes, I think Poppy Cullender exists in most small towns in the period we're talking about. You know, this is an interesting thing. People say, Did you use So-and-so? It will turn out that you could have used So-and-so from any town at all. People write me letters from Texas, or Maine, or wherever, saying, You must have known So-and-so in our town.

PG  Is there a quota? One per town?

AM  I don't know. It seems that there certainly are recurring types of people, and I suppose these people were the people who were interested in . . . well, it's a bit hard to say beauty, but they were interested in things, in interesting objects.

PG  But we didn't understand. You understood them.

AM  I didn't understand them then. I would have been, as the narrator is in the story, very put off with the oddity of a person like that.

PG  But later you can come back and see through your writerly eye that there was something there.

AM  The whole question interests me because it's a person choosing what would seem to be a very difficult role to play. The person who is like this is choosing to stay in a harshly unsympathetic environment and casting himself in the outsider's role and maybe getting some satisfaction out of it. This is what I was getting at. Is it because the person doesn't see other possibilities, possibilities of moving out? It may be something as simple as that. But I think it is something more interesting. I think it's carving out an identity, which for Poppy is the identity of the outsider, the identity of the freak. Not exactly choosing it, because the choice is made for you, but maybe revelling in it a little bit? Acting the part? Just getting the most mileage out of it even though some of what you get is certainly unpleasant.

PG  I'm hesitant in a way to even ask you this, because I know and appreciate and I understand the offensiveness of saying, You're the narrator and it's all autobiographical or something. I don't want to do that.

AM  I'm glad you understand that.

PG  Not that I know if it's true that Alice Munro is not the narrator and Dalgleish is not Wingham, Ontario. You live in a small town?

AM  Yes.

PG  You're an outsider because you write, with a capital W. Your stuff appears in *The New Yorker*. You're a literary celebrity. Is there any link between your understanding of your role and your appreciation of Poppy Cullender? Do you write partly out of your own sense of outsiderness?

AM I write out of a remembered sense of outsiderness. I don't have that sense now because I live in a small town which is tolerant and friendly. I'm a grown-up woman with enough clout not to be ridiculed for what I do, even though it is a fairly unusual thing to do. People are not judgemental about it so it's nothing to do with my life now. But I can remember having a very strong sense of being an outsider as a child and an adolescent, and I identified probably with anybody who was an outsider in the small-town life.

PG You were an outsider because you read and thought? I don't think that is quite what you mean.

AM No, no, that isn't quite it. It was like having a different make-up. It was in a way like being a different colour, but it was nothing that could be identified. It was very hard for me to know why I felt that. I think most writers feel like this because you're the observer and you're still in the body of a child or a young girl. People don't know what's going on.

PG Are you writing it down, then, at the age of eight, as an outsider?

AM No, I was a little older than eight when I decided to be a writer, and that was after discovering writing.

## PART TWO

PETER GZOWSKI You are reading from . . . ?

ALICE MUNRO This is from the story "The Stone in the Field," and the narrator, who is a child, has gone with her family to visit her father's aunts, who live in the back country. They've gone inside the house.

The floor was pine and it was white, gleaming, but soft-looking, like velvet. So were the chairs and the table. We all sat around the kitchen, which was like a small house tacked onto the main house; back and front doors opposite each other, windows on three sides. The cold black stove shone too, with polishing. Its trim was like mirrors. The room was cleaner and barer than any I had ever been in. There was no sign of frivolity, no indication that the people who lived here ever sought entertainment. No radio; no newspapers or magazines; certainly no books. There must have been a

Bible in the house, and there must have been a calendar, but these were not to be seen. It was hard now even to believe in the clothes-pin dolls, the crayons and the yarn. I wanted to ask which of them had made the dolls; had there really been a wigged lady and a one-legged soldier? But though I was not usually shy, a peculiar paralysis overcame me in this room. As if I understood for the first time how presumptuous any question might be, how haz-ardous any opinion.

Work would be what filled their lives, not conversation; work would be what gave their days shape. I know that now. Drawing the milk down through the rough teats, slapping the flatiron back and forth on the scorched-smelling ironing board, swishing the scrub-water in whitening arcs across the pine floor, they would be mute and maybe content. Work would not be done here as it was in our house, where the idea was to get it over with. It would be something that could, that must, go on forever.

What was to be said? The aunts, like those who engage in a chat with royalty, would venture no remarks of their own, but could answer questions. They offered no refreshments. It was clear that only a great effort of will kept them all from running away and hiding, like Aunt Susan, who never did reappear while we were there. What was felt in that room was the pain of human contact. I was hypnotized by it. The fascinating pain; the humiliating necessity.

Okay.

PG  Okay for you; I'm still thinking about it.

AM  Well, these people, the child's father's family, live on an isolated farm, and I was trying to bring out some quality of this life of isolation and also of ritual. To show how completely different this is from what we've probably accepted as the North American ideal of life, which is a life of change and movement and procuring things and better-ing yourself and learning things. This is a double story, and the first half of the story, called "Connection," is about the mother's family and their drive and their notions of themselves. They're rather dra-matic. They believe in having fun. They believe they're being effec-tive. Then we go to the father's family, who seem at first withdrawn.

Well, they are withdrawn, but at first glance, people like the child's mother see their lives as lives of total failure to be effective in any way. They don't own a car, they drive a horse and buggy — this is the late forties or mid-forties — and they don't have a telephone.

PG  This is very grim stuff, the work that they do.

AM  But it isn't grim to them. I was trying to think about the pattern of this kind of life, where the work is seasonal and repeated over and over again and oddly satisfying. They don't ask questions like, Am I happy? or, Is this a good life? This *is* life. It's not even so much that they reject change — they don't recognize it. I find this interesting. I remember people like this.

PG  You don't have to remember. There are such people right now.

AM  Oh, yes.

PG  So, you do all those things, and I've done some of those things, and I see other people doing them.

AM  But I think if you have a job in a factory now you want to be well paid for it. People now don't find satisfaction in such things. I've done housework now for many, many years and housework is repetitive work. I could see that. I don't mean to be romantic about this kind of work. I think what they're taking satisfaction in is not exactly the work. The scrubbing, by the way, is done with lye.

PG  That's the whiteness in the wave that goes across the floor and that scours the old fingers.

AM  It's not entirely the work, it's the whole pattern of life which is seen as somehow inevitable if you don't think about other possibilities. I know many people who do take a great satisfaction in hard work. I think it's something you find in traditional communities.

PG  It's interesting to watch you talk because it's almost as if you're discovering for yourself what you're talking about.

AM  Yes, yes, because I haven't thought about it. When I write I don't think things out this way. I just know I have a picture. I have a picture of those women, and I want to get into what I think is the quality of their lives.

PG  But what you are doing is to get the quality of their lives onto paper, not to be judgemental.

AM  I'm not making a judgement. I'm not completely a non-political person, but I'm not a political writer in any way. This is one of the points the story makes. The mother looks at this and thinks, How awful, if only they could learn a few things. If only they would get the hydro in, for instance, and make their lives easier. It's not even that they *can't* do these things — they're not disadvantaged. They *choose* not to do them, the way that they've *chosen* not to get married. It's a kind of defence against life before life has a chance to move in on you. I have known people like that. It's in my heritage. It's not altogether connected with work, or social class. I think maybe it's a Scottish Protestant or Scottish–Irish Protestant attitude. An extreme attitude. You were taught to be very thrifty and very careful and not to take chances, and the people who learned these lessons too well just didn't take any chances at all.

## PART THREE

ALICE MUNRO  I realized when I looked at this passage that it ties in with what I read yesterday, which was about all of the old-maid aunts. I'll read the first section [from "Bardon Bus"].

I think of being an old maid in another generation. There were plenty of old maids in my family. I come of straitened people, madly secretive, tenacious, economical. Like them, I could make a little go a long way. A piece of Chinese silk folded in a drawer, worn by the touch of fingers in the dark. Or the one letter, hidden under maidenly garments, never needing to be opened or read because every word is known by heart, and a touch communicates the whole. Perhaps nothing so tangible, nothing but the memory of an ambiguous word, an intimate, casual tone of voice, a hard, helpless look. That could do. With no more than that I could manage, year after year as I scoured the milk pails, spit on the iron, followed the cows along the rough path among the alder and the black-eyed Susans, spread the clean wet overalls to dry on the fence, and the tea towels on the bushes. Who would the man be? He could be anybody. A soldier killed at the front or a farmer down the road with the rough-tongued wife and a crowd of children. A boy who went to Saskatchewan and promised to send for me, but never did, or the preacher who rouses me every Sunday with lashings of fear and promises of torment. No matter. I could fasten on any of them, in secret. A lifelong secret; lifelong dream-life. I could go round singing in the kitchen, polishing the stove, wiping the lamp chimneys, getting water for the tea from the drinking-pail. The faintly sour smell of the scrubbed tin, the worn scrub-cloths. Upstairs my bed with the high headboard, the crocheted spread and the rough, friendly-smelling flannelette sheets, the hot-water bottle to ease my cramps or be clenched between my legs. There I come back again and again to the centre of my fantasy, to the moment when you give yourself up, give yourself over, to the assault which is guaranteed to finish off what you've been before. A stubborn virgin's belief in perfect mastery; any broken-down wife could tell you there is no such thing.

Okay.

PETER GZOWSKI You just read a dirty passage.

AM Oh, it wasn't that bad.

PG No, but that's erotic stuff.

AM Well, it's an erotic story. It's a story about erotic obsession, and I start off with, in the narrator's mind, a casting back to a time when an obsession would be experienced quite differently. In a way, the perfect way of experiencing obsession of this sort would be to be in love and have the love never consummated and to go on your whole life treasuring a kind of dream in this quietly mad way. Our narra-tor is getting over a brief affair and its withdrawal pains, and that's all it's about. She just feels obsessive.

PG You can't talk so easily about what it's about without dealing with the tremendous sensuality of that passage. It's very sensual stuff, the words and the images.

AM There's more in the story.

PG Yeah, it's a wonderment.

AM No, I mean there's something important in it for me about dress shops, and clothes, and the way women wear make-up and the way they get dressed and this feeling of — almost of desperation. You can feel it sometimes if you go around shops where women are buying clothes. I set it at the end of summer because that's when everybody is thinking about a new image, and that was important to me in the story. What I want the reader to feel is this almost hysterical, erotic climate. It doesn't much matter to me what happens at the end — well, I won't say what happens at the end, but it really doesn't matter very much. It's the pulse of experience.

PG Does that woman's erotic obsession interest you partly because it happens next to the pine trees and the very faded houses of small-town Ontario?

AM Well, the part I read really is about that, isn't it? It's about the puritanical exterior of a life and the obsession that may be underneath. I think sensuality as a sexual obsession would often be strongest where it's contained in a very repressed way. The character in the story is living the modern woman's life of free choice and various experience, and perhaps one of the underlying things is that she's having this intense response to experience but she's living in a context where you're expected to take things much more lightly. So in a way there is no room to feel what she's feeling.

## PART FOUR

PETER GZOWSKI Now, Miss Munro, you know that you are among my exalted heroes in the world of literature and I'm a huge admirer of everything you've written, including your most recent work, but what I want to know is, are you going to read some more dirty stuff?

ALICE MUNRO Sorry, no.

PG What, you mean yesterday's eroticism, that was it?

AM This is about love, what I am going to read today.

PG Okay.

AM It's a story called "Mrs. Cross and Mrs. Kidd," and it's about two women in an old people's home. What it's really about is the relationships that people manage to keep up in quite a lively way in very difficult circumstances. I'm going to read the part about where these two women, who've known each other ever since they were five years old, meet in the home.

> Mrs. Cross has been in Hilltop Home three years and two months, Mrs. Kidd three years less a month. They both have bad hearts and ride around in wheelchairs to save their energy. During their first conversation, Mrs. Kidd said, "I don't notice any hilltop."

"You can see the highway," said Mrs. Cross. "I guess that's what they mean. Where did they put you?" she asked.

"I hardly know if I can find my way back. It's a nice room, though. It's a single."

"Mine is too, I have a single. Is it the other side of the dining-room or this?"

"Oh. The other side."

"That's good, that's the best part. Everybody's in fairly good shape down there. It costs more, though. The better you are, the more it costs. The other side of the dining-room is out of their head."

"Senile?"

"Senile. This side is the younger ones that have something the matter with them. For instance." She nodded at a Mongoloid man of about fifty, who was trying to play the mouth organ. "Down in our part there's also younger ones, but nothing the matter up here," she tapped her head. "Just some disease. When it gets to the point that they can't look after themselves — upstairs. That's where you get the far-gone ones. Then the crazies is another story. Locked up in the back wing. That's the real crazies. Also, I think there's some place they have the ones that walk around but soil all the time."

"Well, we are the top drawer," said Mrs. Kidd with a tight smile. "I knew there would be plenty of senile ones, but I wasn't prepared for the others. Such as." She nodded discreetly at the Mongoloid who was doing a step-dance in front of the window. Unlike most Mongoloids, he was thin and agile, though very pale and brittle-looking.

"Happier than most," said Mrs. Cross, observing him. "This is the only place in the county, everything gets dumped here. After a while it doesn't bother you."

"It doesn't *bother* me."

PG  It's an old person's story. Now justify that. Explain yourself.

AM  I suppose it's a Canadian tradition. Look at *The Stone Angel*, where this is done so very well. I don't find it at all difficult to imagine being old. I never have.

PG Do you think of yourself now in the prime of life? Do you think of yourself past the prime of life?

AM No. I think of myself just about at the peak. In my prime, like Miss Jean Brodie. I think I am at the stage, and I think you are, too, where you can look ahead and have a pretty good idea of the type of old person you are going to be and you can also look back and see yourself as a child. I notice in the faces of people who are my own age . . . I can see the old person emerging. I can also see the young person I remember.

PG You the writer see more in a lot of faces than other people do. It is a game to think of ourselves as old, but all I can think of is being two things. One is distinguished, and the other is free to speak my mind at long last. I'm going to have licence to say, You're boring me, leave the room, and no one will blame me. They'll say, Forgive the old guy, he's eighty-two now.

AM I wonder if that happens very often. I have a feeling from watching people that we stay pretty much the way we are, and in a way that's disappointing because you do have this feeling that someday you're going to bust out and you're going to say everything.

PG The old ladies in the story, I think they say, I'm eighty-one, and if I was only sixty-two they'd give me heck for doing this, but I'm going to say I don't want any more custard.

AM Yes, I think they do. But they also see our attitudes. You know, if you go in there in a charming, patronizing way, people are going to laugh at that, just as if they were younger. The sense of irony isn't gone just because you've become an old person. Your sense of humour isn't gone. You find this in the nursing home I visit, that people make jokes about things many younger people cannot stand to think about. There's a sort of wild humour. A couple of the ladies I visited would always tell me the news, what had recently happened in the home. This would be often fairly grotesque stuff, but they were laughing about it.

PG Am I invading your privacy if I ask you why you visit the home?

AM Well, my mother-in-law was in the Huron County home — which is called Huron View — for, oh, I think nearly three years, so my husband and I went — when I say every day, I'm exaggerating. We didn't go Sundays. We went every other day unless something came up, so we were there constantly, and I became friendly with people there. After my mother-in-law died I continued to visit. Not nearly so frequently, but I continue to go out to see the people I've made friends with. I didn't do this to be nice. This wasn't the nice lady visiting the home. I did it because I enjoyed these people so much that I wanted to see them.

PG You weren't possibly thinking you were absorbing material that would become . . .

AM Well, I'm always absorbing material wherever I go, be it the corner store or over coffee.

## PART FIVE

ALICE MUNRO  This reading is from the title story, which is the last story in the book. In the part I'm going to read, the narrator has come back into her father's hospital room, where he is waiting for heart surgery, and he has just said as she comes into the room . . .

"What?" I said. I wondered if he had found out how much, or how little, time he could hope for. I wondered if the pills had brought on an untrustworthy euphoria. Or if he had wanted to gamble. Once, when he had wanted to talk to me about his life, he had said, "The trouble was I was always afraid to take chances."

"Shoreless seas," he had said again. "'Behind him lay the gray Azores, / Behind the Gates of Hercules; / Before him not the ghosts of shores, / Before him only shoreless seas.' That's what was going through my head last night. But do you think I could remember what kind of seas? I could not. Lonely seas? Empty seas? I was on the right track but I couldn't get it. But there now when you came into the room and I wasn't thinking about it at all, the word popped into my head. That's always the way, isn't it? It's not all that surprising. I asked my mind a question. The answer's there, but I can't see all the connections my mind's making to get it. Like a computer. Nothing out of the way. You know, in my situation the thing is, if there's anything you can't explain right away, there's a great temptation to — well, to make a mystery of it. There's a great temptation to believe in — You know."

"The soul?" I said, speaking lightly, feeling an appalling rush of love and recognition.

"Oh, I guess you could call it that. You know, when I first came into this room there was a pile of papers here by the bed. Somebody had left them here — one of those tabloid things I never looked at. So I started reading them. I'll read anything that's handy. There was a series on personal experiences of people who had died, medically speaking — heart arrest, mostly — and people who had been brought back to life. It was what they had remembered of the time that they were dead. Their experiences."

"Pleasant or un-?" I said.

"Oh, pleasant. Oh, yeah. They'd float up to the ceiling and look down on themselves and see the doctors working on them, on their bodies. Then float on further and recognize some people who had died before them. Not see them exactly but sort of sense them. Sometimes there would be a humming and sometimes there'd be a — what's that light that there is or colour around a person?"

"Aura?"

"Yes. But without the person. That's about all they'd get time for; then they'd feel themselves back in the body and feel all the mortal pain and so on — brought back to life."

"Did it seem — convincing?"

"Oh, I don't know. It's all in whether you want to believe that kind of thing or not. And if you are going to believe it, take it seriously, I figure you've got to take everything else seriously that they print in those papers."

"What else do they say?"

"Rubbish. Cancer cures, baldness cures, bellyaching about the younger generation and the welfare bums. Tripe about movie stars."

"Oh, yes. I know."

"In my situation you have to keep a watch," he said, "or you start playing tricks on yourself."

PETER GZOWSKI Now here's my question. Does he believe that he's going there or not?

AM He doesn't know. He is a rational man. He's probably struggling to stay rational, but he's tempted to hope. He's appalled at the idea of ceasing to exist.

PG Are you?

ᴀᴍ Yeah. Oh, yeah.

ᴘɢ Were you as a kid? Did you think about this when you were a kid?

ᴀᴍ About dying? Oh, I suppose so.

ᴘɢ I was more interested in it then than I am now.

ᴀᴍ I think that I was, too, and I think this is something age does to you. Have you seen that fifteen-minute cartoon where the guy goes into the doctor's office and the doctor says, Okay, you have fifteen minutes to live?

ᴘɢ No. Why am I laughing?

ᴀᴍ The guy goes through all the classic reactions. Oh, no, why me? You're crazy. Let's get another opinion. Meanwhile, the clock's ticking off the minutes. Well, if you said that to me now, I would certainly be frightened. I would go through all of that too. I think that when I was young, I thought about death far more than I do now, when I'm much, much closer to it. I thought about it desperately and I worked very hard in my mind to defeat the idea. To establish a belief in immortality, my personal immortality. Then all of this pre-occupation faded gradually away.

ᴘɢ Why is that, do you think?

ᴀᴍ I think it's just some protective thing that happens so you can get through life. I remember when I was about eight thinking, I've got to figure out what the meaning is to life, why we're here. If I can't figure this out, how can I go on living? I looked at older people and thought, They must have it all figured out because they go on living. I noticed that whenever I tried to have a serious conversation with middle-aged people, they usually seemed very shallow. They brushed off the subject I was interested in. Then I found that when my own children would talk to me about things like this I tended to brush it off, or I would talk about it but without that deep concern I had had when I was younger.

ᴘɢ That's a very curious thing. When I was ten in southern Ontario, I used to go home from the sermon and wonder about the logic there. I used to have this trouble with a logical flaw. This was the extent of my philosophy aged ten or eleven. I would think, If you are unselfish you'll go to heaven, but if you become unselfish in order to get to heaven, that's a selfish act.

ᴀᴍ Exactly, so how can you win?

ᴘɢ That's right, and that troubled me then, but now I hardly ever think of stuff like that. Am I going to have to wait until I'm on that hospital bed? Is that what that story is about?

AM That's partly what it's about. It's also about the surviving daughter's reaction to death and her feelings about the next generation — her children — as well as her feelings towards her father. What's important is what he's feeling. He can't really share that, and she can't share his fright, really, because to her in a way it seems natural that he's going to die. We can face with equanimity the death of people in the older generation, even those we love very much.

PG Could you have written that story when you were twenty-two years old?

AM No, I couldn't have. I don't know how I would have approached it then. I wrote about very, very weighty, gloomy subjects when I was younger, but I wouldn't have had any real appreciation of what happens in that story.

PG Does it bother you that the story has a kind of tentativeness to it?

AM Not a bit, but it's encouraging to think that I might write it again in twenty years. I hope I'll be writing in twenty years' time. I hope I'll be wanting to write and finding myself able to do it. Someone asked me the other day, If you had a chance to rewrite *Lives of Girls and Women*, would you? I said yes, and then I thought, no, because really I can't imagine writing it now. I've done it so I really can't think about it.

PG I'm curious to know if you write more easily, if things come more easily to you now in maturity than they came to you in youth, or if they come with difficulty.

AM Harder, harder, much harder, yes. I think there's a thinning out of the writer's energy that I'm already feeling. I'm not sure what this is because in the beginning there's the wish to write, to use the material, and then there's a much more crass wish to be a writer. A simple ambition which provides you with lots of energy and determination . . .

PG The wish to be a writer?

AM . . . to be a writer, yes.

PG The trouble is you have to write.

AM Someone else is published and they are a year younger than you are — this is what happens all through your twenties. When I would read work by new writers I would always look at the biographical notices to find out how old they were, and I wanted them to be older than I was. You're driven by very simple competitive forces that have nothing to do with the quality of your work. But later on I've found there's a great dying down of that motivation. It's just gone. So now you only write something if you feel that it's important enough to write, and you may give up on things too soon because of that.

PG But are you a more severe editor of your own bad stuff now than you were?

AM I don't think I'm any harder on myself than I always was. I always worry the story. I keep at it and edit and edit, changing it, trying to get at what I want. I still do that.

PG You are known in certain parts of the book trade as quite a devil for doing that.

AM I made a couple of changes as I was reading that today.

PG Really? Did you really? Did you edit as you went?

AM Yeah, I did a few things. I thought, Oh, I can do that better. But I don't know if I'm right, you see. I will go on writing and rewriting perhaps beyond the optimum point, and I need an editor to tell me, Well, I like this version better, and then we can argue it out and I may see the way it should be. I may go back to the third-last version and present that. I may be trying to get something into it that doesn't really belong in the story. What I'm saying is that you don't get any surer of your judgement. It's the one profession, it seems to me, where you don't get onto a kind of plateau of competence where you're sure of yourself. A surgeon, for instance, learns to do operations pretty well, and he goes on doing them with a fair amount of confidence. He has to be vigilant, but he doesn't go into every operation thinking, Well, this is touch and go, but a writer does. I do.

PG Well, it's working. I thank you one more time.

AM Thank you.

# THE MORNINGSIDE COOKBOOK

*People who looked down their noses at* Morningside *would often say, "Hmm . . . chili sauce again. . . ." And sometimes they were right. But food of all kinds was a constant subject of our interest and our pleasure. This is a compilation of some of the recipes we collected — chosen from hundreds after much discussion. Choosing, needless to say, was very difficult.* Morningside *never did have a test kitchen, but these recipes have been tested by their authors — from premiers to professional chefs to overburdened gardeners. And, yes, there's chili sauce.*

## CHILI SAUCE

This is Toronto chef Hugh Garber's recipe, from the Great *Morningside* Chili Sauce Cook-In of 1988.

*Note: If you don't have a boiling water canner, you can make one. You need a large, deep pot with a tight-fitting lid, a rack that fits into it, and empty jars. Place the jars on the rack so they don't touch the bottom of the pot. The jars need an inch (2.5 cm) of water over their tops, and remember to leave room for a rolling boil.*

| | |
|---|---|
| 24 | large tomatoes |
| 6 | medium onions, diced |
| 6 | sweet green peppers, diced |
| 2 | red peppers, diced |
| 2 | cups brown sugar (500 mL) |
| 2 | cups cider vinegar (500 mL) |
| 1 | tablespoon celery seed (15 mL) |
| 1 | tablespoon mustard seed (15 mL) |
| 1 | tablespoon salt (15 mL) |
| 1 | clove garlic, minced |
| ¼ | teaspoon ground cloves (1 mL) |
| 1 | teaspoon allspice (5 mL) |
| 1 | teaspoon mace (5 mL) |
| 1 | teaspoon cinnamon (5 mL) |
| 1 | tablespoon (15 mL) chopped fresh ginger, or 1 teaspoon (5 mL) ground |
| 6 | pint (500 mL) jars, clean and hot, lids boiled 5 minutes |

Cut tomatoes in quarters. Place all ingredients in a large stainless-steel kettle. Bring to a boil, stirring occasionally to prevent sticking. Cover and let cook on low heat for 2 hours. Remove lid and cook for one more hour, or until mixture is quite thick and no longer watery. Ladle into hot jars, filling to within ½-inch (1 cm) of rim. Lid should be just fingertip tight. Process filled jars 15 minutes in a boiling water canner. Remove and let cool, undisturbed, for 24 hours. Check seals. Makes 6 jars.

*Hugh Garber*
Toronto

## MARSHLANDS CHILI SAUCE

As a former Nova Scotian, I have been making chili sauce for years. This recipe comes from the Marshlands Inn in Sackville, New Brunswick, and it's the best chili sauce I have ever made.

| | |
|---|---|
| 9 | pounds ripe tomatoes (4 kg) |
| 3 | green peppers |
| 3 | cups celery (750 mL) |
| 3 | sticks root ginger |
| 6 | cups white sugar (1.5 L) |
| 3 | cups cider vinegar (750 mL) |
| 4½ | tablespoons mixed pickling spice (60 mL) |
| 2 | tablespoons salt (25 mL) |

Scald, peel, and chop tomatoes. Remove veins and seeds from peppers and cut in thin strips. Combine tomatoes, peppers, and celery in a heavy preserving kettle, then add the remaining ingredients, bring to a boil and simmer until thick. Remove ginger. Ladle into hot sterilized 1-pint (500 mL) jars to within ½-inch (1 cm) of top and screw on lids until fingertip tight. Process filled jars 15 minutes in a boiling water canner. Remove and let cool, undisturbed, for 24 hours. Check seals. Makes eight 1-pint (500 mL) jars.

*Elizabeth Ireland*
Owen Sound, Ontario

## TOMATO MARMALADE

Chili sauce is dandy — but you need to try tomatoes as a fruit, not a vegetable. Try my mother's tomato marmalade. Given unexpected company and no pie, rush baking powder biscuits into a hot oven. Serve hot buttered biscuits with this ultra-deluxe marmalade.

| | |
|---|---|
| 4 | pounds ripe tomatoes (2 kg) |
| 2 | lemons |
| 4 | cups sugar (1 L) |

2 or 3   pieces stick cinnamon
  4   ½-pint (250 mL) sterilized jars, lids boiled five minutes

Blanch and peel the tomatoes. Chop roughly and place in a very large stainless-steel saucepan. Grate the peel coarsely off the lemons; cut up lemons and add fruit and peel to tomatoes. Add sugar and stir well. Add cinnamon. Bring to a boil; reduce heat and boil gently, stirring frequently to avoid sticking, until as thick as jam. (A day without rain gives faster evaporation.) Ladle jam into hot, sterilized jars to within ¼-inch (0.5 cm) of rim. Screw on lids until just fingertip tight. Process filled jars 5 minutes in a boiling water canner. Remove and let cool, undisturbed, for 24 hours. Check seals. Makes three or four ½-pint (250 mL) jars.

*Clare McAllister*
Victoria

## Tomato Jam

I have the best recipe with the least amount of work — no endless chopping of pears, apples, onions, peppers, peaches, and so on. It looks like chili sauce, tastes like chili sauce, but has few ingredients and little work.

12   good-sized tomatoes
2½   cups white sugar (625 mL)
 2   cups white vinegar (500 mL)
 1   teaspoon ground cloves (5 mL)
 1   teaspoon cinnamon (5 mL)
 1   teaspoon salt (5 mL)
 4   ½-pint (250 mL) sterilized jars, lids boiled 5 minutes

Blanch and peel tomatoes; chop coarsely. In a large stainless-steel kettle or saucepan, combine tomatoes and sugar. Bring to a boil, then turn down heat and boil gently for at least 1 hour, stirring frequently. Add vinegar and spices and continue boiling till thickened, stirring frequently. Ladle into hot, sterilized jars to within ¼-inch (0.5 cm) of rim. Screw on lids until just fingertip tight. Process filled jars 5 minutes in a boiling water canner. Remove and let cool, undisturbed, for 24 hours. Check seals. Makes three or four ½-pint (250 mL) jars. Enjoy!

*June Morrison Smith*
Lakefield, Ontario

### GREEN TOMATO CHUTNEY

Don't know what to do with those green tomatoes when the first frost looms? Try this!

| | |
|---|---|
| 3 | pounds green tomatoes (1.5 kg) |
| 3 | pounds apples (1.5 kg), peeled and cored |
| 3 | pounds onions (1.5 kg) |
| 1 | pound sultanas (500 g) |
| 2 | quarts vinegar (2 L) |
| 4 | ounces dry mustard (100 mL) |
| 1½ | pounds brown sugar (750 g) |
| 2 | tablespoons salt (25 mL) |
| 1 | teaspoon cayenne pepper (5 mL) |
| 2 | teaspoons white pepper (10 mL) |

Finely chop tomatoes, apples, and onions. Place in a large, heavy-bottomed stainless-steel preserving pan or saucepan; add sultanas and 6 cups (1.5 L) vinegar. Bring to a boil and cook until tomatoes are soft. Meanwhile, stir together remaining vinegar and the mustard. Add to the tomatoes, then add sugar, salt, and peppers. Boil, stirring frequently to prevent sticking, until the mixture has a jam consistency. Ladle jam into hot, sterilized jars to within ½-inch (1 cm) of rim. Screw on lids until just fingertip tight. Process filled jars 10 minutes in a boiling water canner. Remove and let cool, undisturbed, for 24 hours. Check seals. Makes six or seven ½-pint (250 mL) jars.

*Peggy Swift*
Sarnia, Ontario

## ZUCCHINI PICKLES

There are certain things one would better keep hidden behind the more than passable stand of dahlias, but I somehow feel compelled to reveal all, perhaps in order to support those others across our vast land similarly afflicted. Surely I can't be the only person in Canada who has failed at growing the vegetable even a vegetable can grow — the zucchini!

It began rather well. As a matter of fact, I was probably one of the first Denman Islanders to be sizzling the tiny squash in my frying pan and enjoying them thoroughly. I maintained a humble demeanour, but in my heart I bragged and I strutted. Alas, this time pride went before a raging case of yellow-tipped fruits that got kind of hollow and spongy while the gigantic leaves grew white with mildew and eventually crunchy. Squash ceased to form. I watered more. I watered less. I fish-fertilized. I fretted. I avoided the zucchini patch entirely and wondered why I bother when the damn things are cheap to buy and even cheaper to cadge. I felt ashamed, inadequate. And worst of all, I felt guilty because I really did love the dahlias more.

From past years when different gardens yielded plenty of those fabulous shiny patent-leather monoliths, I recall Zucchini Pickles. This recipe is great to use up those triple-football-sized ones.

| | |
|---|---|
| 1 | quart vinegar (1 L) |
| 2 | cups sugar (500 mL) |
| 3 | tablespoons salt (45 mL) |
| 2 | teaspoons celery seed (10 mL) |
| 2 | teaspoons turmeric (10 mL) |
| 1 | teaspoon dry mustard (5 mL) |
| 4 | quarts unpeeled zucchini, sliced (4 L) |
| 1 | quart onions (1 L) |

In a small pot, combine vinegar, sugar, salt, and spices. Bring to a boil. Place zucchini and onions in a very large kettle. Pour boiling vinegar over vegetables. Let stand 1 hour, then bring liquid to a boil. Pour immediately into hot jars and process 10 minutes. Makes six or seven 1-pint (500 mL) jars.

*Roberta DeDoming*
Denman Island, British Columbia

## ELDERBERRY JELLY

Many years ago, I came across an elderberry patch in a neighbouring swamp. My two oldest children were in school, and I was pregnant with my youngest daughter. Every day I went to the swamp. Every day I came home with my treasure and processed bowls and bowls of berries into elderberry jelly — two hundred jars in all.

| | |
|---|---|
| 4 | pounds (2 kg) ripe elderberries, about 20 cups (5 L) |
| ½ | cup lemon juice (125 mL) |
| 7½ | cups sugar (1.75 L) |
| 2 | pouches Certo liquid fruit pectin |
| 5 | ½-pint (250 mL) sterilized jars, lids boiled 5 minutes |

Wash berries and remove stems. Place berries in a saucepan and crush. Heat gently until juice starts to flow, then simmer, covered, for 15 minutes. Pour into jelly cloth or bag and squeeze out juice. Place 3 cups (750 mL) of juice in very large stainless-steel saucepan. Add lemon juice and sugar and mix well.

Place over high heat and bring to a boil, stirring constantly. Add Certo, bring to a boil again and boil hard for one minute, stirring constantly. Remove from heat and skim off foam with a metal spoon, then pour quickly into hot sterilized jars, filling to within ¼-inch (0.5 cm) of rim. Process jars 5 minutes in a boiling water canner. Remove and let cool, undisturbed, for 24 hours. Check seals. Makes about five ½-pint (250 mL) jars.

*Elsie Herrle*
*St. Agatha, Ontario*

## CAESAR SALAD

In order to have a good Caesar salad, preparation should commence at least five hours before serving. This recipe should satisfy six persons.

*Note: Although the Premier used raw eggs in his salad, you don't need to. The eggs can be left out all together, or substitute ¼-cup (50 mL) mayonnaise. Add it just as you would the egg yolk.*

| 4 to 5 | slices of homemade bread |
|---|---|
| | Butter |
| 4 | cloves garlic |
| | Olive oil |
| 2 | romaine lettuces |
| | Lemon |
| | Pepper |
| | Parmesan cheese |
| | Salt to taste |
| | Worcestershire sauce |
| | Anchovies |
| 2 | egg yolks |
| | Bacon |

Cube the bread into crouton-sized bites. Melt plenty of butter in a large frying pan and dump the croutons in the butter and allow to crisp at low heat. More butter may have to be added during the process. The more butter the better!

Crush the garlic into a medium-sized bowl. Once the croutons are crisp, mix them in with the crushed garlic.

Add olive oil to the level of the top of the croutons and mix thoroughly so that the garlic is spread evenly through the croutons and oil. Cover the mixture and let sit until salad is prepared.

Wash 2 romaine lettuces thoroughly and dry leaves individually. Tear leaves by hand into a large salad bowl. Add lots of lemon. When you think you have enough lemon, add that much more again.

Add pepper. Add Parmesan cheese. The rule for Parmesan cheese is to put in a sufficient quantity so that you are satisfied that you have put in too much — then double the amount.

Add the mixture of croutons, garlic, and olive oil. Add salt to taste.

Perhaps add Worcestershire sauce, anchovies.

Add 2 egg yolks. Mix thoroughly into salad.

Toss salad thoroughly. Serve immediately.

By the way, a generous portion of chopped-up bacon should also be added.

*Joe Ghiz*
Charlottetown

## RED CABBAGE

You can double this recipe or triple it, whatever, just don't throw away red cabbage! It's good to eat right away, but better still if it's left in the fridge overnight, then warmed up.

| | |
|---|---|
| 3 | tablespoons butter (45 mL) |
| ¼ | cup brown sugar (50 mL) |
| ½ | cup wine vinegar (125 mL) |
| 6 | cups shredded red cabbage, about half a cabbage (1.5 L) |

In a large pot, melt the butter. Add brown sugar and vinegar and mix well. Add the shredded cabbage. Bring slowly to a boil and simmer 1½ to 2 hours. Makes 2 cups (500 mL).

*Lillian Pedersen*
Redvers, Saskatchewan

## RATATOUILLE

The beauty of this dish is that it can be served hot or cold and freezes excellently. The addition of a little cooked fish or meat makes a fast and easy one-dish meal on days you are pressed for time. Another beauty of this splendid dish is that the quantities are not critical. If you like lots of garlic, put in lots.

| | |
|---|---|
| 2 | onions, chopped |
| 1 | green pepper, chopped |
| 3 | tablespoons olive oil (75 mL) |
| 1 | medium chopped eggplant and 1 medium chopped zucchini (no need to peel them) or, if one of the zucchinis in your garden has somehow hidden itself under the leaves and grown to monstrous size, use that on its own |
| 2 | crushed garlic cloves |
| 6 to 8 | tomatoes, peeled and chopped |
| ¾ | teaspoon salt (4 mL) |
| ½ | teaspoon pepper (2 mL) |

Wilt the onion and the green pepper in the oil, but do not let them brown. Add the eggplant, zucchini, and garlic, and stir till they are coated with the oil. Add the tomatoes, salt and pepper and stir till everything is well mixed. Bring to a boil and simmer gently, uncovered, till most of the moisture has evaporated and the mixture is yummily thick. Stir occasionally. At this point, I like to add a handful of sliced mushrooms, which only take a couple of minutes to cook. This recipe makes 8 cups (2 L).

And there you are. *Bon appetit.*

*Alice Sinclair*
Kleinburg, Ontario

## Master Mix & Variations

These recipes are from my sister-in-law, who is one of the best cooks I know. The soup is my favourite, but they are all good. Freeze the Master Mix in 2-cup (500 mL) portions and use as needed.

### MASTER MIX

| | |
|---|---|
| 2 | tablespoons oil (25 mL) |
| 3 | cloves garlic, minced |
| 4 | pounds ground beef (2 kg) |
| 4 | cups chopped onion (1 L) |
| 2 | cups chopped celery (500 mL) |
| 3 | tins tomatoes (28 ounces/796 mL) |
| 2 | tins tomato paste (5½ ounces/156 mL) |
| 2 | tins mushrooms (10 ounces/284 mL) |
| 2 | tablespoons fresh parsley (25 mL) |
| 2 | teaspoons dried oregano (10 mL) |
| 2 | teaspoons salt (10 mL) |
| 1 | teaspoon dried basil (5 mL) |
| 1 | teaspoon pepper (5 mL) |
| ½ | teaspoon crushed red pepper (2 mL) |

In a large skillet, heat oil. Add garlic and ground beef; cook till browned. Let cool, place in a large bowl, and add all other ingredients; mix well.

(You may want to mash the tomatoes with a potato masher.) Divide into 2-cup (500 mL) portions and freeze. Yield: 20 cups (10 L).

SHEPHERD'S PIE

 2   cups Master Mix (500 mL)
 3   cups mashed potatoes (750 mL)
 1   tin mushrooms, drained (10 ounces/284 mL)
 1   tablespoon beef-flavoured powdered soup base (15 mL)
 1   cup grated carrots (250 mL)
 2   tablespoons Parmesan cheese (25 mL)

Combine Master Mix, 1 cup (250 mL) mashed potatoes, mushrooms, soup base, and carrots. Pour into 4-cup (1 L) casserole. Top with remaining mashed potatoes. Sprinkle with Parmesan cheese. Bake at 350°F (180°C) for 40 minutes. Serves 4.
Freezes well.

FASTA PASTA

 3   cups dried pasta shells (750 mL)
 2   cups Master Mix (500 mL)
 1   can cream of celery soup
 1   cup cubed mozzarella cheese (250 mL)
 1   cup frozen peas (250 mL)

Cook pasta in salted boiling water until tender. Drain. In an 8-cup (2 L) casserole dish, stir together pasta and Master Mix, soup, cheese, and peas. Bake at 350°F (180°C) for 30 minutes. Serves 4.

HAMBURGER SOUP

 2    cups Master Mix (500 mL)
 2    large potatoes, cut in cubes
 2    cans consommé (10 ounces/284 mL)
 2½   cups water (625 mL)
 1    cup grated carrots (250 mL)

1 cup chopped celery (250 mL)
¼ cup barley (50 mL)

Combine all ingredients in a large stock pot. Bring to a boil, then reduce heat and simmer for 1½ hours, or until barley is soft. Serves 4.

*Mary Grant*
Tisdale, Saskatchewan

### BREAST OF TURKEY WITH LEEKS, PARSNIPS, AND CARROTS

¼ teaspoon kosher salt (1 mL)
¼ teaspoon freshly ground black pepper (1 mL)
4 escalopes of turkey breast, skinned and boned, about 6 ounces (170 g) each
1 medium leek, julienned (white part only)
1 medium carrot, julienned
1 medium parsnip, julienned

#### SEASONED BUTTER

¼ cup packed Italian parsley (50 mL)
½ small clove garlic, finely chopped
¼ cup unsalted butter (50 mL)
1 teaspoon tarragon (5 mL)
¼ teaspoon kosher salt (1 mL)
⅛ teaspoon freshly ground pepper (0.5 mL)

Tear off 4 pieces of aluminum foil, each about 11 x 12 inches (28 x 30 cm). Combine salt and pepper in a small bowl. Using half the mixture and dividing evenly, sprinkle a little salt and pepper into the centre of each foil sheet.

Place 1 turkey breast, smooth side up, on the salt and pepper on each sheet. Divide julienned vegetables and spread evenly over turkey breasts. Season each portion of turkey and vegetables evenly with remaining salt and pepper.

To make seasoned butter, combine parsley, garlic, butter, tarragon, salt, and pepper. Dab each turkey breast with seasoned butter, then wrap up and seal foil packets tightly.

Heat oven to 500°F (260°C). Heat a heavy baking sheet in the oven for about 2 minutes, then arrange foil packets, folded side up, about 1 inch (2.5 cm) apart on the hot baking sheet. Bake for 8 minutes. Serve right away.

*John Bishop*
Vancouver

## RHUBARB PORK CHOP CASSEROLE

On a busy day, you can build this casserole and put it in a slow oven for a couple of hours.

|  |  |
|---|---|
| 4 | pork chops |
| 1 | tablespoon cooking oil (15 mL) |
|  | Salt and pepper |
| 2½ to 3 | cups soft bread crumbs (625 mL to 750 mL) |
| 3 | cups sliced rhubarb (750 mL) |
| ½ to ¾ | cup brown sugar (125 mL to 225 mL) |
| ¼ | cup all-purpose flour (50 mL) |
| 1 | teaspoon ground cinnamon (5 mL) |

In a large skillet, brown the chops in the oil and season with salt and pepper. Remove chops and mix ¼ cup (50 mL) pan drippings with the bread crumbs.

Reserve ½ cup (125 mL) bread crumbs and sprinkle rest into 13 x 9 x 2-inch (33 x 22 x 5 cm) baking dish.

Combine rhubarb, sugar, flour, and cinnamon. Spoon half the rhubarb mixture over the bread crumbs. Arrange chops on top. Spoon remaining rhubarb over chops.

Cover with foil and bake at 350°F (180°C) for 30 to 45 minutes.

Remove foil and sprinkle with reserved bread crumbs. Bake 10 to 15 minutes longer, or until chops test done.

Or assemble, then bake at 300°F (150°C) for 2 hours.

*Lee Anne Bryant*
Stirling, Ontario

## Mussels Marinière

¼  cup butter (50 mL)
½  onion, finely chopped
1  clove garlic, minced
2  pounds mussels (1 kg)
2  cups water (500 mL)
2  tomatoes, chopped and seeded
   Sprig basil, washed and chopped
½  teaspoon salt (2 mL)
½  teaspoon pepper (2 mL)

In a deep skillet, over medium-high heat, melt butter; add onion and minced garlic and sauté for about 5 minutes, or until the onion is soft and transparent, but not brown.

Add mussels and water. Cover pan and cook until mussels open up completely. Strain liquid through cheesecloth, reserving liquid. Set mussels aside.

Pour liquid back into the skillet. Add tomatoes, basil, salt, and pepper, and heat till tomatoes are hot.

Arrange mussels on a serving platter and pour hot liquid over; serve at once. Serves 4.

*Marc Thuet*
Toronto

## Stew

This is a great recipe. You make it, then sit down and forget about it while you enjoy a wee drop in front of the fireplace. I have put this in the oven at noon and served it at six. The vegetables stay firm and whole, the gravy is delicious, and it's great for a crowd. The secret is not raising the lid of the pot at any time.

2  pounds stewing beef, chopped coarsely (1 kg)
1  cup celery (250 mL)
1  cup onions (250 mL)

1   cup potatoes (250 mL)
1   cup carrots (250 mL)
2   cups tomato juice (500 mL)
2   tablespoons minute tapioca (25 mL)
    Salt and pepper

Put meat in bottom of large pot that can go in the oven. Put in coarsely chopped vegetables. (Add a cup of any vegetables you like — turnips, carrots, beans, corn — and use as many as you want.) Add seasoning and tapioca, then pour in tomato juice. Cover tightly. Put in oven at 325°F (160°C) for at least 3½ hours and *do not peek*!

*Doris MacIntyre*
Long Sault, Ontario

## AL'S BEANS

The creator of this dish is our friend and neighbour Al McGeachy, who served us his beans one cold winter evening, much to the tasty enjoyment of all. If you want to, you can use ⅓ cup (75 mL) sugar and ½ cup (125 mL) maple sugar.

1          pound navy beans (450 g)
1          large onion (at least), chopped
6          cups water, or enough to cover beans (1.5 L)
3 to 6     tablespoons chili sauce or ketchup (45 to 60 mL)
½          cup brown sugar (125 mL)
1          tablespoon dry mustard (15 mL)
1          tablespoon Worcestershire sauce (15 mL)
¼ to ½     pound salt pork, diced (125 to 250 g)
           A few drops Tabasco
¼          cup rum (50 mL)

Clean and soak beans overnight. In a large heavy-bottomed pot, bring beans to a boil and simmer for one hour. Drain, saving liquid. Mix together bean-cooking liquid, chili sauce, sugar, mustard, Worcestershire sauce, and Tabasco. Layer beans, onions, salt pork, and sauce in 6-cup

(1.5 L) baking dish or bean crock. Bake for 4 hours at 300°F (150°C); keep beans just covered in liquid during baking. Before serving, drizzle rum over beans. Serve with cabbage salad (an old Boy Scout trick) and thick fresh bread.

*Sandra Paterson*
Edmonton

## "Low-Cal" Fettuccine Alfredo

Don't be put off by the cottage cheese, even if you don't like it — just make sure it's well blended and as smooth as possible. I cannot tell a lie — this does not taste exactly like the genuine article (*mit* the whipping cream), but it *is* good!

|       |                                         |
|-------|-----------------------------------------|
| 1     | cup low-fat cottage cheese (250 mL)     |
| 1     | cup low-fat (1%) milk (250 mL)          |
| 1     | egg yolk                                |
| ½     | teaspoon freshly ground pepper (2 mL)   |
| 2     | tablespoons butter (25 mL)              |
| ½     | cup grated Parmesan, divided (125 mL)   |
| 8     | ounces fettuccine noodles (250 g)       |

In a blender, combine cottage cheese, milk, egg yolk, and pepper; purée until smooth. In a small saucepan melt butter over low heat. Add purée and bring to a simmer, stirring occasionally. Stir in all but 4 teaspoons (20 mL) of the Parmesan.

Meanwhile, cook fettuccine noodles according to the package instructions; drain. Toss with sauce. Sprinkle with remaining Parmesan. Makes 4 servings.

*Audrey Phillips*
Ottawa

## GOOD BREAD

My mother learned to make bread from our elderly next-door neighbour, and it was delicious! As a young bride, I decided I would attempt
the feat with only the help of a recipe book, and with no instruction from
my mother. A whole day later, with only one small banana-bread-sized
loaf to show for my hours of effort, I conceded that perhaps I *could* learn
from my mother!

|  |  |
|---|---|
| 1 | teaspoon sugar (5 mL) |
| ¼ | cup lukewarm water (50 mL) |
| 1 | package dry yeast (1 tablespoon/15 mL) |
| 2 | tablespoons white sugar (25 mL) |
| 2 | teaspoons salt (10 mL) |
| 2 | tablespoons shortening (25 mL) |
| 1 | cup milk — skim is fine (250 mL) |
| 1 | cup warm water (250 mL) |
| 6 to 8 | cups all-purpose flour (1.5 to 2 L) |

In a small bowl, dissolve 1 teaspoon (5 mL) sugar in lukewarm water.
Sprinkle yeast over and let stand 10 minutes.

Into a very large bowl, measure the sugar, salt, and shortening. Scald
the milk and add to sugar, stirring until shortening is melted. Add water,
then add yeast mixture.

Begin adding flour ½ cup (125 mL) at a time until dough is stiff
enough to knead. Knead for about 10 minutes, or until you have a
smooth, satiny ball.

Place in an oiled bowl, cover with waxed paper, and let rise until
doubled, about 1 hour.

Punch dough down; shape into two loaves and place in oiled tins.
Cover with waxed paper. Let rise until doubled, about 1 hour.

Bake at 350° (180°C) for 30 to 35 minutes. Cool on wire racks. Makes
2 loaves.

CHEESE AND ONION BREAD: After first rising, roll dough out. Sprinkle
½ cup (125 mL) grated cheese and 1 tablespoon (15 mL) onion soup mix
on dough, then roll to form a loaf.

CINNAMON BUNS: Spread rolled-out dough with ⅓ cup (75 mL) soft-ened butter; sprinkle with ½ cup (125 mL) brown sugar, 2 teaspoons (10 mL) cinnamon, ½ cup (125 mL) raisins, and ¼ cup (50 mL) chopped walnuts or pecans. Roll up as before. Cut cylinder into 1-inch (2.5 cm) pieces. Place in a buttered 8 x 8-inch (20 cm square) pan, let rise for an hour, then bake at 350°F (180°C) for 15 to 20 minutes.

*Madge Skinner*
Sudbury, Ontario

## THE BEST SANDWICH

Spread two pieces of whole-wheat or light rye bread with mayonnaise. Now slice up some red pepper and cover one slice liberally with the pepper. Here's the crazy part: put a good layer of potato chips over the pepper and then sprinkle on some black pepper and garlic powder. Crush down the other slice of bread, mayonnaise side down. Cut the sandwich in two. You can eat one half and I'll eat the other. Great!

*George Foster*
Way's Mills, Quebec

## BAKED AUTUMN APPLES

| | |
|---|---|
| 4 | baking apples |
| ¼ | cup sugar (50 mL) |
| ¼ | teaspoon ground cinnamon (1 mL) |
| 1½ | teaspoons unsalted butter (7 mL) |
| 4 | pitted prunes |
| ½ | cup icing sugar (125 mL) |

With a sharp knife, peel and partially core apples, leaving bottoms intact. Combine sugar and ground cinnamon. Roll apples in the mixture until outsides are lightly coated.

Put a dot of butter in the centre of each apple, dividing the butter evenly between the apples. Place 1 pitted prune in the centre of each apple. Place apples in a 9-inch (23 cm) baking dish or pie pan.

Sprinkle icing sugar evenly over all four apples, place in 375°F (190°C) oven and bake until apples are tender but not mushy, about 35 minutes.

Remove apples from oven and cool to lukewarm. Spoon some of the juice in the dish over the warm apples and serve. Serves 4.

*Marc Thuet*
Toronto

### POACHED PEARS

2  teaspoons (10 mL) vanilla extract or the seeds and
   husks of 2 vanilla beans
4  Bartlett pears, peeled and cored
2  cups sugar (500 mL)
2  sticks cinnamon
5  cups water (1.25 mL)

In a large stainless-steel pot, combine vanilla, pears, sugar, cinnamon, and water. Place over medium-high heat and bring to a boil. Boil for 30 minutes, or until fruit is soft, but not mushy.

Remove from heat and let cool; place pears and liquid in a dish and let steep overnight in the refrigerator. Bring to room temperature to serve.

*John Bishop*
Vancouver

### BLUEBERRY GRUNT FOR THE MICROWAVE

Here's a theory about how Blueberry Grunt got its name: In an old Boston Cooking School cookbook from the late 1800s, author Fannie Merritt Farmer includes a recipe for steamed blueberry pudding. She suggests cooking the fruit in a covered *granite* kettle, with the dough on top. My theory is that the pudding became known as Blueberry *Granite*, referring to the container in which it was cooked. It probably wasn't too long before *granite* was mispronounced *grunt*. (The same book warns that "Fruit should be cooked in earthen or granite utensils. All fruits contain one or more acids, and when exposed to air and brought in contact with an iron or tin surface, a poisonous compound may be formed.") Graniteware is an ironware coated with a hard, granite-coloured enamel.

⅓    cup sugar (75 mL)
1    teaspoon cornstarch (5 mL)
2    cups fresh or frozen blueberries (500 mL)
2    teaspoons lemon juice (10 mL)
    Pinch of cinnamon
1    cup flour (250 mL)
1    tablespoon sugar (15 mL)
2    teaspoons baking powder (10 mL)
¼    teaspoon salt (1 mL)
1    tablespoon butter or margarine (15 mL)
⅔    cup milk (150 mL)

In a 1½-quart (1.5 L) microwave-safe casserole dish, mix sugar, cornstarch, blueberries, lemon juice, and cinnamon. Heat at high power for 3 to 5 minutes or until juices begin to boil, stirring twice.

Meanwhile, in a medium bowl, sift together flour, sugar, baking powder, and salt. With a pastry blender or two knives, cut in butter. Add milk, and use a fork to stir gently until dry ingredients are just moistened. (Be careful not to overmix.)

Remove blueberry mixture from microwave. Using a spoon, drop dough in small mounds around the edge of the casserole, on top of the blueberries. Cover and cook at high power for 2 minutes and 15 seconds, or until batter springs back when touched.

Remove from oven and let stand, covered, for 3 minutes. Serve warm. It's good plain or with a dollop of whipped cream or vanilla ice cream. Makes 4 servings.

*Mary Mouzar*
Halifax

## RICE PUDDING

What I love about rice pudding is its creaminess. This comes from slow cooking in plenty of milk, either the old-fashioned way in the top of a double boiler — guaranteed no scorching or boil-overs — or simmered in a large heavy saucepan with lots of stirring. Fancy up a bowl with raisins, cinnamon, or nutmeg, or ginger and orange, or apricots and orange — or whatever strikes your fancy.

| | |
|---|---|
| ½ | cup short-grain rice (125 mL), Italian recommended |
| ¼ | cup granulated sugar (50 mL) |
| ¼ | teaspoon nutmeg (50 mL) |
| | Pinch salt |
| 2½ | cups (approximately) milk (625 mL) |
| ½ | cup raisins (125 mL) |
| 1 | tablespoon butter (15 mL) |
| 1 | teaspoon vanilla (5 mL) |
| | Cinnamon |

In a large, heavy-bottomed saucepan, stir together the rice, sugar, nutmeg, salt, and milk. Cover and over very low heat bring to a simmer. Simmer very gently, stirring often, for 20 minutes. Add raisins and cook for 5 to 10 minutes longer or until rice is tender and the milk is thickened and creamy. Stir in butter and vanilla. Add more milk, if desired, for an even creamier pudding.

If serving immediately, spoon into bowls and sprinkle with cinnamon. If serving later, transfer to an airtight container and pour in about ⅓ cup (75 mL) more milk to keep the surface moist. Let cool, cover and refrigerate. Stir milk into the pudding before serving. Makes 4 servings.

ORANGE GINGER OR ORANGE APRICOT RICE PUDDING: Make rice pudding according to the method above. Instead of the nutmeg, use 1½ teaspoons (7 mL) coarsely grated orange rind, and instead of the raisins, add either 1 tablespoon (15 mL) chopped crystallized ginger or ½ cup (125 mL) thinly sliced dried apricots. Omit the vanilla and cinnamon.

TOASTED ALMOND RICE PUDDING: Top any of the versions above with 2 tablespoons (25 mL) toasted slivered almonds just before serving.

*Elizabeth Baird*
Toronto

## *The* Rice Pudding

I spent the first five years or so of our marriage searching for the recipe for the Perfect Rice Pudding my husband remembered from his childhood. I tried every recipe I came across, some starting from raw rice, some from cooked rice. Some came close, some were awful, but at last I was able to consolidate the best points into *The* Rice Pudding. This makes lots of pudding to feed a family of five.

| | |
|---|---|
| ¾ | cup short-grain rice (175 mL) |
| 5 to 6 | cups milk (1.25 L to 1.5 L) |
| ¼ | teaspoon salt (1 mL) |
| 3 | eggs |
| ¼ to ½ | cup sugar, brown or white (50 mL to 125 mL) |
| 1 | teaspoon vanilla (5 mL) |
| ½ | cup raisins (125 mL) |

In the top of a double boiler, combine rice, milk, and salt. Cover and cook over low heat for about 1 hour, or until very thick. In a small bowl, beat eggs and sugar. Stir some of the pudding into the eggs, then stir all back into the pudding. Add vanilla and raisins and stir well. (The heat of the pudding cooks the eggs.) Chill and serve.

*Margaret Pointing*
Mississauga, Ontario

## Christmas Cake in Two Tones

We have a favourite Christmas cake that is a great compromise for those who have trouble making the ultimate fruit-cake decision. It is dark on the bottom, light on top. I first had some when I was living with two other young men in Toronto, fresh out of university. Bill was our cook, and a good one, but his mother was even better. She sent some of her cake back with Bill one New Year's. I think of it as "Mabel's Cake."

DARK BATTER

5 ¼ cups dark, seedless raisins (1.25 mL + 50 mL)
1 ½ cups currants (375 mL)
⅜ cup diced candied pineapple (60 mL)
⅜ cup red glacé cherries, halved (60 mL)
⅜ cup green glacé cherries, halved (60 mL)
1 ⅛ cup chopped mixed candied peel or mixed fruit-cake fruits (275 mL)
1 ½ cups coarsely chopped blanched almonds (375 mL)
⅜ cups brandy (or sherry or apple juice) (60 mL)
1 ⅛ cups butter, at room temperature (275 mL)
1 ½ cups light-brown sugar, packed (375 mL)
6 large eggs
4 ½ tablespoons molasses (60 mL)
¾ teaspoon vanilla (3 mL)
1 ⅞ cups stirred but unsifted all-purpose flour (450 mL)
⅜ teaspoon baking soda (1.5 mL)
1 ⅛ teaspoons salt (5.5 mL)
3 teaspoons cinnamon (15 mL)
¾ teaspoon ground ginger (3 mL)
¾ teaspoon nutmeg (3 mL)
⅜ teaspoon mace (1.5 mL)
¼ teaspoon cloves (1 mL)

LIGHT BATTER

½ cup diced candied pineapple (125 mL)
1 ¼ cups (½ pound) red glacé cherries, halved (300 mL, or 250 g)
1 ¼ cups (½ pound) green glacé cherries, halved (300 mL, or 250 g)
2 ¾ cups (1 pound) light raisins (650 mL, or 500 g)
1 ¼ cups (½ pound) chopped mixed candied peel or fruit-cake fruit (300 mL, or 250 g)
½ cup unsweetened, medium-cut coconut (125 mL)
1 ⅔ cups (½ pound) coarsely chopped blanched almonds (300 mL, or 250 g)
¼ cup brandy (or sherry or apple juice) (50 mL)

1    cup butter, at room temperature (250 mL)
1    cup granulated sugar (250 mL)
4    large eggs
2½   cups stirred but unsifted all-purpose flour (625 mL)
¾    teaspoon salt (3 mL)
½    cup unsweetened pineapple juice (125 mL)
½    teaspoon pure almond extract (2 mL)

Using two very large bowls, combine all fruit and nuts for dark batter in one of the bowls and light batter in the other bowl. Sprinkle the required measurement of brandy (or sherry or apple juice) in each bowl. Toss fruits and nuts thoroughly with the brandy.

Cover each bowl and let soak four hours or overnight. Label bowls "dark" and "light" to avoid any mix-ups. Prepare three 9 x 5 x 2-inch (23 x 13 x 5 cm) loaf pans with a triple layer of buttered waxed paper or a double layer of buttered foil. To make dark batter, in a medium bowl, cream together butter and brown sugar until light, then beat in eggs until thoroughly blended. Stir in molasses and vanilla. In a small bowl, combine flour, baking soda, salt, and spices, then add to creamed mixture and combine well. Add batter to "dark" fruit and nuts, and combine roughly until all fruit is coated with batter. Turn batter equally into the three prepared pans to half fill, pushing batter down firmly and into corners and smoothing surface.

To make light batter, in a medium bowl, cream together the butter and sugar until light, then beat in eggs until well blended. Beat in flour and salt. Stir in juice and almond extract and mix until batter is smooth. Add the batter to the "light" fruits and nuts and combine thoroughly. Divide batter equally among the three pans on top of the dark batter. Push batter down firmly and into corners and smooth tops.

The batter will completely fill the three loaf pans, but it only rises slightly when baked. Fill a pan with water and set it on the bottom rack of the oven. Preheat oven to 275°F (135°C). Set cakes on middle rack and bake for 2 hours and 20 minutes.

Cool, peel off paper, and double wrap in plastic bags. Store in refrigerator or freezer. Cold cake slices perfectly.

*Jamie Hockin*
Ottawa

## MUFFIN DAY MUFFINS

During the war, when I was six, I lived with my grandparents in Kitsilano. One strong memory from that time in my life is Muffin Day. The muffins arrived in a horsedrawn rubber-tired 4x Bakery Limited van. I've been searching for the taste of those muffins ever since, and a generation later, I found it. The recipe is completely forgiving; the muffins will be great no matter what mistakes or changes you make. For example: if you don't have buttermilk, used soured milk — add a few drops of vinegar or lemon juice to sweet milk. If you don't have enough bran, add some wheat germ. If you aren't fond of raisins, use chopped dates; if you don't like dates, use chopped apricots, or peanuts, or chocolate chips. If you're super-busy, line your muffin tins with paper baking cups, but don't try to peel the paper off until the muffins are cool.

    3  cups buttermilk (750 mL)
    3  cups bran (750 mL)
    1  cup oil (250 mL)
    3  eggs
    1  cup brown sugar (250 mL)
    1  cup white sugar (250 mL)
    1  teaspoon vanilla (5 mL)
    1  cup golden raisins (250 mL)
    3  cups flour (750 mL)
    3  teaspoons baking powder (12 mL)
    3  teaspoons baking soda (12 mL)
    2  teaspoons salt (10 mL)

Stir together buttermilk and bran; set aside.

In the largest bowl of your mixer, combine oil, eggs, sugar, and vanilla; stir in raisins. In a separate bowl, sift together flour, baking powder, baking soda, and salt. With as few strokes as possible, alternately add the flour mixture and the bran mixture to the oil and eggs mixture. Spoon into well-greased muffin tins and bake at 350°F (180°C) for 25 minutes.

Makes 40 good-sized muffins that freeze well and taste great hot or cold.

*Patricia Barrett*
Vancouver

## Peanut Butter Squares

½  cup corn syrup (125 mL)
½  cup brown sugar (125 mL)
1  cup peanut butter (250 mL)
2  cups cornflakes (500 mL)
1  cup Rice Krispies (250 mL)

In a small pan, stir together corn syrup and brown sugar. Heat slowly, stirring, being careful not to boil.

When the sugar is all melted, stir in peanut butter, cornflakes and Rice Krispies. Mix well and pour into 8 x 8-inch (20 cm square) pan. Chill and cut into squares.

*Dorothy M. Denston*
Peterborough, Ontario

## Puffed Wheat Squares

This recipe used to be printed on the side of every bag of Puffed Wheat, but they stopped including it some years ago. Imagine my delight to rediscover the old, familiar recipe in the family-farm cookbook. Now I can revive my childhood memories any day by simply whipping up another batch.

⅓  cup butter (75 mL)
½  cup corn syrup (125 mL)
1  cup brown sugar (250 mL)
2  tablespoons cocoa (25 mL)
1  teaspoon vanilla (5 mL)
8  cups Puffed Wheat (2 L)

Melt butter in saucepan. Add corn syrup, sugar, cocoa, and vanilla.

When syrup just begins to bubble, remove from heat. Add Puffed Wheat and mix well.

Put into buttered 9 x 12-inch (23 x 30 cm) pan. Press down well with spoon. Cut into squares when cool.

*Debra Lamb*
London, Ontario

## Easy Chocolate Cake

2    tablespoons espresso powder or instant-coffee granules
(25 mL)

½    cup boiling water (125 mL)

2¼    cups all-purpose flour (550 mL)

2    cups granulated sugar (500 mL)

¾    cup sifted unsweetened cocoa powder (175 mL)

1½    teaspoons baking powder (7 mL)

1½    teaspoons baking soda (7 mL)

1    teaspoon salt (5 mL)

1¾    cups buttermilk (425 mL)

2    eggs, beaten

¼    cup vegetable oil (50 mL)

2    teaspoons vanilla (10 mL)

In a small bowl, dissolve espresso powder or instant-coffee granules in boiling water and let cool.

In a large bowl, stir together flour, sugar, cocoa powder, baking powder, baking soda, and salt. Beat in buttermilk, eggs, vegetable oil, vanilla, and espresso mixture. Beat for 2 minutes.

Heat oven to 350°F (180°C).

Line the bottom of a 13 x 9-inch (33 x 22 cm) cake pan with waxed paper, then grease the waxed paper. Pour in cake batter and place on middle rack in oven. Bake for about 45 minutes, or until top springs back when touched lightly. Let cool on rack for 20 minutes.

Remove from pan and let cool completely. Spread top with chocolate icing (recipe follows).

CHOCOLATE ICING

½    cup sifted unsweetened cocoa powder (125 mL)

¼    cup granulated sugar (50 mL)

4    teaspoons cornstarch (20 mL)

½    cup buttermilk (125 mL)

½    teaspoon vanilla (2 mL)

In a heavy saucepan, mix cocoa powder, sugar, and cornstarch. Whisk in buttermilk and keep stirring until smooth.

Whisking constantly, bring to a simmer over medium heat, then simmer an additional 2 minutes. Remove from heat.

Stir in vanilla. Let cool for 45 minutes or until thickened, stirring occasionally. Makes about 1 cup.

*Anne Lindsay*
Toronto

## Marble Mocha Cheesecake

| | |
|---|---|
| 1½ | cups chocolate wafer crumbs (375 mL) |
| 2 | tablespoons granulated sugar (25 mL) |
| 2 | tablespoons water (25 mL) |
| 1 | tablespoon butter or margarine (15 mL) |
| 1⅔ | cups 5% ricotta cheese (400 mL) |
| ⅓ | cup softened light cream cheese (75 mL) |
| ¾ | cup granulated sugar (175 mL) |
| 1 | egg |
| ⅓ | cup light sour cream or 2% yogurt (175 mL) |
| 1 | tablespoon all-purpose flour (15 mL) |
| 1 | teaspoon vanilla (5 mL) |
| 1½ | teaspoons instant-coffee granules (7 mL) |
| 1½ | tablespoons hot water (7 mL) |
| 3 | tablespoons melted chocolate (45 mL) |

In a medium bowl, combine chocolate wafer crumbs, 2 tablespoons (25 mL) granulated sugar, 2 tablespoons (25 mL) water, and butter. Spray an 8-inch (20 cm) springform pan with vegetable-oil spray. Press chocolate-crumb mixture into bottom and up sides of the pan.

In a large bowl or food processor, beat together ricotta cheese, cream cheese, ¾ cup (175 mL) granulated sugar, egg, sour cream, flour, and vanilla until well blended.

Dissolve coffee granules in hot water; add to batter and mix until incorporated.

Preheat oven to 350°F (180°C).

Pour batter into springform pan and smooth top. Drizzle melted chocolate on top. Draw knife or spatula through chocolate and batter several times to create marbling.

Bake for 35 to 40 minutes. Centre should be slightly loose. Let cool and refrigerate several hours before serving.

*Rose Reisman*
Toronto

## FROZEN CHOCOLATE RASPBERRY MERINGUE CAKE

MERINGUE

| | |
|---|---|
| 4 | egg whites |
| ¾ | cup icing sugar (175 mL) |
| 3 | tablespoons cocoa (45 mL) |
| ¾ | cup granulated sugar (175 mL) |
| ¼ | cup chopped semi-sweet chocolate (50 mL) |

FILLING

4 cups (1L) fruit or chocolate sorbet (I use 2 packages, 500 mL each, Gelato Fresco chocolate raspberry marble sorbet)

SAUCE

| | |
|---|---|
| 4 | ounces bittersweet or semi-sweet chocolate, chopped (125 g) |
| 2 | tablespoons cocoa (25 mL) |
| 3 | tablespoons corn syrup (45 mL) |
| ½ | cup water (or coffee or raspberry juice) (125 mL) |
| 1 | teaspoon pure vanilla extract (5 mL) |

To make meringue: Place egg whites in a large glass or stainless-steel bowl. Reserve. Sift and stir icing sugar and cocoa. Reserve.

Beat egg whites until opaque. Very slowly beat in granulated sugar and continue beating until stiff. Fold in cocoa-sugar mixture. Fold in chopped chocolate.

Spread meringue mixture into two 9-inch (24 cm) circles on cookie sheet lined with parchment paper. Bake in preheated 250°F (125°C) oven for 1½ hours, or until meringues feel dry. Cool.

Meanwhile, prepare filling. Line a 9-inch (24 cm) springform pan with plastic wrap. Soften sorbet and spoon into the pan. Cover well and freeze.

When meringues are cool, trim to fit into another 9-inch (24 cm) springform pan. Place one meringue in the bottom of the pan. Remove sorbet "cake" from the other pan and place over the meringue. Top with remaining meringue. Wrap well and freeze.

To make sauce: combine chopped chocolate, cocoa, corn syrup, and water in a small heavy saucepan. Cook very gently until smooth. Add vanilla. To serve, dust cake with cocoa. Drizzle each slice with sauce. Makes 12 to 16 servings.

*Bonnie Stern*
Toronto


## CANADIAN COFFEE

In the interest of Canadian unity, here is my recipe for *Canadian* Coffee. The secret is to travel across the country to collect all the ingredients, then enjoy the coffee with a neighbour from another province. Cheers!

- 1    ounce rye from the Prairie provinces (30 mL)
- ½    ounce brandy from the Niagara peninsula (15 mL)
- ½    ounce maple syrup from the Eastern Townships (15 mL)

Add coffee. Top with whipped cream from a dairy in the Maritimes or British Columbia. Serve on a coaster that says "Chimo" from either of the territories.

*Stuart W. Holloway*
Acton, Ontario


## HOT CHOCOLATE WITH RASPBERRY SCHNAPPS

My sister and I are hooked on this hot chocolate, which is thoroughly decadent but very comforting on a freezing Ottawa night.

Several spoonfuls of No-Name hot chocolate mix
Boiling water
1   ounce raspberry schnapps (30 mL)
Marshmallows

In a huge pottery mug, mix hot chocolate mix with just enough warm water to make a loose paste. Add boiling water to ½ inch (1 cm) from the top. Stir vigorously. When mixed well, add raspberry schnapps. Top with marshmallows.

*Jennifer Tsai*
Ottawa

# Conversations with Writers II: Robertson Davies, Part I

*"I'm getting to be quite an old party," says Roberston Davies at one point in this, the first of two interviews that appear here. And, I suppose, measured in years, he was — by my calculation he'd have been seventy-eight when we talked this time. But he was also at the height of his writing powers, and, as you'll see, at the height of his gracious and erudite conversational powers, too.*

PETER GZOWSKI The publication of each new work by Robertson Davies is an occasion in this country, and so, I have to say, is a visit by Robertson Davies to *Morningside*. This morning marks both such events. The new work is called *Murther and Walking Spirits*, and to talk about that, as well as perhaps some other matters, Robertson Davies joins me now. Good morning, sir.

ROBERTSON DAVIES Good Morning.

PG *Murther and Walking Spirits*. Do you know where you're going when you write page one?

RD To a very great extent, yes, I do, but I never know exactly how things are going to end, because I find that I can plan a book or view the shape up to about two-thirds of the way through, and from then on it's found its own way and it develops as it will.

PG But quite a lot of the structure exists in your head, then, as you touch page one.

RD Oh, yes, yes, indeed.

PG Because I'm just realizing as I'm beginning this interview: I'm not sure where I'm going, and I'm a little afraid of asides, and I wonder if you're ever afraid of asides when you write, because once again the energy of your mind takes you down every avenue from church architecture to popular culture to . . . And I think, Rein that in. Do you have to worry about that?

RD Yes, I do, and critics complain about it a great deal because they hate that sort of thing. They want you to pursue a kind of straight line right down the middle, but I find from the letters that I get that readers like it. They like a discursive novel and I like to be discursive because I do feel that the odd bits that I put in add to the story and have a bearing on it.

PG I must say I enjoy them and sometimes I chuckle and have quite a good time and sometimes I think you've just put something in perhaps because it amused you at the time.

RD I know. For instance, there's one, I think the first one that occurs in that book, when the man who has been killed suddenly realizes that he's hungry. Now why should a man who is simply a spirit be hungry? Apparently the digestion process in the body goes on for about forty-five minutes after death. I think that's fascinating. A friend of mine who is a biologist told me that, then he told me how it was found out, and it was all intensely interesting and I wanted to get that in because I felt people would like to know.

PG Well, you said the man got hungry, but patently he didn't get hungry until after you found out that his digestive system was still burbling away.

RD Yes, yes.

PG So . . . you went for that.

RD Oh, indeed, I did, yes.

PG Perhaps I'll ask you about ghosts, because ghosts are among your subjects. You're fascinated by them, believe in them, think that they're there. But the ghost of old Gilmartin — if I can leap right to the end, and we're not giving away anything here — here he is hovering around in the spirit world on the other side, and his wife, his widow now, is trying to get in touch with him.

RD Yes.

PG So she goes to a spiritualist in hopes she can make contact with the other side, and Gilmartin can't figure out how to do it.

RD And she can't do it. That's one of the things that I wanted to bring out in the book, and to bring out as amusing as possible but in a determined way. I don't think that communication with dead people is possible, and I think that a lot of what passes for it in seances and so forth is not actually crooked but a kind of delusion. You see, there are a lot of things going on apart from our obvious and tangible life which are very hard to cope with, and the fact that there may be somebody answering those mediums who is not the person they think it is seems to me to be perfectly possible. You know, one of the fascinating things about mediums is that a medium never brings a message from somebody who doesn't sound like the medium. And when the medium is supposed to be talking to Napoleon, it's funny how Napoleon sounds exactly like Mrs. Jones or whoever it is that's the medium.

PG Well, your spiritualist doesn't sound exactly like herself, but she doesn't sound like Gil, either.

RD No, she doesn't. She sounds as if she were in a kind of mystical dream. And I think that is perfectly possible. She's sincere, but she's on the wrong track.

PG But I thought the possibility existed that someone was speaking through her because he says, "Who is that? It's not me speaking through her, but it's not her, either." Doesn't he say that?

RD Yes, I think he does say that. Yes. Well, who is it? I don't know. But I've read a good deal along these lines and I've never read anything that convinced me anyone had made contact with someone who was dead. Though they've often heard strange things in seances.

PG But you were in touch with him?

RD Oh, yes.

PG The late Gilmartin. You were in touch with him?

RD Yes. Well, one of the things I wanted to bring out in the book was what conceivably might happen to a man whose life was interrupted. Gilmartin did not live his life out; he was murdered when he was in his very early forties. And he wanted a number of things. He was very angry with the man who'd killed him. He wanted to revenge himself on him. And he wanted to complete his life and to make a kind of finished thing of his existence. And he couldn't quite do that, but he did discover a way of finding out who he was, where he came from, and what kind of creature he belonged to. And he also discovered that vengeance was for him impossible, but vengeance was possible from somewhere else. And the man who murdered him suffers at the end of the book what I think is a very dismal fate indeed. Nothing crushes him, nothing kills him, as a revengeful ghost might do. But he discovers that he's got to live the rest of his own life, which could be thirty-five or forty years, with a consciousness that he had done a very evil thing.

PG And couldn't have that guilt expiated.

RD No, and Gil couldn't expiate him and neither could anyone else. He wanted somebody to get him off the hook. It couldn't be done. That's real vengeance.

PG Where does that priest come from? The priest who refuses the confession? Wholly from one's imagination?

RD I think you've met him, Peter. He was not entirely imaginary. I knew him quite well. I think you knew him, and a great many people knew him who were in the position of that man who in my book consulted him.

PG And those are enough clues?

RD  I think those are enough clues. If you are looking for a superb, very fine priest in the University of Toronto twenty years ago, and you find a very handsome man with very black eyebrows and extremely elegant shoes, you won't be able to figure out who it is.

PG  That's as close as I've ever heard you come to identifying one of your characters.

RD  Well, yes, but he was a man whom I knew and admired enormously and I tried to portray him as I think he was in my book.

PG  You said that Gil finds a way to complete his life. But he doesn't. You do. I mean the method is an internal festival of films, a festival which turns eternally. But he doesn't go to that festival seeking what he finds there. He goes there serendipitously.

RD  He discovers that he is no longer in charge of what happens to him. He is an object, not a subject. He goes to a film festival expecting to see a lot of fine old historical films. But the films that he sees are depictions of his forebears — the way that they've lived, the way that they've suffered, the things which have almost crushed them and in some cases have crushed them. And he discovers that they have lived lives which, in terms of what they were given and where they were, were truly heroic. And that is one of the points I wanted to make in the book. That so many lives, I think a majority of lives, have a strong measure of heroism in them.

PG  Even the lives of people we don't regard at all as heroic.

RD  Oh, absolutely. The people who slave along, doing the best they can, under very difficult circumstances, people who've been dealt a hand of poor cards in life, but who play it as well as it can be played, these people are heroic. They're not heroic on the Julius Caesar and Alexander the Great scale, but they're heroic insofar as they make it through to the end manfully — or womanfully, if such a word is permissible — and they are people of genuine heroic dimension.

PG  I don't want to pursue this line any farther than this question. And I even apologize as I ask it, because I think it is often demeaning to the richness of the imagination. But it's impossible for the reader even vaguely aware of the details of your own life not to see the parallels between you and the central character, the family and the newspaper business, all of those things. Are the ancestors, from the Welsh badlands and the Loyalists from New York, are they all parallel to your own genealogy?

RD  They form a kind of skeleton on which I've hung the story. Because indeed my mother's family came up from the States at the time of the Revolution. They were Dutch people and they were Loyalists. And my father's people came from Wales, because of grim necessity, as did so many people who've come to Canada. These are facts, but the actual figures, and the way in which they perform, and what they do, is 98-per-cent imaginary.

PG  If I can just come back and talk about the technique for a moment. One of the occasions on which we talked was 1979, as our notes make it around here. Which was, I think, when *Leaven of Malice* was being staged at Hart House, and I had the effrontery to ask you if you would write *Leaven of Malice* differently if you were writing it again in the seventies. And you said, "That's a novel of immense complication among a very large number of people and now I'm interested in inner complication in a single character." Could we have presaged *Murther and Walking Spirits* from that?

RD  Absolutely. You see, essentially everything that happens in the book is a part of the narrator, Connor Gilmartin, and he recognizes this, and he recognizes from what a remarkable background he has come. He sees that he is part of it and he realizes that he is not the end of it, not the completion of it. Because there is a child in prospect. He will occupy a sort of ancestral position towards that child.

PG  That's a very different energizing factor — I should have a better literary term — than some of the other novels, which have taken a single event and followed its ripples through all kinds of interconnected lives, and all carried by the energy of those events, each event blending into another. Now you're working without the net of that plot.

RD  Yes, that's right. I am trying to probe a single character by discovering where he came from and what sort of bricks and mortar he's made of.

PG  Is this a maturing view of the world?

RD  I hope it is. You see, I'm getting to be quite an old party. And if I have got any coherent notion about life it ought to come along pretty soon. And I'm trying to express something of that in this book. I think, from responses I've had to it, it finds an echo in the spirit of a great many people.

PG   Some people are saying it's a more forgiving book, a more under-
     standing book. That you're gentler about humanity's foibles and
     fables than you have been before. I wasn't quite as aware of it.

RD   I would like to think that that was true. I think that the book shows
     a kind of gentleness towards the strange behaviour of humanity, and
     the sources from which strange behaviour springs, than things I've
     written previously.

PG   More . . . tolerant?

RD   Not necessarily tolerant. More understanding, perhaps. Tolerance
     is a rather patronizing attitude. Understanding is not. Sometimes
     people have said to me, "Oh, compassion is the great thing in a
     novel." But it seems to me that compassion is rather a patronizing
     thing. If you are compassionate towards someone, you're rather
     putting him on a shelf below yourself and being very nice to him
     because he is not quite up to your level. I don't look at life that way.

PG   Is the complicated fabric that eventually gives the world Connor
     Gilmartin a uniquely Canadian one because of it?

RD   It is very Canadian, because he is the result of a union of one half
     of his family, which has an American Loyalist background; the other
     half of his family was connected to Great Britain. And that creates a
     tension and a pull in his family life, which is a very difficult one, and
     which has continued for two or three generations. It affects his father,
     as well, the pull towards Europe or the pull towards the United
     States. And these are tensions which Canadians experience all the
     time. What I try to indicate is that, somewhere in those tensions, a
     unity and an understanding and a realization will occur. And the pull
     won't go totally in one direction or the other.

PG   Canadians don't love Canada, you write, we just sort of *are*
     Canadians. I'm not quoting you with precision, but that's the
     thought. We accept a relationship with the country rather than cel-
     ebrating it. Have I got you wrong?

RD   No, you haven't. I think that Canadians in general, the average
     Canadian, if it's possible to use such a term, never thinks of himself
     as loving his country. He would think perhaps it would be pretentious
     to say that. He looks to the south and sees people proclaiming noisily
     that they love their country, and he thinks, I don't want to be like
     that. But people in Canada who think a lot about Canada I think have
     a great deal of worry and disquiet and misgiving about the country,

which is a kind of affection. It is a desire that it should not go amiss, that it should find its path, that some kind of chart should be found for our destiny. Or our destiny should in some way declare itself. Because, you see, at this very moment — as you very well know and as you've indeed said yourself, I've heard you do it — we are in a great crisis in Canada, which I think of as a sort of psychological civil war. And a psychological civil war is a very much more difficult thing to fight than an obvious guns-and-sabres civil war, as they had in the States. And that a country like Canada, which is so reluctant to think of itself, if I may use the expression, metaphysically as Canada, should be confronted with a psychological civil war is a really tough destiny. But we've somehow or other got to find our way out of it.

PG How do you defuse a psychological civil war? At least a physical civil war you can fight.

RD You fight a physical civil war and in the end you have an uneasy peace, as they're having in the United States, where Southerners still think of themselves as Southerners, and when you talk to them late at night you find they still have a very great grievance. Well, now we somehow or other have got to deal with our grievances. Grievances which involve the two founding nations and also the native people, who are making a very, very strong and convincing case for their place in this country. That is a situation of extraordinary complexity and difficulty, and we've got to manage it with a great deal of psychological skill and subtlety. What worries me, and I know worries enormous numbers of other Canadians, is that we haven't got people with the psychological skill and subtlety at the head of things.

PG Can I dare to offer a thought to you which arises from contemplating *Murther and Walking Spirits*, which is that the people who don't love Canada — which isn't to say they dislike it but, as you've been saying, love it without passion — are those of us who are around now. But as I contemplate all of the historical threads in the making of old Gil, I think each generation back is closer to the *land* than the generation before it, and I'm wondering if the people who had to take arduous journeys by canoe to get here, or fight their way across the stormy seas, or were fleeing poverty, didn't have an attachment to the *land* in which they settled. An attachment to the land that was a love and that's missing in our lives because we are remote from our land.

RD  That is true: we're remote from our land, and also there is something historical about it. You see, now an enormous amount of Canadians go south for the winter. That was a thing that nobody could do until the last forty years. Or they travel all over the place or are always meeting someone who's just back from Guadeloupe, or Vienna, or somewhere or other. We travel endlessly. It's really difficult to develop a strong, passionate attachment for your own patch of country when you're always jazzing off to someplace that is entirely different. I think that this is just one of the things that isn't anybody's fault, but I think that it is a fact.

PG  Is this the beginning of another trilogy?

RD  I don't quite see it at the moment. I want to write some books which have all of the things in them that my reviewers dislike, which are entirely discursive — I'm already famous for that.

PG  No plot.

RD  No plot.

PG  Are you going to change characters every couple of pages?

RD  Not even have characters, just opinions and . . .

PG  But you'll have songs? You must have songs. I think you have more snippets of song, hymn: "Life Is Like a Mountain Railway" appears in here. This is one of the great songs.

RD  This is true, and, you see, people, particularly the kind of people I write about, are enormously caught up with music. This is something that James Joyce knew very well, and his great books, particularly *Finnegans Wake*, are full of snatches and parodies of remembered music. I think this is true of a great many people, and I try to get something of that into my own books.

PG  I find more than ever — I don't have your total oeuvre at the fingertips of my mind — but there are more musical references than ever. And in one passage, someone talks about "I hear the books," and there are all kinds of references to Noël Coward as writer . . .

RD  Yes.

PG  . . . or Walt Whitman. I mean, the language is to be heard and many of the sentences in here I think are to be heard.

RD  Oh, decidedly. I write my books — not consciously but because I can't help it, it's the way I have to do things — I write them as if I was speaking them, and I would like it if people heard them instead of skimming them very quickly in their heads. As for music, there are things in that book which I put in because I thought that they were intensely interesting. One is the origin of the song "Yankee Doodle," which began as a British mockery of the Americans, which the Americans took up and made a national song. That's a fascinating change and that's an American revolution in itself.

PG  After you knew that, you managed to find an occasion in which "Yankee Doodle" would be sung.

RD  Yes, because originally it was a song jeering the American troops and I suppose the British soldier thought it was just wildly funny until they discovered what a tough character Yankee Doodle really was.

PG  When is your next book out? Do you have one for next fall you have to come up with?

RD  No! [Laughs]

PG  Why not?

RD  Because, I'm getting . . . well, I keep telling people I'm suffering from decline and waning powers and general debility and all of those awful things you used to read about in advertisements. I've got to have a little time to draw breath.

PG  Well, don't spend a heck of a lot of time drawing breath, we need you writing more.

RD  Well, that's very nice of you to say. Okay, I'll do my best to keep on.

PG  Robertson Davies, thank you.

# CONVERSATIONS WITH WRITERS II:
# ROBERTSON DAVIES, PART II

Anthony Jenkins, The Globe and Mail

*And keep on he did — both writing and, again as you'll see, weaving his spells as he talked. My only regret in all the chats I had with Robertson Davies over the years is that I never did figure out what to call him. Rob? I couldn't bring myself to say it. Dr. Davies? I suppose so. Maybe just . . . the Master.*

PETER GZOWSKI Robertson Davies is internationally respected as one of Canada's leading men of letters, and his productivity has been undeterred by age. At eighty-one he has just published his eleventh novel, called *The Cunning Man*, and in typical Davies fashion it covers a variety of subjects, including, in this case, medicine, cannibalism, and Shakespeare's constipation. Robertson Davies is with me now. Good morning, sir.

ROBERTSON DAVIES Good morning, good morning.

PG I thought you were going to quit. I thought when *Murther and Walking Spirits* came out in 1991, you said that was the end.

RD Well, I know I said that, but the habits of a lifetime are not easily broken, and what would I do if I didn't go on?

PG Well, some of the characters from *Murther and Walking Spirits* appear in *The Cunning Man*.

RD Yes.

PG So does Dunstan Ramsay from *Fifth Business*.

RD That's right.

PG I wonder if some of these people have taken over your life.

RD Well, it could be, but I wouldn't be a good judge of that.

PG But do they have lives of their own? Do they exist for you?

RD In a sense, yes, but I'm hesitant to talk about that kind of thing because some authors are so pretentious about their characters, as though they were real people whom they had mysteriously brought into the world. And that's pushing it a little far.

PG You mean you made them up?

RD I made them up out of my own head. And, as we used to say when I was a schoolboy, lots of wood left.

PG You set a lot of your fiction in Toronto, but *The Cunning Man* is really almost a history of the artistic and religious elements of *this* place and *that* time of the postwar city. Is that a city that's gone?

RD Not entirely. It's a city that's changed radically, but it was a very, very interesting change. And I have been fortunate in having a chance to watch it. I came here to be a schoolboy when I was fourteen, and had a chance to see the city as it was then. And I've been watching it ever since. And the change has been fantastic. From, really, a kind of colonial place to a great big international, metropolitan city.

PG    What about the change of values, though? The values of the time that you write about in *The Cunning Man*, the church defines many of them, the connection with Empire defines many of them. Have the values gone?

RD    Oh, yes, they have. History outside Canada has conditioned that. You couldn't have that gigantic 1939–45 war and the subsequent decline in prestige of Great Britain and that sort of thing without it affecting Canada. And also what goes on in the United States affects us a good deal. And history has a great part, well, everything to do with making Canada what it is today.

PG    What about the changing nature of Canada itself and the way we think about it? Your hero, Jonathan Hullah, talks about our preoccupation with sincerity. He deplores that because he thinks it strips life of beauty. Has that changed?

RD    No. It used to be very much so that a Canadian was regarded as a sort of Honest John, whom you would trust with anything. We still cherish that and cherish a kind of myth of innocence and sincerity — which is a myth, but it's our myth. It's not like the American myth, which is the myth of success, and the clever guy, and the fellow who makes it big in the world. We don't have that quite so much. We tend more to the sincere, good, honest, decent person whose word is his bond. And of course that is very far from being the picture of a typical Canadian, but it's the one we cherish. You see, we have the reputation of being great international peacekeepers. And that is a good reputation to have. But we don't want to have with it the reputation of Mr. Good Guy, you know, who can always be called upon to rush with bandages and a peanut butter sandwich whenever anyone's in trouble.

PG    Do you sense a certain hypocrisy in the way we proclaim our own virtuousness and don't always act virtuously?

RD    Any virtue that is proclaimed is bound to be hypocritical.

PG    Did you just make that up?

RD    No, well, I didn't. It's just the truth.

PG    No, but it sounds as if it should be in *Bartlett* or something.

RD    Well, I don't know.

PG    It will be.

RD    This self-regarding sincerity is bound to be somewhat hypocritical. It is insincere to think about your own sincerity, if you follow what I mean.

PG But if you can fake sincerity you have it made, as people say. What about your fascination with the word "cunning," as in *The Cunning Man*.

RD Well, that is an expression that used to be, and may still be, somewhat current in the remoter parts of rural Great Britain. The cunning man I can remember from when I was a boy and used to visit my father's place in Wales; there were cunning men in the district, and cunning women, too. The cunning women and the cunning men were people who would help you with illnesses. The cunning man was sometimes a bone-setter. He was sometimes a horse doctor. But he was also somebody who might help you to find lost objects, or he might help you if your herd was beginning to look rather peaky. He might tell you someone had put a spell on it, and that he would take the spell off. And if you wanted to put a spell on your neighbour's flock maybe he could be persuaded to do that, too. He was a kind of person people consulted, as I think nowadays city people consult psychoanalysts and the people they call counsellors — people who are supposed to know more than the rest of us.

PG So when did Jonathan Hullah begin to take shape in the way you've described him, both metaphorically and really?

RD Oh, I've been thinking about him for a very long time. And thinking about cunning men and their place in the modern world, because, well, he is a modern cunning man. The old cunning men in the seventeenth century were sort of country wizards.

PG Wizards? Wizards appeal to you?

RD Well, yes. People think of a wizard as a fellow who goes around in a cloak and casts spells all the time. Not necessarily so. He may be just somebody who knows a lot of things that the rest of the neighbourhood doesn't know. He knows who may have committed a robbery, he knows who may have got a girl into trouble and who isn't admitting it. He knows all kinds of things that aren't general knowledge. Maybe a cunning man nowadays might go into journalism. I don't know.

PG Can I ask you a little bit about journalism? This is, in a sense, a digression. One of the premises of the book — one of the devices of the book is to have a younger journalist exploring Dr. Hullah's mind and looking at his life.

RD Yes.

PG    And he muses about whether it's — and this is the theme of the whole book in many ways — he muses about whether she, or anyone, can ever capture truth.

RD    Exactly. And I don't believe they can. Any experienced judge or courtroom lawyer will tell you how extraordinarily varied the evidence may be which a whole lot of obviously quite honest people give about a certain incident. They all see, for instance, an accident in a rather different way.

PG    I don't know if you ever took that undergraduate psychology course which would begin — they would have an unexpected event in front of the class. Someone would fake a shooting or something, then they'd have various people recount what they'd seen, and they'd all be different.

RD    Yes.

PG    When were you conscious of the limitations of journalism? When you were a young journalist?

RD    Oh, yes. You see, I grew up in a family that were all journalists. All my family were in the history of the business. And we were very well aware of the fact that although we did the best we could, as honestly as we could, we weren't uttering final truths. How were you going to find that out? Often you did find out something — long after it had been reported and had vanished from the public consciousness — that offered a whole perspective on what had happened.

PG    You must have been a very good young journalist, because I didn't know that. When I was a young journalist I thought I was writing truth and then entering it in the daily press every day. Maybe not truth, but accuracy, which is probably not always the same thing. But I was quite sure then, and later — certainly as a magazine writer, I had the conceit that a magazine profile could actually summarize somebody or tell the truth about them.

RD    I don't think profiles can possibly do that even when they are extremely searching, because it is one person's personality sifted through another, and inevitably the sifting personality colours what is said. I'm very much aware when I'm interviewed by some newspaper people that what is going to appear is in actual fact a portrait of the interviewer. Because they bring with them, when they come to see me, presuppositions and ideas of what I am and what I ought to be and what I am not. And then those somehow will find their way into what they write. This is not necessarily the whole truth. In fact, I don't know how you get at the whole truth. I don't pretend to know the whole truth about myself.

PG  Are novels true?

RD  No, novels are creations, which are supposed to have the ring of truth. But again it is a thing which admits a second look. Now you read a very great novel, like Tolstoy's *War and Peace*. And you can think about the characters in it and get an idea of them which is entirely different from that which Tolstoy has described. And it is interesting: at the end of that book the beautiful, charming, delightful, irresistible girl Natasha is gradually getting to be a fat housewife who wears spectacles and is pretty sharp with her husband. If you developed that you'd get a very interesting story.

PG  Does it bother you when people see *clefs* in your *roman*?

RD  Not particularly. Sometimes they are perceptive, sometimes not. Now, for instance, in this most recent book there are two ladies who are engaged in the arts who live together, and people have already been saying that they are two ladies who did that in Toronto a few years ago.

PG  Frances Loring and Florence Wyle.

RD  Yes. I never knew them. I was aware that they existed but I never knew them. And there could be no possibility of it's being a portrait of them.

PG  But the idea would come from them, would it not? They were "the girls," and your two friends are "the ladies."

RD  Ah, but I knew some other girls. I knew a lot of them.

PG  You've got this twinkle now.

RD  Actually I knew a lot of those lesbian couples in England, more than in Canada. So I knew quite a bit about them and had many friends among them. And so it's not Miss Loring or Miss Wyle, whom I didn't know.

PG  I'm disappointed that you didn't know them. I had hoped you'd met, because I've always wondered what they were like. They must have been very charming, because they did have salons, as true ladies have salons.

RD  Yes, they did. I think they were rather exclusive and they didn't see the likes of you and me.

PG  Well, I've got the feeling I wouldn't have got to go to the ladies, either, because they didn't like writers, for one thing, your ladies. They liked musicians.

RD  Well, you see, I present my characters so that the reader can make up his mind about them. The ladies are not entirely likeable, and they are not infallible, and they do some awfully silly things.

PG  Chips is likeable.

RD  She's likeable, but Chips realizes before the end of the book that a very important thing in her life has been a gigantic mistake. That's a sad recollection, and she goes back to England and not long after she dies. To realize that your life has been built on a mistake or a falsehood is a very serious blow.

PG  Has the Governor General who walks across the stage got any relationship to Vincent Massey?

RD  Oh, yes, of course. It says specifically that this was the first Canadian to become a Governor General. Well, Vincent Massey was the first Canadian to be a Governor General. The character in the book is not exactly like Mr. Massey, but he has certain of his characteristics. And what he goes to see the doctor about is not necessarily Vincent Massey, but it is a thing which such a person might go to see a cunning man about.

PG  Now, Colborne College is Upper Canada College?

RD  Oh, yes, of course.

PG  Was there a Curfew Club when you were at Colborne College?

RD  Oh, indeed, yes. Many people living would remember it.

PG  How did you get in?

RD  I got in because I was editor of the college magazine.

PG  You got in *ex officio*?

RD  Yes.

PG  You didn't have to achieve anything?

RD  No.

PG  Now was conversation at the Curfew Club possibly as learned as your three friends . . . ?

RD  Oh, my dear man. The conversation of eighteen and nineteen is more learned than it is ever going to be at any other time of life. They have certainty and long memory, which you can never really maintain into adult life. They were terrific arguers. They knew everything. You know what Mark Twain says: when you're young you know everything, and later on you gradually go downhill. And that is the way it is. I remember in the Curfew Club the certainty and determination of the arguments was fantastic.

PG  Now, what's the source of your medical knowledge?

RD  Oh, I'm just very interested in medicine. I'm a hypochondriac. I'm always reading about medicine.

PG  You're not a doctor *manqué*?

RD  Well, I think I might be, but I'd make a terrible doctor because I would get bored with dull patients and do something awful to them. It's a very lucky thing I never did it.

PG  This is the source of Dr. Hullah's musing that it's unfortunate a doctor doesn't get to choose his patients and that's one of the problems with being a doctor. Where did you learn "Some inherit valuable possessions and can find lucrative foreign investments constantly available"?

RD  Well, I just know that to be true.

PG  No, but that's a mnemonic. That's the mnemonic for the opening of the right — the points of opening of the right . . .

RD  Oh, well, I was told that by a doctor who had been through the University of Toronto medical school and knew an awful lot of mnemonics that they used to detail anatomical things. Without those things I don't know how they'd manage it. The feats of memory that used to be demanded of medical students were absolutely inhuman. I'm not surprised that so many of them, once they're qualified, never use their heads again, because they've been driven mercilessly before they got their M.D.

PG  But that's all they require is knowledge, they don't require wisdom.

RD  Well, that's exactly it.

PG  Robert Burton's *Anatomy of Melancholy*, published in 1621, is Hullah's favourite book. Why is this? Are there premises here that provide you with your own views of medical practice?

RD  Yes, it is because it was said by Sir William Osler — who was a Canadian, a very great doctor, and a very great collector of books — it was the finest work on medical science that had ever been written by a layman, and it is. It's a fantastic book. It's about neurosis, and if Sigmund Freud had ever got hold of it he would have picked up a few tips. Burton could see through a brick wall just as well as Freud could. It's a wonderful book and hilariously funny to read.

PG  Sir William Osler is very important to Hullah. He also appears in John Irving's latest book. Did you put John Irving onto Osler?

RD  I don't know. I know John, but I don't remember ever discussing Osler with him. But Osler was a very, very great man, and we should be very proud that he was a Canadian.

PG  Was he really an expert on bad breath?

RD  He writes about it in his *Practice of Medicine*.

PG  What's the origin of the bad breath contest that appears in *The Cunning Man*?

RD  Well, you know, here in the city of Toronto there was a quite good tavern, a very decent tavern, out on Bloor Street West, where they used to have one of those things every year. My students told me about it. They used to go to it.

PG  So there is a *clef* behind that *clef*. You're just having sport with your . . .

RD  Oh yes, yes, yes. My students used to go and come back and tell me with roars of laughter about the contest. It wasn't exactly the way I describe it, but I built on it.

PG  What about the story that cannibals find the flesh of white people almost inedible because they eat too much sugar?

RD  Well, I was told that by a master at Upper Canada College when I was a schoolboy. He had been in the navy — he'd been in two navies. He'd been in the British navy and the French navy, and he'd been a lot in Africa, and he said that the cannibals had told him that white men were not very good eating because they have a kind of nasty sour taste which came from their eating too much sugar.

PG  Isn't experience in two navies also the background of the person who makes that comment in the book?

RD  Oh, yes, Mr. Daubigny. Well, a great many people who went to Upper Canada in my day will remember Commander de Marbois, who is very like that. Jean Punier de Marbois. He was a wonderful teacher. He taught geography and German.

PG  Have you ever forgotten anything that you have experienced?

RD  Not really, no. I'm not a forgetter, I'm a rememberer.

PG  Is it true that banks used to spy on social gatherings in Toronto to suss out civil libertarians?

RD  Why do you say *used to*? You see, this is one of things which is important to my book, Peter. There are all kinds of people in a big city

like this, where a lot of important things happen, who want information, and they get it from people who are called private investi-
gators, or something of that kind. But they're really just snoops,
gumshoe men, and they're paid usually quite substantially. The interesting thing is that the police do not pay their informers very generously. But some of the financial houses have informers, and the
insurance companies, and they pay pretty well.

PG   So this is a comment from the Toronto that's in the book to the world
as it is now?

RD   Yes. The idea that the world is full of secrets, and that you can get
away with things if you just don't attract too much attention, is a
great mistake. This comes from my old experience as a journalist.
There are no secrets. One of the things you find out when you work
on a newspaper, particularly in a moderate-size place, as I did, is that
behind every suicide was a story which you couldn't possibly tell in
the paper.

PG   The rules about that have changed, substantially, in our time. In
some places the old rules were the better rules, about what could be
said and what couldn't be said. There have even been instances in at
least one paper you used to be associated with, the Kingston *Whig-
Standard*.

RD   Yes.

PG   Are we now too . . . Is your old profession or craft now too nosy?
Does it have too much licence?

RD   It depends entirely on the men who are controlling the paper.
Sometimes they interfere and publish information which is necessary,
which the public ought to know about, because it influences the
public good, and it influences — as in the case that you speak of —
a lot of other people, who are not able to protect themselves, very
young people.

I'll tell you a tale that came within my own experience, which was
about a bank manager in a moderate-size place who went out
hunting. When he was alone, he had a hunting accident, and it killed
him. Well, everybody knew that it was suicide. A great many people
knew why. He had been getting into money which wasn't his, and
he had been getting into it because he'd had to associate with men
who had much more money than he had and he thought it a dis-
advantage. So he had set up some phony accounts and was getting

money into them and using it for his own purposes. Now, his number two, his assistant manager, knew that, and he had had a great crisis of conscience. Should he inform headquarters or should he leave things alone and not be a squealer? He decided not to be a squealer. Well, when it all came out the bank was very hard on that man. They thought he ought to have been a squealer, and they punished him. They punished him quite severely. They put him in a department of his bank in which there would have been no promotion ever. Now that's the kind of way things happen that you don't hear about and that you can't publish in the papers. You can publish when an organist is abusing choirboys.

PG   Ought you to?

RD   Yes. I think you should, because it is a scandal which has to be brought out or else many boys will fail. In the case you spoke of, one of those boys committed suicide and two had very serious nervous breakdowns because they were not the natural prey of that kind of man. They were people who were sucked into it because they couldn't resist somebody who was in authority.

PG   But if there are cases where unpalatable personal truths should be reported when the law is involved, and if there are cases where they should not be reported, who is to decide which is which? All journalists are not as wise as you and I . . .

RD   No, and you have to depend on . . .

PG   . . . and I'm not sure about us.

RD   Well, I'm not sure about us. But you see all of that hullabaloo that went on about the Prince of Wales and that unwise telephone call or letter or something he wrote, there was no reason to blat that all out in the papers. It really didn't change anything or harm anybody. What people say in circumstances of great intimacy, sexual intimacy usually, is nobody's business but their own.

PG   Even when they're Heir Apparent to the Crown?

RD   Yes, yes. There is not one of us who has not said things to somebody that we were deeply involved with that we would not want to have blatted out in the papers.

PG   We ought not to be so foolish as to say them on the telephone, I suppose.

RD   Well, I suppose so. I was told by my father when I was very young that there was no dirtier, more corrupt press than that of Great Britain. Ours over here looks like Sunday School in comparison.

PG  We're getting better.

RD  Yes.

PG  Was Shakespeare constipated, in your view?

RD  No, that was a story where a bright boy was tempting the Curfew Club into a kind of discussion to which they were not accustomed. It was a joke.

PG  The argument is that Claudius . . .

RD  King Claudius in *Hamlet* . . .

PG  He's constipated?

RD  Yes, he is, because you see he doesn't know where to look for the body of Polonius. And the body of Polonius is in the privy, but the king hasn't been to the privy for several days.

PG  Did you just make that up one afternoon sitting there at the typewriter?

RD  Yes, that's my trade.

PG  Is it still fun for you, writing?

RD  Oh, yes, it's great. I enjoy it enormously.

PG  Are we two-thirds of the way through another trilogy here? Do we know?

RD  I can't tell. You see I've got a lot of work on my plate that I have to get done before I can think about any more novels. I can't tell, but an idea may occur, or it may just gel in my mind, and then we'll see.

PG  You're not making any more promises . . .

RD  I'm making no more promises than I did when . . .

PG  . . . you don't trust yourself to say you're not going to write any more.

RD  That's right.

PG  Because you seem in awfully fine fettle. I'm sure you've got more tricks up your sleeve.

RD  Oh, you ought to see me early in the morning. It's a disaster.

PG  I could give you a call some morning.

RD  Oh, don't. No, no. You know, you get old and you just have to put up with it. But you have to be careful not to become brain dead before it's absolutely necessary.

PG  In ending the book, Hullah contemplates his death and he quotes an Ovid poem that begins: "Then Death, so-call'd, is but old Matter dressed / In some new Figure and a vary'd Vest: / Thus all Things are but alter'd, nothing dies." Is that your philosophy?

RD Yes. It's a very old one, and I think a very good one, and it's not unorthodox, it's not heretical. It is something which fits in very conveniently in the Christian religion, though it's not Christianity as the fundamentalists put it forward.

PG Thank you so much for coming in, as always.

# LETTERS HOME

*Morningside's army of foreign correspondents rarely wrote about what radio people call "current affairs." Mostly they wrote from such places as Butaritari and Ougadougou and Thimphu and Timpale and Pumwani to talk about their daily lives. Their editor, for more than the last decade, was Shelley Ambrose, whose bulletin board collected postcards and stamps and other souvenirs and curiosa from all over the world.*

## NAIROBI

"Ever been to this part of town before?" Frank asks, glancing across at me in the passenger seat of his Nissan Patrol. He can probably tell from the look on my face that the answer is no. I'm ashamed to say that after two years of living in Nairobi, I haven't done much exploring in the city's teeming, sprawling slums where half the population lives. Frank Plummer, on the other hand, is a medical researcher who works here all the time.

"Well, this is Pumwani," he announces, as he eases the Patrol into an alleyway narrower than the living room in my house. "It's one of Nairobi's oldest slums. It covers a square kilometre and fifteen thousand people live here," he says. "It's a rough place, even for those who live here."

I try hard not to look overly perturbed by the squalor, the crowds, the claustrophobic *slumminess* of the place. There is a strong smell of sewage and I suspect we are driving through the source. I have the impression that all fifteen thousand Pumwani dwellers have gathered in this one alley that we are trying to negotiate this morning. Everyone is trying to sell something — old shoes, old curtains, old bedsheets, old brassieres, fresh mangoes or tomatoes. The alley is thick with hawkers and makeshift stalls. Behind those are the houses, wattle-and-daub structures that need to lean on each other to remain standing. I keep an eye out for thieves, the men with slippery fingers who people Nairobi streets, waiting for a chance to grab at bags or earrings through car windows. I wind my window up, right to the top.

I glance over at Frank who is busy winding his window *down*, sticking his head out. "Excuse me," he begins, addressing a swarm of young men, armed with their wares — stacks of second-hand blue jeans. "Could I get through?" he says, sounding every bit the soft-spoken gentleman from the Prairies that he is. The hawkers seem to appreciate Frank's good manners, unusual in a *Big Man* in a *Big Car* in this, their part of town. They take up the call in Swahili, warning everyone ahead that a car is coming through. The path clears. We pull into a littered yard in front of a small bungalow badly in need of a coat of whitewash.

"This is Majengo clinic," Frank says. "*Majengo* means slum. This is where we do our work with the prostitutes. We have eighteen hundred registered patients here. They're all *malaya* — women who sell sex. They work only in the daytime, selling sex to men who are on their way to work or passing by. They have houses, usually just one room with two beds: one for themselves and their children or steady boyfriend at night; one for their daytime clients. They have four or five clients a day. They charge twenty shillings for sex with a condom, thirty without." I am busy taking notes, as my mind flounders through the arithmetic. Twenty shillings for sex. That works out to about fifty Canadian cents. It's not just life that's undervalued here.

I follow Frank into the clinic, which is separated from the bedlam of the Pumwani market by a low wire fence. Amazing lack of security, I think, in a city where security is measured by the diameter of the bars on windows and the height of walls around compounds. Frank has been working here for more than a decade, heading up an AIDS research project that involves the universities of Manitoba and Nairobi. Originally he came to study chancroid, a sexually transmitted disease that causes genital ulcers. It's rare in North America, common in this part of the world. But an epidemic of chancroid in Manitoba in the 1970s sparked interest in the disease. In Pumwani, there was no shortage of chancroid and other sexually transmitted diseases to study. Then in 1985, the research team tested the women patients at Majengo clinic for HIV. The results were shocking — two-thirds of the women were already HIV-positive.

"After that," Frank says with a shrug, "there wasn't much choice but to work with AIDS."

Inside the clinic nurses are busy with files. Frank and I enter the small treatment room where two young Kenyan doctors are pondering what to do with one of their patients. She is young, not yet thirty. She's wearing plastic flip-flops and a low-waisted brown dress of polyester that might have been fashionable back home twenty years ago. But she has trouble standing so she leans against the bed. She's lost co-ordination in her right arm and leg. The doctors, Joshua Kimani and Ephantus Njagi, are assessing the thrush that has appeared on her tongue, and a bacterial infection around her eyes. Joshua tells Frank that she's already been treated for tuberculosis. The woman's eyes are lifeless; she's hacking up phlegm, using a wrapper slung over one shoulder to cover her mouth and wipe her face.

I turn away, gaze out the window, amazed that the raucous marketeering just a few feet from the open window doesn't attract anyone's attention but mine. A purple-and-green minivan has pulled up just in front of the clinic. It has the words CHRIST CRUSADES emblazoned on the side. There is an enormous plastic fish, painted silver, on the roof.

The deafening music seems to be coming from loudspeakers inside the fish. The van door slides open to reveal a wall-to-wall selection of Christian music cassettes and videos. Faith is for sale here, too.

Frank and his two Kenyan colleagues are still examining the woman, deciding that her loss of co-ordination indicates neurologic problems, a sign that she is moving into the final stages of AIDS, of her life. All they can do is nurse her through to the end. The project *does* pay for patients' health care, in exchange for monitoring and studying the sexually trans-mitted diseases among the registered patients. That includes the eighteen hundred sex workers here, sixteen hundred mothers with children in another clinic nearby, and fourteen hundred patients in a city clinic down-town. This Majengo clinic also organizes community projects to help the women find alternatives to the sex trade. The projects bring the pros-titutes together in groups, where they learn how to protect themselves from further infections, learn that together they have a voice and that unity gives them a little power — if all the sex workers in Majengo refuse their services to men who won't wear a condom, the men eventually give in. This protects the men and the women, slows the epidemic. This is a give-and-take project, not, as Frank puts it, "safari research" that gives nothing back to the communities in which it works.

Joshua tells me that 95 per cent of the patients here are HIV-positive. The remainder, the other 5 per cent, are women who have had intense contact with HIV for years and who remain HIV-negative. Which is why I have ventured into this slum with Frank, why Frank Plummer's name and the names of his Kenyan and Canadian colleagues feature large in prestigious medical journals and at international AIDS conferences. Fifty-eight resistant women — a small silver lining in this obscure Nairobi slum — are making and shaping medical history. They are among the first doc-umented cases of people who, for a reason that has to do with the anti-gens on their white blood cells, are resistant to HIV infection.

"It's pretty exciting," says Frank in that deadpan way he has of down-playing the importance of his work. We're heading home, stuck in Nairobi traffic in the city centre. I ask him to elaborate a little on what, in particular, he thinks is pretty exciting. "Well," he says, "for a long time we thought that everyone could get HIV and that once you got it, it was forever and it was fatal. This work in Kenya is helping to shift the paradigm on AIDS, showing us that not everyone is susceptible to HIV.

# A Day in the Life of Morningside

*5:45 a.m. Wednesday, April 30, 1997. Only eight minutes after I've left my apartment in downtown Toronto, I arrive at the Broadcasting Centre. 6:10 a.m. My office day starts with a survey of the mail. Extraordinarily, a day that begins like any other day turns out to be quite special. At the top of my stack of mail is a fax from Bill Richardson in Vancouver. He suggests* Morningside *stage a kind of Prairie social for the flood victims in Manitoba.*

All photos in this section by Peter Paterson.

**6:25 a.m.** *The studio crew, who have been here long before me, work on their preparation. Left, Marieke Meyer, studio director, centre, Leanne Stepnow, associate producer, and right, Carole Ito, technician. Then, below, at precisely* **8:06 a.m.** *(9:06 in the Maritimes and 9:36 in Newfoundland), Marieke prepares to cue me as the theme rolls. The computer to my right is how she'll talk to me as the program progresses.*

*9:17 a.m.* *The producers are hard at work on Bill's idea. Left, Shelley Ambrose is already booking guests.* *9:33 a.m.* *Senior producers Linda Groen and Willy Barth shape the format, roughing it out on our scheduling board behind Linda.* *9:51 a.m.* *Shelagh Rogers, who has already come up with a name for Bill's idea — the Red River Rally — drops in with some* Morningside *letters.*

**10:03 a.m.** Marieke and I take advantage of the six-minute newscast to see how the Rally is shaping up. Executive producer Gloria Bishop is now in charge. The scheduling board Gloria is pointing at is of critical importance to Morningside. For a day as frantic as the one we're planning for Friday, it looks a bit messier than usual. But as we talk and the program rolls on, the producers are calling dozens of possible guests and booking studios all over the country. **10:16 a.m.** Producer Tom Jokinen, who worked for two years in Newfoundland, reads a faxed confirmation that Buddy Wassisname and the Other Fellers will join us on Friday.

*11:05 a.m.* The show is over for the day.
Gloria prepares for our daily story meeting.
*11:17 a.m.* Producer Harry Schachter, on the
left below, who handles all of Morningside's
political affairs, talks to Andrew Cohen of the
Globe and Mail *about a possible appearance
on one of our political forums. We've cancelled
this Friday's because of the Rally, but Harry
always wants to talk politics.*

*11:37 a.m.* The daily ritual of the story
meeting is under way. By custom, we all
sit in the same places every morning. By
edict, we try to end precisely at noon.
By necessity, we seldom do.

*12:46 p.m. With the story meeting finally over, Neil Sandell eats lunch at his desk while he works the phones. Neil's usual responsibility is our regional reports, but today, like almost everyone, he's pitching in to plan the Rally.*

*1:17 p.m. Carole Ito organizes her tapes for this evening's* Best of Morningside. *Carole's work is typical of the new downsized* CBC. *Her technical training has been added to so she can perform most of the functions of the traditional producer.*

*2:20 p.m. We've added a fourth hour for Friday. This complicates even more the work of the versatile and experienced Willy Barth, who looks after everything from our radio dramas to our technical needs. Today, he's booking extra studios, extra lines, and extra satellite feeds for Friday's adventure.*

*2:39 p.m. Life must go on. For all the excitement about the Rally, there'll be* Morningside *tomorrow, and on Monday, and for several more weeks. Producer Meredith Levine, who specializes in discussions that challenge our minds, is talking to one of her possible guests for a future panel.*

*3:03 p.m. Discussions about money must go on, too. At the right, Carol Dawes, who has the unenviable task of looking after our budget, has a friendly chat with producer Ian Pearson.*

*3:14 p.m. Producer Peter Kavanagh, thoughtful as always, contemplates some future plans.*

*3:35 p.m.* Producer Paul Wilson, in the grey sweater, who produced our literary pieces this season, talks with the author Josef Skvorecky and his publicist Jasmine Zohar about an interview they've just recorded with Shelagh.
*3:40 p.m.* Later than I'm usually here, I have a last chat with Shelley about the mail and other matters in my office, which features, of course, an old manual typewriter. This may be the last one at the CBC.

*5:17 p.m.* Long after I've gone home, producer Sian Jones keeps working on the flood story itself. Sian is a former Winnipegger who seemed personally involved with every aspect of the tragedy. *7:03 p.m.* Linda Groen, who as our "Senior Producer, Desk" bears the responsibility for the final line-up every day, makes some last-minute changes on her computer for tomorrow when, well before 6:00 a.m., everything will start again.

Once we understand why that is, we should be able to come up with something to treat or prevent AIDS — absolutely."

Yes, I guess you could call that pretty exciting, if you are prone to understatement, as Frank is.

*Joan Baxter*

## Havana

You can never tell what Havana is hiding behind its decomposing glamour-queen facade. The buildings of the old town, once an ostentatious mix of *fin-de-siècle* splendour and streamlined art deco, have merged into a uniform peeled-paint grey. Corinthian columns and elaborate ironworks sulk, forgotten, in dark alleys. Once-lovely inner courtyard oases act as convenient landing pads for bags of rubbish launched from upper-storey windows. All exterior staircases, especially the ones carved from wood, are suspect. It's rotting, it's rusting, it often stinks, and it's very much alive.

Out walking one grey morning, I saw a colourful class of schoolchildren, aged maybe ten years old. They were waiting to cross the street. Singing and holding hands, two by two, waiting for their teacher to give them the sign to break formation and run for it. I stopped and watched. The signal came. They ran. The teacher was leading the way but an older boy, about eleven, was shepherding behind. I probably wouldn't have noticed him if he hadn't been carrying a framed, three-foot-high portrait of Ché Guevara. I followed them.

They were heading straight towards my hotel. Half a block before they reached it, the juvenile centipede made a sharp left turn into an opening in the wall. I gave the boy with the poster time to pass through then, casually, I walked slowly past. There, open to the street like a French sidewalk café, was a classroom full of six-year-olds. A school. I shouldn't have been surprised but I was. I had walked past that building dozens of times and had always assumed it was yet another rundown tenement. I stood back and appraised the building. Decades ago, it had been an ornate, lovely three-storey private house.

There was a cluster of teachers standing in what would have been the vestibule. One of them, a wiry woman, smoking, in her thirties, caught my eye. I smiled. She smiled back, and suddenly, with a speed nearly unheard-of in Havana, I was touring the school. The six-year-olds were in what had probably been the drawing room. The old dining room, brightly painted ceiling becoming increasingly cloudy, housed a class of raucous nine-year-olds. The eight-year-olds were up one narrow wooden flight in the study. The third floor was for the older students. The rooms were much smaller, servants' quarters probably. It had been a beautiful house. But that was a long time ago, before the paintings on the walls had been replaced by posters of revolutionary heroes. Certainly before the schoolchildren had been born. Probably before most of the teachers had been born.

The rooms were sparse, the desks and chairs old, the blackboards rubbed brown. Most of the children, some barefoot but all well-fed and keen, were using notebooks that had clearly been used many times before, their pencilled notes erased at the end of each year.

I pointed at one of the omnipresent faded posters of Ché and asked my hostess, now on her third cigarette, about the poster the young boy had been carrying in the street. She got excited. She spoke fast when she got excited. Two cigarettes later, I finally figured it out. The primary school was preparing for one of the most important days on its calendar, the day when the six-year-olds are inducted into grade one. The day when the grade-threes ceremoniously exchange the blue scarf they have worn for the past three years for the red one they will wear for the next three. The school was preparing to commemorate the day Ché Guevara died in a hail of bullets in Bolivia. My new friend invited me to attend tomorrow's show. I said I'd be honoured.

At nine the next morning, I walked down to Revolution Park, the small patch of widened street and disheartened flora directly in front of the Ministry of the Interior and across a thundering boulevard from the Museum of the Revolution. The students were already there, spiffed up, divided into classes and surrounded by beaming relatives. I spotted my friend. She was so frantic, she wasn't even smoking. My boy was still carrying his Ché poster, but now he stood just a shade more erect. Graduation day.

Then, suddenly, it started. Class by class they sang. Graceful young children stepped out of formation to make heartfelt speeches. A sparkling twelve-year-old raised her voice in an achingly beautiful solo, chorused by her classmates. A young cadet from the Ministry of the Interior, not more than seventeen or eighteen, took the makeshift podium and spoke with the fervour of a preacher. The same phrases echoed throughout: *Seremos como Ché*; *Amigo Ché*; *Ché, Commandante*. The square was charged with emotion, reaching a climax when the young ones, around eight years old, formed a V and faced the podium. A parent flanked each child and, on cue, awkwardly untied the student's blue neckerchief and knotted in its place a red one. All glowed with pride and love.

I turned to the grinning Cuban next to me and asked what had just happened. He explained that the blue neckerchief symbolized that the child was willing to "die in a hail of bullets for Socialism." But now that they were older, they were eligible to "die in a hail of bullets for Communism," just like their hero Ché.

The ceremony ended with the playing of a scratchy record of a speech by Ché. It was the root of many of the songs, poems, and speeches that had been made by the young students. It ended with the impassioned cry: "*Patria o Muerte*"; homeland or death. And while most children fidgeted like any child who, after an enforced period of good behaviour, sees the end in sight, some had tears in their eyes. They were the tears of a patriotic American hearing "The Star-spangled Banner" or a Christian hearing "Onward Christian Soldiers." They were the tears of faith.

*Cleo Paskal*

## Hong Kong

The character representing rice is contained in the characters that mean China, and so it is only natural that food and eating are central to the consciousness of people here. Of course, gone are the days when the colony made any attempt to grow their own food. Even at the best of times, the arable land could not support the population, and less so now. Western travel writers are fond of noting that Chinese people greet each other with "*Neigh sik fan mah?*" Have you had your rice yet? Well, in the modern Hong Kong, with so many educated in England, Canada, and the United States, this quaint way of saying hello has been replaced with "Have you see the Heng Sung Bank Index this morning?" or "Did you score the Quenella at the races last night?"

Some wag once wrote that the Chinese will eat anything that has legs so long as it is not a table. I'm not sure of this statement's political correctness, but like all clichés, there is some truth in it. Everything is fair game because in China — and by extension Hong Kong — there are many mouths to feed and hungry people will not look at food with the same preciousness that some *gweilow* — foreigners — might have about what should or should not be eaten.

On my second morning here I raced down to my favourite tea house, tucked in a back alley, to meet some old friends who had invited me to *Yum Cha*. Westerners have mistakenly referred to this meal as "Dim Sum." *Deem-sum* means "to dip the heart" and refers, idiomatically, to little portions or bite-sized dumplings. Most Chinese would actually invite someone to *Yum Cha* — to have tea, just as Westerners would casually say, "Let's go for coffee." *Yum Cha* is a modest invitation to sit down and gorge on an infinite variety of steamed shrimps mixed with bamboo shoots wrapped in sheets of rice flour, minced ginger pork balls in wonton paper, taro root covered with a light batter and fried golden brown, radish cakes speckled with ham and bits of shrimp — I could go on, but you get my drift.

That afternoon, my second cousin telephoned — he is my *only* second cousin and therefore does not require a number, like first cousins number one, two, three, and so on. Robert invited me to a picnic at "birthday bay." As children, whenever one of the cousins had a birthday, all thirty-two cousins were invited to celebrate. A small army of nannies and parents were also in attendance, requiring a mini-flotilla of launches to take us all there. Today, we went aboard his yacht. The island is still untouched. We dropped anchor and immediately a little one-oared sampan pulled up beside us. The fisherman was hawking his catch of the day. We bought two catties of shrimp. Robert's coxswain, our boat driver, boiled them, in their shells, for one minute, then served them, piled like a hill on a large platter. To eat, we plucked off the head, peeled the shrimp, and, holding it by the tail, dipped the meat in a ginger, white wine vinegar, and chili sauce. Ambrosia!

On my last evening, my cousins invited me to a farewell dinner. Something special, "Memories of Hong Kong," just like those bottles you get in grocery stores in Canada, they said. I wondered what exotic delicacy might be on the menu. I once ate monkey's brain when I was a boy. It's outlawed now. Back then, it was served after a tongue-tingling soup. The waiter would bring in a small, live monkey — brains must be fresh, you see. The creature's head was already shaved. The waiter crawled under the round dinner table and pushed the top portion of the monkey's head up through a hole in the centre of the table. A second waiter arrived with a mallet, split the skull like a coconut and peeled it back to reveal a white-grey blancmange. Diners then scooped out a spoonful and swallowed the brain like an oyster, washing it down with an expensive cognac. I was given a teaspoonful of the grey matter but had to wash it down with a Coke. Old enough to eat warm monkey's brain but not old enough to drink. No, it did not taste like chicken. It didn't taste of anything, actually. That meal was more memorable for the event than for its brains.

So you can imagine that I went to my farewell dinner with a little trepidation. A Chinese, unlike a Westerner, would never dream of announcing the menu ahead of time — not even to family members. It is considered the height of rudeness to do so. A greater sin would be for one to examine the contents of the dish before eating it. No. The invitee is expected to pop food into the mouth, chew with delight, swallow, and smile approval.

At the restaurant's front door, I looked up at the sign. It said KING KONG RESTAURANT. Eating, like life or business in Hong Kong, can be a high-risk adventure.

*Simon Johnston*

## BHUTAN

### I

I awake to a cool, grey morning. Outside, the sky is heavy, and the north end of the valley is a wall of mist. But we are approaching the end of the monsoon — September 23 is Blessed Rainy Day, officially the last day of the summer-long rain, but since there is no such thing as official weather, the monsoon stops whenever it feels like it. When the clouds finally lift, it will be autumn, warm days with skies so clear they hurt your eyes, and in the hard, bright light, every rock and fold and ridge in the surrounding mountains will stand out sharply. After the monsoon, I always feel like I have bionic vision.

The end of the monsoon is the start of tourist season in Bhutan. Last year, almost five thousand people paid $200 (U.S.) a day to visit a country that sells itself as "the last Shangri-La." The government-imposed tariff, which will rise to $250 (U.S.) next year, serves two purposes: it ensures a conservative *number* of tourists each year, and an older, quieter, conservative *type* of tourist. One government document I read referred to this type as "well-heeled." And the tourists do look well-heeled, in Tilley Endurables and sturdy shoes, with their books on Tantric Buddhism tucked into their vest pockets. Tourists to Bhutan tend to be museum curators, university professors, management consultants. There are no backpackers. Thimphu has no tourist area, like Kathmandu's Thamel, with its cheap lodges and way-out little bars serving cappuccino and lemon torte. Tourists in Bhutan must come in groups through a registered Bhutanese tour operator, who arranges everything from accommodation to the daily program. There is little time or chance to wander off the beaten track.

Bhutan opened its doors to its first tourists in 1974, for the coronation of the fourth king. It wasn't until the mid-eighties, however, with the advent of flights into Bhutan, that tourism began to pick up. There is no set limit on the number of tourists, but whenever the royal government feels there are too many, the tariff is raised. There are sometimes complaints: for $200 (U.S.) a day, visitors want their money's worth. They don't want to be told that the electricity has gone off for the rest of the weekend, or that there will be no water, hot or otherwise, all day, or that they have just spent nine hours waiting at the airport only to find out that the flight is cancelled because it is raining in Bhutan, and the pilots have to be able to see the Paro Valley before they land the plane in it.

There is definitely a tourist hierarchy in Shangri-La, and I wonder if this is common in other unusual destinations. Tourists who have been coming to Bhutan for several years behave as if they discovered the place single-handedly. One American woman I know who was planning a trip here was refused information by a man who has been visiting since the early eighties: "When I started going to Bhutan, there were no tourists," he said. "Now *everyone* is going and they're *ruining* it." Five thousand people a year hardly constitutes everyone, and perhaps the only thing the tourists are ruining is this man's notion that Bhutan is his personal Shangri-La.

This tendency to want to make Bhutan your own special place is very strong. People who have been here a few times return as tour-group leaders; they are now experts, pointing out the colourful phalluses painted on the houses, smiling at lesser members of the royal family, gently correcting the pronunciation of the uninitiated — "Boo-tawn, it's Boo-tawn, you see." Somehow, they have pulled themselves out of the ranks of mere tourists. They have their own unique relationship with Bhutan, outside of the mundane group they are leading.

In Nepal, the group tourists are scorned by the backpackers. Dressed in baggy cotton trousers and cheap tie-dyed shirts, the backpackers snigger as the air-conditioned buses return tourist groups to their five-star hotels. *That's* not travel, they claim. Real travel means wandering through rice paddies in the dark searching for the path, sleeping in a shack at the side of the road because you missed the last local bus back to Kathmandu. Real travel means you can exchange a few words in Nepali with a couple of shopkeepers whom you know by name. It means knowing the cheapest places to stay and eat, bargaining down the toughest rickshaw driver, surviving a variety of ailments, from Delhi belly to typhoid. It means you will have tales to tell when you get home.

In Bhutan, well-paid consultants working for big international aid agencies look down on the overseas volunteer workers, whom they wrongly perceive as being poorly qualified and inexperienced. The volunteers, in turn, look down on the consultants, who live sheltered lives in Thimphu with imported china and a fleet of household helpers. They also look down on the group tourists in Bhutan and Nepal. Upon being mistaken for a tourist, they are indignant: "I'm not visiting! I *live* here!"

I know this because I felt the same way when I lived in eastern Bhutan. In the beginning, I felt privileged. For a long time, in fact, I felt privileged. And then I became arrogant. Here I was, living in one of the remotest places on earth, buying my vegetables at the weekly market just like everyone else in the village! I remember rolling my eyes at the tourists at a local festival, at their inappropriate casual dress and video cameras. It has taken me a while to realize that we are all visitors. Whether you stay for two weeks on a group tour, or two years as a volunteer, or even if, like me, you get married and stay and stay and stay, it takes a lot more time, and a lot more than time, to become more than a visitor.

## II

Being married to Tshewang has been an interesting study in conflicting superstitions and beliefs. I won't walk under ladders, he won't cut his hair or fingernails after dark. I cross my fingers to avert bad luck, he won't travel on a Thursday or take chilies directly out of my hand. He claims, quite correctly, that at least his superstitions have explanations: Thursdays are unlucky for him, and handing chilies or any other "hot" food directly to another person will cause a fight. I've had to learn a whole new set of rules of etiquette: do not sit with your legs crossed in front of a high official, do not point at religious objects, walk around all holy monuments and temples clockwise, always refuse whatever is offered once or twice, even if you really want to accept, and always accept things with both hands. A few things I still haven't mastered, like the art of drinking from a communal bottle, Bhutanese style. To prevent the spread of germs, the Bhutanese tip their heads back, hold the bottle a few centimetres from their mouth, and pour the contents in without ever letting their lips touch the bottle. It's actually a very hygienic practice, and it doesn't look so very difficult. Unfortunately, my first attempt at this resulted in a soaked shirt and prolonged choking, and now I bring my own water bottle, or just go thirsty.

When we moved into this bungalow a few months ago, we arranged to borrow a truck, which was only available on Saturday. After we had moved all our furniture in, Tshewang announced that we had to go back to the old house to sleep.

"Sleep on what?" I asked, incredulous. "The bed is here. The blankets are here. Everything is here."

"It doesn't matter," he explained. "It's extremely unlucky to move on a Saturday."

"But we've already moved," I said.

"Yes, but as long as we don't sleep here, we haven't technically moved," he replied.

"Is there anything else we can't do here today?" I asked grumpily.

It turned out that there was almost nothing we could do in the new house: we couldn't light a fire, take a bath, cook, or eat. We sat around shivering all day, and then went to sleep at a neighbour's house.

Our son was more than two years old when he had his first haircut. His very fine, curly hair had become knotted into dreadlocks, and I was anxious to cut it. No, no, my husband said, a lama must cut his hair for the first time.

"Does it *absolutely* have to be a lama?" I asked.

"A lama or a maternal uncle," he insisted. "Absolutely."

It would have to be a lama, then: Pema's maternal uncle was on the other side of the planet.

It had to be the right kind of lama, though, and an auspicious time, and a good place, and I soon lost track of the requirements and gave up. Meanwhile, Pema's hair grew longer and wilder, and to keep it out of his face, I tied it back in a ponytail. I thought he looked like a very cool two-year-old, but then someone told him that only girls wore ponytails and Pema refused to let me tie his hair back any more.

One Saturday morning, I told Tshewang that I was taking Pema to a temple — any temple — and asking a lama there — any lama — to cut Pema's hair. "But today might not be an auspicious day," Tshewang protested, and we began a huge argument, which was interrupted by a knock at the door. We opened the door and there was a lama. Like many lamas, he had left his monastery to beg for alms, part of the spiritual discipline that cuts attachment to worldly comforts. Tshewang and I looked at each other. His unexpected arrival seemed pretty auspicious to us — it did cut short a whopping argument, after all — so we called Pema, who was playing outside.

The lama asked us to bring a bowl of clean water, a bowl of milk, and a pair of scissors. We sat a very nervous-looking Pema on a chair, and the lama then bent his head and prayed, a lovely, half-sung, half-chanted prayer, but a bit too long for Pema, who slid off the chair and tried to escape to his toys in the yard. We reseated him, and then the lama asked for a small leafy branch. I fetched one from a willow tree, and the lama dipped it into the bowls and splashed Pema first with water and then with milk, still praying. Pema giggled. The lama took the scissors, clipped a tiny lock from Pema's hair, and instructed us to burn it outside. We then gave the lama some tea and some money, he said his thanks and told us to take good care of Pema, and that was that.

After he had gone, I expressed surprise that the lama had only cut a tiny piece of hair. "They're lamas," Tshewang muttered, "not *barbers*." And we took the scissors and trimmed the rest of Pema's hair ourselves.

## III

The monsoon ends abruptly. One morning you wake up and the sky is swept bare. The heavy clouds are gone, the light is different — it is hard, harshly bright — and the air is dry. Gardens are still in bloom, but the summer flowers — roses, dahlias, zinnias — are crowded out by masses of orange and rust marigolds, and you notice the fields are turning brown at the edges. You shiver getting out of bed. You hear the sound of fire-wood being cut and think about lighting the woodstove. It is fall.

The most gorgeous thing about fall is the light pouring down from the sky, which is so empty and blue it hurts your eyes. Lines stand out sharply; you can see the details of every rock and ridge and fold in the mountains. Snow peaks suddenly appear where there had been for months only a curtain of cloud. If you got up to a high enough peak or ridge, you could see all the way to Tibet.

The downside to all this glory and clarity is that winter is coming. Never mind quoting that "if Winter comes, can Spring be far behind" business to me. It's not that winter is longer here, or colder — after all, I'm from Sault Ste. Marie. The temperature in Thimphu in winter, which is eight thousand feet above sea level, ranges from minus ten to plus ten Celsius between midnight and noon. Hardly cold at all, compared to a good Calgary cold snap or a Sault Ste. Marie blizzard. The difference here is, there's no central heating, and so it's often minus ten to plus ten *inside your house*. For three months! This makes spring seem pretty damn far behind to me. It seems especially far behind the three or four times it snows in Thimphu: the snow causes power blackouts, and while I am huddled in bed in my cold dark house, I wonder why I just don't unplug the phone, lock the doors, and hibernate until spring.

Most Bhutanese houses are equipped with a wood-burning stove, called a *bukhari*, in a central room. *Bukharis* burn up a lot of wood, but they do keep a whole room warm. In less central rooms, people use little electric space heaters, which are relatively effective under the following circumstances: they have to be new (after a few weeks of use, they throw as much heat as a Bic lighter), and you have to be sitting right on top of them. Being electric, they do require electricity: this means they are useless when it snows and the power lines are down. I spend most of the winter shuffling around swaddled up, waiting for bedtime, because in bed, you see, in thermal underwear and a track suit, under three quilts and two blankets, I am warm. I cannot *move*, but I am *warm*. As the winter tightens around us, we go to bed earlier and earlier. Sometimes I have to force myself to stay up until eight o'clock.

But fall — fall is nice. The days are still warm, and the direct midday sun is positively scorching. The poplar trees turn bright gold, and the fields are a mix of ochre, green, and brown. Pink and white cosmos grow wild everywhere. The river diminishes slowly from its swollen, brown monsoon form to a turquoise rush. Farmers begin to harvest rice in the paddies, laying it neatly in rows to dry. Later, it will be threshed by hand, and the discarded stalks will be raked up and bundled into stacks. A good number of bird species migrate down from higher altitudes, but you can hardly hear them over the incessant buzz of the cicadas.

In the fall, nomadic herders from northern Bhutan come down to Thimphu to sell yak meat. People buy it in sections — half a yak, quarter of a yak, a couple of legs — depending on the size of the household. The meat is cut into strips and then hung to dry, usually over clothes-lines. It's quite a revolting sight at first, these strips of bloody flesh hanging in a cloud of flies, but I don't mind it so much now, because the meat dries quickly in the bright autumn light, and the end product really is delicious. Dried yak meat is chopped into small pieces and eaten with a hot chili sauce. Beef is dried, too, and pork, as well, although this usually means pork fat, which is a great favourite of the Bhutanese. The pigs in Bhutan eat a lot of wild marijuana, which is of course fat-soluble, and I often wonder if this has anything to do with the popularity of big slippery hunks of pork fat. Chunks of fat (sometimes hairy chunks of fat, depending on the butcher) are cooked with large, white, bitter radish and dried chilies. I haven't managed to acquire a taste for this dish yet, but then, I must confess, I haven't really tried.

Chilies are also dried at this time of year. Large green chilies, a staple of the Bhutanese diet, are spread out on rooftops, where they slowly turn crimson. Sometimes the green chilies are immersed in hot water first and then put out to dry. In the hot sun, they turn white. The dried chilies are strung together in bunches and hung from windows. Oranges, grown at lower altitudes in southern Bhutan, have already appeared in the weekly market. They are still small and bitter and green — the really sweet ones won't appear until December. Apple season has just ended. I eat apples here that I would not even glance at in Canada — withered, spotted, misshapen apples — and when I do go home, I am amazed at the round perfection of every piece of fruit in the supermarket. It seems unnatural, somehow: where are all the other apples, the real ones?

In the fall, people begin to serve butter tea, called *suja* in Bhutan. These days it is usually made from cow butter, not rancid yak butter (as promised in all those Tibetan adventure stories). It is mildly salty, and very good on a chilly evening, although some people have to think of it as broth in order to get it down. *Suja* is often served with rice crisps, called *zow*, or dried pounded maize, called *tengma*. The *zow* or *tengma* is usually soaked in the tea and eaten with a spoon when it becomes soft (a highly recommended practice, since people lose fillings eating *tengma*).

In the fall, I begin to wear my *kira* again. The *kira*, Bhutan's national dress for women, is an ankle-length piece of cloth, wrapped twice around the body and belted tightly at the waist. Silver brooches are used to fasten it at the shoulders. It is worn with a silky under-blouse and a little bolero-type jacket over top. In the fall, men wear long underwear beneath their national dress, which is an elegant knee-length robe. The *kira* is not really comfortable, and all those heavy layers and folds, especially around the upper part of the body, make me feel like a freight train pulling into the station, but it is warm, and by the end of the short fall season, that's all I really care about.

## IV

A few weeks ago, I attended the death anniversary *puja* of the late Father William Mackey, a Canadian Jesuit who died in Bhutan last year. A *puja* is a religious ceremony. In Bhutan, *pujas* are performed on the first, seventh, twenty-first, and forty-ninth days after a death, with the final ceremony one year later. It did not seem odd to any of us that a tantric Buddhist ceremony was being performed for a Canadian Jesuit; in fact, it seemed perfectly in keeping with Father's unusual life.

Father Mackey came to Bhutan from his mission in Darjeeling in 1963, at the invitation of the royal government. His job was to help establish a secular school system in a country that had been closed to the outside world for centuries. For twenty years, he worked in the remote eastern district of Tashigang, starting up several schools and Bhutan's first junior college. When I first met him in 1989 in Thimphu, he was chief inspector of schools. He wore full Bhutanese dress and spoke fluent *Sharchhop*, the language of eastern Bhutan. When he did speak English, it was with distinct Bhutanese inflections, but his expressions were my grandmother's: "Nothing doing," he would say, or "By golly." He told us stories of his early days in Bhutan, how on the first visit to Tashigang, he had to carry a big bag of salt; there was no currency in the east at that time, and he bartered the salt for rice, vegetables, and accommodation. He seemed to have taught everyone in the country at some point, from his own office assistant to the king of Bhutan. Another Canadian teacher confirmed this: Father Mackey was a legend, he said, even to the smallest students who had never seen him. He had once sat in on one of Father's impromptu math classes, as enthralled as his students as Father Mackey explained how to balance both sides of an equation: "There was once an old Tibetan king," Father had told the rapt class, "who had twin boys named Impo and Dimpo. And whatever you did to Impo, you had to do to Dimpo." Later, I learned that Father Mackey was one of only a handful of Westerners to be granted Bhutanese citizenship, and that he had been awarded an even rarer honour, the *Druk Thuk Sye* medal, which means "the heart son of Bhutan." The first Canadian teacher in Bhutan, Father Mackey was the start of the long and friendly relationship between the two countries.

When he died last year, he was eighty-one years old and had lived in Bhutan for thirty-two years. During his brief illness, dozens of former students and colleagues stayed with him at the hospital, taking turns to give him sips of water, tuck in his blankets, hold his hands. Several Jesuits from the Darjeeling mission came to administer last rites. Outside in the hallway, Father's friends and driver, Mindu, wept and murmured Buddhist prayers. The morning after his death, the Jesuits took the body to Darjeeling for a Catholic burial, and Father Mackey's students and friends organized the series of Buddhist ceremonies that would guide his soul through the afterworld to a happy rebirth. Father Mackey would have approved of the dual ritual. He had a deep respect for the religion of Bhutan, and although he was an active member of the Jesuit order, he never once in his thirty years in Bhutan tried to convert a single Bhutanese.

Father's final *puja* was held in one of Bhutan's oldest *dzongs*, a massive fortress on the hillside overlooking the Thimphu valley. In a small temple, seven silver bowls of water were set out on the altar, representing offerings of food, drink, flowers, incense, light, and medicine. Small ritual sculptures, made out of butter and flour, were laid out amidst baskets of rice crisps, biscuits, bread, and flowers. Dozens of butter lamps flickered in the room. We laid our white scarves — the traditional offering — on a little side table, under Father Mackey's picture, and sat amongst the rows of monks and religious students.

The *puja* began with a series of prayers in classical Tibetan. The prayers are both sung and chanted, each ending with a burst of ceremonial music:

the deep blast of long horns that extend to the floor, the shrill, mournful cry of smaller horns, the beating of drums, the trill of a conch shell, the silver chime of a bell. The first time I attended a *puja*, I was completely overwhelmed by this discordance: I didn't know whether it was the most awful noise or the most beautiful music I had ever heard. Now it is still rather unearthly but totally familiar to me.

Near the end of the *puja*, we were all given a butter lamp to hold for the final prayer. These are small, goblet-shaped lamps lit with melted vegetable oil. The room danced with light. The *puja* ended, and everyone was served salty butter tea and sweet rice. We talked a little and then stood up and stretched.

As we prepared to leave, I tried to piece together what I believed. My four-year-old son, Pema, had asked me repeatedly where Father Mackey had gone, and I wasn't sure what to tell him. To heaven? To another life? To God? Which God? To Jesus or Buddha? Then I realized that Father Mackey himself would have said, "Both." On our way out, we set the enormous prayer wheels in motion and walked into the night to the ringing of bells.

## V

"So what's it like," people often ask, "to be married to a Bhutanese and living in Bhutan? I mean, what's it *really* like?"

In many ways, my life is probably not so different from the life I would be living in Canada. Mornings are a rush to get my son off to nursery school and myself off to work. In the evenings Tshewang and I cook dinner and play with Pema. We don't have a VCR, and television is still banned in Bhutan, so we have more time to read and talk and write letters. On the weekends, we might take Pema for a walk up the valley, or to lunch at our favourite little restaurant. There's not much pre-packaged entertainment in Thimphu, so we spend a lot of time with friends. I belong to a book club that meets once a month, and a women's writing group. Occasionally, Tshewang and I go dancing at the X, Thimphu's only disco, but the knowledge that we have to get up at dawn with a four-year-old sends us home early.

There are times, however, when I think, "Well, *this* would never happen in Canada." Like the time my mother-in-law, who lives in the hot, steamy southern foothills, sent us up a very large chunk of cow. The —

alas — unrefrigerated truck broke down on the six-hour journey and the meat was already reeking by the time it reached us.

"We can't throw it out," Tshewang said, thinking of the cost of so much meat.

"Well, we can't eat it," I said, thinking of maggots and food poisoning.

"We'll dry it," Tshewang said. He cut the meat into strips and laid it to dry on plastic sheets on our roof. The next day, it began to rain, and I returned from the office to find the garlands of rotten meat festooned all over the house — in the kitchen, the sitting room, the hallway. The smell was overpowering, and I gagged. "Tshewang, honey," I said, breathing through my sleeve, "I know your mom paid a lot of money for that meat, but do we have to let it dry inside the house?"

"The rain will probably stop tomorrow," he said. "Then we'll put it back outside."

But the rain didn't stop. And the smell grew worse and worse. I could hardly breathe inside the house, and even when I was miles away, the smell clung to my clothes. On the third day of rain, I came home from work and made an announcement: "Tshewang, there is a limit to even my adaptability. Get that meat out of the house right now, or we're divorced."

Luckily, the rain stopped, so I never got a chance to find out if rotten meat is considered adequate grounds for divorce in Bhutan.

Another big difference is family visitors. Like all Bhutanese, Tshewang has a million relatives who expect to stay with us when they come to Thimphu. During school breaks, we have up to ten extra people in the house. Last year, we lived in a two-bedroom cottage, and the constant stream of visitors, both expected and unexpected, announced and unannounced, began to drive me crazy. "I have no room, no space, no privacy," I kept telling Tshewang. He seemed sympathetic, but it was hard for him to understand. Bhutanese children grow up in large, extended families, sharing bedrooms and bathrooms and clothes, and even adults don't like to be alone much. "Why don't you just tell them no?" a friend asked. I tried to explain: "Everyone's family comes to stay here," I said. "People coming to town from their villages don't have money to stay in a hotel, and even if they did, why would they want to stay with strangers when they could stay with family? It would be the ultimate insult, to tell them they couldn't stay." We solved the problem by moving to a bigger house, where I could have a room of my own.

"What do you miss?" people ask. Believe it or not, the material things are the easiest to give up: microwaves and washing machines, subways and shopping malls with a million billion things to buy. And there are lots of things I am glad to be without: television, for one thing, and the constant bombardment of ads. Senseless murders and the rush of everything.

But there *are* things I miss about life in Canada. I miss the free exchange of views, debate, public dissent, the stimulation of a critical press. Bhutan is a very hierarchical, conservative society, and the Bhutanese have a profound respect for authority. Once, while discussing graffiti with a senior class at the college, I wrote as an example on the board, "Question authority before authority questions you." A few students looked nervous; the rest looked bewildered. Authority in Bhutan is to be obeyed. To question authority is to show disrespect and disloyalty.

To say that I find this oppressive does not really say much at all. Try as I do, I am unable to get completely outside my upbringing. Bhutanese culture developed for centuries without any contact with the outside world, and there are aspects that will always be foreign to me. I also recognize that some of those very aspects I personally find oppressive are responsible for the social stability and safety I value so much. It's a hard call.

So what's it really like? After eight years, it's like home. After eight years, it's still not home. It's harder in some ways, easier in others. Will I stay here forever? Maybe, but probably not. Anyway, Buddhism teaches us that nothing is forever. I'm here for now, and that's enough.

*Jamie Zeppa*

UGANDA

It is Bev Peden, a fellow Canadian, who invites me to the play.

"A play?" I reply. "Here? In Kabale?"

Since the last time I was here, a year ago, and since last year's massacre just across the border in Rwanda, things *do* seem to have picked up in this one-horse town in Uganda. As Bev and I walk past the UPET gas station this morning, there are seven World Food Program trucks waiting for a fill-up. The main street is overrun by trucks carrying food, containers — just about everything — south to Kigali or Goma. Looks like Rwanda has become lucrative business.

It hasn't, however, had many spin-offs for the people, mostly farmers, on this side of the border. Here, they're still picking up and rebuilding after decades of their own wars and Idi Amin–style, state-orchestrated massacres. Yoweri Museveni, at the helm of the new Uganda, seems to be doing a great job. But there isn't all that much that *can* be done to turn back the clocks for farmers whose land and soils have run out. Or for the many in the region who are HIV-positive. About one in four . . . or is it now one in three? That seems to be the most immediate effect of all the traffic passing through this small town that used to be out of the way, nestled among the spectacular terraced mountains of southwest Uganda. Not a place I'd immediately associate with plays or theatres.

"Yes, a play," Bev continues. "The women's group wrote it. It's about the man who drank his daughter."

How can I possibly resist?

We're late getting to the theatre that afternoon. Except it's not really a theatre. It's a women's house, one they built themselves, with their own savings and their own hands. Yes, there have been some benefactors. Bev, for one, who has lived here for years, and a Dutch woman, who helped with roofing sheets and cement. The rest of the costs the women covered themselves by selling their baskets or tree seedlings from their nurseries. In front of the simple whitewashed structure, they're waiting for us — more than forty women of the Abedkundire Women's Group.

They usher us inside and follow to sit on mats on the packed mud floor. On the rear wall, brown letters in a shaky hand welcome us all. The rest of the wall is plastered with informative posters about "slim," as AIDS is called here. A blackboard is propped against a side wall, underneath some geometric designs and a very geometric rendition of the alphabet. On it is a list of words: *beach*, *book*, *bag*, *door*, *wall*, *pencil*, and *window*.

Beside me, on the chairs reserved for guests and for group leaders, sits Faith. She tells me she's a recent recruit to the group. She teaches the women reading, writing, and arithmetic on Wednesday afternoons. Today, she says, the women would like to sing some songs they've composed. After that they'll perform their play.

I try to get comfortable on the chair. To be honest, I'm hungry and tired. We've been clambering up and down farmers' fields all day, at angles that would make a downhill skier think twice. Babies are crying, and as the women stand and prepare for the performance, I wonder what I've got myself into.

Thunder rumbles across the hilltops. The view out the door is breathtaking: green sensuous mountains carved into a million terraces, with blue-black clouds riding the late-afternoon sun. But mobs of children are blocking the doorway and the windows and the light. In the gloom inside the women look, to me, like the weary and worn farmers, mothers, and wives that they are.

But then they start to sing. Their faces begin to glow — or is that a trick of the sinking sun toying with the stormy light? Their voices raise goosebumps, cause my eyes to prick. I haven't been to church since I was a child, but suddenly it all comes back to me — the joy of believing, of faith, in people.

Faith whispers to me that they're singing about the new laws the government has passed that give women rights to, for example, land. An elderly woman cavorts to the front of the group, urged on by forty smiles and voices. She's as nimble and buoyant — and yes, jubilant — as a beauty queen. Bev tells me that her name is Irene, that a few years ago Irene's husband wanted to take a second wife. To afford this, he needed to sell the land that he owned and that Irene had worked for many years, to feed, clothe, and school her children. Irene didn't agree to the sale of the land so her husband came at night, with a friend, and broke her thumb, forcing her to apply her thumbprint to seal the deal. Make it legal.

Is it dark enough that these silly tears in my eyes don't show? How can this be? A group of half-literate women in the back of beyond has brought me to tears? Not even the horrendous footage from Rwanda did that.

But these women are not finished with me yet. When the songs are done, they disappear behind the curtain, ragged bedsheets on a wire that they've rigged up to turn their house into a theatre. They re-emerge as queens of the rag bag, wearing the usual discards from the second-hand market, where everyone shops. But this is unthinkable. Some are dressed as men, in torn blazers, trousers, shirts. Women in Kabale aren't even permitted to ride a bicycle, because bicycles are for men only. Faith translates for me as the woman in man's clothing, the star of the show, drinks away the family fortune. First to go is the goat, then the land, and finally the daughter, all to pay for his local brew at the neighbourhood bar. It's obvious from the laughter in the house that the reprobate husband staggering about and falling down drunk is not a stranger to these women.

As the final curtain is pulled, as the daughter is dragged off weeping by the man who has bought her, I glance outside, where the darkening hills are being split by jagged blades of lightning. And I know that these women will pull through everything life drags them through. They have faith in themselves, they have humour, and they have each other.

I also know that the hundreds of camera crews that went to Rwanda to focus their sights only on the horrors on the other side of those hills out there were missing an awful lot of the story Africa has to tell.

*Joan Baxter*

## TOKYO

I am staying at a Japanese-style inn, right in the heart of a charming old district in north-central Tokyo. This is my first visit to Japan, and amongst other things, experiencing the famous Japanese public bath was a priority on my to-do list.

The Japanese practice of communal bathing made its first appearance in the sixteenth century, when the Tokugawa Shogunate outlawed private bathing. We modern-day Westerners might think that private bathing was banned for some exotic and downright decadent reason, but it was, in fact, a purely pragmatic decision. It seems that homes (and neighbouring buildings) had a tendency to burn down because of the fires that were lit to warm the bathing water, a risk that was greatly reduced in properly constructed bath houses.

Having always been in favour of the "when in Rome . . ." axiom, I asked the innkeeper to direct me to an authentic, Japanese-style public bath. She handed me a towel, advised me to bring my own soap and shampoo, and pointed me in the direction of one of the 1,669 public bath houses currently in Tokyo.

From the outside, it curiously resembled a Buddhist temple. Just inside the entrance, an older gentleman was buying soap from a woman seated behind a reception counter. He turned and looked at me, and his mouth broke into a wide grin. I suddenly felt as though I had a huge letter *F* for *Foreigner* stamped upon my forehead. I leaned towards the woman behind the desk and whispered in my atrocious Japanese, "Men and women bathe *together*?" She broke into a hearty laugh. "No, no!" She pointed to two sets of curtains, separated by a thin piece of wall. "Men go in *blue* curtain, and women go in *red* curtain."

Just over a hundred years ago, the bemused gentleman and I would have bathed together, and it was amidst great protest that the two sexes were separated in 1885. Evidently the Japanese were perfectly comfortable with communal bathing, but Western missionaries assured them that it was a recipe for moral collapse. I glanced heavenward and thanked Queen Victoria, hastily paid my 340 yen, and slipped through the red curtain, praying that there were no peepholes in the walls between the two.

I entered a spotless, bright room with a sofa, neat stacks of wicker baskets, and a finely polished wooden floor. There were mirrors everywhere. Two naked elderly women sat daintily on little towels on the sofa, chatting. They turned and looked at me for what felt like an eternity, then turned away and resumed their conversation. I began to wonder if I would have the nerve to go through with my plan.

I resisted the urge to bolt and ask for my money back. My typical Western middle-class self-consciousness was going to ruin the experience if I didn't suspend judgement and go through this with an open mind. I quickly stripped, threw my clothes into a wicker basket, and wrapped my towel around my body.

I peered through a set of glass doors, and saw at least a dozen women crouched on a tile floor in front of individual mirrors and faucets, in various stages of soaping and scrubbing. I took a deep breath, pulled myself up to my full, five-foot, two-inch height, and charged into the bath area as if I owned the place.

I grabbed a wooden bucket from a stack by the door and hastened to a faucet in the centre of the room. I knelt down on the tiles and slowly poured hot water over my body from the bucket, while I used my peripheral vision to peek at how the other women were performing their own baths.

The women scrubbed each body part slowly and carefully, and then rinsed and scrubbed again. And again. I had always been under the impression that the Japanese are just, well, *fastidious* people, but like most cultural differences, there is more to it than meets the eye. In truth, Buddhist temples in Japan used to include hot baths as part of their purification rites, and that's why many public baths were later designed to look like temples.

Indeed, the bath appeared to me to be a somewhat hypnotic ritual, with each woman in her own world, seemingly mesmerized by the feel of the soap, water, and scrub brush, and the soothing image in the mirror.

There is no narcissistic element to the widespread use of mirrors in the Japanese public bath house. Actually, even the mirror has cultural and mystical significance: legend has it that the sun goddess, Amaterasu, the spiritual ancestor of all Japanese people, become very depressed and hid deep in a cave, bringing darkness to the land. In desperation, religious leaders finally placed a mirror at the entrance to the cave, and the trick worked. Amaterasu was lured out of the cave by the shiny object, and once again the people and the land were blessed with sun. To this day, mirrors figure prominently in Japanese daily life.

As I discreetly observed how the other women went about their bathing practices, I would occasionally notice one of them peeking at me as well. After all, foreigners very rarely visit public bath houses in Japanese cities, where private facilities are available in hotels. Perhaps they were curious to know if I am *pink* in places where they are *brown*; if my Western body is essentially the same as their Eastern ones. I imagined them duly noting that we are all, in fact, very much the same. And so, satisfied that there were really no aliens on either side, we all carried on with the business of cleansing ourselves.

Three huge tiled tubs stood before me. The water in the one on the right was a sort of greenish colour — perhaps it was salty. The water in the one on the left was brownish — maybe there were minerals added. The one in the middle was clear. I felt like Goldilocks, confronted with the momentous decision of which bowl of porridge to choose. Like Goldilocks, I went for the middle one — it looked just right. (Besides, it was the only one that was empty.) I gingerly slipped into the water and stifled a gasp. It was *hot*! A thermometer at the edge of the tub registered forty-five degrees Celsius.

I think I lasted about thirty seconds in the hot water. My skin turned bright pink and I thought I might faint, vanish under the surface and be cooked like a lobster in a pot. Women continued to sit in the other tubs quietly chatting in small groups or half-dozing. I though that perhaps *my* tub was hotter than the others, but a quick check of *those* thermometers revealed that all were the same.

The dinner hour was not far away, and the change room was now filled with laughing women. In days gone by, the proprietor would sit on a high stool and exchange gossip with the customers on one side of the gender barrier, and then pass it along to the other side. The bath is still a popular meeting place, where people gather at the end of each day to get clean and catch up on the latest news, where self-consciousness doesn't exist, and no one takes notice of wrinkles and aging bodies.

I suddenly felt very lonely. I slipped out onto the darkened street and hurried back to the inn.

*Jane Hamilton*

## BUTARITARI

This is not my story. It belongs to Winnie Powell, the indomitable medicine woman of Butaritari. It belongs to her and to her island, which isn't really an island but an atoll in the Central Pacific. Butaritari belongs to a country no one has ever heard of called Kiribati. It's a real country, and this is a real story.

I only know it because I got sick. I went to visit Winnie on Butaritari and within thirty-six hours was curled up on a pandanus mat, shivering with fever and suffering from what Winnie knowingly called "the flu with a touch of 'epatitis."

Winnie insisted I eat. She offered me the full range of local dishes: bananas, fish, paw paw, coconut, and swamp taro. That was it. The full range. Oh, granted, there is a world of difference between roasted swamp taro and grated swamp taro, but being deathly ill allows you certain privileges and it gets to the point where you grab those privileges by the throat and scream into their collective face, "No more swamp taro!"

And that was when Winnie told me this story. It starts, as all good stories do, once upon a time, not so very long ago . . .

The dolphins and humans lived in separate but equal worlds. The dolphins kept watch over the sea and the humans oversaw the land. There was mutual respect and liking but they rarely saw each other socially. In fact, there were only two families on Butaritari who had the knowledge to "call the dolphins."

Calling the dolphins was difficult and dangerous and only undertaken in times of hunger. When the Caller was asleep, she guided her dreams towards the land of the dolphins. There she could speak to them directly.

The Caller was invariably well received. The dolphins loved company.

Once introductory pleasantries were over, the Caller started the real reason for the visit. "I have been sent to invite the dolphins to a dance in our lagoon. Can you come?"

That always thrilled the dolphins. "Oh, yes! Yes, of course, we would be happy to come!" Invitation delivered and accepted, the Caller then politely excused herself and quietly faded back into consciousness.

The next day, just before high tide, the whole village went down to the lagoon to watch the sea channel expectantly. Soon the dolphins started to arrive. The teenagers and young adults of the village took off their clothes and hung them on trees. Then they dove into the lagoon and paired off with the dolphins. The humans murmured sweet nothings while gently holding onto their hosts. As parents and siblings watched from the shore, singing and dancing encouragingly, the human-dolphin couples frolicked in the crystal aquamarine waters. Occasionally, a mischievously adventurous pair even went out into the darker blue waters of the open sea, returning only hours later.

Eventually, the tide faltered and the time came to end the dance. The dolphins knew what to do next. One by one, they beached themselves, always in the same spot and always facing the same direction. The swimmers quietly got their clothes from the trees and stood watching. Emotions crackled in the air. Sorrow, pain, gratitude, love and, darting about like an embarrassed streaker, hunger.

Some of the stronger men picked up the hatchets that had been lying on the cool grass since the morning and, caressing the lean and still wet dolphins with one hand, hacked them to death with the other. As soon as they beached, they were butchered. The meat was quickly and equitably distributed all throughout the island.

Everyone got a piece. Everyone except the Caller of dolphins. She had known the dolphins as friends, she had spoken with them. It was unacceptable for her to eat them.

She also paid another price. The Caller always died young and, when she died, she was not buried on the island. Just off the coast of Butaritari there was a dark blot on the turquoise ocean, a bottomless hole in the sea floor that people believed led into the home of the dolphins. The body of the Caller was brought to this spot and placed in the water. Other bodies would have floated away, but hers sunk, down, down, reuniting her again and forever with the dolphins, who were always happy to have company.

That sacrifice, dying young, forever being separated from her family, the caller of the dolphins was willing to make for the honour of being able to provide food for her hungry island.

And that was the end of Winnie's story.

She looked rather pointedly at the now cold dish of roasted swamp taro.

"Boy," I said, "that swamp taro sure looks good." I started munching away dutifully.

And Winnie smiled.

*Cleo Paskal*

# CONVERSATIONS WITH WRITERS III:
# W. O. MITCHELL

*In the introduction to the book I put together about* This Country in the Morning *in 1974, I wrote: "When I grow up, I want to be Paul Hiebert. On the way to growing up, I want to be W. O. Mitchell." I'm still working on it. He is, however, one of a kind.*

PETER GZOWSKI  W. O. Mitchell looked tired when I met him, and no wonder. This was last Thursday afternoon, and all week long he'd been rehearsing his performance in Toronto of a kind of musical "Jake and the Kid" — a performance, by the way, that earned him and Billy Mae Richards — who came back to be the Kid to Bill Mitchell's Jake — a fifteen-minute standing ovation. As usual, too, he'd been promoting his newest novel (this one is called *For Art's Sake*, and you'll hear him read from it later on) and getting ready for a very special occasion, a kind of delayed celebration — the real anniversary was in August — of fifty years of marriage to his beloved Merna. Merna is known to some Mitchell intimates as "For Bleep's Sake Merna," after Bill's most frequent form of address. That celebration, it turned out, was a lovely evening. I dropped in on it briefly on Monday night. It was in Peterborough. Now, to complicate things even further last week, W. O. Mitchell has been fighting some illness lately, even though, as his friends know, it's going to have to be some illness indeed if it thinks it's going to mow him down. Anyway, we talked for a while, as we have over the years, and what follows are some moments from our conversation. They begin with a reference to one of his most recent honours: his appointment, along with a few other distinguished Canadians, to the Privy Council. Hi.

W. O. MITCHELL  Hi, Peter.

PG  What do I call you now? The Honourable? The Right? No, the Honourable. The Honourable W.

WOM  You know, when Doug Gibson at McClelland and Stewart heard this, we were over in England, and Brian Mulroney phoned me there. My daughter-in-law thought it was a bloody hoax. We were in Yorkshire, and it was a real shocker. We went upstairs to Orm and Barbara sitting on the bed and laughing their heads off, and then Orm said, "It figures, Bill. Queen's Privy Council. Who's more familiar with privies than you?" That's pretty witty. Then Doug, in answer to your same question, said, "Where does the Honourable come then, before or after?" I said, "I don't know." "Well," he said, "we know one thing for sure, it took something as dramatic as this to make an honourable guy out of you."

PG  Has it worked?

WOM  Maybe.

PG  Are you honourable?

WOM  I try.

PG  You've always been honourable in my book.

WOM  I try to be. Like you, I try.

PG  What do they give you? Do you get anything?

WOM  In the way of?

PG  I don't know, a cheque or a seat or privy.

WOM  Yeah, I got a ribbon and a medal.

PG  Did you?

WOM  Yeah.

PG  Are you wearing it now?

WOM  Yeah, and I just got a Centennial Medal that suddenly came out of the blue. As a matter of fact, I heard on the news the other day that Honest Ed got one, too, so I'm in pretty good company. What the hell am I going to do with all of these things? And then again Merna said, "Hang it on your butt."

PG  Have you got a wall somewhere or all of this stuff in a room?

WOM  No, I just stash them away and never look at them again. They're in a drawer somewhere, I don't remember where it is.

PG  What is the most treasured award you've been given? You have the Officer of the Order of Canada, you've got honorary degrees, you've got the Governor General's Award, you've got the Leacock Award. You've got . . .

WOM  I think the most exciting one was one of the first ones, when *Who Has Seen the Wind* came out. That award, because it was the first I ever received, was pretty nice, but actually I have to make a public confession: they're labels, they don't mean all that much to me. Well, I think mainly because I once realized . . . I was in the bathroom — I think I was shaving — and it suddenly hit me that art is something that somebody does for its own sake, and it does not involve a win-lose, victor-vanquished, adversarial relationship. And therefore, like when I get asked, What's your favourite novel you've written? I can't answer that. Well, I do say, The one I'm working on now. It's not an Olympic event, with a bronze, silver, and a gold. And these medals, singling somebody out in their relationship and their success against each other, do not really mean that much to me.

PG   What do you think of living in a country that gives an award for humour? I've always . . .

WOM   This has been embarrassing, Peter.

PG   Has it?

WOM   I really mean it. I'm as serious as hell. Twice! And a third time I was up, and I breathed a sigh of relief when I wasn't given the Leacock Award for the third time, though I admired him tremendously. I read him when I was in high school in Florida. It's damaging because reviewers who are *Sturm and Drang*-ers, either-or, cannot take seriously a piece of fiction that has humour in it, and wit. They've never heard of Shakespeare's expression of comic relief. They think it should be either all tragedy or all slapstick comedy, the two worst forms of writing I know. Not that it matters, either. So very frequently there will be reviewers, because I made them giggle or laugh, say, This can't be a serious piece of work. So it has been a little discomforting getting that Stephen Leacock Award twice.

PG   Did you know him? Did you ever meet him?

WOM   I never met him, and I would love to have. I'll never forget when I first read him. I was in St. Petersburg Senior High School in Florida, and my beloved drama and English teacher, Emily Murray, said to me, "Billy, you're from Canada?" I said, "Yes." She said, "There's a very fine Canadian writer," and she introduced me to Stephen Leacock. I think I was eighteen or something when I first read him. That's only sixty years ago, and I've admired him so much over the years.

PG   Where's Mark Twain in your life?

WOM   Mark Twain?

PG   You look like Mark Twain.

WOM   I've been told that.

PG   Well, I knew him well.

WOM   Yeah, he was an untidy bastard too.

PG   Leacock wasn't exactly sartorially elegant.

WOM   No, but he was an academic, as well. I learned to read very, very young. My father was in the last stages of what killed him in 1921, before he went to the Mayo Clinic, and one of my greatest visions is of the white sheet and that yellow foot sticking out. He taught me to read with the phonic approach, sounding out words from the Regina *Leader-Post*, and the day that I pronounced "tuh tank ah man" at the age of four, he boasted all over town about his kid.

Now, he was a tremendous reader, and our living room — three sides were stacks of books, and that was where I read every single one of Mark Twain's books in hardcover. He had a whole collection of them, and that's when I fell in love with Mark Twain. Not just for his humour, but I remember loving *Tom Sawyer*. I remember being confused with *The Adventures of Huckleberry Finn* when I was six or seven or eight. Then, years later, I did my novel *Since Daisy Creek*, in which Mark Twain is a character — a guy is doing a biography of Mark Twain — and I reread it. You see, what happened with Mark Twain — when my son Orm went to university and came back, for the first time I knew he had been given the proper respect that he deserved and that he had become hot stuff within the English departments of American Literature in universities. So I reread *The Adventures of Huckleberry Finn*, and hurrah for Sam Clemens. That is the finest — that is the great American novel. *Moby-Dick* can take second place. *The Adventures of Huckleberry Finn*, thematically and every way, except for about the last thirty pages, when for commercial reasons he drags Tom Sawyer into the thing. So what I learned from Mark Twain — you don't generally learn from other writers, but I think what was fixed very early for me is that you write out of your own cultural and geographical context. His Hannibal in Missouri ain't too bloody different from the Saskatchewan or Alberta Prairies.

PG   What's the Great Canadian Novel?

WOM   The Great Canadian Novel? Well, again, because it's not a silver and a bronze and a gold, it's hard for me.

PG   Yeah, but you did the American one, so . . .

WOM   Oh, there are others, too. I mean I'm fond of Steinbeck. Virginia Woolf is a favourite of mine. I got to tap Margaret Laurence.

PG   *The Stone Angel?*

WOM   I think *The Stone Angel* is pretty great. I think so. As a matter of fact, it's interesting to me that as Canadian novelists have come into prominence, from very early, I mean very early, being Canadian back in the forties was not a handicap. There had already been Thomas Raddall, Sinclair Ross — I read him first, something about the sign on the door in *Queen's Quarterly* — and Ralph Connor.

These had already become internationally established, and what was then the case, not so much now, was publishers were interested because we were enough of the same, and they had this goofy notion, the romantic notion of penguins and Eskimos and Mounted Police and wilderness. It was still understandable to people south of the forty-ninth; in fact it was a bit of an advantage. It made Canadian writers stand out.

PG  Can I tell you a story?

WOM  Yeah.

PG  I was asked to go and take part in a concert of a choir in a little town in Ontario. It was a choral concert, and the choir was going to sing, and I was supposed to go and talk in between the songs.

WOM  Yeah.

PG  Don't look at me like this. Oh, I should tell you how I quote you all the time when I'm making public speeches.

WOM  I know you do, Peter, and I love you for it.

PG  Mostly what I quote you on is the night you got up some place in Alberta, and you were on late in the evening. Everybody had made their speech before you did and it was . . .

WOM  No, this was in Toronto, when I was on *Maclean's*.

PG  . . . and they said, "W. O. Mitchell will now give his address."

WOM  Yeah.

PG  And you said?

WOM  I said, "My address is 350 Springdale Boulevard and, damn it, I'm going there right now." That was a Canadian Authors Association thing that Art Irwin made me go to, and I was preceded by people who came in first, second, and third in poetry, in short story, in everything else.

PG  My punchline is W. O. Mitchell's address is High River, Alberta. I didn't know it was in Toronto. Now I'm going to have to change my routine.

WOM  It was while I was in Toronto. I was on the fiction desk at *Maclean's*, and Irwin made me go there. I had already fallen out of love with the amateur association, and I wasn't surprised at what happened. But I wasn't ready — sitting there and waiting and waiting, and they said, "We will now have W. O. Mitchell's address." I didn't behave, Peter: I said, "My address is Springdale Boulevard and, by God, I'm going there right now."

PG   So, that's not the story I'm going to tell you. This is the story: I'm supposed to sing with this choir, I'm going to talk with this choir, and I say, "I haven't got enough to say on my own between the choir pieces. Can I read you something?" The young choirmaster said, "Yeah, read something. Read whatever you want. Read something Canadian." So I said, "I'm going to read the last page and a half of *Who Has Seen the Wind*."

WOM   Oh, boy, I never knew that, Peter.

PG   No, no, wait, I'm not finished yet. I remember when you read that for us on *This Country in the Morning*, in the library in High River, about twenty years ago. I said, "I can't pretend to be Bill Mitchell, but the words will do it for themselves." So I get halfway down — I'm up in the country, and I get halfway down to Toronto, and oh, God, I haven't got a copy of the book with me.

WOM   Oh, my God.

PG   So what will I do? I go dashing into this young choirmaster — he's about twenty-seven years old, a terrific guy. I said, "I wanted to read *Who Has Seen the Wind*, but I haven't got it with me." He said, "Just a minute." He went back to his house and he brought out a dog-eared copy. This is just a young guy who had never been to the Prairies. That book was as important to him as it is to me and to hundreds and hundreds of thousands of other people. Just that one moment, just that one book, him bringing that out — I thought, that makes it all worth it. Everything, I mean everything. That book is a part of that guy's soul, just as it is of mine. So maybe *you* wrote the Great Canadian Novel.

WOM   I didn't know you had done that, Peter.

PG   I do that all the time. I talk about you all the time.

WOM   I'll be getting in touch. I'll be getting legal advice, see what I can do about plagiarism. No. Thanks.

PG   It's not plagiarism, it's theft.

WOM   No, I know it isn't. I'm not behaving.

PG   What I would like to do is get you to record a piece of *For Art's Sake*, but let me ask you about it first. *For Art's Sake* is dedicated to Merna?

WOM   Yep.

PG   I don't want to say publicly what everybody who knows you and Merna knows what you call Merna — it's "For Bleep's Sake

Merna." The love between you two has survived for fifty years, and I don't know if any of the other books have been dedicated to her. This book opens with Art remembering . . . Art is the centre.

WOM  Merna's my life model for Irene, and all through the novel he talks to his dead wife and she talks back to him. I think it's probably one of the most moving sequences that I've ever written.

PG  Is it a thank-you to Merna?

WOM  Well, you see, it's my ass. (Pardon me.) I'm in trouble if I show Douglas Gibson at McClelland and Stewart a finished novel before Merna sees it. All our married life Merna has been my first editor. She could have been a leading editor for any leading publisher. It's a partnership, truly a partnership, and we read each other's minds — she'll say something that I just thought to myself. I think we're unusual and we're extremely lucky. I didn't realize that until about the time we moved into Calgary, and a number of people we had known — they had waited until the kids grew up and they broke up. We had no clue about that. I think it's unusual and damn lucky. I remember being very, very moved by a short piece by Greg Clark, who was a dear friend of mine, and the name of it was, "May Your First Love Be Your Last." It was extremely moving, and it summed up the way I feel and we feel about each other.

PG  That's nice. You once told me something else that Greg Clark told you, but we can't say it on the radio. It was about advice.

WOM  Ah. No — you can say that on the radio.

PG  *I* can't.

WOM  *You* can't, but *I* can.

PG  I know — and you're going to.

WOM  Look, I'm vulgar. So was Greg Clark. It was when I was fishing with Ralph Allen and Greg Clark in northern Saskatchewan, and as a matter of fact it was for Arctic grayling. I had a fly that my young son Orm had invented using mallard feathers on the side. I'm getting kind of off the subject, but Greg was fishing downstream from me. The first time he came up he said, "My God, I've had six on." I had lost count. Orm nicknamed the fly the Mitchell Killer, and Greg insisted that Orm make him twenty of them for his fly collection and for the book he was going to do on flies. Anyway, while we talked, as we did in the bunks at night, Greg, who was quite a bit older than I was, and by this time maybe I was beginning to wonder about age, and he said, "Don't knock it, kid. From the time you were born life takes you by the end of your penis and pulls you all through, and then all of a sudden when you hit sixty, seventy, eighty, it lets go — and it's *beautiful*!" Now I said that, not you.

PG   I know. When you first told me that, the penis wasn't particularly called a penis.

WOM   No, it wasn't.

PG   Never mind, though, that's fine. When this is on the air, I will have seen you briefly at yours and Merna's fiftieth. It's not really. It's a celebration, but the anniversary was in fact back in the summer.

WOM   My younger son did that at the lake. We had a lot of friends at the lake, but this is the real one, because, Peter, we've got ten times more friends. Merna and I hang on to our friends. You're one of them. Tiff Findley's another one. June Callwood's another one. We hang on to our friends, and I'm really looking forward to touching base with all of these old buddies.

PG   Well, your friends sort of hang on to you, too, you know.

WOM   Yeah. Yes, they do.

PG   It's good to see you. Thank you, W. O. Mitchell.

# Some of the Best Minds
# of Our Time

*One of the real privileges of working at Morningside was the opportunity to encounter people whose intellects had taken them into exotic, fascinating, and often important aspects of the frontiers of knowledge and to give them a chance to explain their work and their thinking in terms that even I could understand. Here are some of our encounters.*

## HUBERT REEVES
### *October 1994*

PETER GZOWSKI Montreal-born astrophysicist Hubert Reeves has a worldwide reputation as a scientist and philosopher. Many people consider him the foremost expert on the Big Bang theory, but in English-speaking Canada, Hubert Reeves still remains something of an unknown. That will change, we hope, with the release of English translations of his books in Canada. Hubert Reeves joins us from Montreal. Good morning, sir.

HUBERT REEVES Good morning.

PG Can I ask you about something I saw on the news last week? As I clipped it out I said, Aha, Hubert Reeves will explain this to me. It turns out that the Milky Way, the galaxy that includes our solar system, may not have a black hole at its centre.

HR There are black holes in the centre of many galaxies, and many people would like to have one at home, but it turns out the evidence for such a thing is becoming smaller and smaller, and we may not have one.

PG Does this change my life?

HR I'm afraid it won't change it too much. You can reassure yourself there are many other black holes in many other galaxies.

PG You come back to Montreal every fall to give lectures.

HR Yes, one month in the fall and one month in the spring, I give lectures in cosmology at the University of Montreal.

PG Are they restorative? Is it good to get home from time to time?

HR Oh, it is very important to me. I feel I'm coming back home every time. I see my friends and parents and I don't have the feeling of being away.

PG How did we lose you in the first place?

HR I went to Brussels to give some lectures thirty years ago and found a group already involved in this subject. They asked me to work with them. I found it very exciting and decided to stay most of the time. I decided also to always come back here and spend part of my time in Canada. Actually, if you wanted to do the best science, you would be in the United States. Of course, the United States is half the world in science, but it turns out that I prefer living in Europe or in Canada.

For me the life in the United States is a little bit boring, a little too conventional.

PG Nature is important to you, your farm is important to you.

HR Yes, for me it's fundamental. It's vital. I can work all the week, but I have to go in the fields and work in my garden and walk in the woods, where I see no one. I need to walk. If I don't, I don't feel very well. It is a contact with nature that I find indispensable for my life and for my work.

PG As you walk through your farm, Malicorne, do you take a tape recorder with you and speak your thoughts?

HR Yes, I have done that often. When I come home I organize all my notes and eventually make something like a book out of that. I find that an agreeable and fruitful way of working.

PG Is a specific piece of writing triggered by a specific glimpse as you walk, say the sight of a dragonfly?

HR Yes, sometimes. I find here what is wonderful is the colour of the trees. I can walk many hours and it can always inspire me. I manage to come back every fall. The official purpose is to give lectures, but my very important purpose is to walk in the Laurentides looking at the trees.

PG You ponder ideas that are, to me, imponderable. What was there before time?

HR Yes, that's a big question. No one knows. We would like to know. We use physics, astrophysics, observation with the telescope of the satellites. We try to have a picture of how the universe evolved, where it came from, how it has changed with time, and we have some reasonable answers for such questions. But there are questions that will remain mysterious for a long time, perhaps forever.

PG What is your hunch about "perhaps forever"? It seems to me we could never know what there was before time.

HR It's true we know things that for a long time we never thought we could explore, and we're exploring fields of the cosmos which were thought to be unreachable. How far can we go in exploring the world? My hunch — it is just a personal hunch and it may be quite wrong — is that we will not come to a point where we know everything. In fact I would find that very boring.

PG We'd be like the United States, we'd know everything and be boring.

HR I hope this will not come. Last century, some people thought the universe was determined, that everything was fixed. I think there are things you could have predicted. For instance, you could have predicted that there would be stars, there would be atoms, that there would be molecules, but you could not have predicted a particular star. This is something we learn today through what is called the Theory of Chaos. It tells us that we could have predicted the major lines of development but never the particular event. That is the prevailing view today and I quite agree with that prevailing view.

PG But prevailing views change. They've changed in our lifetime.

HR It's the strength of science that it can always put itself into question. Tomorrow we may have a new observation and we may say, for instance, well, the Big Bang was a nice idea but it is just wrong. Science is never definite.

PG Does that mean there's no truth?

HR I wouldn't say that. I would say our picture of the world is quite believable, quite plausible. The Big Bang is a quite believable theory.

PG This whole struggle with randomness and chaos boggles my mind. I can't understand how chaos can be analysable.

HR It does seem sort of contradictory. I would say what we discover is that nature is determined to a point, but not in great detail. If you try to predict ahead of time a specific event, like for instance the tossing of a coin, if you have a good coin you cannot predict which side it will fall on.

PG I know a guy who can, but he's cheating.

HR An honest coin and an honest player, you cannot predict. Nature is not determined in great detail. It is determined only generally. Meteorology is a good example. Our weatherman can predict the weather for tomorrow with a good chance, the next day not so good, but if you ask him what the weather will be in Montreal or Toronto in a year, he is quite incapable of telling you. If you live in the desert of Africa you can say what the weather will be next year at the same date. It will be nice because it's always nice. It never rains. But in Montreal or Toronto you cannot do that. Life would be dull if everything were determined in advance, if you knew or could know exactly what will happen for the rest of your life.

PG  The whole idea of play is important to you. Your work is play, your life is play.

HR  Right, that's true. Play is very important.

PG  Why did I come out of school not understanding that thought was play? What did you learn from a Trappist monk when you were a child that convinced you that what you do is play?

HR  The problem with school, of course, is that the teachers have forgotten to play. They've forgotten that to teach is first of all an emotive event. You have to give passion to the student; we have to be taught to discover by exploration. A friend of our family, a Trappist monk, was a geneticist, a biologist, a botanist. He enjoyed his life as a scientist. When I was four or five years old, I was very impressed by this man who seemed to enjoy so much. He would take us in his laboratory, walk through the woods, show us the flowers, and for me it was a very important experience. I decided that was the kind of thing I would like to do.

PG  Can you tell me about the sunset you saw in Vancouver?

HR  Yes, that was a very important experience for me. I was a student at the University of Montreal and I had a summer job at an astrophysical observatory in Victoria, British Columbia. I used to walk in the evening in a beautiful park, I think it's called Beacon Hill Park, where you can see the sunset on the sea, on the Olympic Mountains. And one day looking at this sunset, I was struck by the fact that this colour, this light, all this beauty was, after all, related to equations of electrodynamics and physics. Then came to me a question: When you know how this happens, does that not destroy the beauty? Is it better not to know how this happens, the physics of it, the light and so on? Is it possible to keep on enjoying the sunset, knowing how it happens? It is like dismantling your toy. And it took me some time to understand. My book, *Malicorne*, was about how I came to understand that I could at the same time understand physically what happened and still marvel, still be in an attitude of wondering about the beauty of life. This problem gave me a big headache that evening. Today, I can like and enjoy both science and its explanation, and science does not destroy for me the sense of beauty in nature.

PG  Thank you very much for this time this morning.

HR  Thank you.

## WERNER ISRAEL
### *January 1992*

PETER GZOWSKI It's been almost twenty-five years since the term "black hole" became part of our astronomical vocabulary. Black holes are thought to be the corpses of burnt-out stars, corpses so heavy that the gravity prevents matter and light from escaping. Dr. Werner Israel has studied black holes for a number of years. For the past couple of years, he's been concentrating on the insides of black holes. Good morning, sir.

WERNER ISRAEL Hello.

PG I need a refresher course. A black hole — tell me what it is.

WI A black hole is a region of empty space in which gravity is very, very strong, so strong that nothing can escape, not even light.

PG So if I were in a black hole you couldn't see me.

WI No. But you could see me.

PG I could?

WI Yes, because light can certainly fall into a black hole, although it can't get out. So you would still be able to see the outside universe.

PG What would it look like?

WI Pretty normal, for a good part of the way. If you fell into a black hole you would still see the stars shining overhead. If you had one of these monster black holes that people believe lurk at the centres of galaxies, you could fall for twenty or thirty minutes without noticing anything very unusual. I think perhaps the only alarming feature would be a spreading pool of blackness beneath you.

PG How fast would I go?

WI Well, you have to give the velocity with respect to some stationary observer, and inside a black hole nothing is stationary, so you have no frame of reference with respect to which to measure your acceleration and your inward velocity. You would just have to say that you're falling completely freely inwards, and this would continue for twenty or thirty minutes, and then suddenly without warning you would hit something which is a lot harder than a brick wall. And this would be the central nucleus of the black hole.

PG Now what is at that nucleus? Is this a singularity?

WI Yes, it is a singularity: a place where the density of matter has increased to about ten to the ninety-fourth. That is one with ninety-four zeros times the density of water.

PG Wait a minute. This is ten with ninety-four zeros after it. You multiply the density of water by that figure, and you have reached the density of . . .

WI The density inside the nucleus of a black hole.

PG What's the difference between that and infinite density?

WI Well, for practical purposes, of course, almost nothing. If you considered a tiny speck of this material, let's say one-trillionth of an inch across, about the size of the nucleus of an atom, this would weigh as much as the universe. In the case of a black hole about the size of the sun, for example, the nucleus would stretch across several miles. The whole of this nucleus stretching for miles and miles consists of matter having this incredible density. It would mean that the mass of this material inside the black hole, at the core of the black hole, is enormously greater than the mass of the whole universe. This is very speculative stuff. We asked ourselves the question, What happens to an observer, to ourselves, if you like, if we fall into a black hole? What sort of experience do we have? What do we find inside?

PG And how do you ask yourself that?

WI One peers into this abyss equipped with nothing but pencil and paper, and sitting very comfortably in an armchair. That's one of the delights of this work.

PG Are these ideas quite real to you? When you talk about matter that is ten to the ninety-fourth more dense than water, is that a real idea for you?

WI I think anyone whose mind doesn't reel thinking about this kind of thing doesn't really understand. We do not have an adequate theory to describe what happens to matter at densities of ten to the ninety-four times the density of water. All our theories break down. But we can describe what happens up to the moment when densities reach this level.

PG If there are black holes in our universe, and if within those black holes are these singularities, these unimaginably dense entities which in themselves weigh more than the universe, how can that be? How could any object carry within it an object that weighs more than itself without adding that weight to itself?

WI  It's a good point. The black hole is formed by the collapse of a star. And the original black hole weighs no more than the mass of the star that collapsed to form the black hole. But then something very strange happens: the black hole, once it's formed, quivers for a while, rather like a soap bubble settling down into a perfectly round, smooth shape. This quivering dies down, but it never completely disappears. It fills the inside of the black hole with the fine drizzle of gravitational waves. Close to the core of the black hole, close to what we call the inner horizon of the black hole, this drizzle is transformed into a torrent of hail. These hail stones are incredibly heavy, and they pour into the core of the black hole and enormously inflate the mass of the core, so the core becomes heavier than the mass of the entire universe. But nobody outside the black hole will ever discover this fact, because the news of the tremendous increase of the internal field of the hole propagates a gravitational wave travelling with the speed of light, and we know that nothing that travels with the speed of light can ever escape from the hole.

PG  Is there any way to prove that hypothesis?

WI  Well, there is no direct way to do that unless you are willing to commit suicide and fall into a black hole and actually discover it. The fate of an astronaut who falls into a black hole may very well be the ultimate fate of the universe itself. The expansion of the universe is slowing down and there may come a moment, billions of years in the future, when the expansion might stop altogether. At this point the universe will slowly begin to fall back in on itself, finally ending up after another few years in a big crunch where everything comes together. In the last hour of this crunch, all of the black holes in the universe will merge and they will form one gigantic black hole. And we would be inside this black hole — assuming that we can have survived up to this point — because there's no space left on the outside. We would then certainly discover that the inside of a black hole is a great deal heavier than the outside.

PG  What's the closest black hole to earth?

WI  The closest that I know is an object called Cygnus x-1, which is several thousand light-years from here. It's a blue giant, and it's orbiting a small invisible companion which is very, very massive. It's much too massive to be a normal star, a black or white dwarf or a neutron star. And so, by a process of elimination, we believe it's a black hole.

What we believe is happening here is that the black hole is breathing in the atmosphere of the blue giant, and the gas collects around the black hole in the form of a disc, which gradually spirals in. Then friction heats the gas, heats it up to about a hundred million degrees, and it then emits X-rays before it disappears down the hole.

PG When you look back at your career, it must amaze you how much thinking has moved in your lifetime and mine.

WI Indeed. When I started out I had never heard of black holes. In fact the name had not yet been coined. The whole subject was highly disreputable.

PG Would you like to visit a black hole if it were physically possible?

WI Oh, I'm an armchair theoretician. I'm not very adventurous. I wouldn't even want to go on an Arctic expedition, never mind a black hole.

PG You could go on an Arctic expedition just with a pencil in your hand. Thank you so much for coming by this morning, Dr. Israel.

BRENDA MILNER

I: *April 1983*

PETER GZOWSKI I welcome now from Montreal a person who's been studying the brain, or parts of it, and memory for more than thirty years, Dr. Brenda Milner, a neuropsychologist at the Montreal Neurological Institute. Good morning, Dr. Milner.

BRENDA MILNER Good morning.

PG I don't know if you get weary of telling the story on which some of your work is based. I would be fascinated to know what happened with the man — I assume it's a man — known only as H.M.

BM I think I'm never really tired of talking about H.M., because the fascination doesn't decay with the years. This was a young man at the time — I'm learning not to call him a young man any more — whom I first saw in 1955. He had undergone an operation for the treatment of epilepsy when he was a patient of a Connecticut neurosurgeon, Dr. William Skoville. The operation was carried out because the patient had very severe seizures that were interfering with his life, and they couldn't be controlled by medical means. The operation involved destruction of tissue deep in the two temporal lobes of the brain, the left and the right, involving the amygdala, an almond-shaped nucleus, and the hippocampus, which is shaped like a little marine animal. The operation did help his seizures, but was followed by a totally unexpected loss of memory.

PG   And a very specific kind of memory.

BM   Yes. I was invited to study this patient, and I have followed him over the years. He still doesn't recognize me. I've worked hours and hours with him; he has no idea who I am. Patients of this kind teach us a lot about the mechanisms of normal human memory. His intelligence, as measured by standard tests and also as measured in his response to everyday situations, was completely normal, unchanged by the operation. His ability to attend to what is going on, his immediate memory span, is normal. He will retain a series of digits immediately and give them back to you in a normal way, but the moment his attention is diverted — and life is always diverting us and distracting us, there's no way in which the focus of our attention cannot shift, it has to — at that moment, what happened just before seems to be lost, irretrievable. There is no continuity in his life. In his own words, it's as though he's waking from a dream. At this moment things seem clear, but what happened just before is lost.

PG   So if I were to give to him a small series of numbers and not distract him, he could repeat those numbers back to me. But if I were to clap my hands or open the window blind or turn on the television, those numbers would vanish from his recollection.

BM   Well, he's not particularly distractible in that way. But if you were then to give him something else to do . . . I gave him three numbers — five, eight, four — to remember once and I walked out of the room and had a cup of coffee and came back a quarter of an hour later, and he knew five, eight, four, because, he said, Well, five, eight, and four add up to seventeen, and you divide by two and you have nine and eight, and then you divide again, and you have five, eight, four. He said, It's very easy. And I said, That's excellent. I was surprised. I was very naive in those days about memory disorder. And then I said, Do you know who I am? And he said, Well, no, I have trouble with my memory. (He always had insight.) And I said, Well, I'm Dr. Milner and I come from Canada. (It was about the tenth time I had told him that that morning.) He said, That's very interesting, and he made a little remark about Canada geographically.

And then I said, Do you still remember the number? And he said, What number?

PG Does he not also retain the events that happened before the operation?

BM That is true. Not the events leading up to the operation. You usually have what we call a retrograde amnesia, an amnesia going back a surprisingly long way sometimes, maybe covering several months before the operation. But the earlier memories seem to be well preserved. That is why their intelligence is well preserved, because this long-term store of knowledge is preserved. Although if you follow these patients over many years, as I have done, I think you find that their knowledge about where places are, what the capital city is, what the Vatican means, these notions become progressively a little vaguer. This makes me think that we are normally giving our long-term memory little boosts every time we rehearse something by reading about the place in the newspaper. But in general one can say that the old knowledge is retained, and so is the ability to attend intelligently and appropriately to the present situation, but there is no continuity. You can't make new friends. People can become fond of you — we have become very fond of this patient — but friendship is built up through shared experience, which is remembered and enriches the relationship. And this is impossible. So it's a very bleak existence, I would say.

PG Is the scientific, psychological significance of the lessons of H.M. that there are many degrees of memory, rather than just a simple thing called short-term and another simple thing called long-term?

BM Oh, exactly. That is really the big lesson. For example, even back in 1955 I was able to show that H.M. could learn motor skills. If you tried to trace an outline of a star by seeing only your hand and the star reflected in a mirror, you'd make a pretty poor job of it the first time around. But as you practiced it a few times you would learn to make the right corrections at the corners and not to be fooled by the mirror. I found that H.M. could learn this completely normally. I tested him and trained him over a three-day period. He had no idea at the end that he'd ever done this before, but he was keeping beautifully within the narrow confines of the star. I think many kinds of skills are learned independently of this particular deep temporal system. Probably how to skate, how to swim, how to pronounce a foreign tongue, though not, of course, its syntax or its vocabulary. Things we can't introspect about or have images about, things we learn by doing.

PG The old folk saying about riding a bicycle is valid.

BM I think it is, and I think this involves other systems of the brain.

PG What I understand to be short- and long-term memory have been explained to me in a very simple way using telephone numbers. The idea is that a telephone number with seven digits is an acceptable chunk of information.

BM Yes, that seems to be about the average we can handle.

PG If you were to tell me a telephone number now, and I were to move over to a telephone and try to dial it, I would not have that number by the time I got to the telephone. Particularly if you were to give me two telephone numbers, they would be beyond my ability to retain short-term.

BM Yes, I agree with that. You see, you have a limited capacity of short-term memory — we all have.

PG Yet if you were to ask me my home telephone number, or the one at the office, or numbers I use a lot, I could recite them easily to you. I have them in instant recall, in my long-term memory.

BM That is correct.

PG But H.M. has told us that there are subtleties in between.

BM We can comfortably depend upon our beginning long-term memory (or secondary memory) process to take over without having to worry about it. H.M. can't do that. But we can't do that the first time we try to remember a new telephone number and another number, because there would be a lot of interference from the second set of digits. We can certainly remember events — you would remember that that inconsiderate Dr. Milner gave you two numbers to remember.

PG Five, eight, four.

BM Excellent. That, you see, is what H.M. couldn't do in spite of all the rehearsal.

PG Your discipline is just beginning to understand many of these things.

BM That is true, yes.

PG Dr. Milner, we must talk again. I want to know more about what you know about memory.

## II: *April 1983*

PG  Five, seven, four. Were those the numbers you talked about with your patient?

BM  That's very good.

PG  Your work with H.M. led to some really interesting questions about how different kinds of brain injuries might impair different kinds of memory. Do you know quite a bit about that now?

BM  Yes, I think so, from studying patients who have injury to one particular part of the brain in one hemisphere. What we were talking about last week was the devastating effect on memory of bilateral damage to structures deep in the temporal lobes of the brain, and the hippocampus particularly.

PG  What does bilateral mean in that sense?

BM  Bilateral means involving both the hemispheres of the brain. Most injuries, fortunately, involve only one side of the brain, so there is no loss of continuity in your life, because the structures in the opposite hemisphere can keep that continuity going. In most right-handed people the left hemisphere is important for language, especially for prepositional speech, and therefore injury within the left temporal lobe may be associated with particular difficulty in remembering words. People with this difficulty often say they have terrible memories, which isn't true. You find they have a completely normal memory for faces and places and tunes, but our culture values words so much that anyone at a loss for words feels they have a general memory difficulty. It isn't so.

PG  Does that mean, then, that there are physical places in the brain where different sorts of information are stored?

BM  Yes. We don't know the form of the storage, but we do know that there is specialization of corresponding areas on the two sides. For example, if you have an injury in an area in the right temporal lobe, you'll have no problem with remembering words, but you will have difficulty recognizing photographs of faces. If you study a little array of faces and then have to pick them out again a few minutes later, you do a poor job. You try to remember the faces by saying to yourself, Oh, that one has a necklace of a particular kind, or that one has straight eyebrows, and then you find there are lots of faces like that in the ones you have to choose amongst. Your memory is not idiosyncratic enough to help you. What happens when we are remembering the world around us is that we code this information in more than one way. We will label something verbally. For example, we see a picture, it has a name, it's a picture of a boat, it has the name *boat*. But it also has this image, this representation of what it looks like. And it's very important to realize that the two halves of the brain are in communication all the time. There is so much tendency to contrast the two halves of the brain these days.

PG Yes, we have the whole left-brain, right-brain way of looking at the world.

BM That's right, but they are really working together, and this is what makes for the relative efficiency of our memory in everyday life.

PG Tell me a bit more about our memory of where we put things, about absentmindedness. Do I know where I put the pencil I can't find at this moment, but I just can't find that bit of information in my memory?

BM Well, you don't necessarily. You can be thinking of something else and not really pay attention to what you're doing. Now, we can't really blame our memory systems for letting us down if we haven't paid attention in the first place. This is why it's so efficient to have regular habits, to put things in particular places — then you can depend upon yourself to do these things automatically.

PG Do mnemonics work?

BM Within limits. For example, if some psychologist wants you to remember that *elephant* goes with *bouquet* — a rather unusual link — if you picture in your mind an elephant holding a bouquet, then even if you have a poor left temporal lobe and a poor memory for words, when somebody says *elephant* to you, you will get back this picture of these two things interacting and then you will be able to say *bouquet*. You can also use spatial associations. Orators in ancient times were told to do this because they had no typewritten manuscripts to read. They were supposed to imagine each point of their speech, then deposit each point in a well-known building. Then they would visit these places and retrieve the points of their speech. These little tricks only work, of course, if you have some continuity. Somebody like H.M., someone with a total loss of memory, forgets the mnemonic just as much as he forgets the information. Which reminds me that the number is five, eight, four; you startled me when you said five, seven, four. You interfered with my memory. I reconstructed it by using H.M.'s mnemonic. I knew that five, seven, four didn't add up to what Henry's number added to, and so I realized it was the seven that was wrong. It didn't come immediately, it came by this process.

PG  Dr. Milner, you're wonderful. We shall talk again, I hope.

BM  Thank you very much.

BRIAN LITTLE

*November 1994*

PETER GZOWSKI  Carleton University psychology professor Brian Little has been researching introverts and extroverts. Dr. Little, good morning, sir.

BRIAN LITTLE  Good morning.

PG  Now, I take it you know what you are yourself?

BL  I have a pretty strong suspicion.

PG  And?

BL  Well, I think at first blush I seem to be rather extroverted, but upon reflection and upon looking at some of the physiological research, I suspect the answer is really the reverse. I'm introverted physiologically and extroverted superficially. The term I use to describe this is "pseudo-extrovert."

PG  What are the signs of a pseudo-extrovert?

BL  The first thing you notice is that they are apparently extroverted and outgoing. They tend to be optimistic in their interpersonal behaviour — they stand close for comfortable communication, have lots of eye contact, lots of body contact. They are fast-paced. You've probably spotted them driving into work.

PG  Driving into work?

BL  You can see them in their cars. They tend to move around a lot, often with the music. I think many of our daily functions and the things we feel passionate about, our roles in life, the projects we commit ourselves to, demand that we act in that extroverted fashion. And yet, in many cases, this is a guise, a subtle acting out of a role that sometimes compromises what I call our first natures, which are physiologically based. A pseudo-extrovert isn't being phony when she's acting in this outgoing fashion — it's often in the service of something about which she feels very passionate, such as teaching. She's animated behind the podium, yet often you can tell through very subtle cues that she has been playing out a role. Sometimes those cues aren't obvious until the performance is over. Then there are peculiar things pseudo-extroverts will do. For example, I used to go down to St-Jean-sur-Richelieu, Quebec, to teach. As an apparent extrovert, I would put on a performance for a couple of hours. But then I would need to escape, so I would walk by the Richelieu River, which ran by the building where I was lecturing. I wasn't looking at the sailboats, I was trying to get myself composed, to lower the level of stimulation so I could go back and create the illusion of competency for another hour and a half. Alas, the campus moved and the river stayed where it was, so I had to find another place to go. Now I take advantage of a place called the washroom. I can be spotted there after performances such as this, typically in cubicle nine, if it's a nine-cubicle washroom.

PG  You can escape no longer, Brian. You've just given away your hiding place. Are shyness and introversion the same thing?

BL  Very close. Introversion has maybe six or seven other attributes, but shyness is one aspect of it, for sure.

PG  Are there other symptoms of a private introversion under an external extroversion?

BL  Yes — one thing is that we have a strong tendency to seek out and be guided by structure. So, for example, I arrived early for this morning's presentation. That's classic introversion. Extroverts are likely to come in a little late and bang on the window saying, Am I on yet? I also notice that in the middle of a presentation, if we take a little break, I need to get away. A classic extrovert would talk and mingle. The problem is that we may be misconstrued as unsociable, and that's not the case. We may quite love the people with whom we're interacting, and desire to be with them. But introverts tend to become overstimulated in a particular part of the brain, and you cannot carry on a coherent discourse if you are overstimulated. Consequently you learn to escape, get off on your own. It's unfortunate when you are not given the latitude to find those niches in which you can indulge your first natures.

PG  Are most people mixtures?

BL  Yes, indeed. On personality scales of extroversion, most people are going to peak in a range we call "ambiverts," right in the middle.

PG  Now the physiology. This is all biologically determined?

BL  Much of the research that's been done has been biological in origin, and there is some evidence of a genetic component — you spot introverted tendencies even at four days of age in watching a baby orienting to stimuli, turning away from loud noises and so on. That's the beginning. But our culture places a premium upon extroverted conduct, and we've been raised in an atmosphere where extroverted characteristics of interaction are rewarded and reinforced from a very early age. That can be an overlay on top of the biology, and on top of that is the sense of values, the projects that matter to us, the tasks to which we've consecrated our lives. These may impel us to act out of character — it's called professionalism. It's also called love. For fifteen years you may act as a protracted extrovert because Ned loves you that way, then all of a sudden you realize at thirty-nine that it's not really you, and you have this aching sense of emptiness. That protracted disingenuous conduct can take its toll — we burn out, we feel empty. We need to be very sensitive to the ones we love; it's important to acknowledge their first natures.

PG  The signs are there in infancy?

BL  Yes.

PG  What would you look for?

BL  A tendency to seek out stimulation or avoid it. And there are, for example, differences in pain threshold.

PG  What's the test with the Q-Tip and the lemon juice?

BL  The Q-Tip test is something I often do as a demonstration. If you want to measure neocortical arousal you want to use an electroencephalogram rather than this test, but my students enjoy it. It involves a Q-Tip with a thread attached to the centre so that when you hold it up it's balanced. You need a small container, like an egg cup, of concentrated lemon juice — it has to be concentrated or the demonstration doesn't work — an eyedropper, and the willing tongue of someone whose personality is going to be measured. You put one end of the Q-Tip on the tongue and hold it for twenty seconds. You then take it off, put four drops of concentrated lemon juice on the same tongue — it has to be the same tongue. Then put the other end of the Q-Tip on and hold it for twenty seconds. Then hold up the Q-Tip. With one of the groups, the Q-Tips stays parallel. With the other group it tends to tip. And the group that tips happens to be . . . can you guess? It's the introverted group.

PG  No, I wouldn't have guessed. What was the clue in there?

BL  They tend to be overaroused, so any sensory stimulation causes a compensatory reaction: they tend to salivate more when you put lemon-juice drops on, so that end of the Q-Tip weighs more. The evidence is pretty clear that there is a genetic base, and it seems to have most of its source in the neocortex. There are some peripheral nerve differences, as well, but for me the central point is that there are overlays of cultural and social and personal value factors. The intriguing thing psychologically is where you have disjunctions between those and people act out of character. We're tempted, I think, to put ourselves in pigeonholes, a place I'm not even sure pigeons ought to belong. That's why I'm hoping you don't ask me to read some of my questions. People sometimes write them down and then confront George when he comes home . . .

PG  Like those magazine things you fill in and then you know you're not suited for your mate, or you shouldn't wear blue . . .

BL  Exactly. You indict George on a charge of extroversion without realizing that perhaps the best way of construing George is to look at his particularly Georgian qualities, which are singular.

PG  I appreciate your desire to stay away from the specific questions, but you can't fight curiosity.

BL  I have to go to the bathroom now.

PG  Cubicle nine is full! We're talking here about characteristics within complex personalities. Can I get a question or two?

BL  Sure, a couple of them. (I typically ask ten.) I ask people to rate themselves between zero and ten on a set of personally descriptive characteristics. The first one I usually go through slowly: Do you see yourself as an outgoing person? If you see yourself as outgoing give yourself an eight or a nine or a ten. Not to be confused with going out. If you are a reserved person, give yourself a two, a one or a zero. And if you see yourself as in between, give yourself a number such as four, five, or six. The second one is: Are you easily bored (high scores) or not easily bored (low scores)? If you're bored already, be appropriately guided in your answer to the question. Are you a fast-paced person or a slow-paced person?

PG This is all self-assessment, isn't it?

BL One of the most heretical things I teach my students in personality assessment, Peter, is that if you want to understand what a person is all about, ask them — they might just tell you. I begin with what I call the credulous approach. People do know where they stand. I start by asking people to evaluate themselves. I ask them what they do when they are completely unconstrained in their actions. When you're on *Morningside* you act *Morningside*. When you're at a funeral you act funereal. But what do you do when you are by yourself in the cottage and nobody's around? Do you turn up the radio to a hundred and ten decibels and invite in the neighbours? Or do you take out a book and curl up with the cats and go into introvert heaven?

PG A being extro and B being intro.

BL Yes.

PG I'm out of time. Thanks, Brian, very much.

BL Goodbye.

## MICHAEL SMITH
### *October 1993*

PETER GZOWSKI Last Wednesday, Dr. Michael Smith woke up to hear on the radio that he'd won a Nobel Prize in Chemistry. Not a bad way to start the day. Dr. Michael Smith is director of the biotechnology lab at the University of British Columbia. This morning he's in our studio in Vancouver. Good morning, sir, and congratulations.

MICHAEL SMITH Thank you very much.

PG Have you been able to get back to the lab since you got this?

MS Well, just to drink champagne, that's about all. The interest from TV, press, and radio is overwhelming. Even when I went around town, people would come up to me and shake my hand and congratulate me. It's so moving. It's clear that the whole community is getting an enormous amount of pleasure out of it.

PG  Explain to me what it is you do. I could read you a little part of the background material about your research interests. It tells me that the primary, mutagenic method being used in these experiments involves synthesis of oxyo-nucleo. . . . Whoa! Help!

MS  Well, it's oxyoligonucleotide, which is little bits of DNA — oligo means short — and using short, chemically synthesized bits of DNA, which are deliberately made different from a normal DNA that might be in any gene from whatever organism you're studying. You then take advantage of the fact that DNAs are double-strand (the two strands stick together) to incorporate your chemically synthesized DNA into a full-length DNA strand — one of the two strands in double-stranded DNA. Then, if you put that in a living cell, the DNA replicates — that's one of its properties — and you get a line of progeny derived from the strand which has your synthetic bit in, and that gives you a mutant DNA. People have asked me, Well, okay, what does that mean and how do you use it? The analogy I've given is, suppose you're a completely unsophisticated individual and you've got in front of you an automobile with the engine running. You want to know what it is in that vehicle that makes the engine run, and what's part of it but not necessary. You replace bits. Supposing it's a green car and you take one of the green doors off and put a blue door on, the engine doesn't change its tune. You take the exhaust pipe off and put a different-shaped one on, and the noise of the engine changes but it keeps running quite evenly. Then you remove one of the electrical wires to, say, a spark plug, and you replace it with a piece of string. You realize, bingo, that's involved, because it starts to run irregularly. This sort of replacement of different components of a complex thing, in my case a gene, allows you to find out what are the really critical parts of the gene for doing whatever function it might have to do — usually to produce a protein, an enzyme or a hormone or muscle. You want to find out within those proteins which particular amino acids are crucial for the particular function the protein has to carry out.

PG  But you're working with little bits of matter that are so *small*. What do you actually do?

MS  On Wednesday morning reporters wanted to come and see my lab. They said, Well, show us a genetic-engineering experiment. And I said, Well, you see this little test tube (it was about an inch long and less than a quarter-inch in diameter) and you see that drop of liquid in the bottom (it was smaller than a drop that might drop off a tap). Well, that's a genetic-engineering experiment. It's very frustrating when the university has an open house — the physicists have lasers zapping around, the engineers have earthquake machines. The molecular biologists are doing something equally dramatic, or maybe even more dramatic, but it's very hard to give it a visual image that people can react to.

PG  Does *Jurassic Park* make sense?

MS  No. It's good science fiction, of course. The whole trick with good science fiction is getting a transition between science which is known to something which is an extrapolation, and make that seamless, so people don't quite know what is proven and what isn't. The flaw is DNA could stay around for sixty-five million years, but there would be chemical reactions taking place all the time, so it would be damaged. DNA that's derived from a dinosaur would be so badly damaged it wouldn't function. That's one problem. The second problem is it would be in pieces, and you'd have to be able to reassemble those pieces in a great long string to make a chromosome. In one chromosome there might be a thousand or hundreds of thousands of pieces, and you would have no way of knowing what the correct order is. So, it's a cute idea but it's not feasible.

PG  The whole idea of genetic engineering is at once one of the most exciting ideas the mind can comprehend, yet there's something terrifying behind it, as well — the idea of trying to improve or somehow make better people.

MS  Well, it depends what you mean by better. If you're talking better for someone who is ill, I have no trouble with that. For instance, cystic fibrosis: I think no one has any trouble with the idea of trying to get a normal form of the cystic fibrosis gene and put it into people with cystic fibrosis. I think the kind of better you're alluding to is making a better athlete, or having a better intellect. It's a new manifestation of the concern about eugenics and selective breeding.

PG  Except now we can do it.

MS  No, all those things you're thinking about — intelligence, athletic ability, size — they involve so many genes, and we have no idea what genes are involved. And even if we did have the information, we're always confronted with ethical problems. I think some people have the impression that genetic engineering has created a whole new set of ethical problems. I don't think it has. It has the potential for adding more ethical problems, but I think society has always been adapting in that area, just as we adapted when the automobile came along. You can't just drive anywhere — you have to have some rules about where you drive and where you don't drive to minimize accidents. I think the benefits of genetic engineering far outweigh the potential lack of benefits. None of these things people worry about are things that have happened. They're all science fiction.

PG  When were you the smartest in your life?

MS  Well, it's an interesting thing. People in areas like mathematics and theoretical physics seem to make their really brilliant discoveries quite early. That was the case, for instance, with Einstein. In my area of science, which is experimentally based, you accrue wisdom through time. Like everybody else you make mistakes and learn from them. With experimental science, if you're really doing research, things go wrong all the time. If things went right all the time, you clearly wouldn't be doing research. You wouldn't be looking at new things.

PG  Was there a moment when you knew you were on the right path?

MS  Well, yes, it was very exciting. The model studies we'd been doing had been directed to one end: to use chemically synthesized DNA to isolate a gene. I'd been collaborating with a scientist, Ben Hall, who's at the University of Washington. We isolated a particular gene from yeast, and I wanted to know what its sequence was, the arrangement of building blocks along the chain of the gene. This was in the mid-seventies, and it was very hard to do DNA sequencing, but one lab was developing new techniques, in Cambridge, England. I'd arranged to go on a sabbatical to this lab to work on a project — they were working on the DNA sequence of a small virus. As we acquired information, I realized we needed a really precise genetic tool to analyse how the different genes in that virus were working. I knew from the chemical work that you could make a double strand where you deliberately had a mismatch. I knew that would form a stable structure. So we discussed how we might develop that into a method for making a mutant, and we talked about it over cups of tea and coffee in the canteen. Then I came back to Vancouver in the fall of '76 and said,

Look, here's an experiment we designed. Would you try it out? It took quite a bit of work to make the chemically synthesized DNA (it wasn't easy to do in those days — now you can do it with an automatic machine), but they made the fragments of DNA we needed and then went ahead and did the experiment. We saw the first results, and it was so exciting. It's an amazing feeling of exhilaration you get when an experiment works well. There are two kinds you get: One is when you're doing one experiment and it doesn't work right and you see something else that's even more exciting than the thing you wanted to do. The other thing is when you try to do something which you know is a big challenge and it really works and you're on cloud nine. You can't go to sleep at night.

PG Do you wake up in the morning with solutions?

MS I've done it on occasion. Not routine, thank goodness.

PG If you just had a pencil and paper, could you continue to do your work? You need all that hardware, don't you?

MS Well, I need a lab. I'm not what I would call an intellectual scientist. My good ideas in science have come out of observations made while experiments are being done.

PG Wouldn't it be nice if there was some young woman in Cape Breton this morning, listening to you and your pleasure in your work and the sense of excitement, who said, You know, I think I'll go do that. I think I'll become a scientist.

MS I think that would be wonderful.

PG You'll have to get used to this. Thank you so much for this, and congratulations again. All of us feel very, very proud.

MS Well, thank you very much, Peter.

HENRY MINTZBERG
*April 1996*

PETER GZOWSKI Henry Mintzberg is a professor of management. He divides his time between McGill in Montreal and the European School of Business in France. He's in great demand, but this morning he's my guest. Good morning.

HENRY MINTZBERG: Hi, Peter.

PG   You're in Toronto because you're leading a two-day forum on management. Your forty senior corporate types come to listen and to talk to you. I presume they paid the big bucks. Are these guys listening to you? Do they hear what you're saying?

HM   I certainly hope so.

PG   What sort of questions do they ask you? What are they looking for from you?

HM   Well, one of the things I make clear at the beginning is that I'm not giving quick fixes or easy answers. There's so much hype in management, I think it drives everybody crazy. I try to get people to understand better what organizations are, how they work, what goes on in the manager's job. We need to focus. We deny the past. Everything is always *current* and *hot*. I try to get away from that.

PG   You're not a consultant?

HM   I consult sometimes.

PG   But you don't give strategy?

HM   No. I don't sit there and pronounce strategy, and I don't tell people what to do. I try to get people to ask the right questions, or I ask questions that provoke. I think that's the most important thing.

PG   You have said that executives who hire consultants to give them strategy should be fired.

HM   Yes, exactly. For a number of reasons. Number one: Their job is to do those things. Number two: Strategy doesn't come immaculately conceived. Strategy has to evolve and be tailored and crafted over time. If you get it from a consultant, it's like pigeon consulting — they fly over, drop the strategy, and keep going. It's not very good.

PG   Do you understand how ideas get fashionable in the world of business? What drives some thousands of how-to management books to the top of the best-seller list? Do you understand the cycles?

HM   You probably understand that better than I do because I think it has to do with the media; it has to do with hype.

PG   One does fall victim to it. You hear people talking about stuff. You say, I want to know how that works, so you bring the people in and it becomes self-perpetuating.

HM   And everyone wants to know what's *hot* and everything's got to be *current*. That's true on television — everything's got to be up to date. But in management, *current* is not necessarily the most important thing. What's important is to understand situations, customers, production processes.

PG How did downsizing get out of control? People are now downsizing because . . . Why *are* they downsizing? Because that's what everyone else is doing?

HM That's exactly it. These companies that suddenly discover they need to take 25 per cent out of their workforce — if the workforce is so fat in 1996, wasn't it fat in 1990? How come they didn't do it five or ten years ago? And in downsizing, they're getting rid of the most crucial part of the organization: the middle managers, who know what's going on. One fellow wrote an article called "Top Middle Up Down Management," in which he argues that middle managers are as much people who carry messages *to* senior management as they are people who carry messages *from* senior management. They're critical linking devices between the people serving customers and making products, and the senior manager. I like to describe organizations not as top, middle, and bottom — I think that's a distorted metaphor. There's no top management. Management doesn't sit on top of anything except the chart.

PG And the pay scale.

HM Yes, with a vengeance. That's part of the perversion of modern management. A much better way to view it is, management sits in the centre. On the outer edges are the ones who are intimately connected to the outer world. Those people, they see very sharply, very clearly, because they see specific customers, specific products and processes. But they see very narrowly: they see only their own segment. The people in the middle and the centre see peripherally. They see all around, but only very vaguely, because they're far from the specifics. So the key is to marry the people who can see clearly but narrowly with the people who can see broadly but vaguely. Middle management plays a key role in making those connections.

PG When did we begin to think there was such a thing as abstract managing? That someone could move from the towel business to the monkey-wrench business and not have to learn anything?

HM That developed over the whole century, I think. Peter Drucker was probably the best-known writer on management. His book *The Practice of Management* promoted a lot of those ideas. The M.B.A.

very aggressively pushed the idea that anybody who's trained can manage anything.

PG You won't teach M.B.A.s.

HM No, I refuse.

PG Why?

HM Conventional M.B.A. programs for young people teach the wrong people in the wrong ways for the wrong reasons.

PG But other than that they really work well.

HM Other than that they're great. The wrong people, because they're too young. The wrong ways because you can't create managers in a class-room. If they don't have experience you teach them a lot of analyt-ical technique instead of the nuances of management. The wrong reasons because we're creating an aristocracy, people who think they have the right to manage because they've got credentials, not because they've earned the right by showing leadership.

PG I spent my childhood in an industrial town in southwestern Ontario where the factories seemed to be citizens. They seemed to care about their employees, about the communities in which they lived. Now all you hear is, I'm paying off the shareholders.

HM There's a lot of that going on. There are still a lot of corporations that are responsible, but there's clearly a trend to a more callous view of the world. It's very dangerous, and it won't help corporations ultimately.

PG But you say perhaps the current malaise about government is that it's acting too much like business, rather than not enough. We've got governments all over — there's one that surrounds us in this province — using the language of business. "We're a business not a government."

HM You noticed that? [Premier Mike] Harris doesn't hide that one very well.

PG Hide it! They buy ads to talk about it. "We have a business plan for health," they'll say. Every department has a business plan.

HM What I say is, business isn't good and government isn't bad. Business is the right thing for buying and selling and making automobiles, and it's not particularly effective for delivering health care or education. Let government do what it does well and let business do what it does well. There's a lot of cynicism about government, perhaps because it's starting to get too much like business. We're only rarely customers of government. Mostly we're citizens, in the sense that there are all kinds of complex trade-offs; we're subjects, in the sense that we respect laws and regulations; and we're clients, in the sense that we get a lot of professional services from government.

PG We'll all of us all four of those things.

HM Yes, we're all four of those things concurrently. Of the four — clients, subjects, customers, and citizens — the least is customers, I think. The idea that government has to be more like business is perverse, not because business is perverse, but because government has different things to do than business.

PG What were you doing with my friend Bramwell Tovey in Winnipeg? You were following him around. Were you learning or teaching?

HM I was learning. I've been following a whole host of different managers around for a day each, like the commissioner of the RCMP, some deputy ministers in government, various business people, and I wanted to follow an orchestra conductor. Mostly I sat in rehearsals. I wanted to expose the myth about the manager as orchestra conductor. There's this image of the perfect manager who sits up on a podium . . .

PG And waves his baton . . .

HM And everything happens . . .

PG The accounting department comes in on cue . . .

HM Exactly.

PG So what did you learn?

HM I learned that the caricature is perfectly correct in a literal sense: he does stand up on the podium. It's a perfect image of management. Here's the manager with seventy people all around him. When he points the baton you get seventy people suddenly playing in unison. And when he does something else, God knows what, they all stop. But it turns out to be a subtle form of management. For one thing, management is involved in culture-building in a large sense — for the whole organization — and team-building in a smaller sense. Well, here you've got culture-building and team-building all wrapped into one. Imagine trying to harmonize a team of seventy people. The other thing I found intriguing is that an orchestra conductor is a foreman and a chief executive all rolled into one. In the course of one day he's in rehearsals, perfecting the delivery of product, in a sense, very much as a foreman would be worried about getting a product out on the line, but then in the evening he turns around and goes to the maestro's circle, which is like being invited to the home of one of the members of the board of directors. One of the things that worries me most about management is the cleavage between managing up and managing down. The people in the executive suites manage *up*, to the stock market and the big shots and government, and the foremen manage *down*, into the operations. They don't talk much to each other, you get a split, and that's very dangerous.

PG  Tell me about "Look Out the Window to Save the Constitution." This is a lovely idea.

HM  It's a book I did in September on the situation in Canada. My argument is, people get very mad about the situation in Canada, but they don't get mad at each other. French Canadians and English Canadians get along remarkably well as individuals. If people looked out their window at their friends and their own private life instead of getting mad at the abstractions on television, we'd be a lot better off. There was a book some years ago by two professors saying, Let them go — the bon voyage argument. They were saying, We've suffered the longest constitutional crisis in the history of any country on earth. And I'm saying, Who cares? Look what's happened in those years. The UN has named us, three times out of four, as the best country in the world in which to live. Three or four of our cities have been picked among the best cities in the world, and all this happened during our constitutional crisis. Let's keep it going.

PG  You have an interesting view of what compromise means as we seek solutions here.

HM  In problems like this, compromise just doesn't work. I draw on the wonderful writings of Mary Parker Foley who said you can solve a problem by domination, by compromise, or by integration. Domination doesn't work because the side that's being dominated will rise up. Compromise means everybody's unhappy, so everybody comes back for more. Integration means you find a creative solution. She has this wonderful story of sitting in a library. Another guy wants the window open for fresh air, and she wants the window closed because she doesn't want a draught. They open the window in the next room, so they get fresh air without the draught. I use that metaphor for some fresh air for Canada.

PG  And you write a very on-one-page constitution of your own at the end of your slim and thoughtful volume.

HM  France developed its constitution, when they brought in de Gaulle, in a hundred and twenty days.

PG  I don't want de Gaulle.

HM  But when there's crisis you need a visionary. De Gaulle was a visionary. Not with regard to Canada — he didn't know anything about Canada first-hand. But he certainly knew about France, and he was able to bring them to a constitution which has given France incredible stability and prosperity since 1958.

PG  Thanks very much for spending this time with us.

HM  Thanks, Peter.

# The Sixth and Last (and This Time I Mean It) Morningside Papers

*Although its means of transmission changed quite dramatically over the years, as first the fax and then e-mail became part of our daily correspondence, the spirit of our letters and their importance to us never changed — even after we published our fifth book of* Morningside Papers, *which at the time I recklessly suggested would probably be our last. Here, from the last several years, is the last.*

Galoshes! Haven't heard that word for years! What memories it brings back of painful frozen toes and fingers. You did not even mention the kind of galoshes I remember best as a girl child back in the thirties, when winter in Toronto was much longer and snowier. They were made of a black velvety-looking stuff and had black fur around the tops and down both sides of the front opening. They had a tongue, and were laced up through metal eyelets hidden in the fur. When new, they looked very spiffy.

However, as they got older, they took on a scruffy alleycat look and drove me to tears. The fur got shaggier and shaggier as you gradually pulled frozen tufts of it out looking for those dratted eyelets. Then either the metal around the eyelet or on the tip of the lace would come off, making it almost impossible to thread the lace through, even if you could find it. Then a lace would break and it would have to be tied together in a knot and yanked through the eyelet. These problems always seemed to need bare hands, and always to happen on the coldest days.

I can remember my mother gripping the top of my galosh and hollering, "Push harder!" as we struggled to get the heel of my shoe down into the heel of the galosh. And then the struggle to get them off again. And I can recall the smell of wet fur in the girls' cloakroom at school.

But most of all I remember the tingle of nearly frozen toes while sitting on the curb waiting for the Santa Claus parade to come along, or while sitting on the front porch steps waiting for my father to come home from work so I could help him shovel the snow. And the pain was even worse when you got inside the house and tried to warm up those poor little toes.

So much for the good old days of galoshes. Now I just slip into my winter boots, and no matter how cold or snowy, my feet are always warm and comfortable — thank goodness!

*Elaine Oakes*
Toronto

Ah, yes — galoshes! It may come as a surprise to you, as it did to me, that galoshes are an item of military issue, or at least they were about five years ago when I began basic training for a primary reserve infantry regiment. As a militia unit we were nearly always short of many essential pieces until they could be scrounged from other bases or from the regular force, and at the end of my first year I still had not been issued with the complete list. However, my very first of many lineups at QM stores was rewarded with, among other items both useful and otherwise, a pair of galoshes to be cherished, guarded, worn, and paid for if lost. These were not ordinary zipper-fronted boots, but were exalted by the title of something like FOOTWEAR RUBBER OVER followed by a four-part thirteen-digit number that laid out in perfect military logic (right up there with "intelligence officer") exactly what I was gazing upon so wondrously. Following all this was a month and year, stating in plainer language probably the date of manufacture. Had the date on the pair I held been of the previous century I would not have been astounded, but it told me that these had been built a mere twelve years earlier. Since my leather combat boots were size eleven, I leave it to your imagination what dimensions my gumboots, gumbies, or rubber clumsies must have been.

The same military logic that encumbered me with these anachronisms decreed that our rucksacks were to be packed in a certain precise and predictable way, usually with one or more junior NCOs bellowing, "Move it — move it — move it! You're like a #@!* bunch of brownies!" The reasoning behind this was that the bag could be unpacked rapidly and unerringly by you or a buddy, in total darkness or in frantic haste — in short, flawlessly under any conditions. If you suddenly required some particular item, you would know exactly whereabouts in the bag it was, usually near the far end. This system made no allowances for variables such as weather, and I experienced at least one session of kneeling in the cold spring slush with my rucksack contents soaking up the chilling rain of a sudden downpour as I frantically rooted inside (to the usual energetic urging of an impatient master corporal) for the gumbies to secure from the rain my already saturated footwear.

On one march over the rutted trails of a forested area the order came down to don the rubber clumsies and we did so dutifully. Before I had gone half a mile the huge clompers attached to my feet had raised painful blisters on both heels and on most of my toes; by the time the hike ended I was practically reduced to crawling. That night in the armoury I spent my whole allotment of free time before lights-out nursing my tormented feet with such inadequate elastic strips as were available, all the while suffering in the knowledge that those poor appendages must surely endure it all again tomorrow.

That was the worst experience of the course, though, and the few other occasions on which we were forcefully encumbered by these items of modern warfare were endured with less discomfort. Once the recruit course was over and I emerged with my hard-won private's stripes, the hated gumboots were flung to the back of a closet, never to be disturbed again until a workplace accident three years later compelled my discharge. In the great load of kit that I returned to Her Majesty's Armed Forces were a number of items which had never been used or worn and had been written off; these I was allowed to keep. Not the gumbies, though. They went back onto the shelves to bring comfort and joy to other innocent recruits in the years to come.

In retrospect I am certain that our FOOTWEAR RUBBER OVERS were created during the chill of the Cold War by a vengeful adversary and slipped undetected on our equipment lists to cripple and maim the infantry arrayed against him. Had it ever come to conflict, I know one rifleman who would have fallen victim to his foul design.

*Larry R. Bird*
Harwood, Ontario

Galoshes, like tuques, are more than part of the collective Canadian unconscious: they are items that occupy a place in our individual minds such that our senses of self and place are shaped. As children, we compared galoshes; lost galoshes; favoured galoshes; contemplated galoshes; and abandoned galoshes. We return to galoshes as middle-aged men only when, I believe, we have lost the self-consciousness of adolescence and have accepted the limitations on our childlike omnipotence. It's wet, so we cover our feet. It's simpler.

Since my childhood, I have long been fascinated by firefighters. I've tried to figure this out over the years. I watch my two-year-old son play with his favourite firetrucks — "fuddys," in his parlance — and I in some vaguely understood way share his delight. One of the highlights of my medical-school days was a trip to a firehall: I enjoyed it so much and so obviously it was embarrassing. Supposedly, we were to study the occupational-health aspect, but my agenda was different. I asked all my stored-up questions of my unsuspecting hosts; I'm somewhat surprised I stopped myself before wondering if they would mind letting me sit in the pumper. I was in some sort of reverie that had transported me back in my own history. Those guys were undeniably cool. Their equipment was ultra-cool: their tools, their gear and — their galoshes. Of course: that explained it. The galoshes evoked everything. They could wear these massive rubber boots all the time, anywhere they wanted. They could track through a person's house, right past the dreaded living-room carpet barrier. No "Take your boots off!" ever greeted them at the back door. No, sir, these men were heroes, and their moms did not tell them what to wear. They wore their galoshes when they did brave, wonderful things, not just as they daydreamed walking to school on a cold winter morning.

*Tim Gofine*
Toronto, Ontario

It was a Thursday night and I got a call from my mom and oldest brother: our family home had been sold. I listened in disbelief as they celebrated the fact it was only on the market for one week. How could this be happening? I knew it was for sale (a fact that I had trouble dealing with) but I was counting on the slow real estate market. Surely it would still be ours when we went home for our summer vacation. Tears welled up in my eyes, and before long they were spilling over as I tried to hide my heartbreak from Mom. She was relieved and happy — something I couldn't share — but I didn't want to take that from her. Mom and Dad had raised eleven children in our home and they always had a steady stream of friends and extended family coming and going. With my father's passing six years ago, all the grandchildren getting older and more self-absorbed and our lives getting busier, the house was getting quieter and lonelier than Mom could bear. The days of sacks of flour, cases of butter and Carnation milk and fifty-pound bags of potatoes were gone forever. It was time to sell.

I kept myself somewhat composed until I got off the phone — and then lost it. My husband, who had recently gone through the sale of their family home with ease, was at a loss. I cried for a long time. I had to let go of the secret dream of me buying the house and telling my two children that this three-bedroom bungalow was once filled with thirteen people. I had to realize that I wouldn't be taking fresh bread out of that oven as they came in from school, and on their lunch hour I wouldn't be able to challenge them to see "who can run the fastest to the Co-op for me?" I cried as I realized that the little girls I saw in my swings and in my back-yard rink were me and my sisters and not my daughters.

Mostly I cried because I hadn't said goodbye. It was already the end of January and the closing date was the third of February.

On February first, with a baby by the hand and one in my arms, I walked across the runway to board my flight — a convoluted eight-hour, three-connection one — to Gander, Newfoundland. It didn't matter that I had to rearrange several appointments, miss a few already-paid-for programs, burden our meagre budget, or travel alone with two small children. What did matter was I was bringing my children home for one last time and I was going to be able to say goodbye.

There were tears in my eyes, as always, as they announced our arrival at Gander airport, but there was also the contentment one can only feel from being home.

That Saturday night there was a gathering of the Dwyer clan at 23 Read Street for one last time. There were no tears, just story after story about growing up in that house. We all laughed as we remembered the details of a small house with thirteen people. The next generation sat in awe, hanging on to every word and adding some memories of their own.

I'm back in North Bay now, and life goes on. But in my heart I took 23 Read Street with me. It will always be where I belong.

In my kitchen you can sometimes get a whiff of salt beef and pease pudding. And — though infrequently — the sweet smell of homemade bread fills the house, too. I only hope my children will feel the same love for their home as I did for mine.

*Maureen Dwyer Clout*
North Bay, Ontario

Three beautiful unquilted quilt tops are among the many treasures I have from past generations. The first, a hand-stitched Sunshine and Shadows log-cabin design, was made by my great-grandmother Anastasia (Young) Browner, 1838–1924. My mother recalled sitting by her knee as a very small child, selecting pieces from her basket and suggesting to her grandmother, whom she loved very much, "Put this piece next." I estimate this particular quilt top was made circa 1905. The second, a rather intricate red-and-white pattern, entirely stitched by hand, was made by my grandmother, Catherine (Browner) McKinnon, 1870–1947. The third, a traditional hand-appliquéd fan design, was made by my mother Anne (McKinnon) Godwin, 1900–1985. I also have a lovely silk and velvet log-cabin wall hanging created by my mother, each piece undoubtedly with a story to tell about a dress made for a special dance or a pretty blouse to accent her beautiful black hair. To keep the tradition alive to the fourth generation, I am now completing my first quilt, a log-cabin design like my great-grandmother's some ninety years before, and as I guide the needle through the layers to form small and even stitches, I look at my fingers bearing the three wedding rings so lovingly worn by the matriarchs in my maternal line.

*Catherine Godwin*
Dominion, Nova Scotia

It wasn't a thousand-dollar bill, it was only a hundred. But when you're a kid growing up in a big family in a small Alberta town, even a hundred can make dreams come true.

My eldest son, James, was eleven that hot, windy June afternoon four years ago. He was a bright and friendly kid, a top student, a talented athlete. His sharp eyes were forever spotting money in the grass, on the sidewalk, on the floor of the grocery store near the cash register. Usually it would be just a penny or two, but sometimes he'd find a dime or a quarter. Having been blind since birth myself, I was secretly rather envious of this talent, since the only way I could find money was to go barefoot, an approach which was painfully lacking in efficiency.

James and two of his friends were walking home from the baseball diamond for supper when he spotted the bill fluttering in the poplar fuzz beside the curb just around the corner from our house.

"Gosh, James," said his twelve-year-old sister, "you're so lucky. You're rich."

"Can I keep it, Dad?"

"This money belongs to somebody," his father said.

"But, Dad, I found it. It was just lying there on the ground. There wasn't anybody around it."

"Well, then, I guess we'll have to call the police and let them handle it."

"Please, Mum." Somehow James knew I was a softer touch. And, yes, I knew exactly how he felt. Our family could use one hundred dollars.

We had five kids, three of whom would need braces, a mortgage, base-ment bedrooms without ceilings, and a roof that needed replacing. My husband was our only wage-earner, and his health was uncertain. One hundred dollars would pay down the credit-card bill or buy a week's groceries.

Two hours later a police car pulled up in front of our house. By then the neighbourhood, if not our entire town of nine hundred souls, had heard about the one-hundred-dollar bill. A parade of our children's friends had been to the house to see it. Now a whole circle of curious kids, and a few curious adults, too, gathered around James and the RCMP con-stable. The officer asked James where he'd found the bill and when and how. He took the bill from my son's hand and examined it. Then he said, "I'll take this back to the office."

"What are you going to do with it?" asked James.

"Well, we'll put it in the safe, and if nobody claims it after sixty days then I guess you can have it," said the officer.

But, of course, somebody would claim it. Anyone could go to the police station and say it was theirs. There was no secret about where the money was found or how much it was. In fact, over the next few days James assumed the status of a local celebrity, telling and retelling the story of how he had found a one-hundred-dollar bill, *one hundred dollars!* and his parents wouldn't let him keep it.

He got our last year's Sears Christmas Book and the Canadian Tire cat-alogue and the Toys "R" Us flyer. What would he buy if he had that hundred dollars? A new bike, a video game, another hockey stick? Why, he could get three or four hockey sticks with one hundred dollars!

Sixty days! That was like forever. But the school term ended, and with holidays, hockey school, and summer camp, the catalogues were forgot-ten. James started mowing lawns to earn enough to buy the things he wanted.

Then one morning late in August the sergeant of the local RCMP detachment was on the phone. "Tell James he can stop by and pick up his hundred-dollar bill."

After James and his father picked up the money, they didn't head straight home. James had an errand to run. He went to the Treasury Branch next door to the video store and across the street from the drug-store where chocolate bars were on sale two for ninety-nine cents, and deposited the hundred-dollar bill, all of it, in his bank account.

There have been some big changes in James's life, in all our lives, since that summer of 1991. We still live in the same house on the same street, and the poplar fuzz still piles up against the curb in June. But two years ago, James's father died, and he found himself suddenly the man of the house. He's a teenager now, still bright, still a top student, and the highest-scoring player on his bantam hockey team. His sharp eyes still spot pennies in the grass and on the sidewalk. On Valentine's Day, a young lady, whose name he declines to reveal, gave him a gorgeous red rose. He slipped it into the bouquet of carnations that he and his brothers and sisters bought for me.

Sure, he has a few pimples, he misses a bag or two when he takes out the garbage, and his bed is never made. (He must like it that way because I never make it for him.) But he's just an all-round terrific kid growing up too fast into a fine young man.

I wonder. Would it have anything to do with that hundred-dollar bill?

*Donna Cookson Martin*
Sedgewick, Alberta

My two best childhood friends are dyslexic. Staying in touch with them has always been a challenge: Harry writes on the order of a letter every two and a half years and Keith has put pen to paper maybe three times since we all left home twenty years ago. Our only irregular communication has been by telephone. Harry writes more letters than he sends, he claims, but because he cannot stand to look at the finished product his letters seldom find their way to an envelope, much less to a mailbox. Keith used to get his wife to write letters for him, but since their kids came along their letter-writing has been abandoned. Harry's letters are always an exploration in cryptography, an adventure in decoding. They are, in truth, exhausting to read because of the multiple spelling mistakes and grammatical train wrecks and syntactical snafus. Keith's few letters were equally difficult, and while I always welcomed letters from these two old and dear friends, I also found it time-consuming and fatiguing to cut through the learning disability to the content of their lives as revealed and obscured in their correspondence.

And then, for about eight months last year, Harry had an e-mail account. Suddenly I was getting a letter every two days, usually a page or two in length — double per letter what Harry had produced previously.

Harry's e-mail was littered with spelling mistakes, incomplete sentences, mangled syntax, and all the baggage that his learning disability imposes on him. The quality was unchanged, but the quantity was dramatically and abruptly increased.

I suspect that Harry found it easier to send electronic mail than to print off a word-processed letter, which he would then have to take responsibility for in some manner. As he explained it to me, it was the effort of proofreading his snail-mail that usually dissuaded him from sending it. But that problem never confronted him with electronic mail. It seemed easier for Harry to hit his F5 key twice and have done with it. He never had to handle and fold into an envelope a piece of paper that he knew to be littered with incomprehensible phrases. For reasons I cannot begin to fathom, reading his electronic mail was easier than reading his snail-mail, too — even though the actual content was unchanged. Something about the medium itself made it easier for Harry to send his letters and easier for me to read and understand them.

When Harry let his account lapse, his output dropped to its ante-electronic level. But for a brief eight months it was wonderful to log on and find a mailbox with two or three letters from him.

I can't wait for him to reopen his account.

*Craig Jones*
Kingston, Ontario

In answer to your guest who worried about whistling anaesthetists, my husband is a general practitioner and an anaesthetist, also a wonderful whistler with a varied repertoire of tunes.

In our small country hospital he whistled up the corridors, in the library and parking lot, I'm sure most of the time unaware he was whistling.

It was accepted behaviour that he often whistled while administering the anaesthetic, until one day the surgeon looked up sharply. He was whistling "Nearer My God to Thee."

*Bettie Hames*
Kenton, Manitoba

I really had to laugh when you talked about spring cleaning. Now, I am well-versed in that topic, taught by the best of German-bred housewives! But at the same time you were discussing Q-Tips for window sashes, I was fully engaged in my spring cleaning — using a pitchfork, front-end-loader tractor, and rubber boots. Not my house, but the henhouse. And there is a fine art to that, too. Warm enough weather for the "girls" to spend outside but not so warm that the ground begins to thaw and the tractor gets mired. Do it in summer, and it's very hot, dusty, miserable work. This was wet, very aromatic but manageable. Next come the corrals. Maybe the house will get done in June (it's still spring until the twenty-first). By then we won't be using the wood stove and the fight with fly ash in the house takes a hiatus.

All the best with your housecleaning. I charge ten dollars plus airfare — and I supply the boots and pitchfork. You supply the tractor.

*Brenda Giesbrecht*
High Prairie, Alberta

I heard your cross-country garden panel and must warn you: you have obviously gotten yourself involved with a bunch of expert gardeners. This situation needs immediate remedying, so I have decided to share some insights from a true Canadian garden klutz.

A garden klutz is one who loves gardens perhaps a trifle more than gardening. She or he devours seed catalogues and gardening books with religious fervour and has grandiose horticultural intentions. While she tries hard to be organized, tidy, hardworking, and consistent in her gardening habits, she is in fact rather sporadic in her efforts and woefully lacking in follow-through. She might even be ever so slightly lazy. In its creatively chaotic fashion, life happens to her; and while she intends to be digging and hoeing, weeding and thinning, she ends up, well, doing other things. For instance, intending this year to "do it right," I put the stakes in, tall and straight, next to the tiny baby tomato plants, but somehow, what with all those summer guests, I plain forgot to tie the growing plants to the stakes.

Much more could be said about the garden-klutz syndrome, but I must save some time and energy to get out there and do some gardening this afternoon. Though I will mention that it helps considerably to have a partner with a bad back who, though he loves the results of a beautiful, in-control, cultivated veggie garden and yard, would rather — well, be doing other things. A dog who eats fish compost, lives to unearth bulbs, and who will dig vigorously to China to get near one single grain of bone meal comes in handy. It is also helpful to have a few grown children who borrow tools without first asking or fail to return tools they borrowed two weeks or two months ago so that when you go looking for the rake or the pickaxe it is simply gone, whereupon a rotten mood ensues and the need to find the tools kills the longing to create beauty, and the aspiring gardener goes into an afternoon-long sulk, festering with resentment towards her children, who she becomes increasingly convinced must have had a rotten mother and been brought up in a barn.

Back to your experts. I must take exception to what one of your guests dug up about bulbs. Why grow these banal little nuggets, it was implied, when everyone else does? They are too easy, too mundane. I mean, really, not all of us are wanting to have stinky old oversized fritillarias parading pompously about our foundations. And while your guests were getting hot and bothered over those lovely species tulips, many of us unjaded, simpler folk still love the crocuses, grape hyacinth, scilla, chinodoxa, anemone, and, of course, the golden daffodil — the simple bulbs of our youth that naturalize perfectly delightfully. We shall not be intimidated by persons who, face it, are teetering fairly dangerously close to the edge of botanical snobbery. Furthermore, many of the other things in life that everyone else does and that are quite easy to accomplish are quite delightful, and I, for one, have no intention of abstaining from any of these activities, including the enjoyment of the common spring bulb.

I have known one of your guests for twenty years. Des Kennedy and I live on the very same island. Even garden amateurs like myself enjoy and appreciate his book *Crazy About Gardening*. There is no one I would rather kibitz with than Des. I am crazy about Des Kennedy. But Des, please — something must be happening to your nasal buds or whatever makes us able to smell. It must be caused by an overdose of heady fumes from those fragrant English roses you and Sandy grow. Des's household and mine shared that priceless load of fish compost to which he referred and, to my nose, it was redolent of Grandpa's pipe tobacco and old barns. Perhaps Des could painlessly grow those smelly fritillarias, and while he's at it why not try some cleomes, a fantastic annual that grows four feet tall like a fancy perennial? It has spidery flowers of purple, pink, and white. Not only does its foliage smell rather musky and skunky, but it has thorns, too! It is a good one for filling in big blank spots in the garden really fast, just for the summer season. One of my expert garden neighbours tells me that cleome seeds can be easily saved for next year.

Well, I must get back to the garden. First, maybe I'll have another cup of tea. But before that — do you remember that little Mother Goose rhyme, "A man of words and not of deeds/is like a garden full of weeds"? That little rhyme used to make me feel awful about talking too much and not doing enough. It made me feel inadequate for being an unfinished, Winnie-the-Pooh, lacking-in-expertise sort of person — for being, among many other radiant inadequacies, a garden klutz who has embarrassingly too many weeds in her garden. A few years ago I saw an illustration accompanying this little couplet in which an old man leaning on his garden rake is sitting on a stump in a wildly overgrown and weedy garden. Next to him stands a child whose attention is on the man who I am certain is telling a wonderful and timeless story.

As I write, the crickets thrum, an occasional songbird trills, an early October breeze shivers the laburnum and plum leaves, and I need right this minute to close the window. My lawn, which I prefer to call "green stuff," is chock-full of uninvited clovers and plantains. Of course it also sports scores of cheeky ever-present dandelions, who are taking turns nodding their heads under the weight of the occasional fat bee who sips their sweet yellowness.

One final word about the garden klutz. To qualify, one should, like me, keep one's bone meal in an empty yogurt container with a label that clearly reads *Spaghetti Sauce*.

*Roberta DeDoming*
Denman Island, British Columbia

One of our newspapers recently had an item that spoke of saving time by not having to commute. Time behaves in an interesting manner. I, too, have my office at home, and the following is a sequence of events that took place a few mornings ago . . .

As I finish getting dressed in the bedroom to go to my office, it is difficult to ignore Schooner, our golden retriever, who, in a language that is unmistakable, pleads to have his tennis ball thrown for him to fetch. On the ball-launch site, the back sundeck, I discover a very large fir branch blown down by the previous night's easterly gale.

While I ponder about how to deal with this problem, Schooner has found the ball in the underbrush of our back-yard jungle and has come back for another go. This involves first wrestling the ball out of his mouth. Someday I must teach him to drop.

While dragging the large branch to the wood pile to deal with some other day, I notice two apples on our only apple tree have been partially eaten. Raccoons have rediscovered our kings.

Schooner has brought back a double. Two tennis balls in his mouth. He's been known to handle as many as three at a time.

Last year I tried anointing the undamaged apples with a mixture of oil and cayenne pepper, hoping that the raccoons would have at least as much problem with the heat as I do when I mistakenly order Thai food that's too spicy. They must have loved the peppery dip better than the apples themselves, as the following morning every apple was licked clean but otherwise untouched.

Schooner has retrieved a ball again, but now is happy to lie down and shred the ball into little green slimy bits.

While looking for wire fencing to deal with the raccoon problem, I have to digress to find binoculars so that from my hillside I can better see a sloop on English Bay. Its colourful spinnaker seems difficult to control in the gale leftovers and demands attention, even from the shore.

I construct a temporary wire sculpture around the apple tree which the raccoons will believe to be some kind of trap and thus keep away — I hope. Finally I get to my desk. My office is about six feet from the bedroom.

Elapsed time to get to at-home office: forty-seven minutes.

Travel time to office when it was downtown: twenty-six minutes.

*Al Vitols*
West Vancouver

A discussion about the flag brought back for me a memory of my father, former senator Eugene Forsey. At the time of the flag debate, Dad wasn't convinced that there was any need for a new national symbol; he was more concerned with the real and practical dangers presented, even then, by the pressures to devolve more and more powers to the provinces. Responding to some proposal for decentralization that he considered particularly foolish, he put forward his own suggestion for a new flag: "ten jackasses eating the leaves off a single maple tree."

In the context of the then-popular "two nations" theory, and with his flair for nonsense verse, Dad also had a proposal for a new national anthem:

(Please sing)

O Canada, we don't know what you are,
Nation, we thought, but that Lesage doth bar,
And a colony you have ceased to be,
So we know what you are not,
And we stand on guard, though it's rather hard
When we're not quite sure for what —
O Canada! great Undefined!
O Canada, can't you make up your mind?
O Canada, can't you some status find!

*Helen Forsey*
Ompah, Ontario

In a tribute to Emmett Hall, someone raised the question: "Who was the father of medicare, Emmett Hall or Tommy Douglas?"

Emmett himself answered this question. He said that he and Tommy sorted this out between themselves. "Tommy and I agreed," he used to say, "that Tommy was the father of medicare because he brought it to life in Saskatchewan — the first such program in North America. I took his plan, added to it, made it a national program and enshrined it in Canadian law — that makes me the father-in-law of medicare."

Although they were miles apart in many ways, these two men were great friends. Emmett used to love to tell this story:

When Mr. Hall was still in the East, Mr. Douglas, by then an elder statesman, was struck by a bus in Ottawa and almost killed. Mr. Hall heard the story on a news flash and immediately phoned Mrs. Douglas. She told him how serious it was, that Tommy was in intensive care and unconscious, but that she would have the hospital admit Mr. Hall to visit him.

Mr. Hall tiptoed into the room. He was startled to see how tiny Tommy Douglas really was: "He looked like a little kid under the sheets."

Tommy was obviously badly hurt, but as he lay there drifting along somewhere between this world and the next, there was a beautiful smile on his face.

Moved, Emmett sat down, took Tommy's hand and began to pray.

Think of that picture: the two old adversaries, the Tory and the Prairie socialist, the chief justice and the former premier, the Prince of the Catholic Church and the Protestant minister — different in every way but united in mutual respect, in caring for others, and in pure affection.

Tommy began to stir. He was coming back. He opened his eyes and, heaven still with him, said with delight, "Oh, Emmett, are you here too?"

Once upon a time we had lawyers and politicians like that. I believe the genes are out there somewhere, waiting to come back to us.

*Don Leitch*
Craik, Saskatchewan

Your tribute to Robertson Davies reminded me of the five days I spent with him in 1975. I was a young assistant director working on a production of "Question Time" written by Mr. Davies for Toronto Arts Productions. The action of the play took place on Les Montaignes des Glaces, a fictitious mountain range somewhere in Canada. Prime Minister MacAdam crash-lands on this mountain range and upon waking experiences Jungian visions of his own life through which he gains insights into the Canadian identity. Typically, it was a big show conceptually as well as being theatrically demanding.

I was assigned by the director to take care of Mr. Davies during tech week at the St. Lawrence Centre. Tech week was when an awesome number of lighting, special effects, sound, costumes, props, and other cues were rehearsed into a seamless whole. A two-hour play usually took five days of technical rehearsals. During this time, the full attention and co-operation of all members of the company both on stage and backstage was required for a gruelling sixty hours. Everyone was on edge during this complicated process. My assignment really meant that I was to keep Mr. Davies away from company members so that they could get on with their jobs without the meddling of a nervous playwright distracting them with notes about the interpretations of their roles or with the odd rewrite.

I saw this assignment as an opportunity to get some professional advice about my own plays. So, with a hubris I put down to naiveté, I asked if he would mind reading some of my work. He was very obliging and accepted the slim envelope. That took about thirty seconds. I had five days left. We sat together that first morning and watched the rehearsal as it coughed, sputtered, and hiccoughed like a car trying to warm up on a very cold day. Mr. Davies got increasingly agitated as he watched the actors mangle his lines, the technicians blow every cue, and costumes rip at critical moments. Finally, he could stand it no longer and demanded to be taken backstage so that he could speak to the "bumbling jackasses" who were ruining his play.

I sprang into hyper gear. My job at the theatre depended on my ability to keep him away, and my future as a writer depended on Mr. Davies's opinion of my abilities. My only solution was to take him backstage but to get conveniently lost on the way. We ended up in the bowels of the building. Tired of walking, he stopped and plunked himself on some packing crates. We called for help, and when none came, he sent me off to look for a way out. Meanwhile, he said that he would read my manuscript. I went around the corner and pretended to walk off, but stayed and watched as he read my material. He turned the pages stonefaced. When he finished, he replaced it in the envelope, closed his eyes and let out a sigh. What did that mean? That was my cue, and I walked up to him and told him I had found the way out. Of course, the company had broken for lunch, so it was not possible for him to speak to any of them.

When we returned to the auditorium, Brenda Davies was waiting for us. She had brought a hamper. Could I find them a nice quiet spot for a picnic? Not outside, because it was snowing, but inside — in the theatre. I led them to a large landing to the left of the auditorium. There, the Davieses set out a tablecloth on the floor and pulled out endless cold dishes of chicken, salad, cold cuts, pickles, fruit, cheese, and wine. I was invited to join them for lunch. As we sat down, I was bursting with curiosity but could not bring myself to ask him what he thought of my writing. Suddenly, the lights in the auditorium went out. The house technician had switched all the lights off before leaving for his lunch break. Without missing a beat, Mr. Davies flicked on his cigarette lighter, reached into the basket and fished out two candles, which he lit and placed at the centre of the picnic.

We had lunch like that every day for the next five days and talked about everything in his life, in Brenda's life, and in my short life, which sounded so pale in comparison to what they had experienced. We spoke, it seemed, about everything except my play. As the days passed, rehearsals improved and Mr. Davies was able to relax and enjoy the performances which had irritated him so much at the beginning of the week. On the final day, at our regular candle-lighted lunch picnic, I could stand it no longer and plucked up the courage to ask him about my play. I must have displayed a mild annoyance that he had not even mentioned it in the last four and a half days. He leaned in to catch the candlelight which bathed half his face in an amber glow and cocked one eye. He said: "But, young man, we have done nothing but talk about your play." I was dumbfounded. Did I miss something? "Indeed," he said, "you want to hear about dialogue, structure, plot — that is not playwriting. Life is what you want to experience, a lot of life. The rest is just a tedious tech week."

Now, twenty years later, I realize that those five days with Mr. Davies were not just lessons in playwriting, they were more — much, much more.

*Simon Johnston*
London, Ontario

I had occasion to encounter Robertson Davies in 1967 — though I didn't know it at the time. It was spring, and my girlfriend Pam and I had driven into Toronto from Galt, to experience the famous "Love-In" in Queen's Park. Our long hair was freshly ironed, our eyes circled with the obligatory black liner. We were decked out in rainbows and beads, and carried giant gaudy papier-mâché flowers.

As we walked through the University of Toronto campus a bearded man in scholarly robes bustled towards us and asked us what was going on that brought so many strange and colourful people to his neighbourhood. He was distinguished and formal, though friendly and clearly bursting with curiosity.

We explained that it was a Love-In, a celebration of love, peace, and happiness, and I handed him my big pink papier-mâché flower. His eyes twinkled and he told us to wait while he hurried back into Massey College. A moment later he re-emerged bearing a bottle of fine red wine, which he gave us as he wished us a lovely day. We thanked him and headed off to a day full of sunshine and music in Queen's Park.

We shared that wine with the people sitting around us, and I'll never forget that mellow yellow afternoon, sweetened by the gracious gesture of the robed and bearded gentleman.

*Helen Aitkin*
Arthur, Ontario

How does one remember the matriarch of Canadian poetry?

I know many people in Canada's literary community who have opinions about Dorothy Livesay, not all of which, I might add, are necessarily glowing. Dorothy was a controversial woman. She dared to write about female sexual passions, not *just* about being in love. She certainly wasn't one to keep her mind to herself.

I discovered this in September 1992, when I was issued my first major arts assignment for the *Vancouver Sun*. My task was go to Victoria and visit Livesay in the seniors' home where she was staying.

This is how I will choose to remember Dorothy:

Dorothy was the woman who met me in the foyer of the seniors' home dressed in a shocking-pink cardigan. She reprimanded me, insisting that I was late when, in fact, I was early. "Oh," she said. "I forgot what time." Her memory loss was the reason for her being there.

Dorothy was the woman who, within ten minutes, informed me that her name meant "Gift of God," and that it wasn't pronounced *Dor-thy* with two syllables but rather *Do-ro-thy* with three.

She was the woman who insisted that her eyes were blue like the sea — not *regular* sea blue but rather *deep* sea blue — almost green. And indeed, they were.

That afternoon, we planned to take a trip to Beacon Hill Park for some soft ice cream. We'd do the interview on a bench looking out to the Olympic mountain range that faces Victoria from across the ocean.

But before we could go, *Do-ro-thy* asked if I'd accompany her to her room. "It'll be windy," she said. "I'll have to dress warmly." In her small, bare bedroom she walked to a dresser and pulled from a drawer a pair of flesh-coloured stockings.

Grinning — and without a self-conscious note in her voice — she asked if I could give her a hand. I awkwardly cinched the stockings up her small, frail frame. When I finished, she laughed. "I bet you weren't prepared for *this* when you came, were you?"

No, I wasn't. Nor was I expecting this occasion to inspire me today as much as it did that sunny afternoon, eating soft ice cream with one of Canada's great poets.

Dorothy's passion suggested a female Walt Whitman. She was in awe of life. Whether it be a tree, the wind, or, as she put it that memorable afternoon, our conversation spiced by "the black crow's yack."

Life, even at eighty-two with a fading memory, was still very much worth living. In her poetry, may Dorothy Livesay be remembered.

*Kim Heinrich Gray*
Toronto

One morning in November 1976, I bought a copy of Paul Hiebert's *Tower in Siloam* from the book table at a church bazaar. I was curious to read what else this former chemistry professor had written besides *Sarah Binks* and *Willows Revisited*. I got home just in time to turn on the CBC and hear you talking with Paul Hiebert in Carman, Manitoba.

The coincidence spurred me into writing my first fan letter. I wrote to tell him what fun we had had quoting Sarah at university in Winnipeg, how she had lifted our spirits while we struggled with footnotes and references in our theses for grad school and helped put things in perspective when confronted with academia.

To my surprise and delight, his reply was quick, very funny and equally serious about his spiritual development and beliefs, and very generous. He invited me to become a member of PHCSLF, his organization, "known in more expanded form as the Paul Hiebert College Sweetheart Lunch Fund." He explained that he and his wife had extra money and that he had decided to use his share to take old college sweethearts out to lunch, but that at his age, eighty-four, he was running out of sweethearts from college days. As a result he was beginning to have to put the money into bonds he didn't really want. So instead he wanted to use the money from the Sweetheart Fund to send copies of his latest book, *Doubting Castle*, to people who might like to have it. He hoped I wouldn't object to receiving it in this indirect way from all those other women. They were all very nice, he said, and in fact his wife complimented him on his discrimination.

Of course I accepted. And that was the beginning of a wonderful correspondence.

Just in case you have not come across these parodies here is "Tree Fever," based on John Masefield's "Sea Fever."

I must decorate the damn tree again, the too tall tree and high
And all I ask is a step-ladder, and no one around or nigh,
And all I ask is to be left alone, and no one's constant yacking,
And no sighs, or smothered cries, when the ornaments are cracking.

I must string up the lights again, and find the ones that are out,
The used ones, and the fused ones, and the ones put away in doubt,
And all I ask is no advice, or be told that the tree is wilting,
Or the dear little angels are upside-down, or the whole damn tree is
   tilting.

I must decorate the tree again — it's part of the Christmas life,
And all I ask is no one's help, and least of all the wife's —
And all I ask is no wise cracks from some laughing fellow rover —
Just a long rest, and a long drink, when the job is over.

*Angela Graham*
London, Ontario

Christmas is always a magic time for me, I think because my parents believed in its power and weaved unforgettable moments to be treasured by their five children.

For most of my childhood, my father worked eighteen hours a day. We did not see much of him, but he always took time off to be with us at Christmas. Each year we would sit in front of the bare fir tree while he showed us how to properly string the lights, which branches to choose to hang the ornaments, how to cut the treetop for the red-and-white tinfoil star. He would place angel hair around each bulb, and smother every branch with icicles made of aluminum strings. When everything was to his satisfaction, he would turn off the lights in the room, then plug in the Christmas tree. The first burst of sparkling lights was enchanting. Around each light floated an angel, each with a differently coloured halo.

If my father was satisfied with the tree, he declared it ready for Santa Claus. This pronouncement marked the beginning of Christmas time, and we would start to speculate what presents Santa would bring us.

When I was four years old, my family moved from our second-storey apartment into a three-bedroom house on the outskirts of Mont-Laurier, a small town two hundred kilometres north of Montreal.

As our first Christmas in the new house approached, I started to worry. We had a beautiful tree, but no chimney. When I asked my mother about it, she assured me that we had a chimney in the basement, and that Santa Claus would come that way. I was a precocious child, rarely taking anything at face value, so I decided to check out this chimney. I went downstairs and saw a very narrow column of bricks with a small round flap way above where I could not reach. As the furnace started to rumble, the flap moved back and forth.

Instead of reassuring me, the sight of this chimney made me even more worried. I could not imagine how Santa could come down such a narrow space, even less how he could come out through that flap without tearing his beautiful red suit. On top of everything, if he succeeded, he would surely break his neck falling from so high a distance to the floor.

The problem continued to preoccupy me, and despite all my mother's reassurances, I went to bed on Christmas Eve convinced that even with all Santa's goodwill, he would have to bypass our house that year. A few hours later, my mother gently shook me awake and took me in her arms. She spoke softly to me, saying she wanted to show me something in the basement. As we went downstairs, I heard, "Ho! Ho! Ho! Is this the little girl who thought I couldn't come down her chimney?"

My mother put me down and I walked toward him. There was Santa, I marvelled, standing right beside the tiny chimney, with a bit of soot on his beard, and a big bag of presents on his back. He took me in his arms, like the jolly man he was, and he brought me upstairs where my two little brothers waited with my mother. After distributing the presents, Santa left by the front door since, he explained to me, it was much easier to go down a small chimney than to go up.

To this day, I have never figured out how Santa Claus could fit in such a small space, with his big bag of presents. Such is the magic of Christmas.

I only wish my father would have been with us to see him, but he returned from Midnight Mass a few minutes after Santa had left.

*Dominique Benoit*
Nepean, Ontario

No one ever says anything nice about turkeys. In fact, until just a few months ago, not even I would have given this particular fowl a second thought. But that was before Lurkey.

How we ended up with Lurkey is unimportant. Although I am, admittedly, nuts for chickens, turkeys did not appeal to me particularly much. First of all, they look really weird. All those globby, hangy bits — yuck! And, of course, they're stupid. In fact, I was told, they are so stupid that when it rains you have to get them into the barn or else they will stare up at the sky and drown. I knew all that. But, nevertheless, Lurkey, a Bourbon Red turkey hen, came to live with us. She seemed to fit in well enough with our other assorted fowl, caused no particular problems, and was reasonably attractive, considering, so I didn't pay much attention to her, really. Except that, in the spring, Lurkey constructed herself a nest and began to lay eggs. This behaviour distressed me. Being a mother myself, I recognized the forces of nature that were at work here, and so I set about to find Lurkey a mate. Enter Lurch. He was big. And, as it turned out, bad. And, depending on your point of view, ugly. However, Lurkey was infatuated, and a torrid relationship ensued. Lurch, in the meantime, terrorized everyone. He attacked my children, he chased my elderly mother down the driveway, he went next door and threatened the neighbour's two-year-old. And yes, he even "foomped" (I hadn't realized there was an actual word for it).

Unfortunately, what we didn't know at the time was that he was also brutalizing poor Lurkey. Now, far be it from me to cast aspersions, and perhaps it was done during the heat of passion, but Lurch, it seems, was an abusive husband. He had to go. Lurch was promptly crated and sent to auction, where he fetched thirty dollars. Meanwhile, Lurkey was in bad shape. My friend Debbie, usually unfazed by animal injuries no matter how disgusting, was not at all optimistic about Lurkey's chances for survival. "Oh, yuck, I can see her insides!" Debbie announced bluntly, during the examination. Nevertheless, we decided to give it a try because, as Debbie put it, "This was a clear case of domestic violence, and we women have a responsibility to support one another." She began to sew. And sew. And sew. The surgery took nearly two hours, during which time my husband, George, sat at the kitchen table holding Lurkey, and I ransacked the bathroom cupboard for medical supplies. Despite our efforts, the prognosis was far from good. Lurkey was dressed in a stretchy bodysuit to cover the wounds, confined to a cage, and left in George's studio to recover from the operation. We didn't think she'd make it through the night. But she did. And, miraculously, the next night, and the next. Lurkey was going to live. During the month that followed, Debbie came three times a week to change Lurkey's dressings and administer strange homeopathic remedies. It was truly a heroic effort. Naturally, we developed quite a relationship with this bird and a deep respect for her remarkable ability to overcome physical pain and emotional trauma. She is certainly a true survivor.

Now, what I had failed to mention was that before Lurch was sent packing, Lurkey had produced a small clutch of fertile eggs. These were given to an enthusiastic banty hen who, four weeks later, hatched herself two baby turkeys — the offspring of the ill-fated union of Lurkey and Lurch. Almost simultaneously to their hatching, Lurkey was released from confinement and went in search of her long-lost eggs. Of course, they were no longer there. But, conveniently, our peahen, Betty, had recently laid some eggs and so I snatched these and gave them to Lurkey, who was delighted to have something to sit on. Four weeks later, Lurkey became the proud mother of three baby peacocks. She has proved to be an exemplary parent — gentle, attentive, devoted. Truly, this is a bird who has triumphed over adversity. As for her biological children, they roam the yard in search of their identity. I believe that, in time, they will come to terms with their true ornithological heritage, and that Lurkey, in her wisdom, will accept them as friends, at the very least.

As Thanksgiving approaches, I am filled with doubt. Not that Lurkey *herself* would be in any danger, but now I look at *all* turkeys differently. They are not stupid. They are not ugly. They do not drown in the rain. I think perhaps for Thanksgiving dinner we'll have lasagna. Vegetarian lasagna.

*Evelyn Raab*
Millbrook, Ontario

# A Not Always Flattering but Sometimes at Least Frank Gallery of Cartoons

Aislin, *Montreal Gazette*

Graham Harrop, *Globe and Mail*

# CONVERSATIONS WITH WRITERS IV: MARGARET ATWOOD

*Although I'm sure I talked to Margaret Atwood as often as to any other Canadian author, I never knew what to expect. She could be scholarly, feisty, lyrical, or sometimes just playful, but always a delight.*

PETER GZOWSKI Margaret Atwood does not use ellipses. I can't think of a sentence of hers that starts out to say something and changes its mind in the middle. Maybe it's because she's Canadian and ellipses aren't, or maybe it's just because she's Margaret Atwood. Margaret Atwood writes straight ahead. Together, the lines of her sentences make a surface, which when you first stare at it seems to reflect the light, but later you realize it's like a prism. You can look through it and see things out the bottom in different ways. Reading Margaret Atwood is like standing under a cold shower except you're on the third floor and someone is in the basement playing with the hot-water tap. It's a distinct prose style, and I can try but I can't imitate it. So I welcome the person who worked it out in the first place: Margaret Atwood, good morning.

MARGARET ATWOOD Hello, Peter.

PG I can't do it.

MA I liked to hear your imitation.

PG It's not an imitable style, except as I read through the book I promise we'll mention and talk about and get you to read from, it started to ring at me, and I realized there is something Atwood in the world.

MA There's something Gzowski in the world.

PG No, no, no, never mind. No, but there's a way you do it. Now, are you aware?

MA Well, I like to think that I do different things at different times. However, there is an adjective now appearing in academic circles, "Atwoodian."

PG What does it mean?

MA It means Atwood-like.

PG What does that mean?

MA I'd like to tell you that my sister-in-law was having dinner the other night and some strangers were introduced to her and they said, "Oh, Atwood. Are you related to the famous Atwood?" and she blushed modestly and looked down and murmured that she was and they said, "We love your furniture." You know there's a store called Atwood's Traditional Interiors?

PG Yes, yes. Are you related to the famous Atwoods?

MA Probably very distantly.

PG  Is that a cousin of yours, Atwood furniture? Do they make furniture the way you make prose?

MA  I don't think so. Well, I haven't checked it out, but I kind of always read their ads just to see whether there is a family resemblance.

PG  Have you ever put ellipses into a sentence?

MA  You mean brackets?

PG  No, I mean those little three dots that Tom Wolfe uses all over the place.

MA  Those three dots. I don't like them. I sometimes put four dots at the end of a sentence but I don't like those sort of gaspy, breathy dots. I use dashes instead of dots. Does that reveal anything?

PG  Well, I think it was what I was trying to get at when I was trying to capture the way you write, which is this incredible directness. I mean it is the cleanest prose around.

MA  Thank you.

PG  Not necessarily a compliment, because sometimes there are moments for ornament.

MA  Yeah, I've done that in novels when I've had more space, but this particular book is very, very short pieces of prose fiction.

PG  Or poems.

MA  Or prose poems, yes. Some of them are towards the prose-poems end of things, and some of them are definitely towards the fiction end. In fact, there's a mini science fiction in it, and a couple of other forms that are very, very condensed. "Happy Endings" is plots for about six novels done in about three pages.

PG  "Happy Endings" starts — and they are all the same people — "Happy Endings" starts with John and Mary, and you see John and Mary, and that becomes version "A," and in the next version you have John and Mary and someone called Madge, who becomes the extra person, and it takes you about a paragraph to write what could be a short story. Would that have been a short story? What are you doing when you do that?

MA  I think in "Happy Endings" I was talking about endings and the fact that people, when they read a novel and they get to a point when the hero and the heroine get married, they think that's a happy ending, right? Of course it's not the ending of those people's lives. It's just the end of the novel.

PG  I think — at the end of that piece I think you say that's what happened, now how . . .

MA  How and why.

PG  . . . how and why are the questions that remain there for the novel-ist to pursue always.

MA  Yes. That's why novels are long and "Happy Endings" is short. "Happy Endings" is just the plots.

PG  One of the reasons — when I tried to do my little instant caricature this morning, satire, ah, imitation, the sincerest form of flattery — I made it about writing parody is because a lot of this book — whose name we have not yet mentioned — is about writing, and writing itself interests you, the writer.

MA  How could it not?

PG  Did it ever occur to you that it might interest you the writer more than it would interest me the reader? Do you have a concern about that?

MA  Well, most of my work isn't about writing . . .

PG  No, I know that.

MA  . . . and this one is, and it's probably the first and last time I'll ever say anything about it, because that's about the extent of my interest in it.

PG  That's true, although you write works of criticism, and you're an essayist.

MA  It's not about my writing. It's about other people's writing.

PG  Yeah, that's right.

MA  Even this is not about my writing, it's about writing as an act that you do and as an event that you participate in.

PG  The book is called *Murder in the Dark*, and "Murder in the Dark" is also the title of one of the longer pieces. I'm going to ask Margaret to read it, and it is a short piece, but I think from what you're saying about writing as an act, it's a good thing. Would you read the entire title piece from "Murder in the Dark"?

MA  All of these pieces are quite swift. Oh, "Murder in the Dark," by the way, is also the name of a game, which you may or may not know, but you are about to find it out.

This is a game I've played only twice. The first time I was in Grade Five, I played it in the cellar, the cellar of a large house belong-ing to the parents of a girl called Louise. There was a pool table in the cellar but none of us knew anything about pool. There was also a player piano. After a while we got tired of running the punchcard rolls through the player piano and watching the keys go up and down by themselves, like something in a late movie just before you see the dead person. I was in love with a boy called Bill, who was in love with Louise. The other boy, whose name I can't remember, was in love with me. Nobody knew who Louise was in love with.

So, we turned out the lights in the cellar and played *Murder in the Dark*, which gave the boys the pleasure of being able to put their hands around the girls' necks and gave the girls the pleasure of screaming. The excitement was almost more than we could bear, but luckily Louise's parents came home and asked us what we thought we were up to.

The second time I played it was with adults; it was not as much fun, though more intellectually complex.

I heard that this game was once played at a summer cottage by six normal people and a poet, and the poet really tried to kill someone. He was hindered only by the intervention of a dog which could not tell fantasy from reality. The thing about this game is that you have to know when to stop.

Here is how you play:

You fold up some pieces of paper and put them into a hat, a bowl or the centre of the table. Everyone chooses a piece. The one who gets the x is the detective, the one who gets the black spot is the killer. The detective leaves the room, turning off the lights. Everyone gropes around in the dark until the murderer picks a victim. He can either whisper, "You're dead," or he can slip his hands around a throat and give a playful but decisive squeeze. The victim screams and falls down. Everyone must now stop moving around except the murderer, who of course does not want to be found near the body. The detective counts to ten, turns on the lights and enters the room. He may now question anyone but the victim, who is not allowed to answer, being dead. Everyone but the murderer must tell the truth. The murderer must lie.

If you like, you can play games with this game. You can say: the murderer is the writer, the detective is the reader, the victim is the book. Or perhaps, the murderer is the writer, the detective is the critic and the victim is the reader. In that case the book would be the total *mise en scène*, including the lamp that was accidentally tipped over and broken. But really it's more fun just to play the game.

In any case, that's me in the dark. I have designs on you, I'm plotting my sinister crime, my hands are reaching for your neck or perhaps, by mistake, your thigh. You can hear my footsteps approaching. I wear boots and carry a knife, or maybe it's a pearl-handled revolver, in any case I wear boots with very soft soles, you can see the cinematic glow of my cigarette, waxing and waning in the fog of the room, the street, the room, even though I don't smoke. Just remember this, when the scream at last has ended and you've turned on the lights: by the rules of the game, I must always lie.

Now: do you believe me?

PG  Now, that's the piece from which the title is taken, and it appears a third of the way through somewhere. The book is divided into sections, which are?

MA  The first are many, many fake autobiographies.

PG  Are they all fake?

MA  No, they're not entirely fake. I should say fictionalized.

PG  "Boys' Own Annual, 1911" is not . . .

MA  Fictionalized.

PG  Fictionalized. But there are childhood scenes and then there are Mexican scenes, and there are writerly things . . .

MA  Then there are other things, which get off into an area which is difficult to discuss. That's your prose poems. But I think that further towards the end of the book we're getting into what writing actually does to you when you read it, because what writing really is is a kind of computer programming that you play through your own head when you read it, and the difference between you and the computer is that you participate. When you're reading a piece of fiction you are actively engaged in the imagining of that fiction. In that respect it's different from movies and television, which supply more sensory information for you. But with reading you just have the words on the page and all of the sights, sounds, smells, touch — all of those things — you are supplying out of your own brain. You're interacting with the book. It's one of the most active forms of entertainment.

PG  Did you conceive the book as a book? Or are those pieces that you would write and then assemble?

MA  No, I didn't. I was just writing them. They were orphan pieces for a long time because they didn't seem to fit anywhere. They weren't short stories — they were too short — and they weren't poems, and what were they? So I didn't really think of them as being a book until I found that I had quite a number of them.

PG  Then you look for a pattern to impose on them . . .

MA  Then I looked for . . .

PG  . . . or did you do what James Thurber did? Take them up to the top of the stairs and throw them down and push them into six different piles with his nose, I think he once said.

MA  Well, he would have to, he was very near-sighted. Whenever I arrange a book consisting of small bits like poems or anything, what it usually involves is a large floor, and I do lay them all out on the floor, and then I shuffle them around like shuffling a deck of cards, and I try to arrange them into some kind of order. Because the other thing about a book is you can't just present it to people as these things on a floor. You have to put it into an order with pages. Something has to come first. It's the nature of books. So, then you start looking for what should be at the end, and I usually work from the end back towards the beginning. I can usually figure out what should be at the beginning and what should be at the end, but as it says in "Happy Endings," the in-between part is the most difficult.

PG  I want to ask you one more question about the structure, but first, just about the pieces themselves. When you begin to write those — pieces is my word, but that's an old journalist word. They're prose poems, or . . .

MA  You can call them pieces, just like piano pieces.

PG  . . . do you know where you are going when you start at sentence one? Because there's an inevitability about much of them, but some of it is an inevitability that is out of control, as your imagination grabs it and goes with it. I go with you all the way, but do you know where you're going when you start?

MA  Let's switch to music and call them improvisations. You have a theme, you have a melody, if you like, and then you are playing with them, and I never know where it's going to end up when I'm writing something. I do a lot of improvising.

PG Do you start to write about Murder in the Dark, the game, without aiming toward any conclusion about the writer's perception of herself?

MA I started with a description of what happened. What actually happened. That's real.

PG Yeah.

MA I *did* play Murder in the Dark when I was in grade five, and I *did* play it in somebody's cellar, and all of that was . . .

PG And there was a poet and six normal people?

MA This is true.

PG And the poet tried to do somebody in?

MA That's what somebody told me.

PG Oh, tsk, tsk. So that's all real, and then you start to play, and then your imagination just goes somewhere.

MA Yeah, that's what happened.

PG About the structure. One of the reviews I read — I've only read one review, come to think of it — Elspeth Cameron in *Saturday Night* is imposing a kind of order on it. Now, is that an academic coming in in the same way academics impose or make up words like "Atwoodian"? Or is she trying to see some symbol of plot or lack of plot?

MA Well, it isn't a novel, number one — it's *not* a novel. And I have to confess I have not read the review yet, so I can't talk about it. But my general feeling about criticism is, if they can see an order there and they can support it with evidence, that's valid.

PG Even though it's an order you may not have known about?

MA Yeah. Now, if I have a contrary theory and there's more evidence to support mine, then I would go for mine. But often you can learn things from people who see things you didn't see, but it's there. And that can be valuable.

PG This book is by Coach House Press, which is something of a return for you, right?

MA Yes. I never have published with Coach House before, but long, long ago, just before Coach House started and just — sorry, just *after* Coach House started, and just after I started, I almost did a book with them, and the book was *The Journals of Susanna Moodie*, which later got done by Oxford. But I've always wanted to do a book with them, so in a way it was a kind of fulfilling of something I probably should have done many years ago.

PG   It's called *Murder in the Dark*, it's by Margaret Atwood, it's published
     by Coach House Press, and what are you doing now? Have you got
     a big one this fall . . .

MA   And I did the cover.

PG   And you did the collage that's on the cover. It says it's by Bart Gerrard
     — now, it's not, is it? It's by Margaret Atwood herself.

MA   Yes. Those are little clouds of caviar floating in the sky.

PG   I thought they were just neat little black things. You're putting stuff
     in there that I didn't even know about.

MA   I cut them out of . . . I think it was *Vogue* magazine. Pictures out of
     *Vogue* magazine, made into the cover.

PG   Now you're not going to tell me if you have a major work coming out
     in the fall?

MA   I have a book of poetry coming out, called *Interlunar*, but I'm still
     at the floor stage with it. And I can't tell you anything beyond that
     except that I'm working on longer fiction.

PG   Thank you for coming by, Margaret Atwood.

# LIFE WITH JESSIE

## by her mother, Nancy Huggett

⌒

*We first heard about Jessie when Nancy Huggett, whose business card describes her as "writer and mom, sometimes in that order," wrote a letter about Jessie's birth in 1990. We were moved and enthralled by it, and suggested Nancy keep a journal. More than five years later, we began presenting that journal on the air in Nancy's voice, which she recorded for us in Ottawa. We came to look on Jessie almost as one of the family, and feel blessed to know her.*

## BIRTH

"Who does she look like?" the nurse asked as she placed this scrunched-up bundle of life into my open and waiting arms.

"Dr. Sim," I joked, referring to my Asian obstetrician, who was impishly grinning at me through my legs.

Dan laughed, for the first time since we had entered the hospital, since I had entered labour. He reached out to hold Jessie, but I couldn't let her go. I wanted to touch and kiss every part of her body. I pulled him to us and we grinned and laughed and put our arms around each other.

The next morning, as Dan was finishing the jubilant phone calls to friends and relatives, a strange doctor walked into the room. She slowly pulled the white curtain around my bed and stood there silently, waiting for Dan to finish talking on the phone. My whole body stiffened when I saw her.

"There's something wrong . . ." I said, hoping that if I said it, it wouldn't be true.

"Yes," she said, "we think your daughter has Down's syndrome . . ." She continued to tell us that there might be some problem with her heart, that she would be mentally retarded with the IQ of a five-year-old. She emphasized that it was not our fault. It was nothing we had done, just a sort of genetic roulette and Jessie had drawn an extra chromosome. She said many other things that I don't remember.

I do remember the soft folds in the white curtain that surrounded my bed, the shuffle of slippered feet, the clipboard the doctor held in front of her as the words came out of her mouth and bounced around the room in a kind of random soundscape. I tried so hard to focus on the information she was giving us, on asking an intelligent question, on not tearing the sheets off my body and wailing loudly into the echo of that hospital.

"I want to see her." It was a statement that erupted out of my body, not a question. I needed to hold her, to look into her eyes, to feel her heartbeat, touch the soft spot on the top of her head.

I pulled Dan to the nursery, and then stopped. It was a sea of Plexiglas bassinets filled with newborns. Having just given birth with sweat and tears and ecstasy to this new life, I was sure I would recognize her as soon as I saw her. But in that ocean of swaddled babies I had to look at the little pink and blue name tags and find the one attached to "Baby Huggett."

She was sleeping. She was beautiful and tiny and peaceful, all six pounds of her. I expected her somehow to look different, but the only difference was that the tiny wisps of hair that had stuck to her head after birth had dried into a reddish blonde halo and she didn't seem as scrunched up and red. Dan and I held hands tightly, a river of questions and fears flowing between us. This was our daughter, Jessie.

We had decided long before the actual birth that if it was a girl we would name her Jessie after my grandmother — a strong and intelligent woman. When she found out that Jessie had Down's syndrome she called to say that she was honoured to share her name, and hoped that in doing so she would also be able to share her strength.

Others asked if we were still going to call her Jessie. As if when we found out that she had Down's syndrome we would change her name to something more appropriate. Like what? I mean, what is more "appropriate" for a child with Down's syndrome? A less valued name? A name that would reflect her IQ?

In the days to come, the most precious people were those who saw Jessie as a baby. Our friend Polly, who walked softly into the room and asked if she could hold Jessie and looked into her eyes and cried — not because Jessie had Down's syndrome, but because she was a tiny, beautiful baby. Kim and Aydin, who sent flowers, flowers that I nursed for a long time because we didn't get many flowers. They must have had a huge "stop order" at the florists when people found out that Jessie had Down's syndrome, thinking that flowers might not be appropriate. Let me be perfectly clear on this point. Flowers are appropriate. I hated peeking into other mothers' rooms and coveting not only their perfectly healthy babies, but their profusion of flowers and balloons.

People did make other insensitive and downright stupid comments. Comments that shocked me into silence because I was not yet used to people's reaction to difference. "Are you going to keep her?" As if this precious life were something we could drop off at the dog pound on our way home from the hospital. "Keeping" Jessie was not an issue, it was not even a question. I loved her from the moment she tumbled out of my womb, and while there were many things I didn't know as we stood there peering at this swaddled life in a Plexiglas bassinet, I knew with a certainty and clarity I had never felt before that I would fight for her life with every breath left in my body.

## GRIEF

Jessie slept a lot those first few days in the hospital, and rarely cried. I, on the other hand, cried until I thought that if I cried any more there wouldn't be enough fluid in my body to produce milk. The hormones after giving birth wreak havoc on any kind of logic.

I cried because I couldn't understand why it had happened to us. I cried because I was filled with love. I cried when I made up songs and rocked her in my arms for hours on end. I cried out of frustration when she wouldn't get on my breast. I cried when she only had two sucks from the bottle and then fell asleep. I cried when she cried for the first time because she was hungry.

I cried because I had to grieve. And what I was grieving was not Jessie's birth, but the death of a set of expectations. We expected a so-called normal child, and without realizing it we had a whole set of futures planned for that child. The coos of grandparents, exclamations of beauty, walking, talking, learning the names of seashells, driving, creating, going to university, reading *The Alexandria Quartet*. I had to grieve the death of a child that had never been born, that had lived only in our imaginations.

Dan and I spent long weepy winter hours balanced on that single hospital bed with Jessie nestled between us. We touched her and cuddled her and tried to catch and hold her sparkling blue eyes. A doctor told us that the sparkles were actually common in Down's syndrome — the result of some physiological or chemical imbalance — but we really didn't want or need to know that. The sparkles were, to us, a magical dance of life, a laughing intimation of Jessie's character.

I thought long and hard in those hours of rocking and singing and crying about what it was we wanted to share with our child anyway. Already we had shared tenderness — was that so different from other babies? She and I had shared the trauma of the first bath where I was certain I was causing her grievous bodily and psychic harm and I'm sure she felt the same way. We wanted to love her, to challenge her, to lead her into the beauties of the landscape of a changing tide in Maine, to teach her silly spider songs, to go fishing. I wanted to be able to lead my child to herself, to have her love and honour herself and grow to the best of her abilities, whatever they might be.

None of these experiences, these opportunities, had been taken away from us when Jessie was born. If I focused hard enough they actually seemed to multiply, because when you take away all the externals of achievement, what you are left with is what really matters. I mean, did it really matter if she understood the theory of relativity (which we certainly wouldn't be able to explain to her)?

My biggest fear was that I wouldn't be able to love her right. That I would want to change her. I wanted to know everything there was to know about Down's syndrome so I could accept her the way she was.

The doctors were helpful. They told us all the things she wouldn't be able to do, and they were numerous. She would never speak very well, she would walk much later than other children, she might never be able to read, she would go to a special school, and she would always be dependent. When we asked for something we could read they gave us a medical text on birth defects published in 1958: clinical descriptions, complete with photographs, of every kind of birth defect imaginable.

It described the physical features of Down's syndrome with close-up shots of protruding tongues and slanted eyes. We kept looking at the book and then looking at Jessie. They weren't the same.

They weren't the same because the book described the condition, not the individual. And while Jessie has Down's syndrome, she is not Down's syndrome. She is Jessie! The reality is not in the things she can't do, but in the things she can do, the gifts she has to share, the relationships she has with those around her.

I had a hard time sorting out the facts and my feelings. I would sometimes retreat to the cafeteria, and it was there that I met Anne. I must have looked forlorn and confused as I nursed my juice and this cheery woman next to me asked what I was in for. "I had a baby," I said. "She has Down's syndrome." I was trying the phrase on for size, as I would find myself doing for the next two months or so.

"Oh, how wonderful!" she said. I looked at her, wondering if she had heard me right. She smiled. "My son Scott has Down's syndrome. He's seventeen, and what a boy!" She laughed with pride and love.

I knew it was time to go home.

## COMING HOME

We have been invaded by cloth diapers and disposables, infant chairs and rocking chairs, a cradle and a crib, not to mention friends and relations. The most noticeable new acquisition, besides Jessie herself, is the breast pump. Not one of these little hand-held jobs, but the great big industrial model. The lights in our apartment pulse when I hook myself up and turn it on. I feel like a cow, but at least I don't feel like the world's worst mother anymore.

The day I admitted defeat I sat in a corner in the living room and cried. I was sure I was not going to be able to do anything right if I couldn't even get her on my breast. I was convinced that her whole fragile future depended on it. My mother, who had come to stay with us for a while, hugged me, told me I wasn't a failure, that I was doing a great job, and cooked liver and onions for dinner. For some reason it tasted delicious and I looked at her in awe.

But Jessie is getting my breast milk even if she didn't get on the breast. It certainly wasn't for lack of trying. La Leche League meetings, droppers, teaspoons, trying every conceivable position, and more than twelve hours with a lactation consultant who said that Jessie certainly was persistent — in sucking the wrong way. I drew the line at sticking my finger down her throat and watching her gag as I tried to massage the part of her tongue that she was supposed to use to draw milk from my breast. I guess we'll have to watch what we teach her in the years to come.

I've been reading everything I can get my hands on about Down's syndrome. Articles on genetics, heart defects, muscle tone, speech and education. But my favourite book is the one that my twelve-year-old cousin found for me in his school library called *Our Brother Has Down's Syndrome*. It's written for children and has lots of pictures. Pictures of a three-year-old boy with Down's syndrome eating ice cream, getting into trouble, hugging his sisters. It's the book I go back to again and again because it's warm and human, and it gives me hope.

Hope for what? I guess that Jessie will just be a kid, like this little boy in the book, and that others will see her that way.

I have this urgent need right now to tell everybody that she has Down's syndrome. I can't help it. The first time I went to our corner health-food store with her they all oohed and aahed and said what a beautiful baby. "Yes, and she has Down's syndrome," I replied, watching them.

Waiting. But there was no explosion, no withdrawal, only comments about her delightfully blue eyes. I don't know why I need to tell strangers that she has Down's syndrome. Maybe it's my way of getting used to the idea, of desensitizing myself. Or maybe I just want to get it over with so we can get on with life and they can be as amazed and impressed as I am when she smiles or turns her head to a sound.

I am living in a constant state of exhaustion. What on earth did I do with all my time before Jessie was born? Between feeding and pumping and rocking and reading I spend a lot of time cutting out pictures from magazines and drawing black-and-white patterns and faces on paper plates to put up around Jessie's crib and change table. We've hung rattles and tin pie plates and small bells in places where she's likely to hit them by mistake and make a noise. We massage her feet and her head and her belly and move her arms and legs while singing nursery rhymes and trying to remember all the words that somehow disappear after the first two lines.

Bev, our infant-development worker, has lent us a great book with lots of songs and rhymes and Jessie seems to love these. Bev. What would we do without her? It seems that giving birth to a child with a developmental delay has all sorts of bonuses I never knew about. Bev is one of them. She comes into our home once a week and works with us so that we can do all we can to help Jessie grow. She shares in our celebrations, is a keen and caring observer of Jessie's development, and is able to hook us up with the resources that are available for Jessie and ourselves. More than anything, she supports us as parents, giving us the information and courage that we seem to need to forge ahead. I know all parents celebrate with delight their child's first gurgles and smiles and steps. But already I notice a difference. We can't assume that Jessie will just do these things, we have to set up situations that will lead her to them. Bev gives us ideas and is there to celebrate each tiny step she takes.

My biggest problem is that Jessie doesn't sleep between two in the afternoon and midnight! The doctor says this is her social time, but at around seven I run out of "social" steam and so I bundle us up, Snugli and all, and we walk the streets, ending up at the club where Dan's doing his show. Of course, as soon as *he* puts the Snugli on, she falls asleep. I thought babies with Down's syndrome were supposed to be lethargic, sleepy, without much energy. But that describes me, not Jessie. She's wide awake, alert, and demanding.

The payoff is — she smiles! Just when you're ready to have yourself committed for ever having had sex, they smile! It's not gas, its not a weird reflex. It's a smile. At first I wasn't sure, because it seemed like just a flicker of a grin. But in the last week she has developed a great big toothless smile that seems to eat up the whole world. And the best part is, she smiles at me! She looks at my face and smiles with delight and I can feel this electric current run between us. She knows, of course, that now I'll do anything for her. I'm hooked. For life.

## Give Me a Sign

Jessie has brought a whole new language into our life. Sign. I've always moved my hands when I speak, gesticulating with rather random abandon. Now my movements can have meaning.

Jessie doesn't have a hearing impairment, but like many other children with Down's syndrome her receptive language skills far exceed her ability to communicate using words. Or words that others can understand. I don't really know why, and at this point in time I'm too busy trying to keep up with her rapidly growing signing vocabulary to find out.

Brenda, our speech therapist, suggested that we try using Signed English with Jessie to help her communicate, and what a world it's opened up! We started with "power" signs, like *more* and *stop* and *play* and *no*. Words that would give her the ability to ask for what she wanted, to see the effect of communicating. Sign *more* and more Cheerios appear. Sign *play* and your Mom plays with you. Wow!

Jessie changed almost overnight from a very frustrated toddler into a blossoming grinning child reaching out to explore the world. We had no hesitation about using sign, about trying to give her the tools to express herself and to make sense of the world. And I certainly didn't mind the attention it brought as she and I signed in the playground or the grocery store. I've met some parents who don't want to use sign because it calls too much attention to their child, it makes them even more different. But I can't figure out why you wouldn't want to give your child the power to talk about the world around them, to ask for what they want, or to express the connections that they are making. What is a world without language?

Besides, I don't mind the attention. People come up to us and ask questions when they see us using sign, and it gives us a chance to explain some things about Down's syndrome. Really important things, like the fact that Jessie understands a lot more than you might think if you just listened to her talk. People are impressed by sign, and amazed that a little kid with Down's syndrome can speak with her hands. I think it makes them do a double-take, makes them question their first reaction when they see her. If she can sign, then what else can she do?

And she *can* sign! Now that she's got the concept she's frustrated by my inability to keep up with her. My sign book is worn and I realize my memory is not as good as it used to be. I practise Little Red Riding Hood and the Three Little Pigs and the Three Billy Goats Gruff before I go to bed at night because I don't want to be caught in the middle of a story having to look up a key word or phrase. Have you ever tried to read and sign a picture book? You need at least four hands.

My pet peeve these days is that Sharon, Lois & Bram don't sign. They do all these wonderful actions with their songs, but they don't sign. Wouldn't it be just as easy, if you're going to do actions, to do actions that have meaning for kids who are hearing-impaired or who use sign? Even kids who don't need to use sign love it, and pick it up very quickly. Most of the signs, at least at the preschool level, make quirky sense and have a kind of spatial–emotional resonance. For *milk*, you move both your hands as if you are milking a cow; for *love*, you cross your arms in front of your chest and hug; for *want*, you pull your hands towards you.

We had to work on *want* for a while. It was a big jump from labelling to making two-word sentences that involved a verb. Instead of just *snack* or *ball* or *book*, we were trying to get her to say and sign *want ball* or *want book*. Then one day when we were in The Papery she saw a row of shiny sparkling stickers that made her eyes light up. She leaned forward in her stroller and fiercely signed *I want*. I was so excited! "You want those stick-ers," I said, trying to contain my glee. I really wanted to shout to every-one in the store, "She did it! She signed *I want*!" And then my heart fell. I didn't have any money. She signed *I want* and I couldn't respond to her first use of the sign. What good is *I want* if it doesn't work? I put my own pride in my pocket and asked the sales clerk if we could have two stickers, that I'd pay for them later. When I explained why, she gave me the whole sheet. Jessie grabbed on to them and signed *I want* all the way home, laughing and giggling at her own power.

The teachers at playgroup, Sandy and Darlene, have really gotten into learning and using sign in the classroom. The other children have picked up on their enthusiasm and I now get calls from parents who want to know what their child is saying with their hands. It's piqued everyone's interest, and Jessie has become the resident expert on sign. If one of the teachers doesn't know a particular sign, they ask Jessie. And for once Jessie has the chance to teach her peers something, to be the leader instead of the follower.

The photographer came to playgroup last week. All the children were dressed in their best clothes. Some didn't want to smile, some squirmed. But when he told them to say cheese, they all, every last one of them, put their palms together and signed *cheese*, without even thinking about it. Now that's a photograph!

## LETTING THE WORLD IN

Jessie is almost two and a half years old. She finally has hair, beautiful blonde hair, she loves books (our current favourite being *Farmer Duck*), she walks, she talks and signs, and she has brought more people into our house than any typical family would care to imagine.

Many I don't know what we would have done without; others we just have to put up with, like the Handicapped Children's Benefit worker who said that having a child with Down's syndrome must be a joy because they are all so happy. I looked at her and smiled (she helps determine whether we get financial aid) and thought, Come visit our house around dinner-time. If children with Down's syndrome are all so happy then I must really be doing some permanent damage because Jessie is not always happy.

Jessie is Jessie. And these days that means a fierce and persistent drive for independence. That's why Barbara, our special-needs worker, is such a godsend. She knows how to make every fine-motor and conceptual activity Jessie's idea.

Last week Barbara was at the house when our speech therapist arrived. Jessie was being her usual nine a.m. self — reacting to some of the pictures the therapist brought with her then going to get one of her own toys, then pointing to "The Bag."

You have to understand here that each therapist comes with a bag of toys: the infant-development worker comes with a bag of toys, the speech therapist comes with a bag of toys, the occupational therapist comes with a bag of toys, the psychologist comes with a bag of toys, and even the physiotherapist sometimes comes with a bag of toys. Jessie expects all adults entering our house to come with a bag of toys specifically for her.

"The Bag" was opened and the asked-for toy procured — a bath for the baby, which held her attention for about two seconds. The speech therapist asked if we were doing much "table work" with Jessie these days. Table work basically means sitting down at a table and focusing on a specific task. Barbara and I eyed each other and began to explain what we did do (both of us knowing full well that we did almost no table work at all).

There is a subtext here, of course, one that all parents of special-needs children might be familiar with. We thought that the therapist was commenting on Jessie's lack of attention, lack of ability to focus on one task for a period of time. Both Barbara and I were trying to defend Jessie's action and, more importantly, ourselves, our ability as caregivers to meet Jessie's needs and to encourage her development.

There is this funny thing that happens when therapists and experts enter your life. You feel watched, judged. Your child's development depends on your intervention. Now this is true of all children, of all parents. But rarely do parents of so-called typical children have so many people watching and taking notes. I didn't just write down Jessie's first smile, her first step. I had massive checklists to fill out — her first gurgles (exact sound and intonations, please), pincer grasp, hands together at mid-line, stacking two blocks, three, four, *ad infinitum*.

As a mom or a dad you can slip so easily into trying to create the perfect little person, and it's funny because you might think that because Jessie wasn't "perfect" to begin with, we wouldn't have to wrangle with these feelings. But they are as prevalent in parents of children with a disability, just the reference points are different.

The only way for me to keep centred is to remember that, to me, being a good parent means allowing her to be who she is and to give her the chance and the opportunity to grow at her own pace. It doesn't mean trying to make a good impression on therapists, family members, or other parents. Let's face it, making a good impression with a two-year-old is almost impossible when they go limp and then kick and scream as if you were beating them to death as you try to stop them from electrocuting themselves in an open socket at the museum.

The difference, perhaps, between myself and any other first-time parent is that I am asked to become an expert in a number of different areas that are all new to me. And I'm never sure what behaviours are due to an extra chromosome or just the result of being two. Do all two-year-olds repeatedly throw sand out of the sandbox at preschool? And what about shoes? Every child that I know with Down's syndrome throws their shoes out the car window. Can an extra chromosome control such things as throwing shoes out car windows?

At each step of Jessie's life I've had to learn new powers of observation, assessment, and intervention. I've had to keep up with research on language acquisition, heart defects, and integration. Because the truth of the matter is, I can never feel that Jessie will get the services and therapy she needs, will be able to lead the life she deserves, if I just leave it up to the powers that be.

Each time we begin to get comfortable — in the infant-development program, our local preschool — it's time to think about the next step, to learn the ropes of a new system, to fill out more forms and to meet new people. And meeting new people often means either convincing them that Jessie belongs or educating them about Down's syndrome. I've got the energy and excitement right now, but sometimes I get tired. Yup, I'm a parent.

Jessie learned her first joke last month. She knocks on the table and you say, "Who's there?" She says, "Boo," and signs *blue* (she's a little confused about this issue). You say, "Boo who?" and she rubs her eyes as if she is crying and then laughs out loud and says *yoke* for joke. She is really quite proud of herself. Now I just have to get Dan, who taught her this fine example of turn-taking in communication, to teach her that after doing it three times in a row it will be hard to get someone, other than your parents, to laugh.

## GYM CLASS

I thought it was a good idea.

Natalie and Drew, two of Jessie's classmates from preschool, have been taking gym classes once a week during the year, and they love it. They get to run around, climb and clamber, jump on trampolines, and balance on beams raised to incredible mom-defying heights.

Now I know running is something kids just do, something most parents try to control. But for Jessie, even though she took her first step at a relatively young age, running is not something she just does. Fast, now, fast she's good at — fists clenched tight, knees stiff, eyes concentrated and fierce, and her little feet barrelling across the expanse of open space. But if you don't lift your feet up high and risk that moment of balancing on one foot, you don't run. You kind of, well, waddle fast.

And if you don't or can't run when you're a three-and-a-half-year-old you miss out on all kinds of opportunities, like being the first one to the tricycle or being a part of a game of chase.

So gym class, besides leading us to this very definite goal, would be fun. Right? Jessie thought so. We went to visit the gym club and she stood riveted to the window as she watched other children bouncing on the largest trampoline she had ever seen, climbing up the tallest ladders and rolling and balancing in brightly coloured tunnels. "My turn?! My turn?!" she kept signing and saying as I tried to explain to her that we were just here to watch. I promised that we would come back to "gym" and she could have a turn. As I watched her I knew this would be a great idea.

I called the club and registered her for a Thursday-morning class. I explained that she had Down's syndrome, liked to go fast and climb high and used sign language. No problem, they said. I breathed a sigh of relief.

I still get tense when I make phone calls like that. I used to first explain that Jessie had Down's syndrome and then ask if we could participate, not knowing what kind of attitude I would run into. Instead of being reactive, I'm now more proactive: here we are, how can we do this? And to be perfectly honest I have yet to run into a problem, but I've always picked our activities carefully — the Y, the library, places that I knew were guided (at least in theory) by inclusive philosophies. Places that I knew wouldn't or couldn't slam the door in our faces.

So we got ready for gym class. I bought Jessie new shorts and a top, we practised jumping and talked about the big trampoline. The big day arrived. I had Jessie so pumped up she tried to leave the house before breakfast in only her diapers. "Jessie! Where are you going?" "Gym," she replied as she marched out the door. Dan rescued her and then we let him go to work, promising to call later. We did the dishes and played trolls waiting for it to be time to go. Finally we headed out the door to the car. Which wouldn't start.

I should have gone back to bed right then, but having convinced Jessie that gym class was her destiny, and myself that the first class is always the most important, I blithely marched into the house and called a taxi.

When it arrived, she wouldn't get in. "No taxi, no taxi. Gym! Gym!" I tried to explain that we were taking the taxi to gym. But in Jessie's mind a taxi ride was a taxi ride and gym class was gym class. Mommy drove the car to gym, and a taxi ride, well, a taxi ride was just foreign territory. I wrestled her into the car, the taxi driver just gritted his teeth and drove. Jessie fell in love with not sitting in a car seat. When we got to the gym club she refused to get out. "No out. No out. Taxi! Taxi!" I wrestled her out of the car and left the driver with a big tip and a big grin.

Inside Jessie thought she had died and gone to heaven. All this stuff just for her! There were at least six other classes going on at the same time, and Jessie had a hard time figuring out where she was supposed to be, who her teacher was, and what she was supposed to be paying attention to. I stayed to sign and to try to keep her with her class.

It was impossible. The last thing Jessie wanted was for me to direct her, and it seemed that the last thing the teacher wanted was to have to deal with Jessie in addition to five other three-year-olds. Jessie wanted to jump and explore all the equipment; she had her own agenda and was not going to be swayed. I wasn't sure what to do. Halfway through the class, having battled with Jessie for most of it, I carried her out kicking and screaming. I couldn't blame her for wanting to try everything, but that wasn't the way the class was set up. I sat her down in the grass by the fence, turned my head away and started to cry. Out of anger, out of frustration, out of fear.

We'd had such an easy time of it up to now. Everyone welcoming Jessie's presence and really trying to find ways to include her. Gym class felt like the beginning of the end. Reality hitting us in the face.

It's fine to say that your program is open to people with disabilities, but you have to do more than just open the door. You've got to find ways for them to participate in a meaningful manner. I was angry. Angry at them for saying no problem, when in fact Jessie posed a problem. Angry at them for putting her in such a confusing situation, for not giving her the time to explore or finding ways for her to follow her class. But more importantly I was angry at myself for not doing more preparation, not going in to talk to them about Jessie and her needs, for assuming that when they said no problem, they meant it.

We haven't gone back to gym. We'll find some other place to run and jump and climb. A place where Jessie is welcomed.

## DANCING AT DINNER

I am ready for school to start. It's been a long, hot summer and I am tired. Tired of doing battle with a very stubborn five-year-old. Dan says she comes by it naturally and looks at me sideways in a knowing manner. Okay, okay.

But my greatest fantasy is to wake up, see Jessie's smiling face, say good morning, and have her say good morning back. Instead, the first word out of her mouth to me is "No." It doesn't really matter what I say, I just provoke this automatic response in her. She has also taken to stamping her foot, turning her back to me, and sticking her nose in the air in an attitude of "you can't make me do anything!" I am exhausted with my very concentrated efforts at patience and consistency. And when I lose it . . . well, I know what the Queen of Hearts in *Alice in Wonderland* is based on. That overwhelming and irrational cry of "Off with her head" is a very good likeness of me around dinnertime at the end of a long, hot summer day.

I go to bed at night with parenting books trying to figure out my options. The most appealing is a long holiday by myself, which is just about as likely as winning the 6/49. So I find solace in other mothers of five-year-old daughters. We remind ourselves that five is a difficult age as our daughters strive for independence and separation. We trade ideas on how to give them responsibility that they can manage without causing anyone bodily harm, and brainstorm natural consequences. We all agree on one thing. When our daughters reach adolescence we're leaving home.

My biggest battle with Jessie has to do with her sense of time, or lack of it. As a toddler I didn't expect her to fully grasp the concept. After all, wasn't it her job to explore every diversion between home and playgroup or the park? The double acorn, the crooked front steps, the feel of grass as you lie looking up at the sky and can't figure out why your mother is closing her eyes and counting to ten. Playgroup starts when you get there. Isn't that the way the world works? Oh, if only it did. Any transition, any movement from one location to another could last as long as three or four hours if we went on Jessie's schedule. And then she would miss so much — like school, playing at the park, and swimming lessons.

Jessie loves swimming. This summer she took lessons every morning and finally mastered this breathing thing. Fearless as she is in the water, flailing and grinning with wide-open eyes, it has taken her a long time to realize that you take a big breath *before* you put your head in the water.

But when you finish swimming you have to get dressed and go home. Well, I guess you don't have to, but hanging out in a locker room for a couple of hours every day is not my idea of fun. I guess I'm too driven, in too much of a rush to get on to the next thing. But I would like, just once, to be able to go from point A to point B without having to plan for each step in order to avoid a battle with Jessie over getting out of the pool, getting into the locker room, not going in the whirlpool, getting in the shower, getting out of the shower, going to our locker without climbing inside every other locker (there are more than a hundred of them), putting on each piece of clothing, and so on. One day I followed her lead and we got out of the locker room two and a half hours after her lesson. And while I'm willing to do this sometimes, there is no such thing as sometimes with Jessie. If you change the routine or don't follow the well-mapped-out plan and forget to be consistent you are right back where you started — prodding, reminding, ignoring, coercing, and, on really bad days, yelling. Sometimes I feel like giving up, but I don't because I want, so much, for her to be independent, to do the things that she can do by herself. And the look on her face when she gets her bathing suit on by herself or gets the paints out is worth every one of my own personal battles with frustration, anger, guilt, and exhaustion.

This summer seems to have been extra hard on both of us, and when Dan comes home from work I just want to go to bed with a good book and dissolve into somebody else's world.

But dinner is the time for us to be together as a family, share moments of our day and reconnect. It's a time I would like us to savour and enjoy. It doesn't always happen. We're tired, it's hot, Jessie wants to play trolls with Dan, and there's Mom with this image in her head of the happy family around the dinner table. It's Dan's turn to do battle with Jessie about staying at the table until she is finished; I've given up. For the seventh time she pushes her chair back from the table and just as we are about to tell her that her place will be cleared, she says, "I will dance for you."

Dan and I close our eyes, weighing the consequences. We should say, "You can dance if you are finished your dinner," we should be consistent, we should follow through. Instead Dan turns on the music.

We sit and watch Jessie dance. She sways and moves her shoulders and turns and pirouettes. Her eyes are half closed as she listens to the rhythm of the jazz and is moved by it. Some of her awkwardness is transformed into a delightful quirkiness that is both cute and very serious.

As I watch her dance in the fading summer light I realize with a pang how much she has grown. She's developed her own way of moving, of listening to the music that is this life around us. My only hope is that we've given her enough courage and comfort to always want to dance at dinner.

The music stops. She bows and looks at us expectantly, defiantly, with pride. Waiting for us to clap. We do. Not because the dance is finished, but because it continues.

## Happy Endings

Jessie is six years old. She has lost her first tooth, can write her name if you help her with the S's, has mastered the tuck jump, has told me to change my attitude, and is learning to read.

One day last month, as we were approaching the schoolyard, Jessie looked up at a street sign and stopped. "Mommy. Look. I know that word. It says *school*." She beamed from ear to ear. "School. I know that word!" She had stopped underneath the sign that said SCHOOL BUS LOADING ZONE, and the delight in her eyes mirrored a sudden revelation that she could read not only the word, but the world.

Nothing, however, quite matches my pride as I watch her learn. She has a sight vocabulary of at least one hundred words, and we just moved into families of words: the *-at* family, as in *cat, hat, mat,* and *bat.* What amazes me is her ability to play with word order and meaning. The unrestrained delight in her eyes as she turns a simple sentence into a silly one by switching one word and then waiting for me to laugh.

I spend my evenings cutting out pictures, writing words in bold black print, creating books, and making up games. That Jessie would read was never a question, at least not in our minds. Our house is filled with books, and if any child had it in her genes to read, it would be Jessie. Reading and writing is what both Dan and I do for a living (if you could call it that) and for sheer pleasure. But I never thought it would be this easy or this much fun.

Some people would say, well, yeah, sure, but she's high-functioning. I'm getting tired of that phrase. Sure, integration works for her because she's high-functioning. High-functioning . . . just what exactly does that mean? Sometimes it means that it's more difficult for other kids to figure her out. Because at six, kids are into mastery. Who's better than who. And there's a general order that they have figured out that is closely hooked to age. When you lose your first tooth, when you turn six, all these rites of passage are tightly tied to the ability to do something. To read, to ride a bike, to draw a figure, or write your name. Pushing Jessie on her tricycle the other day we met Tim on his two-wheeler. "Why are you pushing Jessie?" he asked. "Because she's just learning," I replied. Tim looked at me for a moment, then up at his mom for support. "She can't ride a bike? But Jessie is six!" This is inconceivable to him.

If Jessie were just always behind, if her effort and difference were just a bit more pronounced, I sometimes think the other kids would have an easier time of it.

"How come Jessie can read?" asks Tess one day at our house. She was a little put out because she's used to being better than Jessie at most things. Having finally figured out that, even though Jessie turned six before she did, Jessie was really like somebody a bit younger, she now had to reassess her whole world because Jessie could do something that she couldn't. I could see her little face struggling with this new view . . . exactly where, then, did Jessie fit in? That is the million-dollar question, and the best "educational opportunity" any of us will ever have.

Jessie continues to be an enigma, a child who is and is not a peer. She knows her colours in French better than most of her classmates, can recognize a variety of birds, can read many of the signs around the classroom, but she can't ride a bike, doesn't run very fast, and still grabs toys as a way of getting attention. She can, however, do the macarena, a kind of line dance that's a big hit in the schoolyard. And while the macarena might never show up on her IEP, it's an important part of her education. An education that she could never get in a segregated setting.

The hard part is not so much in the day-to-day things, but in the things that go on outside our immediate lives. The undercurrent of cutbacks, legal battles, dealing with therapists, preparing for grade one, making myself clear.

There is an air of desperation these days that makes me very nervous. People are losing their jobs, school boards are claiming that they can't afford the services our children need. Never mind that integrating children into their neighbourhood schools actually costs less than putting them in a segregated setting. Parents are being told that their child can get an integrated placement, but they can't promise any supports. But without supports it's not integration, it's dumping. Jessie would never survive and thrive the way she is without supports. I am so proud of Jessie, of her classmates and her teachers and of the school community. But there are moments when I get this vision that Jessie and others like her will only be this weird blip in time, this strange generation of kids who grew up and went to school together and learned something about meaning and value and caring. I shake my head and clear my eyes. I cannot believe that what we're doing is not right, is not a step forward, and I can't bring myself to think that at some point Jessie or the children following her will be forced into segregated settings. Settings that maximize their difference, that deny them the day-to-day opportunity to make friends, to feel good about what they have to offer the world. It's not that we don't struggle with how she fits in, it's that we're taking the chance to figure it out. Without that struggle we would not have the moments that make it all worthwhile.

The best moment, the moment I would trade all others for, is the moment when, hidden in the closet behind a sheet and amongst the pillows and stuffed animals that I was ordered to supply, Jessie and Claire got the giggles. Singing funny troll lullabies in their own imitation of how a troll would sing, they began to giggle with each successive phrase as each one topped the other in silliness. Nestled there among the pillows in the dark cave of the closet they wriggled and giggled and I stood quietly in the hallway holding that moment to my heart. They are so few and far between and I want, more than anything, Jessie and her friends to know what these moments feel like. Moments of connection and delight. Moments when Jessie's sense of humour and playfulness are appreciated and treasured.

That night as I was tucking Jessie into bed, she turned to me and said "Mommy, I like happy endings, do you?" I do, Jessie, I do.

## Falling in Love Again

I'm still reeling from the expanse of a full day before me, trying to adjust to Life *without* Jessie, since Jessie is in grade one and at school all day. I miss her. I miss her more than ever this fall because something wonderful happened over the summer. I fell in love with her all over again.

You know, the terrible twos lasted a long time for us. About four and a half years, to be exact. And while my love and delight in Jessie never stopped growing they certainly hit a number of rocky patches. Patches where the thought of waking up and battling over getting dressed, or walking to school, or brushing teeth just made me want to stay in bed. But this summer I can honestly say I finally reached a point where I found her persistence admirable.

It has allowed her to learn to swim, to get on the swings by herself, to talk to other children, to continue to try to play tag and hide-and-go-seek when she can't quite keep up. And this summer Jessie and I were actually able to do things together without either of us insisting on going in a different direction.

Perhaps it's because she has the skills to be more independent now and doesn't need as much support — she can get most of her clothes on by herself, get her own breakfast, look both ways before she crosses the street, answer the phone, get out her paints. She doesn't always have to ask for help or have me in there interfering in her life. Or maybe it's because I eased up this past summer.

Not by choice, mind you. I had grand plans: swimming lessons, summer camp, reading, writing. We were going to get a head start on grade one and really work on developing friendships. We were going to have a "productive" summer.

But just as our "productive" summer was about to start, my aunt began to lose her battle with cancer. My Aunt Kathy. I don't know how to describe who she was or what she meant to me except to say that she was a perfectly ordinary woman with an extraordinary impact on my life. She loved me. But I mourn the space that her dying has left in Jessie's life. A space that has no real meaning to Jessie but that strikes me hard and at awkward moments. Jessie needs people who just love her. People who will continue to love her and support her through the different stages of her life. And Kathy won't be one of those people, which is unfortunate, because Kathy knew how to love unconditionally. That was one of her gifts.

So this summer I spent as much time in Montreal as I could, needing and wanting to be with Kathy and our extended family. Trying to give back a small measure of what she had given me, and scrambling to learn how to love as she did.

When I was at home in Ottawa, a bit dazed and saddened, and thinking, in that way that you do when you are losing someone you love, about life, I found myself watching Jessie. Not with eagle eyes, but with open, curious eyes as she splashed and giggled and did tricks in the pool or as she transformed herself into a princess and demanded that I be the frog. "No, not that way. You have to hop, Mom."

I listened as she tried to join in on conversations with other children and invented a brother and a sister that lived with her in her house. "A long, long time ago my brother and my sister . . ." And instead of seeing the falseness of her conversational offerings, I was impressed with her ability to understand that she had to share something that was on topic, which in this case happened to be siblings. Searching for something appropriate, and finding only what her imagination could conjure up, she boldly offers it and waits for a response. I don't intervene right away because I don't want to interrupt the flow of the conversation, the back-and-forth jangle of five-year-old banter, in which my daughter is an active participant.

It felt so good to watch her get excited by the prospect of a new day, of going to the pool, of painting, of having a friend over. It felt so good to watch her being happy. I had forgotten, in our struggles over process, just what a joyous, curious, excitable, perceptive, and creative child she is. I hate to admit it, but I had forgotten to let her be happy, to let her be. And Kathy's dying made me more aware of just how important it is to be.

The summer passed, not without pain, but certainly with a lot of love.

Jessie drew many pictures for Kathy. Pictures that surrounded her at home, in the palliative-care unit, and when she died. Pictures of family, of birds and sunshine and rainbows. The last picture Jessie drew for her was done in bright green paint — a picture of Kathy in bed in the hospital. And beside her she drew pictures of all the things she thought Kathy would like with her: "Toys, a book, coffee, a ball and you and Grams. She would like you and Grams to be there. Oh, but there's no room . . . ," and she pointed to the full page and looked at me with disappointment as she struggled with how to get two more figures on the page. "That's okay," I said. "Our spirits are with her." While Jessie might not have known exactly what those pictures meant to all of us, she certainly put her heart and her love into them. I was reminded, between Jessie and Kathy, that the most powerful and enlightening force is love.

I fight for Jessie. I advocate for her, I speak to doctors and students, I sit on committees, I stay up late reading and stay out late at meetings, I find resources for teachers, I struggle with existing systems and for changes to the system . . . because I love my daughter, Jessie. That is the underlying force, the ghost in the machine. Sometimes I forget why I'm doing all these things, and they take on a life all their own. Sure, they're all noble and challenging commitments, and often they're necessary parts of planning for Jessie's inclusion. But this summer I began to realize that if all these other activities only lead me away from loving Jessie, from having Jessie know and feel that love, then I've got to stop doing them. I get tired of having to struggle and be polite and find ways to support the people who are supposed to be supporting us. I get tired of being an advocate and want to shout, "Just let me be a mom!"

Jessie loves grade one. She gets off the bus smiling, ready to play or paint or do homework. Happy to see me, but also happy because school has been such a delight. She proudly shows me her home reader and says, "We have homework," then she pauses and looks at me. "What's homework?" As I explain it to her I realize that she has been doing homework all her life. It's time to play. To follow her lead and delight in the messy black paint we are using for the witches' tower she has created or to act out, once again, the story of Cinderella.

This morning on the way out the door to school Jessie and I pause for a moment on the front porch. The wind chimes that Kathy gave us tremble and gently ring in the cool wind. "Listen, Mom. It's Aunt Kathy's spirit," Jessie says with joy and delight. And I think about how much I miss Kathy, and how much I miss Jessie. Sometimes you have no choice but to let go. And it's only in the letting go that the joy and delight shine through.

# VOICES FROM THE NORTH

*Both of the writers in this chapter grew up on the land, and both have gone on to remarkable careers — in Michael Kusugak's case, as one of our most celebrated children's authors, and in Ann Meekitjuk Hanson's (although she, too, is a published author), as deputy commissioner of the Northwest Territories. Anyone who has heard me talk about my own affection for the North knows of my regret that more Canadians don't see this awesome landscape for themselves, but reading Michael and Ann may well be the next best thing.*

## IQALUIT, BAFFIN ISLAND

### I

Inuit believe each season has a gift for its living beings. We have about eight seasons in one year. Each has a description of purpose — seasons according to animals, their usefulness for survival; seasons describing the norms of weather to fit the times: almost winter, winter, time of longer daylight, almost spring, spring, summer, almost autumn. Each season is carefully observed for future comparison.

October is *Ukiaq*, almost winter. This is one of our favourite times. We look forward to quick frozen meats, meats that freeze as they are cut. The taste and texture are like no others. It belongs to *Ukiaq*. Air is fresh and crisp. Snow makes everything bright and new. The seas are black, dotted with white caps clashing with the rugged coast, struggling to change one season to another.

This is also polar bear season in many of our Eastern Arctic communities. The bears come to communities in search of food. They stay around until freeze-up. After freeze-up, they can then hunt for seals away from the communities.

My cousin who lives in an outpost camp outside Cape Dorset saved her husband from a polar bear attack a few years ago. Her husband was carving a stone outside their home. She was doing some chores. When she looked up from her work, there was this bear so near her husband. She whispered, "*Haang* [Inuit version of *dear* or *darling*], don't move, there is a bear near you." She stealthily groped for the axe, which she remembered was nearby, while staring at the bear and her husband. With the axe in her hand, she let out a scream and ran with both arms up in the air. The bear fled one way and my cousin ran in the opposite direction. She hid behind her house. She stuck her head out around the corner of her home. To her horror, the bear did the same from the other side of her home. She peeped again, and so did the bear. In the meantime, her husband had managed to get into their home and got the rifle. He shot into the air and scared the bear away. My cousin now laughs about the time she and the bear had a peeping game.

Martha Ashevak of Clyde River informs me the polar bears are so plentiful around her community this time of the year that they have to escort their children when they go trick-or-treating at Halloween. The children are told not to wander off from the houses and are told to be with other children at all times. Before venturing outdoors, one sticks one's head out and checks all corners of the house and beyond.

This season is also the time of sea lift. Sea lift is when a ship comes in and unloads your winter supplies. The ship comes from Montreal and makes its rounds to each community. It is a very exciting time, almost like Christmas! Northern living would not be complete without sea lift.

Here is an example of our shopping list for the whole year. I figure out how many soups I plan to have each week, tomato, mixed, vegetable, or any other. I count how many soups for the month and then multiply that by twelve. I plan how many loaves of bread I will bake a week. How much flour it will take. How many packages of yeast, salt, vegetable shortening, dried milk. The staples — rice, flour, tea, salt, tins of vegetables, tomatoes, mushrooms, pop, soups, raisins, cereal — are quite simple, once you have figured out from the previous years how much a family uses. It is the dry goods, such as toilet paper, detergent, paper towels, toothpaste, deodorant, face soap, and shampoo that are more difficult for me, because the shopping list involves the whole family. We try to figure out how much of what each family member uses and how often. I know store-owners, restaurants, hotels, and hospitals have a much bigger shopping list — they have to plan for the whole community for one year! In the years before scheduled flights, if we ran out of something by April or May, we went without until the ship came in after break-up, around July or August. In bigger communities like Iqaluit, it is not really necessary any more to order sea lift, but it is cheaper, and old habits are hard to change at times. Older people like me compare sea-lift goods with friends over a cup of coffee and complain about not having enough space for bulky items.

Knowing simple math comes in handy around March when you have to shop for the whole year and book a space with Transport Canada for your supplies. New shopping-list items for the nineties? Computer paper, batteries, floppy disks, new keyboard, video games.

The High Arctic community reporters submitted their weekly news to our CBC Radio Inuktitut program, *Tausoni*, about unusually heavy ice conditions in their regions. They said the ice did not melt or go away. The seas, which are usually almost ice-free for a few weeks, were packed.

One community, Grise Fiord, Canada's northernmost hamlet, was affected the greatest. The supply ship could not go through the ice and went to Pond Inlet instead. The ship carried the Co-op's supplies for the year, personal sea lift, and building materials. The High Arctic MLA, Levi Barnabas, brought this dire news to the House at Yellowknife last week. The elected officials suggested that air lift will be necessary when the ice completely freezes in the bay.

Larry Aulaluk, a community leader at Grise Fiord, said the late spring, ice sticking around all summer, and early coming of winter prevented the supply ship from going to the community and the goods from being unloaded. Larry wonders out loud if the global warming is bypassing their region.

I have to go now and observe the almost-winter weather and share my findings with others. The daylight is getting much shorter. It is through understanding and acceptance that we welcome each season, what it offers, what it teaches, and what it takes.

## II

What a wonderful sound: *katap*, *poink*, *fut*, *fut*.

It has been a long, cold, windy, stormy winter. Even as an Inuk, with deep feelings of destined residency in the Arctic, with gifts from the Supreme Being to survive the harshest climate on earth, sometimes I get selfish and feel, "Why me?" Mind you, there are also rewards to our winter. We sleep more hours, spend more time with the family, get to know our mates better. Since we spend a lot of time indoors, we don't wear out our clothes as much. We spend less money on unnecessary things. We get a little bit nutty, but we survive. The humour inside us comes out more often. The other day I was asking one of my uncles to let me know the next time he was going ice fishing so I could go with him. His quick answer was: "I am not going anywhere until a mosquito bites me!" We had a good laugh. He was telling me that even for him, it was too cold to travel.

When we get together with friends or relatives we comfort each other by talking about spring and summer things. Some of the conversation goes something like this: "Oh, it is going to be so nice to go for ptarmigans again. It will be so good to see those little brave birds." "I wonder what the ice fishing will be like in May this year?" "Remember last year? Why, it was so warm that we hardly needed the tent." "Have you made a new tent for the spring?" "Oh, the berries will be showing through the thin, thin ice from the melting snow once again."

One gives a little warm smile with a glitter in the eye, and even if one is alone, one says out loud, "*Takuapikiit*," meaning "How very nice," with a feeling of welcome back and deep appreciation. We also talk about how even the sound of silence in the spring is different. If one understands the difference between the sounds of silence in the winter and spring, then one has a great appreciation for the new season *or* one has been listening to too much of the sound of silence over the long winter.

When you were cheerfully talking to people across the country about spring a few weeks ago, we were in the middle of a very cold, stormy, windy day. I just couldn't believe that there was a warm sunny spot anywhere on earth! I was close to tears, near breaking point as the wind and snow blew outside. I was going to turn the blasted radio off and feel sorry for myself. Our two-year-old daughter, Neevee, came over and gave me a hug and a kiss. That itself was the sign of our spring and gave me the will to keep the radio on and tell you out loud, "The rest of Canada may be having spring, but just you wait. We will have our spring and, boy, when it comes, it comes!"

As I write this, two young girls just came in with frostbitten cheeks but they claim it is a lot warmer. Temperatures are in the minus-twenty and minus-twenty-five Fahrenheit range now instead of steady temperatures of minus forty through the months of November, December, January, and February. The days are longer and much brighter. People are starting to go for walks. The husky dogs look lazier. The ravens fly slower and their caws sound friendlier. People say a pleasant hello more often. The pallid complexions from the long winter of indoor living are starting to look half-decent. People are starting to talk about snowblindness. Teenagers and children are more tolerable. Our tempers are no longer short-fused.

Of all races we may be the most appreciative of the wonders of spring. As our elders say, "If I live through the winter . . ."

Soon we will be comparing this winter with the past winters with a sigh of relief. I am leaving my wintery feelings behind and plunging forward to a new season. Today was the first time that a few drips fell in our house. Very quickly we got our homemade drip cans out of the cupboard — perhaps too quickly, because the drips have since stopped. But I shall keep the cans within reach. When the *katap*, *poink*, *fut*, *fut* starts again, I will place those cans under each wonderful drip!

*Ann Meekitjuk Hanson*

## RANKIN INLET, NORTHWEST TERRITORIES

### I

Summer, O glorious summer. Actually it has rained more this summer than I ever remember it raining. There were no two days in a row in July when it did not rain. Definitely no forest fires this summer. Now the grasses are lush, the berries are ripe, and the berry-pickers are happy.

Simon Ford passed away this summer. He was the principal of the Leo Ussak Elementary School. He died after a long bout with cancer. With him it was a bout; he fought it to the very end. After going down to Winnipeg for massive doses of chemotherapy, he was back at work the next day. He was active pretty much to the day of his death. He went ice fishing this spring, he visited friends and went to ball games at the diamond.

Simon took up principalship at a tender age but knew what he wanted to accomplish. He was fond of saying, "If it's good for the kids, let's do it." He once decided our kids needed pride in their heritage, so he made a rule that every kid in the Leo Ussak School would be called by his or her Inuktitut name. It was a humble beginning but it has led to great and wonderful things. It is so nice to hear kids calling my sons Ka'lak, Inninajuk, and Kusugak. Not only is Inuktitut spoken much more at the school now, but we have wonderful things like the Ajaijaa choir, which is very popular up here. It is wonderful to hear kids singing the traditional *pisiq* songs that were pretty much relegated to the prehistory shelves where most of our culture is stored.

I hadn't realized that he had a difficult childhood and would visit our house early in the morning. My father made him breakfast and they ate together. He would then wait for my brothers to wake up and they would go to school together.

I visited him the day he died. He was thirty-seven.

I have not been idle this summer. As part of the twentieth-anniversary celebrations of my publisher, Annick Press, I was the official storyteller on a steam train in Alberta. We were in between the forest fires and the flooding. The weather was beautiful. We travelled from Stettler to Meeting Creek and back again. The train was robbed by some masked men on horses but the robbers were caught and the loot was donated to charity. It was probably the best touristy kind of tour I have ever been on.

# FROM THE MORNINGSIDE FAMILY ALBUM

*If this is indeed a family album, and it does represent all kinds of moments, places, and people over fifteen years, the rambling old building pictured above was for most of our time on the air the family home. This was 354 Jarvis Street in Toronto, and that's the Morningside office to the right. The building, and our office, were full of mice and dust and cobwebs. But they were also full of history and a sense of belonging. And know what? For a long time you could even smoke in the studios there. Smoke and wave your arms.*

*I saw Vicky so infrequently that when I did visit her in Vancouver, we instantly burst into friendly fisticuffs. Seriously, this is just us clowning around for a newspaper photographer. I like Ms. Gabereau a lot — as who doesn't?*

*I can't remember if I was trying to teach Brian Mulroney how to swing a golf club left-handed when we met in our Ottawa studio, but whatever it was, it apparently amused him. To the right, in a rare moment in the same studio, Stephen Lewis, on the left, Eric Kierans, in the centre, and Dalton Camp — this is rare, too, many people would say — on the right.*

*These are the workers at a Christmas party in Toronto in 1986. The* Morningside *sense of family and collegiality was never more evident than at these affairs. Below are the bosses, or some of them. From left to right behind me, Patsy Pehleman, Hal Wake, Gloria Bishop, and Nicole Bélanger. This was the wrap-up party in Toronto, June 1997.*

*You don't mind if we include two different pictures of Alice Munro, do you? I loved talking to her, both when we caught up on each other's personal news before the interview and in the studio as we talked more about books. As you can see by the clock behind Alice, this was an afternoon pre-tape.*

*Graham and his tom-toms — novelist Tom King with the coffee cup, the actor and singer Tom Jackson in the vest, and the actor Graham Greene awarding me a headdress behind my back. They had just finished making* Medicine River.

*Dennis Kaye, the Incredible Shrinking Man, made it to our studio before he died of ALS. But at home in Quathiaski Cove, B.C., the scene below, is how he spent much of his time when he wasn't writing one of his gallant and funny letters to* Morningside. *What a hero he was.*

Ruth Kaye

Jim Ford

*Northerners on* Morningside. *To the left, Michael Kusugak at his writing cabin near Rankin Inlet. Above, a famous accordionist delivered by Buddy Wassisname and the Other Fellers.*

Arne Glassbourg

*Some of the world's best anecdotalists.
Above, the film director Norman Jewison,
who apparently doesn't know where the
microphone is. To the right, the novelist
and performer W.O. Mitchell, who does.
Below, one of* Morningside's *most famous
moments: Stuart McLean opens the cricket
jar. As you can clearly see (I could, anyway),
Stuart's famous ten-cent cricket was mori-
bund. This moment, by the way, is on the
CD that accompanies this book.*

Terry Hancey

Terry Hancey

George Kraychyk

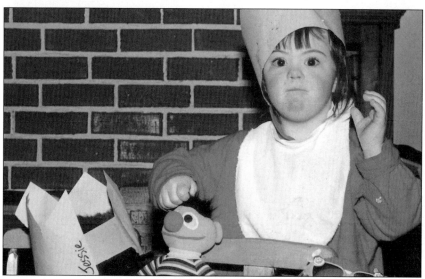

Nancy Huggett

*Various friends. Top left, Moxy Früvous prepares for an outdoor performance. Top right, Shelagh's annual birthday hug provides us with a picture of* Morningside's *favourite laugh. Above, Jessie (see "Life with Jessie"). To the right, Premier Frank McKenna works the room, preparing for a golf tournament for literacy.*

Julie Oliver

Don Hall

Morningside, the Finale: *This is the Temple Gardens Mineral Spa, Moose Jaw, Saskatchewan. Left, Colin James warms up as the TV cameras roll. Below, live, on the air, Colin is joined by Connie Kaldor. Details in the Afterword.*

Don Hall

*To the right, Stuart McLean takes advantage of the last ever* Morningside *program to bring one more example of cheap but transportable wildlife onto the radio. In his hand is Harwood the Hissing Cockroach. Harwood, alas, was indisputably alive.*

Don Hall

I spoke at the Whole Language Umbrella Conference in Windsor, Ontario, at the end of July. My room at the Hilton was directly across the Detroit River from the Joe Louis Arena. I read at the Sechelt Festival of the Written Arts in August. People there told me Joni Mitchell was in the audience. And a couple of weeks ago, I told stories in the Inuit Spirit of the Arctic Pavilion at the CNE in Toronto. The Pauktuutit fashion show was the most beautiful show I have ever seen. It showcased traditional and contemporary Inuit clothing. It had everything: beautiful clothing, gorgeous models (my niece Jacqueline was one of them), great choreography, fun — the little kids who modelled the children's clothes were teasing the young men and women — and wonderful music. Those high-fashion fashion-show people should watch the program. They would be sure to learn something.

This summer has also been a summer for bicycles. I have been riding mine all summer — when I have been here to ride it. Nathaniel, my twelve-year-old son, decided his new bike was a little mundane. He was determined to get himself a BMX bike, so he scrounged around for parts and built one from scratch. I was really impressed to find him riding it when I returned from Alberta. Alas, the ball-bearings were old and not in good shape and gave up the ghost. But I am convinced he will get it back on the road. The outside of our house is strewn with bits and pieces of bicycles that we are not allowed to throw in the garbage. I think I had better get busy and build us a garage so we can at least hide the stuff somewhere.

The weather was pretty rotten here today. It rained again, as if we needed more rain, and the wind was shaking the metal roofing on my shed, where my office is. I guess we better start getting ready for winter. The radio reported snow in Repulse Bay today. It won't be long before it gets here.

## II

How time flies, except when you are waiting for people to send you money. Here it is, summer pretty much gone, the nights get awfully dark already because the sun does not just dip below the horizon any more, it goes down under. And the rains have begun.

A most exciting addition was made to our community this summer: a swimming pool. It is the busiest place on earth. My two younger kids are taking swimming lessons. They spend about three hours in the pool every day. We go for family swim every Tuesday and Thursday. And then there are the open-swim and midnight-swim times. It is a strange experience to see people's legs and feet for the first time, people you have never associated legs and feet with because they have always been covered up. And fun. We throw pennies into the water and dive for them, we play tag, I snorkel and think about what it must be like to be a hippopotamus, and we dive. Our kids take to the pool like ducks.

Sometimes we are reminded we live in very unforgiving territory. My grandfather died on the floe edge when I was a little boy; my father died at sea in 1973. This summer, three young men also died in the relentlessly unforgiving Hudson Bay. They were in a small boat, paddling to check on a boat that was anchored in a small bay, when their boat capsized. There was a very strong wind from offshore and they were dressed warmly, not at all dressed to swim. It was a sad day. We could see the rescue boats from my living room window, going back and forth, looking for their bodies. We suffer the pain of their deaths with their parents, wives, and children. We, too, had known them all their lives. *Ajurnarmat*.

I want to tell you about Moses Aliyak. Who is Moses Aliyak, you say? Aliyak is one of our most upstanding citizens. He was one of the very first people to move into this community in the mid-fifties. He is a lay reader in the Anglican Church and an avid sportsman. He must be in his sixties now. I shook his hand yesterday and told him how wonderful it is to see him alive and well. You see, Aliyak had a fight with a polar bear a couple of days ago and won.

Aliyak, his wife, and their grandson, Kuuk, were getting ready to come home from their cabin. Aliyak climbed a hill to take one last look around. Kuuk was on the roof of their cabin. I don't know what he was doing up there but there he was, watching the whole show unfold before him. Aliyak's wife went out to empty the honey bucket when a polar bear charged her. She said she turned and ran. She returned to the cabin still carrying the honey bucket, went in and started to pray. It was the only thing she could do. She said after she communed with God, she picked up a rifle and went out and there was her husband throwing the bear to the ground.

Aliyak's account is that as soon as his wife went in, the bear attacked him. As the bear charged he remembered his uncle, Kreelak, who once told him about dealing with polar bears: Look at the bear and try to determine which side he favours and step the other way. That is exactly what he did, and the bear missed him. He said the only thing he had with which to protect himself was his binoculars. He wrestled the bear, trying desperately not to be thrown to the ground. He decided that he had a better chance with the bear if he stayed on his feet. Every time the bear's head got too close to his own, he would hit its nose with the binoculars as hard as he could. He said he realized it smarted when he hit the bear's nose and he would gain an invaluable second or two to try desperately to think of what to do next. Once, when the opportunity arose, he grabbed the bear under its arm and shoved. He said he did not shove very hard, but the bear seemed to fly through the air, fell and bounced on its haunches. Then it got up and ambled away. He said it walked down to the beach, joined its cub, and ran away.

Aliyak says he thinks that when he grabbed the bear under its arm to give it a shove he tickled it and it jumped back. How do you like that? A ticklish bear.

Aliyak's advice when confronted with a bear? Always carry a weapon in bear territory; stay on your feet; stay close to the bear, and don't let it get its teeth too close. Me, I'll stay as far away from its teeth as I can — miles away.

The Royal Couple, Queen Elizabeth II and Prince Philip, visited us this summer and I actually got to meet them. They came through here on their way back from the Commonwealth Games in Victoria. It was a very special time for us all.

The organizers had been planning the visit for a long time, of course. I once asked them if I may be allowed to say a few words to Her Majesty on behalf of the NWT Literacy Council, of which I am the president. I also wanted to present Her Majesty with copies of my books along with a plea to her to read them to her grandchildren. One of the things we do is to encourage Northerners to read to their children and grandchildren to get children used to the idea of reading. I think the organizers forgot about me. But Charlie Panigoniak, a great and wonderful singer, and forever considerate, did me a favour. He got a sore throat.

The royal air-carriage with the NWT Air logo on it touched down at three-fifteen in the afternoon on August 22. It was a cool day, overcast and a bit windy, not exactly pleasant. The Royal Couple made their way downtown with hundreds of kids running along beside the shiny black Suzuki Sidekick with flags waving on the hood. The couple greeted people, opened a meeting place for elders and visited the visitors' centre.

Then they made their way to the Sakku building where they were met by my brother, Jose, and his wife, Nellie. Jose is the president of Nunavut Tungavik and he and Nellie were to host the Royal Couple.

The Queen was wearing what seemed to be a woollen or bouclé suit in a fuchsia colour with matching hat and sturdy shoes of the same colour. Both she and the Prince wore coats designed and made by artisans at the Ivalu shop here in Rankin Inlet. The coats were embroidered with the word NUNAVUT on the back. The Queen wore a light-blue one and the Prince wore a royal-blue one. They sat down for some entertainment.

There was a drum dancer from Cambridge Bay, square dancers from Iqaluit, *pisiq* singers from Repulse Bay, and folk singers from Newfoundland.

Charlie Panigoniak's spot had to be filled, of course, and I was the stand-in. Since I could not hope to fill Charlie's shoes by singing, I decided to talk about traditional storytelling, read a paragraph from my book *Northern Lights: The Soccer Trails*, and to play with string. I was so nervous while the others performed. But performing was fun. They laughed and applauded and seemed to have a good time. They are nice people.

After the show, we were introduced to them and I gave the Queen the book I had read from. It was a thrill to see her walking along, talking to people, carrying a book of mine in her arm with the cover in plain view for all to see.

Nathaniel will not soon forget the Royal Couple. He was bothering me no end. He wanted to take pictures of them. I got tired of him pestering me, gave him my camera, and sent him off. He ran ahead and started snapping away. Prince Philip saw him and said to him, "Little boy, your lens cap is on."

Nathaniel said, "Oh, no, I took eight pictures like this!"

The Prince took pity on him and said, "Would you like to take a picture of Her Majesty?"

He said, "Yes!"

The Prince took him by his shoulder and ran ahead with him. The security people tried to assist the Prince but he told them to go away; the Canadian Rangers tried to assist him with a troublemaking boy but he told them to go away. Then he went to Her Majesty and said, "This little boy would like to take a picture." And they stood there and posed for him as he snapped a picture. I am keeping my fingers crossed, hoping the picture turns out. Even if it is blurry and out of focus, we will keep it.

Sandy missed all this excitement. She was down in Winnipeg at a Rolling Stones concert. She is a diehard Rolling Stones fan.

### III

Here I sit in my office once again, a fire crackling in the wood stove. It is a peaceful morning. Kiri Te Kanawa sings so sweetly on my stereo.

Outside my window, the ground is yellow and brown. It seems to be overcast all the time, we get a lot of rain, and the wind rattles the roofing. Freezing rain is not much good for the crops, but that is what you get when you live on the coast. Just kidding about the crops. But the berries are ripe and the people are happy.

Listen to local radio and all you hear is talk about berries. I don't remember if I ever told you about local radio, but it is the greatest thing. When local radio is on, you can call up and say "Happy Birthday, Peter," or anything you want to. They put you right on the air. The only rules seem to be that you cannot be too obviously celebrating Peter's birthday when you call and that you don't put anybody down. These people are pretty quick with their hang-up finger when they hear alcohol on your breath. Local radio is wonderful when you don't know where your kids are and you want them home: "If anyone sees Bubsy Kusugak out there, tell him to go home and eat. We haven't seen him since after school."

These days, the talk is more like, "We filled up a whole ice-cream container-ful of *paungat* in no time at all. Happiness. Where did Sarah go? I thought she was going to meet me at the Dancing Place." The Dancing Place is a rock-strewn rise of land out there, big rocks for miles around. God knows why it is called the Dancing Place. You can hardly walk on it, let alone dance.

*Paungat* are little black berries and they are ripe and very abundant right now. *Kigutanirnat* — tiny blueberries — are few and far between but sweet and just lovely. *Kingmingnat* — tiny cranberries — are also out but hard to pick because there are so few of them. *Kablait* — big, black berries — are always plentiful but taste awful and nobody bothers with them. And *aqpiit* — they look like orange raspberries — are the tastiest of all, but birds or some other animals must like them, too. They go very fast.

Anyway, people are everywhere, picking berries. It is the most wonderful time of year. Even Jeannie, my sister, who would much rather spend her life sitting in her house or playing bingo or some other boring thing, spends as much time as she can lying out on the tundra until her fingers are blue with berry juice and her cheeks are red with cold, picking berries.

The geese are flying around now, too. You see them in long Vs, flying along up there, way up in the sky. I heard them last night, in the dark. I don't know how they can see in the dark but there they were, honking their merry way. The young swans are really big now and move very fast. They are turning white. They haven't learned how to fly yet, but they run and swim faster than I can run.

Everything is turning white: the young Arctic hare are turning white, the baby gulls are turning white even though they still talk like baby gulls — I sometimes think baby-gull talk is like baby-baby talk only in gullese — the baby foxes are big and turning white, and I hear various places in the North are also turning white, like Coral Harbour for instance. Brrr . . .

## IV

I am sure this has been of great concern to you but I cannot decide when the best time is for you to come and visit us. You should just visit a lot. Right now is a good time.

I would not really recommend the hamlet. The hamlet itself is like a giant construction site that the constructors are forever trying to make into a moonscape. There is gravel everywhere; buildings are going up everywhere; people are digging and hammering everywhere. It is wonderful that nature will eventually reshape it into its original natural state.

To really appreciate the beauty of this land you have to get away from the hamlet. There, the fields are adorned with very soft, fuzzy yellowish-brown grasses, dotted with graceful sandhill cranes of the same colour. The eskers are blanketed with a most impressive mat of black, purple, and yellow moss. *Tiraujat*, the black stuff is called. I am sure it began as *tingaujat*, "pubic hair moss." It really does look very much like thick, black pubic hair. But the effect of all the colours and texture is most wonderful. Sharon MacDonald, a friend of ours from Winnipeg, says she would like a carpet just like it. Even the low-lying bushes, which are as close as we get to trees around here, seem very high this time of year.

Going back to sandhill cranes, we saw a flock of about a hundred of them, flying in a V formation the other day. We thought they were just another flock of geese until we heard them. Sandy said, "Those aren't geese. They are sandhill cranes." Sure enough, they were sandhill cranes. I have never seen so many of them flying together in one giant flock. Even at a distance, they are so distinctive, the way they slowly flap their big, delicate-looking wings, giving them that extra little bit at the end of a flap.

The young swans are flying now, too. They are still a light grey colour. We drove up to a family of five swans yesterday. We got pretty close to them. There were two adults and three young ones. It was so nice to see them fly off, all together.

The big news is that the people of Igloolik have caught a bowhead whale. All the old people around here are dying to go up to Igloolik to feast on *muktuk*. Lizzie Ittinuar was remembering the people she is, in one way or another, related to. She was laughing and saying they were not going to remember their poor relative in Rankin Inlet, who is dying for some *muktuk*. She and her husband, Ollie, made a big joke out of it on local radio for the benefit of us all.

*Muktuk* is very rich and tasty. I could never convince Sandy of that, of course: she will not touch any of our oily delicacies. She eats raw fish and caribou but no *muktaaq*, or walrus fat. Ken Dryden, the greatest goalie that every played in the NHL, tried *maktaaq*, though. When he was here, we had a community feast and he ate everything. He even had some cured *muktaaq*, which is a bit green and takes a lot of getting used to. I told him his stomach might try to reject it later but he kept right on eating. I guess he has a cast-iron stomach like the rest of us.

*Muktuk* is whale blubber. Can you believe it, *muktuk* does not appear in any of my dictionaries. *Muktak* is the skin of the bowhead whale; *maktaaq* is the skin of the beluga whale and the narwhal. *Muktuk* and *maktaaq* have a very thick layer of fat attached to the undersides of them that, as far as I know, is called blubber. It is the skin we eat more than the blubber.

Here is the late news: hockey is definitely dead; baseball is definitely dead. I had to walk up to Umingmak Supply — my Honda, too, is defi- nitely dead — to buy a crowbar. Why is a crowbar called a crowbar? I don't know. It looks nothing like a crow to me. Anyway, I walked by the ball diamond, which is next to the hockey arena. There was a bunch of guys, about a dozen of them, all dressed in hockey gear there. They were obviously wearing shoulder pads, they had hockey helmets on, and they were wearing hockey sweaters with Toronto Maple Leafs, Montreal Canadiens, L.A. Kings, and Calgary Flames crests emblazoned on them. Were they playing hockey? No. Were they playing baseball? No. They were playing football right there on the baseball diamond, next to the hockey arena. Well, that's it. I am selling the TV.

V

I was just driving a Yamaha four-wheeler around with my little boy for about four hours, looking for ptarmigan. Not a single one was to be found. It is awfully windy and cold out there. I guess the ptarmigan are staying put.

Boy, five-fifteen and it is already dark. We barely made it back before dark. Why do we go through this "spring forward, fall back" torture every year? We never have enough light to do anything with the kids after school in winter. It gets dark too early.

November, and the sea is still open. Soon the polar bears will get restless and come to bother us until they finally have some sea ice to travel and hunt on. These last two years, winter has come so late. We had rain the day before Christmas last year.

Soon we will have enough snow for snowmobiles. Older people who know this land tell us to beware of thin ice. Taking short cuts across a lake sometimes leads to tragic results. Some years ago a young man and his son were coming back from a hunting trip late at night. They did not return. Next day our search-and-rescue team found the father at the bottom of a lake just out of town, and the boy, wet and freezing to death, in a shack nearby. But we soon forget these tragedies and take our chances. It is nice to have the old and wise to remind us.

The eleventh hour of the eleventh day in the eleventh month draws near. Two years ago my little boy, Nathaniel, got a taste of being a cadet. He had a uniform with buttons missing, a beret cocked just so, ugly boots and all. I thought he was a little young for it, but it made him happy to be marching around with the other kids and getting yelled at a lot. One day he said that, the night before Remembrance Day, he might have to stay up all night guarding some monolithic *thing*. He did not know what the *thing* was, what he was to guard it from, or why he was to guard it at all, but it was a very important job, guarding this *thing*. He was looking forward to staying awake all night with his friends guarding the *thing*. I was just as glad when the people who did all the yelling decided he did not have to guard the *thing* after all. I think we do not appreciate the significance of Remembrance Day any more. Most of us never have.

I remember writing poetry in school, making up feelings about a war I do not remember. The closest we ever got to the war was in 1958 when an airship flew over Repulse Bay. Someone said, "I have heard there is a big war with the enemy somewhere, and maybe this thing is coming to get us." We all got scared and ran away from Repulse Bay. The war had been over a few years but I guess no one had bothered to tell us. To this very day, I do not remember ever having seen a real poppy, dead or alive.

My father-in-law, Stan Belsey, was in Europe during the Second World War. He has all kinds of medals. He has never been vocal about his involvement in the war and he never puts his uniform on and marches with the other veterans on Remembrance Day. But he once gave us a most interesting tour of the war museum in Ottawa. He made it a personal experience.

One morning, I had breakfast with him at a restaurant which claimed to be the home of the Elvis Sighting Society. He ate his eggs in a most peculiar way. He ate all the egg white, cutting carefully around the yolk. Then he took the yolk with his fork and stuffed the whole thing in his mouth. He said, "This is the way we ate our eggs in the army."

I asked him about the war. He said he went to Europe to do a job because Hitler was marching around over there killing young people and he had to be stopped. He was in charge of an anti-aircraft gun unit and actually shot down some enemy airplanes. "Belsey shot it down," he said with an assumed British accent, mimicking the British soldiers he was with.

He also hit a British airplane, which arrived from the wrong direction unannounced. Apparently, the pilot said to him, "Mighty fine shooting, Canada."

I bought some Aeroplan tickets for him to come up to Rankin Inlet this summer. We had a most wonderful time. He brought all his war memorabilia, pictures, and newspaper clippings, and told us some most interesting stories. He has a fork which is made of the lightest metal I have ever seen. It has a swastika stamped on it. He said he found it in an abandoned German camp.

I asked him what his greatest memory of the war was. He said, without hesitation, "I danced with Marlene Dietrich and she call me 'Dahling.' I thought it was very special until I realized she called everybody 'Dahling.'"

I also stayed with Mr. and Mrs. Randall, an elderly couple, who have a farm in Delburne, Alberta, last year. They were so kind and gracious. Mr. Randall would make me a huge breakfast with eggs, ham, bread, homemade jam, and coffee. We would go for a long walk in the cool, fall morning air, looking at huge rolls of hay and deer tracks until I had to go and read in a school or a library somewhere. At night we talked and I read them some of my books.

Mr. Randall was one of those people who flew the Allied bombers in the war. He was organizing the Remembrance Day ceremonies in Delburne. I introduced him to all the kids at the Delburne School after a minute's silence at their Remembrance Day ceremony. I would have preferred that he came up and told stories about the war instead. But I was working and it is my job to tell the stories.

I flew home from Edmonton on Remembrance Day last year. This year, on Remembrance Day, I am off to Goose Bay, Labrador. I am touring for a month. I will be taking in Goose Bay, Nain, Davis Inlet, Toronto, Port Colborne, and New York City (Long Island, Greenwich Village, and all). Except for the fact that I will be away from home for so long I look forward to meeting more interesting people.

*Michael Kusugak*

# CONVERSATIONS WITH WRITERS V:
## MARGARET LAURENCE

Anthony Jenkins, *The Globe and Mail*

*As Timothy Findley wrote in the sad and celebratory obituary he prepared for* Morningside *after her death in 1987, "Margaret Laurence believed, with a passion so profound it almost put me to shame to think of it, that war and hatred must and* can *be put aside, and she devoted even to the point of exhaustion all the latter years of her life to activities supporting this belief." Except through her novels, I never got to know Margaret Laurence well, but I was touched by her, as so many people have been.*

PETER GZOWSKI About halfway through, in fact almost exactly halfway through, an occasionally dreary evening last fall, an evening called privately "The Night of a Thousand Egos" but publicly "The Night of a Hundred Authors," there was a very nice moment when Margaret Laurence was introduced to a lot of people who'd spent a lot of money to have dinner with other people, and there was just a moment or two of genuine applause and appreciation and tribute. Margaret Laurence joins me this morning. I really liked that. Did you really like that?

MARGARET LAURENCE I found it very touching, Peter. I must say I was grateful.

PG Your name came up here not long ago when we were talking about African literature. You have, of course, written about African literature. Can you talk about your involvement there, what that meant to you, what the African experience meant to you?

ML My first novel was set in what was to become Ghana. I wrote two books of fiction out of Africa — the novel and a book of short stories — and a book of critical essays. When we went to Africa, I became so fascinated by it that I wanted to write fiction out of that circumstance, out of those experiences, and for the first time I had an experience of a culture very different from my own.

I think that helped me in two ways. First it helped me to understand some of the conceptual and cultural differences, and second, it gave me a new perspective on my own land and my own people. It probably also saved me from writing a first novel that was one of those rather juvenile autobiographical novels. I think that I might have written at far too early a stage in my writing career a novel out of Canada when I was still not really sympathetic or understanding enough towards my own people. Don't forget, I left my home town when I was seventeen, eighteen, and of course every kid at that age growing up in a small town longs to get away. A wonderful place for a child, but by the time you get to be seventeen or eighteen you can't wait to get out of that little town. Had I written about it at that point I would not have written about it with sufficient compassion and understanding. I came back to that writing when I was considerably older, and I think I was able to see not only the petty rivalries and the gossip and the negative side of a small town, but to see the positive things, such as a sense of community and the strength of some of the people I portrayed in *The Stone Angel*. Hagar is my grandparents' generation. They were very harsh people, but they were very strong people and they endured. They were difficult people.

PG  At seventeen you would have seen the harshness and . . .

ML  You bet, and nothing else.

PG  . . . and not the strength. Because Hagar is beautiful, in a way.

ML  Well, I love that character. In fact, she still lives in my head. They all do.

PG  They're so real for so many people. Do they carry on? Do you have Rachel and Stacey and Morag and Hagar in there all rattling around?

ML  They're all in my head, and they are very real to me. Sometimes people say to me, What happened to, let's say, Stacey after the end of the book? And I have to say I don't know. I don't follow them through the rest of their lives. It isn't given to me to know what happens after the novel finishes. Something happens, but it's not given to me to know.

PG  What a curious sentence, "It is not given to me," as if it were given by somebody, something.

ML  Well, I don't want to sound mystical or anything, but that is the sense that many fiction writers do have, I think. People say, Where do your characters come from? And I have to say I don't really know. They enter my imagination, and through a creative process I don't claim to understand, these people become real. I had the sense when I was writing *The Stone Angel* — and obviously I'm not the only writer who has felt this — that the old lady was there in my mind and was telling me her life story and I was simply putting it down.

That's what fiction writers have to hope for: to find the right kind of voice for their characters to speak, to put it down on the printed page so the reader knows, is *convinced* that is the way that particular character would have spoken. Now, you may remember a few years back we had what in my county we call "the controversy" over *The Diviners*. People would say, Why did you find it necessary to use all those terrible four-letter words? And I would say — and it's perfectly true — with a character like Christie Logan, if I had him talking in a very polite, grammatical, restrained way, it would have been a betrayal of him. I had that character talking the way Christie would have talked. To put it down any other way would have been a betrayal, and of course I feel the one thing a fiction writer has to do is to try to be true to their characters. That's the first responsibility. To be true to your material as honestly and truthfully as you can.

PG  Recently a new campaign was mounted against your books. This time you are fighting back. I hope you win. I'm impartial on this, but I hope you win.

ML  Well, I think we have to win. It isn't just a question of my books. It's a question of all Canadian writers — and indeed all contemporary writers are threatened by this kind of thing. I think that if all our books are removed from high school courses and high school libraries — I'm thinking of Canadian books — our children are not going to know anything about their literary heritage. These books tell us who we are. The senior years of high school are very important in terms of our kids getting in touch with Canadian literature. If they don't then, they may never, and if they do get an introduction to Canadian literature under the guidance of a good teacher, they will very probably go on and read more on their own.

PG  Good. Tell me about the campaign. Where does it stand now?

ML  This village councillor from Burleigh Falls is the person who started it.

PG  This is Helen Trotter?

ML  That's right. She got the support of several of her local councillors, who admitted they had not read the books in question. She is sending a petition to the Peterborough Board of Education, and wanted the Lakefield Village Council to support that petition. They refused, thank goodness. What will be the outcome when the Peterborough Board of Education receives this petition — a demand to take my books off the courses and out of the libraries in the high schools — we just don't know yet. I'm hoping the Peterborough Board of Education will decide as they did eight years ago that these books are not to be removed.

PG  Has she read them?

ML  She claims she has.

PG  When they have these meetings, do you get to go? Do they say, Let's ask the author about these books?

ML  No, they certainly don't, nor would I go. I don't think it's up to an author to do that. On the other hand, this time I'm not maintaining a dignified silence. Last time it was just *The Diviners* under attack, and I thought, Other people have to defend this book, and it will also speak for itself. And many people did defend it. But this time I am not traumatized, I'm not deeply hurt — I am very angry. It's not only *my* books that are threatened but many other Canadian writers, as well. I think the whole principle is dangerous. Now I must say I am personally very much against pornography, the use of women and children in video, films, and photographs. I think it's terrible stuff but . . .

PG   Terrible stuff to the extent that you would impose some form of censorship on it?

ML   It's a complex situation. What I would do would be to have Section 159 of the Criminal Code, the section dealing with obscenity, amended. It will not be easy to amend it but it is about fifty years out of date. When people like Mrs. Trotter group my books with pornography I become outraged. I feel the same about many other Canadian writers whose books have been attacked, people like Alice Munro, W. O. Mitchell, obviously wonderful writers. Our children need to read books like those.

PG   Are they after your works in the area in which you live partly because you live there? Is that a part of it?

ML   I can't think it's a coincidence, but this is the first time my novel *The Stone Angel* has been attacked, and I find this so ludicrous as to be practically unbelievable. That book was published twenty years ago, and in those years I have received thousands of letters from people who said the book helped them understand an elderly parent or gave them an insight into old age. The book has been the subject of essays and theses, articles by academics, articles by students. And the novel is used in many teaching hospitals in Canada in courses on geriatrics to help student nurses understand sympathetically the elderly.

PG   I'm going to go maybe a little bit farther. I want to lay at your door the accusation that you are not an anti-religious or anti-human writer but that you are in fact a religious writer and that you are in fact a writer about humanity and the essence of humanity is central to your work and your life and what you write. And to justify my charges of you being a religious writer I'll cite your background. You are a Christian person. You come from a Christian background. You studied theology at the University of Manitoba.

ML   I did study theology.

PG  You are a Christian, Margaret Laurence, I accuse.

ML  I accept that. I am a Christian. At least I aspire to be a Christian. I come from a Christian social democratic background. I went to a theological college. My work is filled with a kind of Christian faith and outlook. I don't preach in my novels but anybody who reads . . .

PG  No, but there's echoes of it. There's Christie Logan.

ML  He is obviously a Christ-like figure. The name was not chosen lightly. He is a scapegoat, a man who in a sense bears the weight of the community.

PG  He's the town garbage collector.

ML  That's right, he is.

PG  The name has meaning to you and the attitude of the community to him has importance to you?

ML  That's right. All my books are filled with biblical references, both Old and New Testament. And the books are informed with a sense of mystery at the core of life, which some people call God. I think there is a sense — I feel it, anyway — of the Holy Spirit in those books.

PG  It's been a year or two since I've read *The Stone Angel*. I'll go read it again, as a matter of fact. I'll go buy three copies. But what in there is degrading, dirty, or disgusting, in their words? They must point at something.

ML  I have not been able to find out what passages Mrs. Trotter objects to. It's a sympathetic picture of a very old woman who is very stubborn, who's very difficult but who is enormously courageous. Hagar is a difficult woman but she's a brave woman. She's like many of our pioneers. People have said to me, When I read that book it reminded me of my grandmother or it reminded me of my very elderly mother. She has got a kind of indomitable quality that is totally admirable.

PG  You should see the expression on your face when you're talking about Hagar. You really like her.

ML  Really.

PG  But still . . . I've searched. There's got to be something they point their finger at. They have to say this is too sensual, this is too anti-clerical, this is too outrageous, this is . . . I don't know.

ML  Maybe because it portrays old age as I think old age often is. I don't think many old people dance cheerily into death. The concept of the dear old apple-cheeked lady who is totally happy and content —

there may be some people like that, but many elderly people suffer a lot. With physical pain. With a sense of losing touch with the present. With lack of memory, although they may have wonderful memories for things that happened long ago. Many elderly people feel isolated and they suffer and their pain is real. And I don't see how it can be anything except a good thing to understand that elderly people are not objects. They are real, suffering human beings we must try to understand and sympathize with and help.

PG  When you sat down to write *The Stone Angel*, did you have an idea of conveying that? Or was the book something that existed at a whole other level in your writerly mind?

ML  I thought, Will anybody except myself be interested in a story of a ninety-year-old woman who is close to death? And then I thought, I don't care if anybody else is interested. *I* am interested.

PG  Is she Margaret Laurence, age ninety?

ML  Oh, I don't think so, although I have to say there are certain characteristics in me — because I come from the same kind of people — that I'm going to have to watch. I tend to be a matriarchal sort of person. And I've got that same streak of stubbornness. But unlike Hagar — partly because my family was very different from hers — I have indeed been fortunate enough to know how to give and receive love, which is what she had to learn when she was very close to death.

PG  Tell me a bit about life in Lakefield. Tell me about your house. A lot of the people who visit it like to point out that it used to be — was it a funeral home or the funeral director's house or something?

ML  It was a funeral home several families ago. It is a very beautiful old two-storey brick house. What I think is amusing is that a funeral home comes into all of my Canadian fiction. One of my grandfathers was an undertaker. I thought, when I discovered this, how appropriate — I didn't realize it when I bought the house. I've lived there for nearly eleven years now.

PG  May 1, 1974.

ML  That's right.

PG  *The Diviners* was published and you moved into that house.

ML  That's right.

PG  It's about the size of Manawaka, Lakefield, isn't it?

ML Yes, I guess it is. When I left my home town of Neepawa, when I was seventeen or eighteen, I swore I would never, ever, ever live in a small town again. And most of my life I have lived in small towns. I am really only at home in a small town.

PG You had a cottage down the river or up the river.

ML That's right, I had that for ten years.

PG And you used to write in the cottage?

ML I wrote most of *The Diviners* there.

PG But you've given the cottage up.

ML I sold it about four years ago.

PG Now, life in Lakefield. They don't deliver the mail to your house?

ML No, I go down to the post office five days a week or six days a week — we have a Saturday delivery — and pick up the mail, which I really love. If we had a home delivery, in the very cold weather I might not go out at all some days. Going down to the post office gets me out of the house. I meet neighbours and shoot the breeze. It's a kind of social event to go and pick up the mail.

PG You answer all your own mail?

ML Do I ever. I answer approximately twelve hundred letters a year. That's a lot of letters. I never seem to catch up with my correspondence.

PG If you had not written in the order you happened to write in, Africa first and Canada second — and many things to come, as well — would you have been as in command of your technical powers? You are now a wonderfully accomplished technical novelist in every sense. Could you have done that earlier?

ML Every serious writer of fiction, every serious writer of anything, must of necessity go through quite a long period of apprenticeship, of learning what I call my trade. I don't like to call it my art or my profession, although it is my profession. It's my trade. You learn it like a carpenter learns his trade, and you don't learn overnight. It's complex. Obviously a first novel, no matter how brilliant, is a first novel. Now, I can think of a few exceptions where a first novel is absolutely and totally brilliant. One of them would be Adele Wiseman's *The Sacrifice*, but she had been writing from a very young age. I would say that *my* first novel is probably what I would call, in the slightly demeaning phrase that is often used, a promising first novel.

PG  Where do you learn? Who teaches you? Do readers teach you?

ML  Well, I think you learn simply by doing. By writing and writing and rewriting and rewriting. What I always tell young writers is, Read as widely as you can, not in order to imitate somebody else's narrative voice, but simply to learn what can be done with a particular form. If you're interested in writing novels, read a lot of novels, and you begin to see, My goodness, isn't this incredible, that Joyce Cary or whoever can do this with a character, can make a character come alive.

I was extremely fortunate: my mother had been a high school teacher of English, and she always read everything I wrote when I was in high school and was very good about giving me a critical analysis. One of my high school teachers of English also, Miss Mildred Musgrove, went far beyond the line of duty, reading my stuff and giving me a critical analysis of it. But I think that every writer learns to write by themselves.

PG  Did you ever have one of those periods of reading a writer, when you were totally infatuated, and you would sound like a poor imitation of that writer? Did you ever do that?

ML  Oh, I think that every writer at some point does that.

PG  Who affected you?

ML  Well, I'm just wondering.

PG  Hemingway got a lot of people at one point. Short flowed the sentences.

ML  Short flowed the sentences indeed.

PG  And bright shone the light.

ML  And corny were the women.

PG  And corny were the women, yes.

ML  Much as I admired Hemingway when I was in college, and still do in many ways, I think there was a part of me that had been an early or perhaps lifelong feminist. I objected to his characterization of women, which was one-dimensional, always. I never liked that sort of male macho aspect.

PG  You saw that then? You saw that on first reading him?

ML  You bet!

PG  You say that with such certainty. I'm not sure a lot of people did.

ML  I even objected to Milton.

PG  Ban the *Areopagitica*.

ML It wasn't the *Areopagitica* that bothered me. It was such lines as those from *Paradise Lost*: "He for God only, she for God in him." And I thought, Rats to that.

PG I want to know more about your sense of your own growth as a writer. I think you look on all the Manawaka novels as one work, don't you?

ML Well, I do now, but when I wrote *The Stone Angel* I had no idea that four more books of fiction would proceed out of that Prairie milieu. They simply kept coming along, that's all, suggesting themselves to me.

PG They're not in order? It's not a serial or anything?

ML No, no, not at all.

PG I've got to ask you about nuclear power. There's a letter that came into my ken coincidental to your appearance here. You're firing off angry letters about nuclear power.

ML I'm not just firing off angry letters, Peter, I'm participating as much as I can in a number of disarmament and peace groups: Project Ploughshares, the inter-church peace group. Operation Dismantle. A local group in Peterborough. And there is now an excellent organization, Candis, the Canadian Disarmament Information Service, which was formed to try to correlate information from the various peace groups. I think this is the most important practical, moral, and spiritual issue of our times. If we do not solve this one, there's not going to be anyone around to solve anything else. We absolutely must do something to reduce nuclear arms. Both Russia and America now have the nuclear capability to kill every creature in the world many times over! Why are all these billions and billions and billions of dollars going to add to this increasingly dangerous nuclear force when you think that a fraction of that could be used to alleviate some of the pain and misery and hunger and disease in this world? I am incensed. I'm outraged.

PG What incensed and outraged you? Was there some one thing, did one morning you say, I won't do it, I won't take it?

ML No, I think this is a lifelong thing. I think this goes back a long way. I do believe that Canada could have a very great effect in this. I am not suggesting, none of us are suggesting, unilateral disarmament at this point. What we are suggesting is a verifiable reduction of both sides, and in that I think Canada could have a real impact as a mediator, just as some of the Scandinavian countries could. I think it's outrageous if our government permits the cruise missile to be tested in Canada. What we should do is declare our country a non-nuclear area. We could be a great force for peace in the world.

I don't think this was a sudden thing with me at all. It is corollary to my conviction that we really must try to do what we can in terms of social justice. This goes back a very long way in my background. My sense of a Social Gospel has always been very strong.

I think if you look at many of my novels, perhaps particularly with *The Diviners* but not that novel exclusively, you will find a strong sense that some people are being given a very raw deal by society. People such as the Métis. This is by no means a new thing with me.

I think what scares me the most about the possibility of nuclear war is that so many of our leaders — not just in Canada but all over the world, and particularly the two great superpowers — do not seem to have the imagination to understand what would happen. They think that they would go down to their bunkers or they would dig three feet into the earth and cover it with an old door and three days later walk to Becker's for a quart of milk. This is not what is going to happen.

PG  No Becker's, no milk.

ML  No nothin'. This concerns me on behalf of my own children. Almost everybody who has children feels the same love and care for their children as I do for mine, and by extension they are all our children. I think it's appalling that the future of all those generations is being put in jeopardy. If I sound deadly serious, I am.

PG  I know. I don't want to change the subject but there's just a minute or two. More novels. Another novel? Something is in the works?

ML  I'm working on a novel, yes.

PG  Are you done with Manawaka?

ML  I think so. With *The Diviners* I felt in a sense the wheel had come full circle. What I'm working on now is quite a different thing, but of course, as you know, I don't talk about that.

PG  But what is the fight doing to your life in Lakefield? Do you see Mrs. Trotter at the post office?

ML No, no, she lives in Burleigh Falls, which is north of Lakefield. And
 I have had all kinds of support from people in the village, people I
 meet in the post office and the grocery store and at church.

PG Will this fight be resolved? Will we see the resolution in 1985?

ML Oh, I certainly hope so. In fact I'm hoping that the Peterborough
 Board of Education will simply turn down this request to have my
 books removed. But that remains to be seen.

PG Happy New Year, Margaret Laurence.

ML Thank you very much. Same to you, Peter.

# LETTERS FROM SECTION SEVENTEEN

*Fred McGuinness is an editor, columnist, beekeeper, lover of history, publisher, champion of prairie enterprise, a gentleman and a farmer — and now an honorary doctor at the University of Brandon. As I said so many times on Morningside, "From Section Seventeen, just outside Brandon, Manitoba, Fred McGuinness writes:"*

## I

One morning, in the early 1970s, I got off the CPR train in Brandon and went for a particular stroll. I had often thought about it, and now I was going to do it: I was going to retrace the path I followed in 1933–34 as Carrier #5 for the daily newspaper, the *Brandon Sun*.

To me, that carrier route had been a great learning experience. My deliveries covered the heart of the business district. The first was at the Dill Café, a most unsavoury place right across from the railway tracks. It not only served meals, but it also had rooms for rent on the second floor. The sign said they were available by the day, week, or month. Rumour had it they were available as well by the hour.

As I was only twelve at the time, I was not aware of the local belief that in this enterprise, the waitresses laid the tables on the first floor and the customers on the second.

From rumoured debauchery to pious rectitude was only half a block: my second customer was the best-known citizen in the territory, Albert Edward McKenzie. He was known universally as A.E. He not only founded McKenzie Seeds, the largest seedhouse in the British Empire, but he ruled over his fiefdom until he was ninety-four. Rumours about A.E. abounded, and I believed none of them. To me, he was a real gentleman.

I delivered a paper at an implement house, and often watched as workers attached cleats to those old-fashioned steel wheels on early-model tractors. I nipped in and out of the poolroom next door ever so quickly, because my mother had taught me that that was the house of the devil.

The next call was so interesting I could have stayed all day. William Lacey, of Brandon Signs, was a British-taught sign painter. One of his regular customers was the Strand Theatre. For the twice-weekly motion-picture changes, Mr. Lacey painted tall, thin signs, about fourteen inches wide and four feet deep. These stood behind glass on either side of the theatre entrance.

It intrigued me how he captured the mood of the movie with his artistry. If it was a Lon Chaney spooker, it would show ghostly faces and tombstones. If it was a musical, it would be complete with trombones and the treble clef. When he had finished his lettering, the artist would then paint some glue over selected portions, and cover them with stuff that sparkled.

Two doors down there was a barber shop, and I hated this place so much I had to force myself to enter. The barber had a foul mouth. I went in there one day and a policeman told me I had just lost a customer; the barber was in jail for molesting boys. That was the day I learned two things: that there was a word "buggery," and that it was an indictable offense.

My one bulk sale was five copies to the cigar counter at the Prince Edward Hotel. Then I crossed Ninth Street for another hateful experience.

I had two papers to deliver at the old city hall. One was to the janitor, but the second was at the relief office. There were always petitioners at the counter, and they were frequently in tears. The relief officer had a heart of granite. He yelled at people. He wanted every petitioner to exhaust every asset before he would help them. He treated them as if he believed they had gold bars in the mattress.

Then I delivered a paper to the home of a physician, Dr. Peters. His son, Doug, is now a Secretary of State. His daughter, Jean, married Max Freedman. If you are really long in the tooth, you may recall when Max Freedman gave us a commentary from Washington every Sunday noon in an early radio broadcast.

I had plenty of customers on my route, eighty in all, and my deliveries ended at a terrible tenement that could be the subject of a novel by Charles Dickens.

The Imperial Apartments were on the second and third floors over a retail store. There was one toilet per floor, and no tubs. I had perhaps ten customers in there. Two I remember in particular.

I always pushed a newspaper under one particular door, and rattled it a bit, and a cheery three-year-old on the other side would pull it all the way through. Occasionally she would open the door and chat with me. There was another doorway that always opened for me, as if my arrival was anticipated: this was an elderly woman who usually had a cookie for me.

I remember these two customers with great sorrow. That three-year-old one day backed into a tub of wash water, and was scalded to death. Later on, I was going to deliver a card to that elderly customer, to mark her eightieth birthday. But when I started up the stairs to deliver it, I saw the undertaker's men carrying their basket down. She had died that day. A few years later, when I was home on leave from the navy, I saw that card in a bureau drawer.

Well, one day I wrote a memoir of my newspaper-delivery days, and it was published by *Reader's Digest*. It was translated into a dozen different languages. For some months afterward, Brandon expatriates from China, Brazil, Portugal, and other countries sent foreign-language copies home to the Brandon city hall.

It took me a while to recall why these boyhood memories were so pronounced, and then I reached a conclusion.

That paper route covered all the bases: it introduced me to the rich, the poor, the caring, and the despicable.

Come to think of it, that was a great introduction to life.

## II

One recent afternoon I was prowling through the shelves in a bookstore and I saw a Group of Seven pictorial calendar. This triggered a memory of the week in which I had not one, but two chats with one of those great artists.

Now, I cannot tell you this story without providing the background. This is going to take a minute.

In 1957, when I was at the *Medicine Hat News*, the Southam company asked me if I would care to attend a session at the Banff School of Advanced Management. They wanted to send an employee and get some feedback on the educational process. I was a cheerful volunteer, and away I went for the six-week live-in course of training in that mountain fastness.

Before I get to the artistic part of this commentary, I must tell you something about my fellow scholars.

We were ninety-two in number. The dominant group came from British Columbia. They had a simplistic view of the world — they divided the class into two categories: east-slopers and west-slopers. You were a west-sloper if you lived west of the Rockies. Otherwise you were an east-sloper, and hence, in this view, a decidedly inferior person.

Again in this view, the only hope for an east-sloper was to move across that range of rocks. If this happened, there would be a magical transformation to your status in life. At least, that was the theory.

Oh, yes, about the training. It was by way of a series of case studies. In the evening we read the details of corporate problems as outlined in our textbooks; the next day we had to take a position on the *solutions* to those problems.

The rules of the Banff School were quite specific: each class had to have some officers. Through a process I never understood, I ended up as vice-president. A member of the administration patiently explained my job to me: I was to collect money from each student and buy a gift for the school.

Collecting that money really was not a problem: I decided that ten dollars per head was a nice round sum, for surely $920 would buy a gift of lasting value. My fellow students were co-operative. Between the president and myself we agreed that I should try to buy a painting.

After a brief consultation with the artistic types at the school, I learned that there was a member of the Group of Seven still living — and still painting. His name was A. Y. Jackson. He lived in Toronto.

To my astonishment, this man's name was in the telephone book, and to my greater surprise, he answered the telephone himself.

Well, I explained that I had this money and that I needed a painting *right away*. I calculated that I could spend eight hundred dollars for the artistic work and save the rest for transportation, framing, and the appropriate brass plaque.

After I told my story this great artist told me how sorry he was that — at that moment — he had nothing to sell.

Then there was a moment of silence, and then came the question, asked tentatively: "How much money did you say you had?"

I repeated . . . eight hundred dollars.

At this point there was another pause and then came the joyful news: Mr. Jackson said that while he had nothing *right then* — he *would* have something by the end of the week! He asked me to call him the next Saturday.

I did as I was asked. This time he told me he was just wrapping the painting and he would send it to me via railway express. It arrived a few days later and I must tell you that I had a little trouble getting it unwrapped: it had been packaged while still damp.

In the intervening forty years I had completely forgotten the name of the picture; I couldn't even recall what it depicted.

Last week I called the Banff School for some details. Art curator Catherine Crowston was not available for a telephone call, but one of her associates was most helpful. John Burril told me that the painting is "Georgian Bay, October," and he describes it as "a landscape with autumn colours of purple, red, and yellow."

And there you have my story. Some day I will tell my grandchildren that I once purchased an A. Y. Jackson original for eight hundred dollars, and that today, at auction, it is worth a king's ransom.

What I won't tell them is that I'm still kicking myself; I should have bought one for myself at the same time. Why didn't I? For about eight hundred reasons.

## III

One hundred years ago this week there were big goings-on in Brandon.

On the evening of November 25, 1896, the member of Parliament arrived on the CPR train and a crowd of hundreds was waiting for him. His name was Clifford Sifton, and he was a brand-new member of the Laurier cabinet.

When Sifton stepped down from the train, a torchlight parade led him to the city hall, where the mayor was waiting in the council chamber.

Two days later, November 27, Sifton made a speech that created headlines. He announced his plan for a massive immigration program that would fill the Prairies with farm families.

Now, in that speech, Sifton made some comments which must have been viewed as hyperbole: he said he would cut through all the red tape in the Immigration Department, which reportedly had the reddest tape of all.

He said he would induce settlers with promises of free land. This, too, was interesting: the land in question was owned by CPR and Hudson's Bay Company.

He said one thing more that I must admit I like. He was going to offer his staff a performance bonus: they would get extra pay for every new citizen they recruited for Canada.

While these were bold words from a brand-new member of the cabinet, you must consider them in light of the man himself.

This was a redoubtable battler: all he ever asked for was total surrender.

The Sifton motto was: "Never explain, never apologize."

Pierre Berton once wrote that Sifton had a mind like a steel trap, the memory of an elephant, and the hide of a rhinoceros. When Sifton got back to Ottawa, he needed these characteristics, because he had major impediments in his path.

One was the deputy minister of Immigration, the other the deputy in the Indian Affairs Department. There was a lot of heavy betting that Sifton could not remove these two men from office, but those who bet against the Brandon MP may not have known the whole story: Laurier had given Sifton all the power Sifton needed. Those deputies were fired.

At this point Brandon's role in the settlement of the West took positive shape.

Sifton hired Brandon's first mayor, Mayne Daly, to be the head of his legal department. He hired Brandon's second mayor, James Smart, to replace both of those deputy ministers who had been ousted. He hired Will White, the publisher of the *Brandon Sun*, to be his director of press relations in the United States.

Supported by what was called the Brandon team, Sifton went to work.

He flooded Europe and the United States with literature, and every word was carefully selected. The prairie winter climate was described as "bracing" and "invigorating." He once tried — unsuccessfully — to have Winnipeg's winter-time temperatures omitted from the weather reports.

The Sifton program worked. Within a year, settlers were arriving by the hundreds of thousands. And, just in case you think Sifton had an open-door policy, perhaps you'd like to rethink that ideal situation. It was specified that no "Asians, Jews, or Negroes" would be welcome, on the grounds that they were not likely to become good farmers. This was not the age of enlightenment.

In the United States, Will White was having great success, provided all the prospective Canadians had white skins. In ten years, 217,000 American-born immigrants arrived on the Prairies, a few in Manitoba, a few more in Saskatchewan, and the bulk of them in Alberta.

While the eastern Prairies were settled by homesteaders who arrived with little more than the clothes on their backs, those American settlers were the sons and daughters of settled families in Iowa, Nebraska, and the Dakotas. They arrived with boxcar-loads of possessions. By the way, one of Will White's immigration agents received a bonus of three dollars for every one of those settlers.

Clifford Sifton — later Sir Clifford — did not last long in government, but while he was there he transformed a nation.

It is not an overstatement to say that he filled the Prairies with farm families right from the Red River to the Rockies.

What I find astonishing is what has happened in just one hundred years which, historically speaking, is only a blink. Just think: it all began one hundred years ago last week.

## IV

Many, many years ago, in those pre-TV, even pre-radio days, when my little sisters and I tired of playing Parcheesi or Snakes and Ladders, we would get out an unusual household item that gave us countless hours of pleasure.

It was the button bag. It hung on the inside knob of the dining-room door. It was almost as large as a rugby ball. It was made of flax-coloured linen, with a drawstring top. Its sides were decorated with a repeating pattern of pansies executed in cross-stitch.

One of us would carry it to the dining-room table, where we made a fence of flesh with our arms as we dumped it out.

Now, this wasn't *just* a bag filled with buttons; this was a lifetime assembly of buttons and other small memorabilia. My mother had worked on this collection from the days of the family homestead at 22:15:02, west of the second meridian.

Frugality was the order of the day on the agricultural frontier, so no small artifact was ever thrown away. You just knew that if you kept something seven years you'd find a second use for it.

In those early days, every time you discarded an article of clothing you stripped it of every button, clasp, and dome fastener.

We first paired up all the buttons, and this was quite an assignment. We had them in the hundreds. There were buttons plain and buttons coloured. There were buttons with two holes, and three holes, and four.

There were leather buttons, wooden buttons, even toggles from early versions of the parka. There were fancy buttons galore, snipped from ball gowns dating from the turn of the century, perhaps even earlier.

With all the buttons organized, it was time for the memorabilia. At this point the scene changes from the oddments collected by a needlewoman to the very stuff of social history.

We lined up the military badges so neatly they made us think of soldiers on the parade square.

Uncle Fred had been a doctor in the Royal Canadian Medical Corps, and we had his tunic buttons and one hat badge. These were easy to identify: they had the serpents of Aesculapius entwined on a wand, although we didn't understand this at the time.

We had buttons and badges that belonged to Uncle George. He was a soldier in the 181st Battalion, and he died at Vimy Ridge. A man who later worked in the Brandon post office had been with him when he lost his life. He had clipped two buttons off Uncle's tunic, and given them to his mother.

Uncle Roy was a youthful bandsman and we had buttons from *his* uniform. This was heroic stuff. First he was mentioned in dispatches, and later awarded the Military Medal. He ran for help through enemy lines when a small company of men was cut off from the rest of the battalion. We even had that tiny piece of striped fabric that designated his medal. The medal itself was in safekeeping in a bureau drawer, and we were not allowed to touch *that*.

When a real collector sets out to store away the memorabilia of a lifetime, there is no end to the variety.

There was a little nickel (can you remember them?), slightly bent and highly polished. One day on the homestead my mother had found it in the gizzard of the Christmas turkey.

There were tourist souvenirs from Gananoque, where my grandparents settled briefly on their arrival from Ireland.

There was a handful of coins, and we knew the story behind each of them. These were *zlotys*, and *pfennigs*, and some German coins with a story all their own. Uncle Harry had traded them away from a German soldier on Christmas Day when the warriors in the trenches got tired of killing each other and spent the day fraternizing.

There was a collection of thimbles, also from the homestead. Some of them were heavily scarred by work needles. From what my mother told us, *her* mother could sew anything: clothing, binder canvas, even the hides of cattle that had been gored.

Now, I suspect that I will be greeted with disbelief if I try to tell the story of the button bag to some grandchild engaged with Nintendo, but this doesn't matter. It's a precious memory to me. When I went home for Mother's funeral I looked behind the dining-room door — no button bag. One of my sisters got there first.

This is Fred McGuinness, still deep in nostalgia, west of Brandon, Manitoba, on Section Seventeen.

# MOURNING DOVE

*a drama by Emil Sher*

❧

*Right from the time I returned to radio in 1982 and was lucky enough to intro-duce Linda Zwicker's stunning "The Panther and the Jaguar," drama was an integral part of Morningside — though my own role was mostly simply that of listener and fan. Emil Sher's powerful "Mourning Dove," which is loosely based on the case of the Saskatchewan farmer Robert Latimer, but is not history, has now been heard all over the English-speaking world and has garnered, among many other awards, the Gold Medal at the New York Festival's International Radio Competition in 1997.*

## Scene One

*(Outside TINA RAMSAY's bedroom. Sound: TINA's laboured breathing. Continues under:)*

SANDRA: *(Off.)* Doug. *(Beat.)* Doug. *(Approaching.)* Come to bed.

*(Sound: TINA's breathing rises, then fades.)*

This has become a regular habit, you know, you standing there, watching her like some faithful dog. *(Pause.)* I can't remember the last time you came straight to bed.

*(Sound: DOUG coughs.)*

Every night, the same detour. *(Pause.)* Standing there isn't going to change a thing. *(Pause.)* I'm going to bed. You coming?

*(Sound: Faint breathing of DOUG and TINA.)*

Good night. *(Off.)* Good night.

*(Sound: Off, SANDRA closes bedroom door. Sound: TINA moans. DOUG exhales.)*

## Scene Two

*(Courthouse steps. Sound/biz: Media frenzy as REPORTERS swarm around DOUG, shoving and shouting. Continues under:)*

REPORTER 1: Mr. Ramsay, how will you plead?

REPORTER 2: Did you talk it over with your wife?

REPORTER 3: Was it a question of mercy?

*(Sound: "Mercy" reverberates in a rapid succession of different inflections: a statement, a plea, a question, a sneer, and finally, a whisper.)*

## Scene Three

*(Courtroom.)*

COURT CLERK: Douglas J. Ramsay, would you stand up please. Indictment: Douglas J. Ramsay (born 7th of June 1953) in the Province of Alberta stands charged that on or about the 21st day of November, A.D. 1994 in the Province of Alberta he did unlawfully cause the death of Tina Catherine Ramsay and thereby commit first degree murder —

KEITH: *(Off.)* No. He didn't do it. Not Dougie. No, no.

> *(Sound/biz: mumbling and rumbling as court spectators react to outburst.)*

Not Tina. Never, never.

JUDGE: Sit down or you will be escorted out of this courtroom. *(Beat.)* Continue.

CLERK: . . . he did unlawfully cause the death of Tina Catherine Ramsay and thereby commit first degree murder contrary to Section 235 (1) of the Criminal Code. Douglas J. Ramsay, do you understand this charge that has been read to you, sir?

DOUG: Yes.

COURT CLERK: How do you plead?

DOUG: Not guilty.

## SCENE FOUR

> *(Flashback: Medical examination room. Sound: TINA crying out in pain as she lies on table. Continues under:)*

SANDRA: Okay, Tina, that's a girl. Dr. Kovacs is almost done. Almost.

DR. KOVACS: Her left hip has a nice range. The right hip concerns me.

DOUG: She never lies down on her right side.

DR. KOVACS: You can see how the skin on the left side is starting to break down.

SANDRA: She favours that side. You know. It's more comfortable.

DR. KOVACS: I want to try and move her right hip. I'll need your help.

SANDRA: Daddy and I are going to turn you over, sweetheart. Okay?

DR. KOVACS: On the count of three. One. Two. Three.

> *(Sound/biz: TINA cries in pain as her body is shifted. SANDRA whispers words of comfort.)*

DR. KOVACS: Her right hip has no range. It's too —

DOUG: It's too painful.

> *(Sound: A sharp cry from TINA.)*

DR. KOVACS: *(Beat.)* Yes.

## SCENE FIVE

> *(Flashback: Doctor's office. Sound: Off. A baby crying in waiting room. Sound: Off. Phone ringing.)*

RECEPTIONIST: *(Off; into phone.)* Dr. Kovacs' office.

*(Sound: Door closing, muffles waiting room sounds.)*

DR. KOVACS: Tina is going to need another operation.

*(A discomforting silence as the news sinks in. We can hear, faintly, the infant crying in the waiting room.)*

SANDRA: I remember what you did to her back. All those rods and wires. I don't want you drilling any more holes in my baby.

DR. KOVACS: I understand that, Mrs. Ramsay. But you've seen what Tina's hip is doing to her. The pain it's causing.

DOUG: What about drugs? You know. Instead.

DR. KOVACS: I don't think so. We would have to use fairly powerful drugs. If they're taken with the medication she's using to control her seizures there could be some serious side effects. It could be even harder for her to swallow. Food could end up in her lungs. She could get very sick.

SANDRA: No more. *(Beat.)* No more.

DR. KOVACS: Tina's in too much pain to do nothing. Her hip is too far gone.

DOUG: What does that mean? Too far gone.

DR. KOVACS: We have to do what we call a salvage procedure.

SANDRA: Salvage?

DR. KOVACS: Try and picture the ball at the top of Tina's thigh bone, and the hip socket it fits into. There's something called "articular cartilage," a tissue which allows this ball and socket to move freely. The trouble is, Tina's ball has been sitting out of its socket for too long. The ball is damaged and has lost its shape. The cartilage has worn away. We can't put the ball back into the socket.

SANDRA: Why not?

DR. KOVACS: It would be like putting an arthritic hip back together again. It's doomed to continue to be painful.

DOUG: How are you going to do this salvage business?

DR. KOVACS: In simple terms, I have to take away the damaged part and cover the end of the bone with muscles, and hope —

DOUG: What do you mean, "take away"?

DR. KOVACS: Remove.

DOUG: You saw it off, don't you? You're gonna saw off the ball part.

DR. KOVACS: *(Pause.)* The ball part and about the top quarter of the thigh bone.

*(Sound: SANDRA reacts.)*

The surgery is necessary. We have no alternative.

DOUG: That's not the end of it, is it? Half the kids with palsy, they don't make it to their tenth birthday. You told us that. You showed us that study.

DR. KOVACS: Fifty per cent survived past age ten. Tina is twelve.

DOUG: No more operations?

DR. KOVACS: The chances of Tina's other hip dislocating is a real possibility. And because of her weight loss, I expect there may have to be more intervention.

DOUG: Intervention.

DR. KOVACS: A feeding tube . . .

*(Sound: A bereft SANDRA reacts.)*

Or another method of giving her nutrition that would bypass the mouth and swallowing mechanism. But let's not jump too far ahead. We have to schedule Tina's hip surgery. The sooner, the better. I have an opening in three weeks. Let's do it then.

## Scene Six

*(Flashback: RAMSAYS' home. The hallway. Sound: TINA's laboured breathing. Continues under:)*

SANDRA: *(Off.)* Doug. *(Approaching.)* Doug. Come to bed. *(Pause.)* We've got to get up early tomorrow. I don't want to be late for church. *(Beat.)* You look tired. You look terrible. You shouldn't have gone into the store today. Not after what the doctor told us yesterday. You should've taken the day off. You should get some sleep.

*(Sound: TINA's breathing.)*

I'm going to bed. Good night. *(Off.)* Good night.

*(Sound: TINA's breathing continues, cross-fades with a ticking clock in RAMSAYS' bedroom, which continues under.)*

## Scene Seven

*(RAMSAYS' bedroom. Sound/biz: DOUG climbing into bed, SANDRA being roused.)*

SANDRA: *(Groggy.)* I didn't think you were ever coming to bed. What time is it?

DOUG: What's the colour of pain?

SANDRA: What?

DOUG: Pain. You think it has a colour?

SANDRA: *(Fully awake.)* What are you talking about?

DOUG: Today, at the store. Keith comes up to me, he's all upset. A customer had come up to him and said he needed some paint for his pane. What colour would Keith suggest?

SANDRA: A window pane.

DOUG: You know how Keith can scramble words. Like when he carved Tina the mourning dove.

KEITH: *(Reverb.)* To wake her up in the morning.

SANDRA: What'd you tell him about the colour of pain?

DOUG: I told him what the customer meant. But I've been thinking about it ever since. If Tina's pain had a colour, what colour do you think it would be?

SANDRA: Red pain. Blue pain. What does it matter? Pain is pain.

DOUG: A colour might make things easier.

SANDRA: For who?

> *(An uncomfortable pause.)*

I don't think Tina can take much more.

> *(Another pause.)*

DOUG: Today I picked up a forty-pound bag of gravel. You know what went through my mind? This bag of gravel weighs more than my daughter.

SANDRA: Some nights, I wish she would just go to sleep and not wake up.

> *(An unearthly silence as both SANDRA and DOUG absorb SANDRA's statement.)*

## Scene Eight

*(Flashback: RAMSAYS' kitchen. Sound: Bacon frying, kitchen sounds.)*

SANDRA: You going to church dressed like that?

DOUG: I'm going into work.

SANDRA: Can't it wait?

DOUG: I asked Gwen to look after Tina till I got back.

SANDRA: I thought we should both be there. Make our prayers twice as loud.

DOUG: I'll take a raincheck.

SANDRA: Why're you opening up on a Sunday anyhow?

DOUG: I didn't say I was opening up. I have work to do.

SANDRA: Even God rested on the seventh day.

DOUG: God didn't own a hardware store.

SANDRA: I thought if we both went. I don't know. Maybe things would turn out all right.

DOUG: I've said my prayers.

SANDRA: You want me to pick you up at the store, then? On the way back from church?

DOUG: I'll meet you back here.

## SCENE NINE

*(Flashback: RAMSAY's hardware store, back room. Sound: Electric sander. The sander becomes louder as DOUG approaches and enters.)*

DOUG: *(Over sound of sander.)* Keith. *(Beat.)* Keith. *(KEITH shuts off sander.)*

KEITH: I didn't hear you come in.

DOUG: How could you, with that thing going a mile a minute? What are you doing here on a Sunday morning? Store's closed. You should be home.

KEITH: I want to finish this. For Tina. My sander wasn't working. I let myself in. Is that okay?

DOUG: I wasn't expecting you.

KEITH: It's a birdhouse. See?

DOUG: How long do you plan on being here?

KEITH: I have to finish sanding the roof.

DOUG: I got some work to do.

KEITH: You think she'll like it?

DOUG: I'm sure she will.

KEITH: You'll have to put it near her window. So she can look out and watch the birds.

DOUG: I'll be out front if you need me.

KEITH: You think they'll like it?

DOUG: What?

KEITH: The birds. You think they'll like the house?

DOUG: For sure. *(Beat.)* I have to get some work done.

KEITH: For sure.

*(Sound: KEITH turns on sander. Fades.)*

## Scene Ten

*(Flashback: RAMSAY's hardware store.)*

KEITH:  Is it okay if —?

DOUG:  Christ, you scared me.

KEITH:  I didn't want to bother you. You looked real busy. Like you were talking to someone who wasn't there.

DOUG:  How long have you been standing there?

KEITH:  Couple of minutes.

*(Uncomfortable silence.)*

KEITH:  Is it okay if I take a couple of sheets of sandpaper?

DOUG:  Help yourself to whatever you need.

KEITH:  What's the hose for?

DOUG:  What do you mean, what's it for?

KEITH:  I was just asking.

DOUG:  What does someone use a hose for?

KEITH:  For watering.

DOUG:  Well, that's what it's for. It's for watering.

## Scene Eleven

*(Flashback: RAMSAYS' home.)*

CHISHOLM:  *(Reverb/courtroom.)* Most importantly, you will also hear evidence on how Douglas Ramsay, on November 21st, once Sandra had gone to church with the kids, set about going to his hardware store, getting some pieces in terms of fittings and pipes together, getting some rags, putting them in the truck, then driving back home.

*(Sound: Hockey game play-by-play on the television. Sound: DOUG closes door behind him as he walks into house.)*

DOUG:  Gwen?

*(Sound: The game gets louder as DOUG approaches living room.)*

A hockey game at this hour?

GWEN:  Last night's game. I taped it.

DOUG:  What's the point of watching when you already know the score?

GWEN:  I don't know. I kinda like knowing how things'll turn out before they begin.

DOUG:  Tina enjoying it?

GWEN: I don't know. Not like before. She. She doesn't react like she used to.

DOUG: Maybe the game's getting too fast for her.

GWEN: Maybe. *(Beat.)* You want me to stay and help prepare lunch?

DOUG: We're all right.

GWEN: You sure? I don't mind.

DOUG: I'm sure.

GWEN: Okay, then.

> *(Sound: GWEN puts on coat.)*

Bye, Tina. Bye, Mr. Ramsay.

> *(Sound: GWEN walks away. The game continues.)*

Mr. Ramsay?

> *(Sound: More hockey noise. DOUG is lost in thought.)*

Mr. Ramsay?

> *(DOUG still doesn't react.)*

*(More forcefully.)* Mr. Ramsay.

DOUG: *(Startled.)* I . . . I didn't.

GWEN: I forgot my tape.

DOUG: *(Lost.)* The tape.

> *(Sound: The hockey crowd is silenced when TV is clicked off; video tape is ejected from VCR.)*

GWEN: Bye.

> *(Sound: Front door is closed.)*

DOUG: Tina, sweetheart. It's time to go.

> *(Sound/biz: DOUG picks up TINA and carries her in his arms.)*

CHISHOLM: *(Reverb/Courtroom.)* . . . driving with Tina in the truck out to the shed where she was then propped up with the rags while he rigged an apparatus up to run from the exhaust and through the sliding window of the cab and started the vehicle and then eventually shut the vehicle off and returned Tina to her bed in the house and there awaited the return of Sandra and the children.

## SCENE TWELVE

*(Courtroom.)*

PIERCE: I told him I wanted him to listen very carefully because this was a serious matter. I started by saying that we are not here to judge him. I understand the situation you are in and we empathize with you. We have no choice but to do the job we have to but at the same time we'll assist him in getting through this situation as best we can. "We have spoken to several people. Everyone said the same thing, that you are a caring person, a good person. At the same time, we know that this was not a natural death. Your daughter was in a great deal of pain. Doug, after considering all that is known, I have no doubt that you caused your daughter's death." There was no response from him and I noticed that his eyes were glassy with tears. I continued, "This is not something that you wanted or planned to do. You loved your daughter very much." At that point he nodded yes. "This is something that you felt you had to do out of love for your daughter, isn't it, Doug?" There was no reply. "I can imagine this is very difficult for you and I feel bad." I repeated that he was a loving father and I said, "You only did what you felt was best for her out of love for your daughter." Again there was no reply and I repeated it. I asked, "Isn't that right, Doug?" At that point he was close to crying. I said again, "That's what happened, isn't it, Doug? Isn't that right?" He replied, "My priority was to put her out of her pain." I asked, "That's what you thought was right, wasn't it?" and he began nodding his head yes. At this point there were tears flowing freely.

## Scene Thirteen

*(Flashback: RAMSAYS' front steps. Sound: Off. Car engine is turned off; car door slammed shut.)*

DOUG: How was church?

SANDRA: *(Approaching.)* We'll have to wait and see.

DOUG: What does that mean?

SANDRA: Why aren't you wearing your jacket?

DOUG: Didn't notice.

SANDRA: You step out and figure it was still summer?

DOUG: Didn't give it much thought.

SANDRA: Where's Tina?

DOUG: Sleeping.

SANDRA: At this time of day?

DOUG: What time is it?

SANDRA: One-thirty. When did she fall asleep?

DOUG: About an hour ago.

SANDRA: She okay?

DOUG: What do you mean?

SANDRA: How was she when she fell asleep?

DOUG: *(Pause.)* Peaceful.

SANDRA: Well, I hate to disturb the peace, but I gotta wake her up.

DOUG: Now?

SANDRA: She's gotta eat.

DOUG: I'm not hungry.

SANDRA: Are you okay?

## Scene Fourteen

*(Courtroom.)*

PIERCE: I asked him if he wanted to tell me how he did it. He says he drove the truck to the shed with her in it, hooked up a hose to the exhaust and ran it into the cab. I asked, "How long was she in there for?" and he replied, but I don't recall what he said for a time and I asked, "And she just fell asleep?" He said, "Yes, she just fell asleep," and then he added, "If she'd have started to cry I would have taken her out of there," and then again he himself began to cry. *(Pause.)* I said, "Doug, you have told us briefly what happened. I would like you to start at the very beginning and go through exactly what took place. Go slow. I'll put it to paper." He started, "She's been in pain for years. Ever since she was born she's had trouble." He hesitated. I said, "Go on."

*(PIERCE's voice cross-fades with DOUG RAMSAY's.)*

"She had an operation a year ago in August to straighten her back, put rods in."

DOUG: Prior to that her hip was dislocated intermittent so they operated on her back. They knew there would be one on her hip but the hip was secondary, didn't seem that serious. Then since May or June almost full time dislocated. Each time you moved her there was pain so the operation for the hip was planned for this time of year. It was more complicated than what we had expected so we just couldn't see another operation. She'd be confined to a cast for I don't know what the time was so I felt the best thing for her was that she be put out of her pain.

## SCENE FIFTEEN

*(Flashback: RAMSAYS' house. Sound: Anxious knocking on front door. There is no reply. Anxious knocking resumes. More silence, until . . .)*

DOUG: *(From behind door.)* Who is it?

KEITH: Me.

> *(Sound: DOUG opens door. Sound: Off. SANDRA's muffled, animal-like crying. Continues under:)*

I just finished it. What do you think?

DOUG: Very nice.

KEITH: I painted the roof red. They like bright colours.

DOUG: Maybe.

> *(Sound: SANDRA's crying intensifies, can be heard more clearly.)*

KEITH: Is that Tina?

DOUG: *(Pause.)* No.

KEITH: Can I show it to her?

DOUG: *(Lost in thought.)* What?

KEITH: The birdhouse. Can I show it to Tina?

DOUG: When?

KEITH: I'll show it to her. Then we can put it up near her window.

DOUG: No.

KEITH: You don't like it?

DOUG: Not now.

KEITH: I can make another one.

DOUG: Now is not a good time.

KEITH: When's a good time?

DOUG: Leave it here for now.

KEITH: Tina won't see it down there.

DOUG: Leave it here. *(Beat.)* Please.

## SCENE SIXTEEN

*(Coffee shop. Sound/biz: Clatter of cutlery, small talk in booths. GORDON BELLAIR approaches CPL. PIERCE's booth, sets down his coffee.)*

GORDON: Craig, you gotta minute?

PIERCE: You know what the service is like around here, Gordon. I got at least fifteen. What's on your mind?

GORDON: Keith.

PIERCE: Keith made a nuisance of himself in court today.

GORDON: I heard.

PIERCE: He didn't want to hear what I had to say about Doug. About what Doug had told me he'd done. He kept crying out, saying it wasn't true. The judge warned him twice, then threw him out of the courtroom.

GORDON: I know. He dropped by my place this afternoon.

PIERCE: That's not front-page news, Gordon. He spends half his life at your lumberyard, the other half at Doug's store.

GORDON: He didn't stick around. Usually he sticks around. You know. Collecting scraps of wood and whatnot. Today he was all funny like. Real nervous. Just stood around with his hands in his pockets. Then kinda disappeared.

PIERCE: Is there a moral to this story?

GORDON: I drove by Keith's apartment. To make sure he was all right. Mrs. Sanderson, she told me he never showed up for supper.

PIERCE: Keith's not one to miss a meal.

GORDON: He could be in danger. He could be. He doesn't . . . You know what Keith is like.

PIERCE: I don't have a crystal ball.

GORDON: My rifle's gone, too. The one I keep in the office.

PIERCE: Rifle?

    *(The higher stakes suddenly spark* PIERCE's *interest.)*

GORDON: I'm worried.

PIERCE: I'll look into it.

GORDON: I was wondering.

PIERCE: What were you wondering, Gordon?

GORDON: I was thinking maybe there was . . . I don't know. Some kind of connection.

PIERCE: What kind of connection?

GORDON: He was awfully attached to the girl. Always making her gifts out of wood. Maybe what happened to Tina set him off. Scared him. *(Beat.)* You know. They were both . . . *(Pause.)*

PIERCE: Both?

GORDON: *(A considered pause.)* They were both different.

## SCENE SEVENTEEN

*(Courtroom.)*

JUDGE: Good morning. It is your job to decide the facts from the evidence you have heard, then to apply the law to those facts, and, having done that, to try and reach a verdict as to the guilt or otherwise of Douglas Ramsay. You cannot let your passions or your feelings stand in the way of your reason. The questions you must ask here are whether you are satisfied beyond a reasonable doubt that Douglas Ramsay did in fact cause the death of his daughter and, if so, did he do so intentionally. It is convenient here to deal with Mr. Barclay's argument. He says Tina's death should be characterized as a suicide, that all her life her parents were required to make her choices for her, and that they had a moral and legal obligation to make the proper choices — choices that were in her best interest, that she was entitled to commit suicide and that her legal guardians were authorized to make that choice for her because she was incapable of making it herself. I must tell you as a matter of law that this argument is untenable. Mr. Chisholm says that this was a calculated, cold-blooded murder motivated by self-interest. The evidence did not leave that image in my mind and I doubt that most people would see it that way. Mr. Barclay says that if Mr. Ramsay did intentionally cause the death of his daughter by some means of unlawful act, then it was a compassionate act of kindness. That seems to be more likely. Each of you will have your own view, but both characterizations beg the question, which is, did Tina's father intentionally cause her death by means of some unlawful act, namely by putting her in the cab of the truck and polluting it with exhaust, and, if so, was it planned and deliberate? First degree murder is one that is planned and deliberate. Murder that is not first degree is second degree murder. There are only three possible verdicts here: guilty as charged, not guilty as charged but guilty of second degree murder, or not guilty.

## SCENE EIGHTEEN

*(Courthouse steps. Sound/biz: A refrain of the melee that greeted DOUG on the first day of the trial: a media frenzy as REPORTERS swarm around DOUG RAMSAY, shoving and shouting.)*

REPORTER 1: How do you feel?

REPORTER 2: Did you want to speak in your own defense?

REPORTER 3: Do you think the jury believes you're innocent?

> *(Sound: "Innocent" reverberates in a rapid succession of different inflections: a statement, a plea, a question, a sneer, and finally, a whisper.)*

## SCENE NINETEEN

> *(Holding cell. Sound: The clank-and-grind of a metal jail door being closed and locked.)*

SANDRA: What d'you think's going to happen?

DOUG: Don't know.

SANDRA: You might end up going to jail.

DOUG: I might.

SANDRA: For a long time.

DOUG: I know.

SANDRA: Jail is for criminals. You're not a criminal.

DOUG: No.

SANDRA: Are you scared?

DOUG: *(Pause.)* No.

SANDRA: I am.

DOUG: I'll be all right.

SANDRA: You know how sometimes you wish for something. Then it happens. Then you wonder if it would've happened if you hadn't wished so hard.

DOUG: You don't think I should've done it.

SANDRA: I didn't say that.

DOUG: What're you saying?

SANDRA: I feel guilty.

DOUG: I'm the one on trial.

SANDRA: We've been through this together.

DOUG: Always.

SANDRA: From the start. You and me.

DOUG: And her.

SANDRA: And her.

DOUG: I miss her.

SANDRA: It's been hard.

DOUG: What would you have done?

SANDRA:  I don't know.

DOUG:  What was I supposed to do?

SANDRA:  You did what was best for her.

DOUG:  *(Pause.)* That's right.

SANDRA:  No one understands.

DOUG:  No. They don't. *(Beat.)* Sometimes I don't.

SANDRA:  They don't know what it's like.

DOUG:  I don't understand. Not always. Sometimes I don't understand any of this. *(Beat.)* Do you?

SANDRA:  Not always. Not yet.

DOUG:  Green.

SANDRA:  Green?

DOUG:  The colour of pain.

SANDRA:  They found him, you know. Keith. Sitting on top of the fire tower. He won't budge.

DOUG:  It's a green colour, the pain. An old green.

SANDRA:  Her pain doesn't have a colour any more.

DOUG:  I'm talking about me.

SANDRA:  She loves you, still.

DOUG:  *(Pause.)* You think?

## Scene Twenty

*(Coffee shop. Sound/biz: Clatter of cutlery, small talk in booths.)*

ALBERT:  Vultures.

VERA:  Who?

ALBERT:  Those TV people.

ELEANOR:  Today's judgement day. They hand down the verdict. That's why they're hovering like flies.

ALBERT:  They've been swarming all week, trying to make something out of nothing.

ELDON:  C'mon, now. Tina wasn't "nothing."

ALBERT:  Did I say that? That's not what I said.

VERA:  Yes it is.

ALBERT:  It's not what I meant.

ELDON:  What did you mean?

ELEANOR:  He means Doug Ramsay is a good man and doesn't deserve all this . . . all this . . .

VERA: Attention.

ELEANOR: Thank you.

ALBERT: The press people, they love this kind of thing. This circus. They never knew Tina.

ELEANOR: And they don't know Doug. They'd know he wouldn't. They'd know he wasn't guilty.

ELDON: He admitted he was. Told Craig Pierce right to his face.

ALBERT: Just 'cause he did it doesn't mean he's guilty.

VERA: Then what does "guilty" mean?

ALBERT: I don't know the law. I know Doug. He did the right thing. He did what was best.

ELDON: Best for who?

ALBERT: Whose side are you on?

ELEANOR: He's playing devil's advocate.

ALBERT: The devil doesn't need an advocate. He's got those press people working for him full time.

VERA: They're just doing their job.

ALBERT: If they'd stayed away this whole thing would've blown over real quick. They turned this town into a coast-to-coast courtroom. The whole country's one big jury.

ELEANOR: I half expect to see Keith on television any day now. I'm surprised they haven't done a story about him yet.

ALBERT: Keith isn't news. Keith is slow.

VERA: He's been up on that tower all week, like some frightened bird. That's news.

ELDON: What's he afraid of?

VERA: Maybe he wants to set a record or something.

ALBERT: Don't waste your time trying to understand Keith. Keith is Keith. Doug's the one on trial. He's the one who's innocent. *(Beat.)* No one understands that. No one cares.

ELEANOR: He used to feed Tina by hand. Like a baby.

SANDRA: *(Testimony/reverb.)* Her food all had to be blended with no lumps in it.

ELEANOR: Poor thing couldn't so much as hold a spoon.

ELDON: How does a devoted father turn around and do what he did?

ALBERT: You playing devil's advocate again?

ELDON: I'm thinking out loud.

VERA: He loved her.

ALBERT: Like nothing else.

ELDON: I know he loved her.

ALBERT: Since when does being a loving father make you a criminal?

ELEANOR: People do funny things 'cause of love.

## SCENE TWENTY-ONE

*(Courthouse steps. Sound/biz: A quick refrain of the melee that greeted* DOUG *on the first day of the trial: a media frenzy as* REPORTERS *swarm around* DOUG, *shoving and shouting.)*

REPORTER 1: Was justice done?

*(Sound: The word "justice" reverberates in a rapid succession of different inflections: a statement, a plea, a question, a sneer, and finally, a whisper.)*

## SCENE TWENTY-TWO

*(CPL.* PIERCE's *patrol car. Sound/biz: The media swarm, quickly muffled as . . . Sound: Car door is slammed. Sound: Engine is revved. Car drives off.)*

PIERCE: I guess you won't be missing them any time soon.

DOUG: *(Pause.)* No.

PIERCE: I guess they're just doing their job.

*(He waits for* DOUG *to respond.* DOUG *remains silent.)*

Listen. Before I take you to . . . I know I shouldn't be doing this, but . . . I . . . I know it's wrong. You know Keith has had a bad reaction to all this. I guess you know that. Do you know about the rifle? *(Pause.)* Maybe you don't. He had a rifle with him when he first went up the tower. Took a couple of shots at me. *(Nervous laughter.)* He doesn't have the gun any more. Swapped it for food. You know what Keith's appetite is like. He won't come down. He . . . I was thinking you should have a talk with him. You're the only one. Maybe now that the trial is over he'll listen to you. You get along real well. What d'you think? I can't force you or anything. I mean, I shouldn't even be . . . I thought it's something you'd want to do. *(Beat.)* Do you?

## Scene Twenty-Three

*(Fire tower. Sound: Birds circling above tower. Strong wind. Continues under: Sound:* DOUG's *grunts as he climbs up last rungs of tower. He steps onto platform.)*

KEITH: You? . . .

*(Sound:* DOUG *collapses on platform, exhausted from climb.)*

You're here.

DOUG: *(Catching breath.)* Me. You getting enough to eat?

KEITH: I knew you didn't do it.

DOUG: It's cold up here.

KEITH: You loved her too much.

DOUG: That sleeping bag enough?

KEITH: I knew you'd come up here.

DOUG: What's that?

KEITH: What does it look like?

DOUG: A horse.

KEITH: For Tina. I carved it myself. Tina loves horses.

DOUG: You shouldn't have done that.

KEITH: You don't like it?

DOUG: You shouldn't have carved right into the railing like that.

KEITH: They can fix it. They can put in new wood. From Gordie's lumberyard. *(Beat.)* You want a biscuit?

DOUG: I'm not hungry.

KEITH: Some juice?

DOUG: I can't stay.

KEITH: Too cold for you?

DOUG: No.

KEITH: Remember that time I built a fire up here?

DOUG: Keith, you can't stay up here, either.

KEITH: *(Laughing.)* A fire on a fire tower.

DOUG: They're waiting for us down below.

KEITH: I wasn't scared.

DOUG: I promised Cpl. Pierce we'd come down together.

KEITH: Tell him to go away.

DOUG: I can't do that.

KEITH: Tell him this is my tower.

DOUG: When we get down, he'll take you home.

KEITH: Tell him to leave us alone.

DOUG: He has a job to do.

KEITH: You'll drive me home.

DOUG: I can't do that.

KEITH: *(Peers over tower.)* Where's your truck?

DOUG: They're taking me away, Keith.

KEITH: Away?

DOUG: Prison.

KEITH: *(Pause.)* No, no.

DOUG: Yes.

KEITH: No, no, no, no.

DOUG: Yes.

KEITH: You didn't do it.

DOUG: That's not how they saw it.

KEITH: Who?

DOUG: The jury. They announced the verdict this morning.

KEITH: Tina. Tina, Tina. Tinatinatina.

DOUG: She's not in pain. Not any more.

## SCENE TWENTY-FOUR

*(Flashback: Courtroom.)*

BARCLAY: How much involvement did Douglas have in Tina's day-to-day care?

SANDRA: Lots. When he was home I never had to lift her. He would lift her. When she got home I would give her a drink and then he would lift her from her wheelchair to the couch or wherever she had to go. He did all the bathing. Especially the last year of her life. I was pregnant and I couldn't lift her so he'd bath her. I bathed her once in October but I think the rest of the time that year he did all the bathing. If she threw up, he would — he would clean her up. He would bath her. He changed her diapers, wet or dirty. He was — he was just there for her. *(Pause.)* *(Testimony/reverb.)* Her muscles were very, very tight and it was starting to twist her body, twist it very badly. They cut a lot of muscles, like her toes, her heel chords, the outside of her knees, abductor muscles. They put her in a body cast so that her back — it was to try and keep these muscles, like from not tightening up, like to try and keep them loose.

## SCENE TWENTY-FIVE

*(Fire tower. Sound: A strong, menacing wind.)*

KEITH:  She's dead.

DOUG:  She went to sleep and she never woke up.

KEITH:  She — she wasn't a dog.

DOUG:  No, she wasn't.

KEITH:  She was your daughter.

DOUG:  She still is.

KEITH:  She was my friend.

DOUG:  I know.

KEITH:  You killed her like she was a dog. It's what you do to dogs. You put them to sleep.

CHISHOLM:  *(Reverb/courtroom.)* It is not open season on the disabled.

DOUG:  She died peacefully.

KEITH:  How do you know? How do you know how she was feeling? *(Beat.)* How do you know?

DOUG:  I held her in my arms.

KEITH:  Did you ask her?

DOUG:  Ask her what?

KEITH:  If she wanted to die.

DOUG:  She couldn't speak. You know that.

KEITH:  She could laugh.

SANDRA:  *(Testimony/reverb.)* She liked to watch bonfires. She liked to see things that moved. Like, if we were in the car and the windshield wipers were going, that would make her laugh when she was well, like when she was younger.

KEITH:  She laughed when I gave her the mourning dove. Remember? Remember?

*(Sound: Wind fades.)*

DOUG:  *(Reverb.)* Tina, there's someone here to see you. Keith. You know Keith.

KEITH:  *(Reverb.)* This is for you. For your birthday. A mourning dove. To wake you up in the morning. See? *(Beat.)* She smiled. She's smiling at me. *(Beat.)* If you move the dove up and down, you can pretend it's flying. See?

*(Sound: Reverb of* TINA's *laughter.)*

*(Reverb.)* She's laughing. She likes it. She's laughing.

*(Sound:* TINA's *laughter cross-fades with wind blowing across fire tower.)*

DOUG: She used to laugh. When she was younger.

## Scene Twenty-Six

*(Flashback: Courtroom.)*

CHISHOLM: We submit that the Accused is guilty beyond any reasonable doubt of the first degree murder of his daughter. Now, while Tina may have been frail medically, she was fit enough for surgery and indeed there was an impending surgery coming. Before I go further, I just want to read to you one from the Twelve Commandments for Parents of Children with Disabilities and it's just the first commandment. "Thou art thy child's best and most consistent advocate." I certainly suggest that is not what happened here. When we speak about Tina Ramsay, I'm sure the first thoughts that run through everyone's mind is that she was indeed very frail, a thirty-eight-pound, twelve-year-old girl, couldn't walk, couldn't talk, who was totally dependent on everybody for all that she needed in life, and Sandra Ramsay certainly stressed that in fact Tina had seizures every day of her life. Almost everyone involved in this case seems to portray or suggest that Tina's was a very dreadful existence, but I suggest that's simply not so. As Sandra said, Tina liked to sit outside. She liked to watch a fire, and which one of us doesn't like to sit there and watch a fire and think all kinds of thoughts? She would laugh at windshield wipers on the car. She would smile whenever she saw other members of her family because she recognized them all. She could laugh, she could smile, she could cry. What more, for her, did there need to be? Her care was no different than what you would give to one of your babies and, indeed, it's no worse, just different. As Sandra put it, Tina was like a two- or three-month-old baby, and I suggest to you that your decision should be no different here in this case than it would be if the Accused had murdered a baby. Why should it be any different?

## SCENE TWENTY-SEVEN

*(Fire tower. Sound: strong wind.)*

KEITH: Maybe she wanted to live.

DOUG: They were going to operate again. Cut off part of a bone. But the pain wouldn't've stopped. That's no way to live.

KEITH: How do you know what she wanted? You're not God.

DOUG: I'm her father.

KEITH: Not the same.

DOUG: If she'd cried in the truck, I would've taken her out.

KEITH: God decides when it's time.

DOUG: She never cried.

KEITH: God's will.

DOUG: I would never hurt her.

KEITH: My granny says that all the time. God's will.

DOUG: Your granny didn't have seizures. Seizures, seizures, all day long.

KEITH: God's will.

DOUG: Stainless steel rods in her back.

KEITH: I know someone with a steel plate in his head.

DOUG: He isn't Tina. Tina is Tina.

KEITH: Tina is dead.

DOUG: Tina never had a chance. Not a fair one.

SANDRA: *(Testimony/reverb.)* When she was little I cried myself to sleep every night for a year. That's when I grieved. I did all my grieving when she was little. We lost her then.

KEITH: What you did wasn't fair.

DOUG: Don't tell me about fair and unfair. I lived with unfair every day of her life.

## SCENE TWENTY-EIGHT

*(Flashback: Courtroom.)*

BARCLAY: All of the medical personnel emphasized that Tina's parents were in the best position to try and interpret what was going on in Tina's body and in her mind. They were in the best position to assess the pain that she was in and in fact throughout Tina's life Douglas and Sandra Ramsay made every single decision that was ever made by Tina. They decided whether she would eat, what she would eat, how much she would eat. They decided whether she would roll over, whether she would sit up, whether she would have a clean diaper, whether or not — even whether or not she would have a bowel movement. I suggest no one was in a better position than Doug and Sandra Ramsay to understand what kind of pain their daughter was in, and even those who didn't know Tina perceived her to be in excruciating pain.

## Scene Twenty-Nine

*(Fire tower.)*

KEITH: I'm not going down.

DOUG: You can't stay here.

KEITH: I like it here. Safe. *(Beat.)* Safe.

DOUG: It's safer down there.

KEITH: Not for me.

DOUG: Why not?

KEITH: Not for people like me.

DOUG: What are you afraid of?

> *(KEITH doesn't reply.)*

What are you afraid of?

KEITH: *(Pause.)* You.

DOUG: Me?

KEITH: You.

DOUG: Why me?

KEITH: *(Pause.)* Are you going to kill me, too?

DOUG: *(Emotionally winded.)* What?

KEITH: Like you killed Tina.

DOUG: I would never hurt you.

KEITH: You killed Tina. We're the same.

DOUG: You're not the same.

KEITH: Same, same.

DOUG: Not true.

KEITH: Same because we're different.

DOUG: Tina had severe cerebral palsy. You —

KEITH: I've got Down's.

DOUG: You can't compare. It's two different — You don't understand.

KEITH: *You* don't understand.

DOUG: Tina was my daughter. You're my friend.

KEITH: A freak.

DOUG: You're not a freak.

KEITH: Some people say so. A freak of nature. Like Tina.

DOUG: You're not Tina.

KEITH: You killed her because she was different.

DOUG: Because of the pain.

KEITH: Pain made her different. If she had no pain, she wouldn't be different. You wouldn't have killed her.

DOUG: She was suffering.

KEITH: You don't kill something because it's different. It's not right. That's what my granny says.

DOUG: I wasn't thinking of you when . . .

KEITH: When you killed Tina. *(Beat.)* When are you going to kill me?

DOUG: I'm not going to kill you.

KEITH: How do I know?

DOUG: Keith.

KEITH: How do I know?

DOUG: I'm not like that.

KEITH: Tina didn't know you were going to kill her.

DOUG: She couldn't understand.

KEITH: She couldn't protect herself.

> *(DOUG steps forward.)*

Stay away.

DOUG: I'm not going to hurt you.

KEITH: Don't touch me.

DOUG: We can climb down the tower together.

KEITH: I'm staying. I'm safe.

DOUG: You're safe down there.

KEITH: Stand back.

> *(Sound/biz: DOUG steps forward to comfort KEITH. KEITH misinterprets the gesture. They struggle briefly. KEITH begins to cry.)*

Don't kill me. Please don't kill me.

## SCENE THIRTY

*(Flashback: Courtroom. Duelling lawyers.)*

BARCLAY: I urge you, when you look at this case, to look at it and say, what is the right thing to do in this case?

CHISHOLM: What gives Douglas Ramsay the right to wipe out potentially the next thirty years of Tina's life?

BARCLAY: If my client has committed a sin against God, God will judge him.

CHISHOLM: This is but one man's abhorrent decision because he no longer valued Tina's life as he did that of his other children.

BARCLAY: The only thing we're here to deal with today is whether or not the highest legal sanction known to Canadian law should apply to Douglas Ramsay. Should he be categorized as a first degree murderer?

CHISHOLM: I can only state that this was a murder most foul, callous, cold, calculating, heartless, and not motivated by anything other than making his own life easier.

BARCLAY: I don't wish any of you to get the idea that in any way this trial is anything more than the trial of the guilt or innocence of Douglas Ramsay.

CHISHOLM: So the question arises, what is or what was Douglas Ramsay's cause, and I use that phrase because in an interview he said he wasn't taking up anyone else's cause, so what was his cause?

BARCLAY: This is not a cause. This isn't going to start some slippery slope argument that you need be worried about.

CHISHOLM: Are we saying that those who wish or care for us can determine our fate?

BARCLAY: Nothing about this case *per se* legalizes euthanasia.

CHISHOLM: Does the philosophy become, since we brought you into this world we can decide when you leave this world?

BARCLAY: You only have to deal with this set of facts.

CHISHOLM: I would simply ask you just to remember and look at photo 32 in Exhibit P-1 of Tina. Think of her. Just for a moment.

BARCLAY: You only have to deal with what's the right thing in this set of facts.

CHISHOLM: She had presence.

BARCLAY: We only need to be concerned here about the justice of this case and whether or not your conscience would feel right in sending this man away with a conviction for first degree murder.

CHISHOLM: She had the right to live.

## SCENE THIRTY-ONE

*(Fire tower.)*

KEITH: *(Crying; frightened.)* I don't want to die.

DOUG: I don't want you to die.

KEITH: Don't do to me what you did to Tina.

DOUG: No.

KEITH: Just because I'm different.

DOUG: No.

KEITH: I'm scared.

DOUG: I'm holding you.

KEITH: Don't hurt me.

DOUG: Never.

KEITH: You hurt her.

DOUG: I didn't see it like that.

KEITH: You hurt me.

DOUG: I see that now.

KEITH: *(Cries.)* Tina. Tinatinatina. *(Wipes his nose, sniffles.)* Why're you crying?

## SCENE THIRTY-TWO

*(Flashback: Courtroom.)*

JUDGE: There is no joy in this for anyone. I know you believe you did the right thing and many people will agree with it; however, the criminal law is unremitting when it comes to the taking of human life for whatever reason. Life was not kind to Tina but it was a life that was hers to make of what she could. I am left with no option but to order that you be sentenced to imprisonment for life without eligibility for parole until you have served ten years of the sentence. Mr. Ramsay, is there anything you want to say?

DOUG: I still feel I did what was right.

JUDGE: Yes, anything else?

DOUG: Well, my wife mentioned that it's not a crime to cut her leg off, not a crime to stick a feeding tube in her stomach, not a crime to let her lie there in pain for another 20 years. I don't think — I don't think you people are being human.

## SCENE THIRTY-THREE

*(Fire tower.)*

PIERCE: *(Off; from below tower.)* Doug? *(Beat.)* Doug, what's happening up there?

DOUG: We're coming down.

KEITH: What about the horse?

DOUG: Horse?

KEITH: The horse I carved for Tina.

DOUG: Let's leave it here. She would've liked it up here.

KEITH: She loved watching fires.

DOUG: *(Pause.)* She did.

KEITH: You wanna go down first?

DOUG: You go. I'll follow.

*(The End.)*

# Conversations with Writers VI:
## Timothy Findley

*Most people know that Tiff Findley, or Sir Tiffy, as he may yet come to be known, was an actor long before he published his first novel. As you may not know, he was — and is — an accomplished piano player. And, may I say, simply a lovely guy to talk to.*

PETER GZOWSKI  Timothy Findley, "Tiff," as his friends call him, is a man of music as well as a man of words. His last novel, still on the best-sellers list after a year and a half, is *The Piano Man's Daughter*. His new book resounds with music as well. It's a novella, and it's called *You Went Away*. The title comes from a popular song of the early 1940s, "You'll Never Know." Timothy Findley is with me now in Toronto, and to my great pleasure I can say he is at the piano.

TIMOTHY FINDLEY  Hey, hey, hey.

PG  Now what is it with you and the pianoman? There's a pianoman in the novella.

TF  Well, the father in the family plays the piano all the time. Pianos have always been part of my life, Peter. My mom's father had a piano factory in Oshawa, and there was always a piano in the house. Everybody gathered around the piano and we did all that wonderful thing of singing together. When Dad and Mom gave parties and my brother and I were up in our beds as little children, one of my most vivid memories is of the songs drifting up getting drunker and drunker as the evenings wore on. All the old songs — once you've got them in your bloodstream they never leave.

PG  Would you honour us?

TF  I will try.

PG  This is a great moment in Canadian music and literature.

[TF plays]

PG  Incredible. On *Morningside* tomorrow, Oscar Peterson to talk about his new novel. You love the piano keyboard?

TF  Oh, I do.

PG  But in the acknowledgements of the new book you thank Bill Whitehead for denying you the use of the word processor. You couldn't get off page one?

TF  I can't get off page one. I really can't. I stay there for two weeks. It's because you have that visual thing on the screen so that it looks like the printed page. I love the design of writing as well as the content of writing. I love making the paragraphs balanced and the dialogue balanced in such and such a way, and if it's there in front of me, and I have a keyboard that allows me to change it in front of my eyes, I just never get off of page one.

PG  Now in the endpapers there's some of the text in handwriting?

TF  Yeah.

PG  Is this your handwriting?

TF  That is my handwriting.

PG  Do you know what we've done?

TF  What?

PG  Couldn't resist. We took it to a handwriting analyst.

TF  Oh, God, Peter.

PG  Elaine Charal of Positive Strokes. Want to hear some of the things she said?

TF  Yes.

PG  "The writer is a visionary or a dreamer with a rich fantasy life." You look up with trepidation here.

TF  No, not at all. That's wonderful. Go on.

PG  You show an ability to think about and to project long-term plans and goals.

TF  That's not true at all. That's what Bill does, but I'm not sure I do. He stood over me while I was writing that, Peter, guiding my hands.

PG  What is your long-term plan?

TF  Oh, the long-term goals and plans are now taking shape . . . It's sad, in some ways. Bill Whitehead and I are having to leave Stone Orchard, where we've lived now for thirty-two years.

PG  I heard this, and I'm saddened by it. I had the pleasure of visiting you there and I know how rooted you are in that place.

TF  It's just like Mother Earth, the whole place. But our lives are going to be quite splendid in other ways because we've bought a very small house in the south of France where I can go and write.

PG  Are you a knight in France?

TF  I'm a knight, yes, heavens. Isn't it extraordinary?

PG  Sir Tiff?

TF  Or Sir Tiffy, if you like. I'm a Chevalier dans L'Ordre des Arts et des Lettres. It was a wonderful ceremony and great fun and I'm very proud of it. But to go back to the move — the other half of the move, so that people don't think that we're leaving Canada, because we sure as hell ain't doing that — we're going to go and live in Stratford, Ontario. It's a beautiful town. We're going to live that part of our lives in a condo. Something we thought we'd never do, but we have to have somewhere we can walk away and close the door and not have to worry about animals and gardens and that kind of thing.

PG But that lovely place that's meant so much to you — there are occasional moods of . . . echoes of . . . dislocation and being away from home in *You Went Away*, and I wonder if that's part of leaving Stone Orchard, leaving the home you love so much.

TF It's very much a part of it, I think. I don't know how other people remember things in their childhood, but I can remember feeling that the anchor of where we lived was so secure. It was not a very large house but it was beautiful and it had a wonderful garden. You could climb over the back wall and go straight into the ravines of Rosedale and there you were, in this natural world beyond the garden world and you had those two worlds as part of your childhood. That's what living at Stone Orchard has been like, as well, but in the novella, the characters live in the house where we lived on Crescent Road.

PG And Matthew, by my calculation, is born almost at the same time as Timothy Findley.

TF That's right.

PG Is this the first time your characters have been exactly in sync with you in time?

TF Yes, and that's quite deliberate. But it must be made clear that while the pattern in this book, the storyline, the drinking, womanizing father, the mother who follows him as long he's still in Canada during the war (he's in the air force), the discombobulated children always being left behind in someone else's home — that all happened to us, but my father is not like Graeme and my mother was not like Mi, the wife in the story.

PG Mi short for Michael.

TF Yes, she's called Michael Maude. This is what verifies the fact that they are wholly fictional characters: they come with their names. When I met her in my mind, she had a name: Michael Maude. And I thought, What a strange name, but if that's your name, so be it, and I call her Mi.

PG Now, where do the photographs fit in? There's a delicious picture on the cover that I want to ask about.

TF Isn't that a great photograph?

PG Yeah, but who is it?

TF  We don't know. It's from an archive you can gain access to if you want to go through for such things as posters or covers of books.

PG  That's the one photograph I don't think I've found the literary reference to in the text. As you begin, and throughout, you bring the photographs back, so Findley-like. The author is looking through all of these old photographs and putting them into historic —

TF  Well, do you want to know something odd, Peter?

PG  Of course.

TF  They came last. They weren't in the book at first; I had another device. There was a first-person narrative that strung the episodic story together. It didn't work — that stringing through on the first-person narrative was awful. And then this photograph turned up, and I thought, write to the photograph. The minute I started doing that I realized, there's what is going to save the pattern of the book, is to go to other photographs on the way through. Old photographs are just dazzling. They all have this mysterious anonymity, but they have power.

PG  So are there real photographs? Did you look at real photographs as part of your fictional novel?

TF  No, I looked at them in my mind — but I've seen so many in the past, the family photographs that go all the way back to the late 1800s, and the documentation of people's lives. It was the age of the camera, and the rage then was to take out the Kodak and snap a picture. And the pictures all tell stories. Every one of them.

PG  The use of the photographs is evocative to me because I've seen so many similar photographs myself, and I start to see the pictures and think about my own family.

TF  Well, this would all be a period that you would remember, I think, quite well.

PG  I kept looking and looking, thinking, I'm going to catch this rascal in an anachronism somewhere — Murray's wasn't open in Toronto then — but knowing you, you checked everything within an inch of its life.

TF  Do you know the most fascinating thing you can get from the archives in Toronto? You can get the whole of Yonge Street in different years. Every year this was done, and [the archive] tells you what every single building was on both sides of Yonge Street, including private people's houses. They would tell you who the tenants were above the stores, so then you knew you couldn't get it wrong. Having access to that kind of stuff is terrific. There was the Nifty Nook that I used to run across Yonge Street to go into and buy penny candy . . .

PG   I read through the list of penny candy and said you better have jaw-breakers in there. They were there. All the right ones.

TF   And the licorice pipes and cigars, remember them?

PG   With the red dots on them. Talk to me about war. I was five when war broke out. There's an incredibly powerful reminder that for these people, as World War Two broke out, they weren't finished with World War One. I always thought of it as the wars of two generations, but in your view — and you've thought and written a lot about war and those times — it was the same war.

TF   It *was*. It *was* the same.

PG   Graeme's brother was killed in the war in WWI and he had to go to II.

TF   Yes, and the parents of that generation of young men and women suffered it twice — the loss of their sons — because if they weren't lost in the First World War, they were very apt to be lost in the Second World War. My grandmother, too, like the grandmother in the novella, kept looking at the mantelpiece, at the photograph of the dead son, this beautiful young man. They were all so young, Peter, in the First World War. It was just crazy. *And* in the Second World War. All of that promise, gone. The burden, the cloud, it just descended over the families, and so many young women lost the young men they were passionately in love with. That reshaped everyone's life. We all lived under the cloud of memory, and it wasn't just a *memory* of a bad time, it was the *results*. You carried them forward and saw this other war shaping itself and inevitably coming (when it started in Spain and so on) and then it came crashing down at us. I think a lot of people forget . . . they sentimentalize the past, and they lose track of the fact that it destroyed family life utterly. It affected everyone, from the baby in the crib to the oldest living member of the family.

PG   Matthew's fears. The boy Matthew's fears of being killed in the war. Were they real?

TF   Oh, absolutely. When you were imperilled in those times, you were imperilled because you lost — There was no more hand to hold on to. Your parent was gone. There was nobody standing there saying, "Everything is going to be all right." They went off somewhere else and left you in somebody else's charge, or in boarding school, which is what happened to me. I felt totally abandoned.

PG  Did boarding school start with an S and end with an Andrew's?

TF  That's right. It was St. Andrew's, and it had its bleak moments. But there were also these sinking ships, Peter, and if you had a vivid imagination — as I did as a kid — the image of all those children struggling in the water made you feel, but this *is* about children. It isn't just these romantic men who go off and fight in a war — it was reduced to drowning kids. And if you were a kid, that made you feel, this could happen to me.

PG  Did the women in some ways have it worse than the men? They were left behind. They didn't have the comradeship of the barracks. They didn't have the swashbuckling.

TF  I think that it was a terrible time for women, another of the unacknowledged things, because war *does* largely fall on the shoulders of men — they're the ones who have to go and fight on the battlefields. There's a scene in *You Went Away* which I wrote at very high speed — you know, some scenes in books just come, and it's like taking dictation, not inspiration but in the sense that it's unfolding in your mind. In the scene there is a dialogue between a man and a woman who have been very happily married, and still are, but he's gone, and she's gone to visit him — this is while he's still in Canada — and they have a scene in a restaurant where she just lambastes him for not recognizing what the war is doing to all of these women who have just been torn away from the men they love.

PG  This is, don't you realize you're with a man in uniform and we can't . . . ?

TF  Do you remember that? I can remember my father would say that to my mother, "Don't start yelling in here, because I'm in uniform." And they would go and yell in the street. But the tensions that this created, all those tensions, taking place over the heads of the kids. The kids sure felt it, too. It was a dreadful time.

PG  In another scene, the Spitfire flown by Red Wilson, The Ace, comes out of the fog and passes the reviewing stand, and all the romance of war is there.

TF  Yes. Everybody feels this, I think. I think it would be odd not to. The Spitfire. I remember that scene so vividly. It was a foggy day, and there was no sound, and then suddenly you heard this approaching noise. Peter, it was the most beautiful — and remains in my mind the most beautiful — airplane ever designed. This slim, beautiful thing emerged from the fog, and it brought what the Battle of Britain had been about. And it brought the sense that we can win: if this glorious machine and its wonderful young men could bring down the German air force, then we are going to win this war. As a symbol it was magical, and it was the most aesthetically beautiful thing to look at.

PG  Could you have spotted a Stuka dive bomber if it came over St. Andrew's college?

TF  Why, I think so.

PG  They had all of those silhouette things.

TF  Yes, so did we. My brother and I learned them all. We didn't have to, but we learned them voraciously. The Dornier bombers with their glass noses.

PG  If a Stuka had come over Galt, Ontario, I could have told everybody.

TF  Well, they were built to terrorize. The noise the wings made when they did that dive bombing — it was meant to create terror, and it sure as hell did.

PG  You know a lovely touch for me, for other people, too, I'm sure, is the movie stars.

TF  Yes.

PG  Where has that gone now? The movie stars — we could define ourselves by . . .

TF  Yes, yes, it was wonderful in that sense. They had class. I think now everybody comes and goes so quickly we don't have the kind of contact we did with a Bette Davis, a Ronald Colman, a Gary Cooper, a Fred Astaire. Think of the way they looked. It was magical! And their faces were huge on that screen, and you went and sat in the dark with all those other people. That was a magical experience. They were larger than life, and you didn't have access to them except through the magic of that image. People copied them. One of the women in particular in this novel, Eloise, who I really liked writing. That was fun, to write this woman who behaves like a movie star, and she even has movie-star, smart-ass dialogue, repartee. She was a lot of fun to write.

PG Did you say seven pillows of wisdom?

TF Yes. There's a character who has to sit up to sleep, and she puts up the seven pillows of wisdom up behind her.

PG If you get tired of flogging this book or doing all those other things — you're getting a lovely award tonight at Harbourfront?

TF Yes, I'm very proud of this.

PG — you can always come back and play the piano.

# THE TRIAL OF LOUIS RIEL

*One of the wonders of radio is its ability to assemble a range of expertise from virtually anywhere on earth — though Morningside, of course, ranged mostly within Canada — and one of the devices we found worked for us was to use the format of the criminal trial to look at a number of complex subjects. Later, we would examine such issues as Free Trade, Meech Lake, and the discovery of North America, but we launched this device with our own version of a real courtroom drama — the trial of Louis Riel — and when the arguments had been marshalled by some impressive lawyers and historians, we put the question to a trans-Canadian jury. Their verdict? Stay tuned.*

PETER GZOWSKI  A hundred years ago today, the North-West Rebellion was under way along the banks of the North and South Saskatchewan rivers. The rebellion pitted the Métis of the North-West, centred in the communities of St. Laurent and Batoche, against the troops of the Canadian Militia, led by Major General Frederick Middleton. The conflict ended with the capture and trial of the Métis leader, Louis "David" Riel, for the crime of treason, for which the penalty was death. A jury found Riel guilty and recommended mercy. What follows is a re-enactment of part of the speech Louis Riel made in court, following the jury verdict and before the sentence was passed.

LOUIS RIEL  You have asked me, Your Honours, if I have anything to say why my sentence should not be passed. Yes, it is on that point particularly my attention is directed. Up to this moment I have been considered by a certain party as insane, by another party as criminal, by another party as a man with whom it was doubtful whether to have any intercourse. So, there was hostility and there was contempt and there was avoidance. Today, by the verdict of the court, one of those three situations has disappeared. I suppose that after having been condemned I will cease to be called a fool and for me it is a great advantage — should I be executed. At least if I were going to be executed, I would not be executed as an insane man. Besides clearing me of the stain of insanity, clearing my career of the stain of insanity, I think the verdict that has been given against me is a proof that I am more than ordinary myself. And although I consider myself only as others, yet by the will of God, by His providence, by the circumstances which have surrounded me for fifteen years, I think that I have been called on to do something which, at least in the North-West, nobody had done yet. And in some way, I think that, to a certain number of people, the verdict against me today is a proof that maybe I am a prophet. Maybe Riel is a prophet, he suffered enough for it.

PG  The words of Louis Riel on his own behalf at his trial. We all know how that trial ended. Louis Riel was sentenced to death and hanged on a cold Regina morning, November 16, 1885. The debate over that decision still rages, making Riel one of the most controversial figures in Canadian history. Now *Morningside* enters the fray with a look at Louis Riel, what he stood for then and what he means to us now.

We do so in the form of a Commission of Inquiry whose purpose is to answer the question: Should Louis Riel be pardoned? I will adopt the role of Commissioner. I'll be assisted in my inquiry on the one hand by Ian Scott, QC, a Toronto lawyer, Ontario MPP, and former Chief Counsel for the Berger Inquiry. Mr. Scott will act as Counsel for the petitioners, those who favour a pardon for Riel. On the other hand I will rely on the advice of Claude Thompson, QC, president of the Canadian Bar Association, who will act as Counsel for the respondents, those who oppose a pardon for Riel.

Both Mr. Scott and Mr. Thompson will call on two expert witnesses each to help them establish their case. For Mr. Scott, George Woodcock, one of Canada's foremost men of letters and the author of fifty or more books, ranging in subject from poetry to political commentary to history. He's written dramas on the subject of the Riel years and a biography of Riel's closest associate in the 1885 rebellion, Gabriel Dumont. And Elmer Ghostkeeper, a Métis from Alberta, a member of the Constitutional Committee of the Métis National Council — an organization representing Métis across Canada — and a former president of the Alberta Federation of Métis Settlements Association. Mr. Ghostkeeper practises as a private consultant in Edmonton. Those are Mr. Scott's witnesses.

Mr. Thompson's witnesses are Professor Thomas Flanagan, who teaches political science at the University of Calgary and is one of the foremost authorities on the subject of Riel and the rebellion of 1885. He is the author of four books concerning Riel, including, most recently, *Riel and the Rebellion: 1885 Reconsidered*, and he's a major contributor to the University of Alberta's Riel project. And Professor Desmond Morton, who teaches history at Erindale College at the University of Toronto and is a highly respected Canadian historian. He is the author of several books, among them *The Last War Drum: The North-West Campaign of 1885*. He's also written numerous papers and articles on Riel and his treatment by historians and others.

Finally, we have chosen a jury of twelve *Morningside* listeners from across the country. They will listen carefully to what is said here, then give us the benefit of their opinion. Ladies and gentleman of the jury, without further ado I declare this inquiry open. We will begin with some opening statements for the petitioners. Mr. Scott?

IAN SCOTT Mr. Commissioner, ladies and gentleman of the jury, Louis
Riel was executed by the federal government at Ottawa for a treason
defined by an archaic fourteenth-century law. He was executed
notwithstanding the unanimous recommendation of mercy that was
made by his jury. You will hear that throughout his life, and even at
its end, Louis Riel believed in the Canadian Confederation. In 1870
he was instrumental in bringing Manitoba and its Métis population
into Confederation. Without his influence, that might not have been
accomplished. He thus effectively permitted the white settlement of
the West to proceed, so that Sir John A. Macdonald's objective of a
nation from sea to sea could be realized. Long before 1885 the Métis
in Western Canada had a significant tradition. That population had
already advanced in an orderly way to form a viable community
under which its people were self-governed. By the 1880s, however,
the intolerance, lack of understanding, and political agenda of the
John A. Macdonald government at Ottawa sought to impose its own
vision of society on all, including the Métis nation. A rebellion followed. It is our case that Riel was, as a Métis and a Canadian, loyal
to the best traditions of Canadian political life. He was required to
defend those traditions in the interest of his people against an auto-
cratic, remote authority. Among Canadian heroes it is our submission he rightly ranks with Louis-Joseph Papineau and William Lyon
Mackenzie, two other rebels who have fared better at the hands of
history. We will be asking you, the jury, having heard the evidence,
to grant him a pardon. Thank you, Mr. Commissioner.

PG Mr. Scott, thank you, and a formidable task awaits you. Mr.
Thompson, your opening statement, if you would.

CLAUDE THOMPSON Thank you, Mr. Commissioner, ladies and gentleman of the jury. I propose to approach the issue in three different
aspects. First, a pardon perhaps could be justified even after a convicted person has died, if the government concludes that the
convicted person was not guilty, that he had been wrongly convicted. The purpose of that would be to provide some satisfaction and
belated justice to his memory and for the satisfaction of his family.
Now, I believe that my witnesses will explain that Mr. Riel was guilty
of breaking the law of Canada, that he was convicted according to
our laws and to the standards that existed in 1885, and that there is
insufficient justification to say today that he was not guilty.

Second, a pardon could perhaps be justified for a convicted person who, although he was guilty, has suffered enough. The pardon then is a display of mercy by the government that's willing to forgive. Now, in my view such a pardon would only serve to anger those people like the Métis people today who see Mr. Riel as a symbol of the justice of their demands. A pardon that forgives Mr. Riel for his conduct would in my view serve no useful public purpose.

And third, perhaps a pardon could be justified whether Mr. Riel was guilty or not, looking to the benefit of the Métis people and the political causes that have chosen to adopt Riel as their modern champion. Some have used his name, his history, and his myths to justify social action. A pardon for Mr. Riel could be used to support causes including native people's rights, bilingualism, biculturalism, Western Canada rights, and even increased provincial transfer payments. In my view a pardon in those terms is completely unjustified. It would amount to nothing more than an intervention into the modern political arena. It would send confusing, misleading, and conflicting messages across our land, and would satisfy no one.

PG  Mr. Thompson, I thank you among other things for making clear that your case is in today's terms. Mr. Scott, you have two witnesses. I will ask you to call them in whatever order you would like and whatever pattern. If you would like to go back and forth between witnesses, fine.

MR. SCOTT  Thank you, Mr. Commissioner. I would like to begin by asking my witness, Mr. Ghostkeeper, what you think a pardon for Riel would accomplish today.

ELMER GHOSTKEEPER  Thank you, Mr. Scott. I'd like to begin with a prayer. This is a Métis tradition of beginning an important event or celebration.

Oh, Louis Riel
who through the goodness of God
and to give us an example
of obedience
now that you are near to God

Be our advocate
and carry to the God

of Heaven and Earth
the little sufferings
which we endure
and the desire of following the path
which you have so generously traced

We beg
through our Lord
Jesus Christ
that you give us the strength
to achieve the Great Work
which you have begun
for the welfare of the Métis people
and of the world

Amen

Mr. Scott, it is my understanding that the pardon is partially granted, and I can justify this by saying that the Métis are now included in Section 35 of the Constitution of Canada. That section says the aboriginal peoples of Canada include the Indian, Inuit, and Métis, and that the existing aboriginal treaty rights are recognized and affirmed. I've had the opportunity to negotiate that clause, beginning here in Alberta in 1981. It means to me that we do have affirmed and recognized rights in the Constitution. It is now our work to implement those rights. In my mind and the minds of Métis, Riel has been partially pardoned.

MR. SCOTT Thank you, Mr. Ghostkeeper. Mr. Woodcock, how would you characterize the situation of the Métis in the North-West in the years before 1885?

GEORGE WOODCOCK The Métis had been a hunting people. They depended on buffalo herds, and by about 1880 the herds were diminished almost to extinction. Many of the Métis had the foresight to anticipate this and, particularly in the community of St. Laurent, they had established a kind of government of their own which they hoped and the priests hoped would carry them over into a different era, an era when land would become more important than the buffalo herds.

In 1873, they established a community of St. Laurent, with its council with Gabriel Dumont as president. From all evidence this seems to have worked extremely well. It was a well-run community. In 1875, the Mounted Police moved in. There was a small confrontation, but at that time the authorities in Ottawa, and also Lord Carnarvon, who was Colonial Secretary, remarked that the government the Métis had set up was totally justified in the circumstances and they were only to be praised for having established a government where there was no government. So I think the whole matter of civic responsibility, the feeling of civic responsibility, was very strong among the Métis at that time.

Then they began petitioning for land, for confirmation of their holding of the land. The first petition was sent in by the Métis of Qu'Appelle as early as 1873. The first petition from the South Saskatchewan went in, I believe it was 1878. This was seven years before the rebellion. They were already putting their case to Ottawa, and this continued until Riel was invited to the South Saskatchewan in 1884. Through a series of extremely frustrating months it led to the point where the Métis felt that there was no alternative but to rebel.

MR. SCOTT Mr. Woodcock, can you tell us perhaps what the attitude of the Ottawa government was to the Métis in the years before 1885 and the rebellion?

MR. WOODCOCK I think it was largely one of indifference and ignorance. They knew comparatively little about the Métis in the far Prairies. They had the feeling that they'd solved the whole problem in 1870 at the Red River when they had made land grants, so they were not in a hurry to investigate the matter. It was not until a few weeks before the Rebellion that Macdonald announced there was going to be a Committee of Inquiry into the Métis claims to land. So that they were neglected for a long time and this aroused not only their own protest but the protest of church leaders in the West, other people in the West. Even people like Charles Mair, the poet who had been very much against the Métis in the early Red River Rising, warned of the danger of neglecting them, or neglecting their demands.

MR. SCOTT Mr. Ghostkeeper, do you agree with that recitation of the background history?

MR. GHOSTKEEPER  Yes, I do.

MR. SCOTT  Mr. Woodcock, I'd like to ask why the Métis felt obliged to resort to violence as they did in 1885.

MR. WOODCOCK  As events moved to a crisis point, there had been a great deal of dissatisfaction among the young Métis, and people like Gabriel Dumont and his relatives were impatient. Being old Prairie fighters who had fought with the Indians in the past, they felt that one of the solutions to any problem was the solution of force. In my view Riel was a moderating influence. Possibly one of the historic ironies of the situation is that Riel tended to talk about violence, and then when it came to using violence he was very reluctant to do so.

MR. SCOTT  Mr. Ghostkeeper, do you think there was any practical alternative to the rebellion in 1885?

MR. GHOSTKEEPER  No, I do not.

PG  Mr. Ghostkeeper, would you agree with Mr. Woodcock's point about Riel being reluctant to use violence? Riel's reluctance to use violence — Louis Riel continues to be a symbol. Is that part of his importance now?

MR. GHOSTKEEPER  Yes, an important part. Let me give you an example, in 1985, here in Alberta, on the Métis settlements. Métis settlements are areas of land set aside under the Métis Betterment Act with certain rules and regulations, and one of them is permission for right of entry for oil and gas companies. A number of times, the oil companies did not seek permission for right of entry. We've had to put up road blocks to demonstrate that we are the owners of the land and resources. In a similar manner, on a couple of occasions we've had to go to the legal route. Some people would like to use other means, and it's very difficult.

PG  You're saying that the example of Louis Riel helps to plead against violence or against more extreme measures in the 1980s?

MR. GHOSTKEEPER  That's right.

MR. SCOTT  Mr. Woodcock, were there other legitimate complaints that the Métis nation had?

MR. WOODCOCK  I think the land claim was the principal one, because their whole survival, their whole future depended on it. Another grievance was that they had no representative on the council of the

North-West Territories. This was an appointed body, and when eventually a representative was appointed it was a man called Pascal Breland, who was in favour of the government. He had opposed Riel during the rising on the Red River, and so he was not regarded favourably by the Métis. They didn't regard him as a true representative. I think almost everyone in the territory had a grievance about their representation on the council — not only the Métis, but also the people of mixed blood who were of English and Scottish decent, and also the white settlers.

MR. SCOTT  Mr. Woodcock, was there, in the terms of 1885, any practical course that was open to the Métis people other than rebellion? Why did the government treat Riel differently than Papineau and Mackenzie, two rebels who were pardoned?

PG  I don't think Papineau and Mackenzie were pardoned, Mr. Scott.

MR. SCOTT  They weren't executed.

DESMOND MORTON  They were never tried.

PG  Desmond Morton — well, perhaps we'll get Professor Morton on. They were not tried, I think is what Professor Morton is saying.

MR. SCOTT  Well, that makes my point even more graphic. Mr. Woodcock, why is it that the two rebels of Upper and Lower Canada were not tried after their rebellions, and why is it that Louis Riel was?

MR. WOODCOCK  I think they weren't tried after their rebellion because they had departed the country and they weren't available to be tried.

PG  I don't think that's the answer Mr. Scott was wanting to hear, Professor Woodcock.

MR. WOODCOCK  No, but may I continue?

PG  Yes.

MR. WOODCOCK  We have not merely the example of Papineau and Mackenzie, who I believe were given amnesty. I don't think they were pardoned. They came back under an amnesty. We also have all the other leaders of the 1885 rebellion. Only Riel was tried under the barbarous Statute of Treasons, which was initiated by a feudal monarch in the fourteenth century, and it had no place in a democratic country in the nineteenth century. He was the only one tried under that statute. All the rest were tried under the laws regarding Treason Felony, for which the death penalty was not mandatory. In the year after the rebellion there was general amnesty of all of the people involved. This meant that people like Gabriel Dumont, who were at least as responsible for the rebellion as Louis Riel, came back free of any punishment.

PG  You're trying to argue that Riel has been singled out for reasons that are . . .

MR. SCOTT  Riel was singled out. That's our case, Mr. Commissioner. Mr. Woodcock, can you deal with the other part of my question? In terms of 1885 and bearing in mind the neglect of the Macdonald government, was there any other practical course — and I emphasize practical — that was open to the Métis nation?

MR. WOODCOCK  There is always, I suppose, the practical course of following — the example of Gandhi, of course, didn't exist at that time — and carrying out non-violent civil disobedience. That was not in the tradition of the period, and I doubt if it occurred to anyone at the time. Given the traditions of Indian warfare, the violence seemed the obvious way out. In historical terms, there may not have been an alternative. I think that now, with examples of successful non-violent actions like Gandhi's in India, there might be an alternative.

PG  Mr. Scott, I'll give you one more question and then I'm going to ask Mr. Thompson if he has a question or two.

MR. SCOTT  I am satisfied, Mr. Commissioner. That is the case for the petitioners in this instance.

PG  Mr. Thompson, I'll give you a question or two of Mr. Scott's witnesses before you present your own, if you wish.

MR. THOMPSON  Yes. Mr. Ghostkeeper, I think you were telling us that, as far as you are concerned, the question is not whether Mr. Riel was guilty of crimes according to the law of Canada — because I suggest he was — but rather you're interested in having the legitimate claims of the Métis people recognized today? Is that correct?

MR. GHOSTKEEPER  Well, I think that the legitimate claims of the Métis in 1870 and 1885 and in 1985 are the same.

MR. THOMPSON  Yes, but you're not arguing, are you, that Mr. Riel did not break the law of Canada?

MR. GHOSTKEEPER  I'd like to make one point: Riel is representative of Métis people. He was in 1870, in 1885, and he is in 1985, and in my mind he will be forever. One cannot separate Riel from the Métis and the elected provisional government of that time. I think that's a major mistake. It is my understanding that Riel was charged with high treason under a 1345 treason law passed by King Edward III. This law was 540 years old and very antiquated. It's interesting that he was the only one charged under that particular law.

MR. THOMPSON I'm not here to argue against the legitimate aboriginal claims of the Métis people. I'm trying to explore with you and Mr. Woodcock what good a pardon will do. Mr. Woodcock, do you think that a pardon that was saying, Well, Mr. Riel broke the law, but we don't see any purpose in continuing him as a convicted person — would that be useful?

MR. WOODCOCK For a century the Métis have been a people who have been disadvantaged in many ways, largely through the neglect of the majority. I think the pardon only has a symbolic value in the context of a general reconciliation and a serious consideration of the demands of the Métis people. A pardon that said that he had been guilty and that he was forgiven would be useless.

PG Mr. Woodcock, a pardon in your view, then, is as much apology as pardon?

MR. WOODCOCK Yes. Yes.

PG Mr. Thompson, I ask you to present your case, if you would.

MR. THOMPSON I'd like to begin with Professor Morton. I want you to address your mind to one point that was made. In your view, was violence necessary in 1885?

MR. MORTON No, it was not. It's always an attractive option for excited people, and what happened in 1885 was that a Half-Breed Claims Commission was appointed. It came west with the purpose of resolving the land dispute. Perhaps it wasn't enough, and perhaps it wasn't early enough, but it was on the way when the rebellion began.

MR. THOMPSON Professor Flanagan, what was Mr. Riel's role in the rebellion, and what were his motives?

THOMAS FLANAGAN I tend to see his role as central in provoking the rebellion. I think his motives had little to do with a particular grievance about land claims on the banks of the South Saskatchewan River. He had a more grandiose vision. He thought of himself as a divinely inspired prophet. That's why he called himself David, a name adopted from David in the Old Testament. He believed that the Métis were the owners of the North-West, and that Canadian sovereignty didn't apply. On top of that he was engaged in behind-the-scenes dealings, long-distance dealings with the federal government to try to get a payment of cash. He let it be understood that if he received this cash he would leave the country. I think there are a number of strands of motivation quite remote from the alleged grievances.

MR. THOMPSON Now, Professor Morton. It's been argued that Mr. Riel was discriminated against, treated differently than Papineau and others. What do you say to that?

MR. MORTON Papineau and Mackenzie both left the country. After an interval of time they repented their rebellion, quite publicly and quite openly. They were allowed back under an amnesty, as commonly happens after rebellions. Riel decided not to leave, not to escape, as Dumont had urged. The two men became separated in the confusion after the Battle of Batoche. Riel's intention was to have a grand state trial in Ottawa, before the Supreme Court, after which, he explained in a letter to Macdonald, he expected to be invited back to be premier of Manitoba. Whether this suggests that he was insane or simply, as one man said, a pronounced crank, I can't say. He was around in that dangerous period for rebels, when rebellion is just over and the government searches for the guilty parties. And they searched. They investigated quite intensely, expecting to find a lot of supporters for the rebellion. The government attorneys, led by some of the ablest legal counsel in Canada at the time, came to one indisputable conclusion: Louis Riel was the only person who could have launched the rebellion.

MR. THOMPSON Professor Flanagan, perhaps I could ask you, do you think Riel was dealt with the way he was because of his race or his religion?

MR. FLANAGAN No, I don't see any evidence for that proposition. The rebellion was, after all, largely a Métis affair, and the government, as Professor Morton has mentioned, made an assiduous effort to find the so-called white rebels. They thought they were there, but they couldn't find them, and they were left with Riel.

MR. THOMPSON Professor Morton, back to you. What, in your view, would be the consequence of a pardon granted by the federal government today to Mr. Riel?

MR. MORTON  The first argument is to say he was not guilty. I think no one studying the trial in the terms of 1885 could argue that. The second argument, that a pardon would humiliate the Métis people, I can't speak for, because I'm not of that group, but I can certainly understand the argument. The third argument, that it sends a message — it seems to me it would send a confusing and dangerous message. Riel's role in the rebellion was to turn a period of frustration among the Métis — which all of us can understand and sympathize with — into violence. There was no question that Riel preached violence, and if Riel was singled out it was not because of his religion or his race but because of his education and his eloquence. It was that education and eloquence which made him a leader. How often have we seen people of eloquence preach revolution, preach bloodshed, and allow other, simpler people to go forth and commit that bloodshed and carry the consequences? I think that's the message we would be sending forth: that preachers of revolution and rebellion and bloodshed should go free, but those who commit it, simpler, less cultivated souls, should pay the full bloody penalty.

MR. THOMPSON  Professor Flanagan, what in your view would be the consequence of a pardon to Mr. Riel?

MR. FLANAGAN  I'd have to support the extraordinarily percipient remarks of Desmond Morton. Earlier speakers commented on Riel's reluctance to use violence, but that was a personal reluctance. It's true he didn't want to be the one with his finger on the trigger, but he preached it, and the decision to form a provisional government, to cut the telegraph lines, to take hostages, this is traceable to Riel's inspiration. The message of pardoning the man who sparked a turn towards violence is precisely the wrong kind of message.

PG  Professor Morton, are you saying that Riel was a preacher of violence, but was personally reluctant to perpetrate violent acts? Is that the picture that is being offered?

MR. MORTON  In 1885, a number . . .

PG  A sayer, but not a doer?

MR. MORTON  A sayer. In 1870 perhaps a doer, as well, but a sayer in 1885. In the Duck Lake Battle, for example, when the battle was well under way and some twenty people lay dead or dying on both sides, Riel tried to stop his followers from shooting as the police retreated over the hill (incidentally defeating his own purpose in organizing the encounter).

MR. THOMPSON Professor Flanagan, there's another aspect of this perhaps you should tell the jury about. What was the fate of Mr. Scott a couple of years earlier? What happened to him?

MR. FLANAGAN Yes, I couldn't help but be struck by the irony that your counterpart is also Mr. Scott.

PG Ian Scott we have here. I think it's Thomas Scott we're talking about a century ago.

MR. FLANAGAN Thomas Scott staged a rebellion within a rebellion, if you will, in 1870. He was part of a group who tried to overthrow the provisional government in Manitoba, and he was thrown in prison along with several others. He was very difficult to control in prison, and eventually, when the Métis had enough of him, they took him out and shot him . . .

MR. THOMPSON What did Mr. Riel have to do with that?

MR. FLANAGAN . . . without a trial. Riel was president of the provisional government, and he organized a court martial before which Scott was placed. When the court martial gave a sentence of death, Riel okayed it and allowed it to go forth. He could have stopped it. The irony is, here you have a man who is in prison already and could have been controlled. They could have tied him up and thrown him in a corner, let him die of pneumonia if they felt that strongly about it. But no, they took the most brutal and direct way possible. It's absurd to talk about Riel as the opponent of violence. He was willing to use it in a calculated way when he thought it would serve his interest.

MR. THOMPSON Professor Morton, do you agree with that analysis of the Scott situation?

MR. MORTON What Riel said in justification was that, We must make Ottawa respect us. That was his justification at the time for the execution of Scott, which he felt was a legal act by his provisional government. In 1885 he set up a provisional government again, and he said that this rebellion would be not a patch on the 1870 affair, that there would be bloodshed. May I quote a brief phrase cited at his trial by a Scottish Métis named Thomas McKay? McKay was testifying about what was said at Batoche. I'm sorry it's double hearsay, but it's the best evidence we have. Riel says, "You don't know what we are after. It is blood. We want blood. Everybody that is against us is to be driven out of the country. It's a war of extermination." Later he speaks to a doctor from Saskatoon and warns him to go back to Saskatoon and to pray with the people of Saskatoon because they will soon face their Maker.

MR. THOMPSON  Thank you. Mr. Commissioner, those are the questions I have of my witnesses.

PG  Thank you, Mr. Thompson. Mr. Scott, I'll give you a moment or two if you wish to cross-examine Mr. Thompson's witness, and if you'd care to reintroduce either of your witnesses, we have a few minutes.

MR. SCOTT  I don't intend to deal with the Scott incident, which occurred some fifteen years before the events we're now talking about. I'd like to ask Professor Flanagan this. I read your book, *Prophet of the New World*. Professor Flanagan, in your book you say Riel instituted rebellion in the face of the annihilation of his people's way of life. Why have you changed your view?

MR. FLANAGAN  At one time, I have to confess, I accepted the conventional view articulated by Professor Woodcock, that the Métis had very little alternative in 1885. But going back over the evidence in more recent years led me to change my mind and to see that the Métis grievances, the particular grievances of the people in the south of Saskatchewan, were well on the way to being resolved.

MR. SCOTT  Professor Morton, we know a lot more in 1985 than we did in 1885 about the efficacy of Royal commissions. If we accept Professor Flanagan's 1970s view that Riel and the Métis people were facing the annihilation of their way of life, was an appointment of a Royal commission an appropriate governmental response?

MR. MORTON  It wasn't a Royal commission . . .

MR. SCOTT  It was a commission?

MR. MORTON  It was a commission set up to do a specific thing, which it proceeded to do in the midst of a very real debate among the Métis, themselves by no means united on this issue, about what their future should be. Many experts, Métis and otherwise, gave conflicting views. What the government in Ottawa faced wasn't so much indifference to the problem as a very genuine confusion about the right way to go, the right way to satisfy the Métis in a very difficult world. There was no shortage of land in the North-West.

There was a real problem about justifying title and securing it so the same tragedy that occurred in Manitoba after 1870 would not recur in the North-West. I can assure you there are piles and piles of conflicting evidence in the Department of the Interior papers in Ottawa, which few historians have cared to wander through because unfortunately it is very heavy going, indeed. But it was not neglect or indifference; it was legitimate confusion, which in many ways continues to the present day.

MR. SCOTT Professor Flanagan, perhaps the views of latter-day historians, variable as they are, are less interesting than the views of people who were there. W. G. Brookes was a white man and a juror at Riel's trial in 1885. Brookes said, "We often remarked during the trial that we would like to have the Minister of the Interior in the prisoner's box charged with inciting the Métis by his gross neglect and callous indifference." What do you make of that? From an on-the-spot observer who heard all the evidence?

MR. FLANAGAN This is a remark attributed to him more than forty years after the events. Remarks made that late in life aren't always reliable. More profoundly, I'd be the last to say that the federal government made no mistakes in the administration of Dominion lands. I've documented a whole series of delays and regrettable mistakes that were made with respect to Métis land claims. But the government was well on the way towards dealing with these particular grievances before the rebellion broke out. So yes, indeed, the government probably has much to answer for, but it doesn't amount to justifying an uprising. The government had started to do the right thing before the uprising took place.

PG Mr. Thompson?

MR. THOMPSON I'm content to proceed, on this evidence, direct to our submissions.

PG Gentlemen, in that case I'm going to call a brief recess and then listen to closing arguments from Mr. Thompson and Mr. Scott. Mr. Ghostkeeper, I wonder if you have a closing remark?

MR. GHOSTKEEPER Yes, I do. In regards to the Claims Commission, what the provisional government wanted to do was to make a presentation to the federal government, politicians to politicians. They did not want to be dealt with in a bureaucratic manner. Rather than sending the ministers responsible for the North-West to meet with the provisional government, the government sent this Claims Commission. That was unfair.

PG   Mr. Woodcock, anything you would like to say?

MR. WOODCOCK   I would like to talk just for a moment about the collective nature of responsibility. The rebellion was not decided on by Riel, it was decided on by a secret meeting of the leading Métis, which took place on the fifth of March. Eleven people were present, and they all signed an oath that, if necessary, they would proceed by violent action.

PG   That is an important point. Professor Morton, do you have a quick response to that?

MR. MORTON   When that was considered by the people sent out to investigate it, they felt very strongly that Riel was the most powerful personality, the most educated and the most articulate personality. There was no question that this was a rebellion that would not have occurred if Riel had not been present and pursuing an agenda, to establish this fascinating theocratic state on the South Saskatchewan River. As we know now and knew then, this was Riel's real motivation for the exciting events of '85.

PG   Professor Morton, thank you. This concludes Mr. Scott's and Mr. Thompson's presentation of their cases with their expert witnesses from around the country. We will hear closing arguments from Ian Scott, who will argue for the pardon of Louis Riel. Claude Thompson will oppose pardoning Louis Riel in 1985. From across the country we have selected a jury of twelve regular *Morningside* listeners. We will poll our jury and present their verdict and perhaps a closing comment or two from the Commissioner of the Inquiry.

   The question of the pardon of Louis Riel now falls into the hands of the two counsel who have been part of our Commission of Inquiry. First for the petitioners, Mr. Scott.

MR. SCOTT   Mr. Commissioner, ladies and gentleman of the jury, as I said in opening to you, no one disputes the fact of the rebellion, and we are not concerned with the personality of the man Riel. What we are concerned with is history. In historical hindsight, rebels frequently are seen as standing for important values, which later, on account of their efforts, frequently become an essential part of the fabric of our society. Anglo-Saxon history is full of examples. Cromwell fighting against the divine right of kings. John Adams and the Boston Patriots resisting taxation without representation. And at home, Papineau and Mackenzie against the government compacts of Upper and Lower Canada.

The case for a pardon for Riel is plain. It's my submission to you that he was not guilty in a practical sense and the appropriate remedy in the light of history is to grant him a pardon. There are four reasons I ask you to so conclude. The first is that the Métis nation, his people, were provoked, bitterly provoked, by the inactivity or neglect of the Macdonald government at Ottawa. It was right of Mr. Brookes, the juror at the trial, to say that it would have been appropriate to have the Minister of the Interior in the prisoner's box.

The second reason is that Riel, on behalf of his people, as their leader at that time, tried to stand against what Professor Flanagan a few years ago called the annihilation of his people and their traditional society. In this sense, in this critical sense, his rebellion, designed to sustain his people as an entity, was essentially defensive and, as Professor Woodcock indicated, essentially moderate.

The third reason is that Riel stands in history for the fair treatment of the rights of minorities in Canada, and we all know well that majorities must be judged by how we treat minorities.

The fourth reason is that, in the end, and in the light of history, Riel stands for the best and most creative concept of Canadian political life. That this land is no melting pot, but an open federalism in which a variety of communities of different backgrounds, races, traditions, and rules are permitted to exist with their values intact, each contributing in an important way to the national identity.

If we cannot pardon Riel in 1985, we may well be unable to deal with critical problems of minority or aboriginal rights in this country. It is because of that important symbolism that I ask you to find him not guilty and to grant him a pardon.

PG   Mr. Scott, thank you. A question, if I may, about the second of your eloquently stated points. You say it was a defensive move, and you say that Riel stood against the government. I'm curious as to your perception of the testimony you heard. Was this a violent man? Was this man dedicated to violent overthrow of our government? Or was this a man who was preaching for principles and trying to act against the violence that was rampant among his followers?

MR. SCOTT  In my submission, Mr. Commissioner, he was no more violent by nature than John Adams in Boston, or Papineau, or Mackenzie in Upper Canada. What he was faced with was the annihilation of his people. He was not seeking to overthrow any government in Ottawa. He helped create the government in Manitoba, but on the banks of the Saskatchewan he was facing annihilation of his people. In that sense his rebellion, localized there, was essentially defensive and his role, as Mr. Woodcock has made plain and as I think Professor Morton has acknowledged, was essentially moderate.

PG  Mr. Thompson.

MR. THOMPSON  Thank you, Mr. Commissioner. I propose to approach these issues as I began them. First, a pardon cannot be justified because Mr. Riel was not guilty of breaking the law of the land and therefore was wrongly convicted. There was no basis, on the evidence you have heard, by which you can conclude that the trial was not fair, that he was not accorded the justice the system allowed in 1885. Accordingly I invite you to reject the suggestion of a pardon on that grounds.

Second, there's a practice in our country whereby people can be pardoned, even though they're guilty, on the basis of the government displaying mercy. I think you should accept that no witness was prepared to justify a pardon on those grounds. I think you should accept my argument that that would simply be insulting. Insulting to the Métis people. Insulting to the very serious native rights issues which lie underneath this discussion.

We come to the third question. Forget all about the normal basis upon which we are going to grant a pardon. Should we grant a pardon anyway? Mr. Scott says the Métis people were provoked, that they reacted to violence, that they took the law into their own hands. I don't think it's right to deliver a message to Canada, and indeed the world at large, that it was appropriate for them to take the law into their own hands. It's not too long ago in our history that we watched people in the province of Quebec, because of their very strong political convictions, take the law into their own hands.

I ask you to accept the evidence presented by my witnesses, that the rebellion was unnecessary, that there was no urgency in the matter, and that what we had was a violent rebellion that caused unnecessary loss of life.

Mr. Scott says that Mr. Riel was defending his people. The evidence here is overwhelming that Mr. Riel was quite prepared to resort to violence, to stir up violence, to rely on its consequence. It was for that reason that I put the evidence involved in the murder of Mr. Scott before you. Not because Mr. Riel's murder of Mr. Scott was directly relevant to what happened in 1885, but because it puts the lie to the suggestion that Mr. Riel was not committed to a violent process.

Mr. Scott makes the point that Mr. Riel stands for fair treatment of the Métis. Am I against the fair treatment of the Métis? Of course not. Am I against the recognition of aboriginal rights in our country? Of course not. But if we are seriously concerned about these issues, then the way to deal with them is to deliver a message to our governments, both federal and provincial, that we're not satisfied with the plight of the native people in our country today, any more than we were in 1885. Don't deliver confusing, ambiguous messages pardoning a person who is guilty of a crime. If it's appropriate to amend the Charter, amend the Charter. Put in more words of the kind that Mr. Ghostkeeper approves. Turn those words into positive action. Let's do that. But let's not link the legitimate concerns for native rights on the one side with acts of violence on the other. That's what we do when we pretend that a pardon for Louis Riel is anything more than a signal that we're prepared to acknowledge the right to violence in our country provided it is done in good conscience.

I put it to you that the evidence is overwhelming, that we all want to support the concerns expressed by the Métis people, but it is not in the public interest, and indeed not in the interests of the Métis people, for us to grant a pardon today to Mr. Riel.

PG Mr. Thompson, thank you. Mr. Scott, if I may return to you for one moment. Mr. Thompson has carefully raised the matter of the breaking of the law, has said quite clearly that Louis Riel broke the law and has responded to that. You didn't. You raised no points during your arguments about the breaking of the law. Do you concede for the purposes of this inquiry that Louis Riel broke a law?

MR. SCOTT Of course, Louis Riel broke a law. Rebels almost invariably break a law. In Ontario, William Lyon Mackenzie is in our pantheon of heroes because he broke a law. Men died standing for rights that in our culture were regarded as important. Papineau is the same kind of figure in Quebec. It's our position that the Métis nation should be accorded the same respectability to their Mackenzie, to their Papineau, and that that will provide a foundation for a conciliation, as Mr. Woodcock calls it. Not only with the Métis, but with the aboriginal peoples as a whole.

PG Mr. Thompson, I asked George Woodcock at one point . . . I said a pardon would be in effect as much an apology as it would be a formal pardon. I'm not sure you responded directly to that argument.

MR. THOMPSON I would have no objection to the federal government saying directly or symbolically that its treatment of the Métis people over the years was unjust, but the evidence here . . .

PG And you wouldn't see the pardon of Louis Riel as part of that symbolic gesture?

MR. THOMPSON Not at all, because the federal government was right in trying Louis Riel and arguably right in executing him. It was a matter of judicial discretion, government discretion, whether to execute him. Implicit in a pardon of Louis Riel is a statement that what Mr. Riel did was right and what the government did was wrong. Riel was wrong because he committed murder and incited rebellion. The government defended itself. That is what I say about Mr. Riel and his pardon. Have the Métis people been unsatisfactorily or unfairly dealt with over the years and even in Mr. Riel's time? They may well have been, but let's not confuse the two issues. We run the risk of delivering a message to society that we approve acts of violence that are an integral part of the struggle of the native people.

PG Once again I thank our counsel and the expert witnesses who brought us the testimony.

## THE JURY'S VERDICT

PETER GZOWSKI In one way, at least, I had the easiest time of all of the people who have been delegated to make up their minds on the matter of pardoning Louis Riel in 1985 for the crime — treason — of which he was convicted in 1885. The other twelve are jurors chosen from the people who write to *Morningside* from time to time. The reason I say my task — I was Commissioner — was easier than that of the jurors was that I was able to listen to their conclusions as they reached them. And when I asked for a short summary of their reasons, to hear them and add them too to my own deliberations. This is not to say it was an easy task for anyone. Here for example are two of our jurors at separate moments pondering their dilemmas. First Helen Solomon of Ottawa, then Mary Maxwell Pendleton of Saskatoon.

HELEN SOLOMON You know, you say one thing but then you have to qualify it, and I'm afraid that's what I'll have to do. I would pardon Louis Riel but I don't see any reason for doing so. First, he was tried by a British law — a fourteenth-century British law — and I'm afraid I just cannot accept the validity of that law. I'm not talking whether it's a good or bad law. To me that's irrelevant. It's the fact that it's another culture. It's a British law and British to begin with, and the British got the country by force. That's the starting point and we shouldn't forget that.

PG You're voting not to pardon him, but by that vote you're saying some other things as well?

MS. SOLOMON This is not easy. I didn't realize what I was getting into. He's the hero of the Métis, and that's what counts. It doesn't matter whether we pardon him. In fact, I don't think he would care. He would worry about his conscience and his relationship to God. And since it was an illegal tribunal, who gives a damn whether he's pardoned or not? If they pardon him now I think they might do him a disservice. He might then become an excuse for all kinds of ugly politicking. It's better to keep him alive, accentuate his good qualities. Don't make it a legal issue. I don't think it's a legal issue.

MARY MAXWELL PENDLETON I thought I had my opinion before the trial, but I was certainly set back a couple of times, and I really had a difficult time coming to a verdict. I would like to say that Riel ought be pardoned but with some clarification. I don't believe Riel was wrong, and I believe a pardon would not forgive that wrong. I think I'll stick with that, although I was quite swayed by what Mr. Thompson said in the end about whether we're confusing the issue of minority peoples and violence. I think I still will stick with pardoning him.

PG Each of those jurors had doubts even about the vote she eventually cast, and one of them called back to ponder some more, although she stuck with her original ballot. From time to time, as we talked to the jurors, I had the vision of people poised on a fence able to be blown either way by a new force of argument. But other jurors were as certain as the counsel they supported had been about the positions they took, convinced one way or the other either by the force of the legal arguments or by their own understanding of the times and the people they were being asked to rule on. Here are Wendy Payton of Flin Flon, Manitoba, and Rory Waite of Calgary.

WENDY PAYTON I voted no. I believe he was guilty of the charge. He preached violence. There was evidence that he condoned it. He had delusions of grandeur. I think he wanted to be a martyr. Maybe he didn't try to escape. Because it was a political act doesn't make it any less murder. Perhaps the government at the time didn't do enough. Maybe they weren't moving fast enough, as some of the people were saying. They should have done more, but there was confusion, as there is in our time.

RORY WAITE I believe Riel was charged with high treason. And the best definition I could find is that treason is a betrayal of one's own country by waging war against it. I think he had a legitimate complaint as to whether in fact Western Canada was being governed from Ottawa at all. There's a lot of bad feeling about what happened even to this day in this part of the country because it's so much a part of our heritage. When the aboriginal leaders, including the Métis, sit down and talk to Brian Mulroney, the leader of our current government, they still can't come to a conclusion. The bone is still rubbed very raw. Justice has yet to be done.

We are talking a hundred years ago. These people were fighting for their lives, maybe not with rifles and pistols but certainly with hoes and ploughs, just to survive the winters. It was a tough life, and bloodshed in various ways and means and guises was not all that unusual.

George Washington's a hero. Why? Because George Washington won. He was a rebel. He did exactly the same thing. He led a ragtag group of people who were not being properly represented by those ruling his country, and he went against them and he won, so he's a hero. And Riel tried it, and he lost. The issue has never been settled.

PG We called our jurors from across the country, seeking a broad cross-section. It is worth emphasizing that our process was unscientific and ad hoc. Our twelve jurors good and true represent no more than one geographical cross-section of a dozen intelligent Canadians who write to *Morningside*. One point I think is worth dwelling on. Ian Scott, arguing for a pardon, suggested with a touch of irony that the prisoner in the dock in 1885 should have been not Louis Riel but Sir John A. Macdonald and his government of the day. Three jurors concurred with that view. Here are two of them, Edwin Patterson of Beamsville, Ontario, and Max Wolfe of Jemseg, New Brunswick.

EDWIN PATTERSON  I vote for pardon. You presented a hell of a problem. I probably will go on thinking about this for quite some time. Sir John A. Macdonald . . . he, I think, is the culprit at the bottom of the whole thing.

MAX WOLFE  I would pardon Riel and hang John A. Macdonald. The rebellion in 1885 — if that's what it was — really was unnecessary. It could have been avoided by some reasonable action by John A. Those poor guys had been trying to get their titles settled for years, and a stroke of the pen could have done it and prevented the whole problem.

PG  Macdonald, of course, was not in the dock. Louis Riel was. He was tried by a jury of his times, six men, and with a recommendation of mercy he was found guilty. The question posed is whether now, in the light of history and the realities of life in Canada a full century later, he should be pardoned. At first I thought the answer would be clearly that he should not. I thought our jury agreed that he had broken a law and that a pardoning now would somehow condone violent reactions to unjust laws, or could serve no real purpose in the 1980s, or might be counter-productive. But the tally grew from four-to-one against pardon, to four-all, to five-to-four in favour of pardon, then was tied again, then leaned to pardon, and then, with its final ballot, was tied. A hundred years after the original verdict we had a hung jury.

What had begun as an easy job for me, listening to the jurors deliberate their wisdom, turned into an awesomely difficult one as I tried to answer my obligations as Commissioner and to reach a con-clusion. In the end I am ruling in favour of the respondents to our petition for Mr. Thompson's case. In other words, not to pardon Louis Riel. Had the jury findings been in favour of pardon, I could have happily accepted their decision and reported it to you with my endorsement. But in light of the tie vote, I'm exercising my own judgement.

In doing so, I want to make at least one point emphatically clear. With one or two exceptions, those who voted against pardon, and I include myself, were not making a statement about Louis Riel's guilt. That he broke the legal code of his day is undisputed, even by those who argue the code might not have applied to him. Did he break the code of political and social morality we seek to apply today? That question, I think, remains arguable, and in ruling against pardon now I leave it open.

I've been troubled by the Riel case as long I've known about it. There is much about the actions of the government of my great-great-grandfather's day that upsets and offends me. There were grave injustices done in the 1880s, and there are still wrongs to redress. If reconsidering the criminality of Louis Riel leads to a more profound consideration of how to redress those wrongs, then it is a useful thing to do. If our Commission of Inquiry into this matter has raised more considerations, then it has done its job. But all the arguments weighed, I am convinced that a pardon, however nobly inspired, would be the wrong gesture in 1985, and could perhaps give us too easy a way to avoid the questions underneath.

# FIFTEEN CHERISHED LETTERS FROM
# FIFTEEN CHERISHED YEARS

⌒

*Are these my — or our — all-time favourite letters from the* Morningside
*years? Well, not necessarily. We just wanted to wrap things up with some voices
that were at the heart of all the* Morningside Papers *as well as in the soul of
the program itself. So here are fifteen we all liked. Thank you for them — as
well as for all the thousands of letters that crossed my desk from 1982 to 1997.*

It was the first year my husband, Chris, and I planted a garden. Always in May in Ontario, when it is just starting to be warm, the visit to the greenhouse and nursery to get plants is a major event, the true sign of spring. As I am a native of British Columbia, this sign of the end of winter is eagerly anticipated.

When we planted the garden, Chris and I were not yet married. With a September wedding planned, we needed to keep ourselves out of trouble all summer. As part of this endeavour, we took over the family garden at my mother's farm.

Although I have been involved in the management of the garden in the past, I had never been appointed chief organizer and weeder. In my naiveté, I planted the entire package of zucchini seeds, anticipating a few failures. When my mother and I transplanted the seeds out of the hot beds and into the main garden, all the seeds had grown into seedlings. My mother was so appalled at the number of plants that I had to sign a release form accepting full responsibility for all zucchinis.

The first zucchini out of the garden weighed between three and five pounds. My mother laughed, Chris stared, and I bought a new cookbook. As the summer progressed, the zucchinis got bigger. We were only at the farm on weekends, so keeping track of every zucchini was not as easy as I had anticipated. A few we got early, little and tender, edible in their natural form. It got to the point, however, that our families would only accept calls from us if we promised that there was not going to be a night drop of zucchini on their doorsteps.

With the wedding approaching and the zucchinis piling up in our house, Chris and I made an executive decision to make our own wedding cake. Flashing through our recipe books, lo and behold, we uncovered the perfect recipe to deal with both problems in one fell swoop — chocolate zucchini cake!

After fourteen batches of cake batter and one zucchini, two generous cups of grated zucchini per batch, we had three layers — one fourteen inches, one ten inches, and one eight inches in diameter. It was a great cake, and there were two layers left after eighty-five guests.

We did not just grow zucchinis the size of footballs. The one for the cake weighed about five pounds, and was twice as long as a football. Our latest masterpiece, in keeping with the sports comparisons, is the length of a baseball bat and three times as thick as one. My husband will no longer eat ratatouille, fried zucchini, zucchini cookies, zucchini cake or muffins, grilled zucchini, zucchini pasta sauce, Greek salad with zucchini, zucchini lasagna, or much else that includes the z-vegetable. He wants to grow something else next year.

Do you want one?

Jean A. Fulton
Ottawa

I listened with mounting disgust to your mushroom love-in. I could have guessed that British Columbians would eat so many mushrooms. I grew up in Vancouver, and I've been plagued by their fungiphilia for most of my twenty-five otherwise uncareworn years.

As with so many childhood things, my first gustatory explorations were timid and brief. Most vegetables lived in distant realms, the seas around them guarded on the nutritional charts by unappetizing monsters. Through rigorous discipline, time, and inscrutable changes in my biochemistry, I've since come to know the pleasures of the herbivore. Cabbages, kin to the already beloved salad greens, hold terrors no more, and I can foresee next conquering either the steaming muck of the squashes or the hog fodder of the parsnip and allied root crops.

However, in my otherwise insatiable hunger to expand the boundaries of my palate — in my *Drang nach Essen*, as it were — I shall ever retreat from the mushroom.

Mushrooms are primitive, as though they reached their evolutionary zenith during those first few minutes on land, when the last drops from the primordial soup dried on their puffy skin. They even retain gills, the guts of an aquatic oxygen eater, through which, instead, they perversely propagate, casting their spores upon the ground. I don't deny that this has been reproductively successful; fecundity is a trait they have in common with other early evolvers, like sharks and cockroaches. Presumably mushrooms also share with those other atavists the propensity for surviving a nuclear holocaust. Where civilized creatures are to envy the dead, mushrooms thrive. What shape is an atomic cloud?

Who could be attracted to something both bloated and chewy? What is there to admire in so base and parasitic a vegetable? When will people stop larding my dinner with them? Where do they grow, but in dank, unwashed nooks, the athlete's foot of dead trees? Finally, why must you encourage the rest of the country to emulate yet another decadent tendency of the West Coast?

I think you owe me an apology.

*Richard Poutt*
Vancouver

I first homesteaded in this country some twenty-five years ago. I remember one drizzly overcast day in the fall. I had most of my harvest in the bin and I was doing my fall cultivating when I stopped for supper. As I got off the tractor and the world was once again silent and sweet without old John puffing and snorting around the field (old John is my John Deere tractor), I heard what must have been a thousand geese from the sound of them. I ran to the house to get my gun and with some luck perhaps get one for supper. But when I came back out, the geese had not yet arrived. I thought that this must surely be a big flock to be heard from so far off. I stood there for what seemed an eternity, but it could not have been more than five minutes. As I stood there, the noise of all these thousands of snow geese rose to such an intensity that it drowned out any other sound. When they finally came into view, it was not like any flock of geese I have ever seen, but a cloud that darkened the sky. As they passed overhead I stood in awe. I could not bring myself to shoot at such a marvellous sight. The flock was more than a mile long. I know, because my farm is a mile long, and the flock was stretched the full length of the farm. When the last little straggler had finally passed overhead, I wished I had a movie camera to record all this, as surely no one would believe what I had seen, and I didn't shoot even one. But then I would only have to clean it and — well, beans and wieners didn't taste so bad. I had just started cooking my supper when I heard a second flock fly over, and it was as big as the first. I could not believe there were so many geese in the world. This flock was followed by a third flock that was just as big.

During the night as I lay in bed, I heard geese flying overhead as I drifted off to sleep. In the morning when I went out to greet the day, the sun had not yet crested the treetops, and in the pre-dawn light it seemed I was in some magic world, as during the night it froze quite hard and the mist that hung in the air from the day before was now suspended frosty crystals that sparkled and shimmered like a million tiny jewels. As I stood there drinking in this marvellous sight, I thought it must have snowed because my fields looked white, but then it was really hard to see through all those sparkling jewels drifting all about me. I took a step closer so I could see, and then, as if thunder had broken this silent sparkling world, twenty thousand wings of snow geese thundered to get airborne, and with this came the cries of alarm from ten thousand snow geese. For what seemed like only a moment, the world was vibrating with the cries of snow geese and thundering wings. It shook me to my soul. A few minutes later the world was silent once again. The sun broke over the treetops and all the sparkles melted into the sunlight and I stood there wondering if I had really seen this marvellous sight, or was I just dreaming. But as I stood there shivering in my long underwear, I knew that I had seen what perhaps no other man has seen.

*Vic Daradick*
High Level, Alberta

I live in the Red River Valley. I grew up in a small prairie town, moved on, and lived in several others. You know the type; one grain elevator, railroad tracks, train station, general store, and a curling rink with eight sheets of artificial ice. The kind of place people say that, if you blink when you drive by, you'll miss it. Now I live in Winnipeg, and I suppose some may say the same comment applies. But these are just tourists skimming across the valley in their boats or trolling with empty hooks. Valley, they say. Where are the hills?

True, one must travel far to find them — but they're here. Comforting little brown humps on the shoreline. Why do I continue to live here in Winnipeg in the Red River Valley? It's God in a CBC T-shirt, calling to make me think.

I've contemplated moving to Vancouver, where they tell me that the difference between Vancouver and Toronto is that in Toronto people dress up in bizarre costumes and pretend they're crazy, while in Vancouver they really are crazy. I don't mind the crazy people in Vancouver. They're like wildflowers on the side of a mountain, pretty to be looked at from a distance but never meant to be picked and taken home. But I find when I'm in Vancouver that after three days I no longer see the mountains. All I want to do is find a quiet place, huddle down in the sand, and stare at the ocean. And the same thing happens to me when I'm at the East Coast. Why do I live here?

I ask a friend. Grasshoppers and crickets sing from either side of the dirt road. It's not quite a full moon but bright enough for long shadows. Perfect night to play Dracula. It's my turn to wear the cape. The question eats at me, interferes with the game. On the horizon Winnipeg shimmers pink and still. You live here, he says, because you're short. You're close to the ground and if a big wind should come along you'd be safe. And yet you feel tall. Naw, that's not it, my daughter says. We've got a curved sky and living here is like living inside a bubble. A small town inside a bubble, she says, jabbing the air with her sharp fingernail.

It's Sunday and the question rankles as I make my weekly trip through the forest where the thick, dark trees wrestle the granite boulders for soil. I push the speed limit to get to the lake before all the others and finally I find my spot, huddle down into the sand, and stare out across the water. I think: Why do I live here? Eureka! The answer comes to me. It's not the curved sky or the horizon or because I'm short. It's because when I live in the Red River Valley I'm living at the bottom of a lake. When you live at the bottom of a lake you get cracks in your basement walls, especially in River Heights where they can afford cracks and underpinning and new basements. I like the cracks. The wind whistles through them, loosens the lids on my peach preserves, makes the syrup ferment, and the mice get tipsy. In the potato bin, sprouts grow on wrinkled skin, translucent, cool sprouts. They climb up the basement walls, push their way through air vents, and up the windows in my kitchen. I don't have to bother about hanging curtains.

And time is different here. The days piled on top of lake sediment shift after a good storm so that yesterday slips out from beneath today. Or even last Friday with all its voices will bob up from the bottom and it's possible to lose track of tomorrow. You can just say, To hell with tomorrow, and go out and play Dracula.

When you live here at the bottom of a lake you can't pin your ancestors down with granite monuments. They slide out of their graves. They work themselves across the underground on their backs using their heels as leverage and they inch their way back into town until they rest beneath the network of dusty roads and they lie there on their backs and they read stories to you from old newspapers.

Now this is something the tourists can never discuss as they roar across the valley in their power boats churning up the water with their blink-and-you'll-miss-it view of my place. Sometimes a brave one will leap from the boat, come down and move in next door. I've seen it happen. They become weak and listless, like flies trapped inside a house at the end of summer. And you'll see them walking along the highway in scuba gear muttering to themselves or rowing across the lake in search of a hill. I'll admit, sometimes it's nice to surface, to take off the cape and put on my respectable prairie jacket and boots and do a walking tour of Halifax, sniff a wild mountain flower in Vancouver, get a stiff neck looking up at all those skyscrapers in Toronto, or a three-day-party headache in Montreal. But inevitably my eyes grow tired, glazed, and like a sleepwalker I awake to find myself crouched down beside an ocean, a lake, a water fountain, and I know it's time to get back here — to get down in the basement and breathe the wind in the cracks of my walls where, nestled up against the foundation of my house, is the pelvic bone of an ancestor.

*Sandra Birdsell*
Red River Valley, Manitoba

It was during the mid-sixties. I was studying for my degree and working part-time, for a temporary secretarial agency in Toronto. I phoned them one day for a new assignment and was given a choice: the Acme Nut and Bolt Company, or Glenn Gould. "Do you mean *the* Glenn Gould?" I gasped, but the voice at the other end did not seem to know who *the* Glenn Gould was and merely offered by way of warning, "He's not easy to work for. Either the girls [we were "girls" back then, although I was older than twenty-one] refuse to go back after one session, or he won't have them back. But you can give it a try if you want." I wouldn't have been happier if I had been offered the chance to work for John Lennon.

I was further elated to learn that I was to work in his apartment, which turned out to be the ninth-floor penthouse of an elderly building at St. Clair and Avenue Road — a ten-minute walk from my apartment.

I pushed the intercom button in the foyer and was admitted. My panic mounted with me in the elevator: suppose I made a fool of myself? Suppose he didn't want *me* back either. What would I say when I met him? By now the elevator had risen to the ninth floor and my fears quickly ended, for as the doors opened he was waiting outside his apartment, dishevelled, sock-footed, and utterly charming, stepping forward to greet me. "I'm Glenn Gould. So good of you to come." I don't know what I said by way of response; I must have babbled something. I didn't really regain my wits fully until I was in his living room, seated between the Steinway and the Chickering grands, and he was offering me coffee and cakes. So, this was the fearsome, demanding ogre of whom I had been warned; this was the world-renowned artist; this gentle man making coffee and chatting to put me at ease, not mentioning the work for which he had engaged me.

Much has been written about Glenn Gould's eccentricities and it isn't my aim to add to the memorabilia. Suffice it to say that he did not wear gloves or a scarf at home, any more than he ever seemed to wear shoes. You see, what I noticed then and remember so well now was his kindness, courtesy, and especially his wit. He was a very *funny* man, as well as a brilliant musician. He did devastatingly accurate impersonations of various people, from Walter Homberger to Marlon Brando, and could mimic accents with great accuracy, but never did any of these unkindly.

I was already a fan, but that was of Gould the pianist. What I did not know was that his prodigious musical talent was only one of his gifts. His was the most brilliant mind I have ever encountered. No matter how intricate a path he wove in his discussions, with parentheses inside parentheses, I never heard him lose his way, or stop for a moment to say, "Where was I?" Having rerouted a story in the interests of clarification or enlargement, he was able to return to the precise word at which he had left off, perhaps after five minutes of non-stop talking, without a moment's hesitation. Nor need I have worried about my scanty knowledge of music, for his interests and knowledge were eclectic. His musical taste was pretty eclectic, too. I remember his telling me that the first time he heard the Swingle Singers he fell down on the floor and kicked his heels with delight. And while he didn't care for the Beatles, he was a Petula Clark fan.

I remember a very long afternoon when he tried to overcome my prejudice against twelve-tone music by making me listen to interminable (to me) excerpts from Webern, Schoenberg, et cetera, and then relented and said, since I had listened to such difficult stuff, he would reward me with something more to my taste. After this, he put on a record of music I didn't know, but which sounded lyrical and "musical" to me. Having ascertained that I was indeed enjoying it, he cackled delightedly and informed me that I was listening to Hindemith.

I remember the day I arrived to find him puzzling over a pencil sharpener of mine. It was one of those enclosed types, which allow one to sharpen a pencil without spilling shavings on the floor. To my great amusement this fiendish device, which had set me back thirty-nine cents, quite baffled him. I still relish the thought.

I remember, too, his high spirits on grey, gloomy days. He insisted that his mood bore a direct inverse correlation to sunny weather, and spoke longingly of spending a winter at Great Slave Lake. I was aghast at the thought and knew my amazement amused him, although he professed not to understand my reaction: "Miss Rustage, I believe I'll take you along with me. You really shouldn't miss such an experience."

My most cherished memory, though, is of a private Glenn Gould concert. Well, if not a whole concert, certainly a solo performance. Although I longed to hear him play I never saw him touch a piano, until one day, during one of our inevitable conversations when we should have been working, he was explaining some fine point in a composition (alas, I do not remember which) when he suddenly dashed over to the Steinway to illustrate the point, and played through the whole piece. I think I held my breath the entire time, in case I should distract him and bring him back to business. Yes, he did sing as he played and no, it did not detract from the performance for me.

If you are wondering when any work was done, I must admit still to feelings of guilt. I was paid by the hour, you see, and can remember days when I would arrive at ten and we would not begin work until noon or later, the intervening time having evaporated as we talked. When we did work, it was sometimes hard to concentrate on accurate notetaking because what he had to say — whether in a speech of thanks for an honorary degree, an article for a magazine, or notes for a radio program — was always so exciting, or insightful, or outrageously amusing, or all three.

In the end I worked for Glenn Gould for about four months, until financial necessity made me find full-time employment. In the years since I have had a number of jobs, and have enjoyed them to varying degrees, but nothing has ever held for me the excitement, the stimulation, the sheer waking-up-in-the-morning-happy-to-go-to-work pleasure of those months spent drinking coffee, or frantically straining to keep up with the conversation — or the dictation — of my favourite pianist and one of my favourite human beings. I miss him sorely.

*Avril Rustage-Johnston*
Peterborough, Ontario

Monday, January 5, 1987. I'm driving home, late for dinner. I switch on the CBC and hear Margaret Atwood's voice talking about Margaret Laurence. I half listen. Then I suddenly realize that Margaret Atwood is saying "was" instead of "is." Later I go into my study to mourn Margaret Laurence, who was part of my inner life for twenty-two years. It amazes me that Margaret Laurence knew that innermost being and wrote about it. I look back at how much a part of my life she was. . . .

My sister, Betty Lambert, knows Margaret Laurence as a fellow writer. "How did you meet? What's she like?" I ask.

"Well, I went to a party, knowing she'd be there and feeling quite intimidated. I looked for her and couldn't see her. Finally, I noticed a rather plain, frumpy-looking woman sitting in a corner in a beige pantsuit, smoking. She was surrounded by young people. I could never get near her all night. People seemed drawn to her, like so many moths to a flame. She looked so ordinary. I was rather disappointed."

In early 1983 Betty learns she has lung cancer. Shortly after that we learn that our mother also has cancer. Betty begins chemotherapy treatment. She asks me to go to the opening of her latest play in Toronto. We are determined to celebrate life amidst this onslaught of death. Somehow we make it. Betty goes from the hospital to the airport and I meet her there with my little mother-sucker — my nine-month-old son, Daniel — along for the ride.

We fly from Vancouver to Toronto and stay with Adele Wiseman and her husband, Dmitry Stone. They have been Betty's close friends for years. "You can stay in Peggy's room," Adele says. "I'll just go and get some sheets."

I wonder idly who Peggy might be. The room is small and there are books everywhere. I put Danny on the floor to investigate his new surroundings and I leaf through the books. There are markers in the books saying "Please don't remove." They are signed "M.L." I hold one of the markers in my hand.

Adele returns, bearing sheets. "Who is Peggy?" I ask.

"Peggy? That's Margaret Laurence, Peggy to her friends. This is her room — she stays here when she's in Toronto."

Adele moves towards the bed. "Don't change the sheets!" I announce dramatically. "I want to sleep in Margaret Laurence's bed, dirty sheets and all." I fall onto the bed. "She's my favourite writer."

Adele laughs.

A few days later, I am packing to leave. A storm rages outside. Danny and I watch ancient trees fall gracefully over. Power lines break. I hear on the radio that it is the tip of a tornado. There is a knock at the door. I open it to find a windblown Margaret Laurence.

"Hi," she says. "You're Betty's sister, aren't you? God, what a ride!"

She comes in as I stand dumbfounded. It is the same marvellous face that has stared at me from book jackets for years, the face that Margaret Atwood once described as that of an "exotic Eskimo witch." But the face has a body and talks. I am totally unnerved. She's carrying a dishevelled old shopping bag. She plunks it down on a dining-room chair.

"Put the kettle on, will you, and do you mind if I change? These panty-hose are killing me."

I put the kettle on and come back to find Margaret Laurence stripping off pantyhose, prim blouse, tailored jacket, and skirt. She reaches into the shopping bag and produces grungy slacks and a beat-up sweater, which she quickly dons.

"Ah, that feels better. I hate dressing up."

We sit down to tea. "I'm sorry about Betty," she says, as she lights up the first of many cigarettes.

"Yes. It's lung cancer from smoking."

She fixes me with her incredible brown gaze. "I know." She dares me to say anything to her about her smoking. I don't dare. But it's hard to go on acting as though someone is a Canadian literary legend when you've seen her in her underwear. We talk about children. My four sons, her son and daughter. I tell her about the sheets. She roars with laughter. "For God's sake, change them," she orders. "And don't lose my place in my books."

She talks of her work in the peace movement. "It's taking most of my time, but it's important," she says quietly, as she lights another cigarette. "And we can make a difference." She coughs. A smoker's cough. Betty's cough.

Adele and Betty appear in the doorway, very wet-looking. "It's mad out there," says Adele. "If we're going to make your flights we have to go. Right now!"

I am devastated. I want to stay, talk to Margaret Laurence. Tell her how much her work has meant to me, tell her how she's touched me and taught me. Instead I dash around, organizing everything. Adele and I finally get the suitcases in the car, struggling not to be blown away. My emotions are as wild as the weather. I go back in, clutching my camera.

"Just one photo, please, Adele," I beg. "I want to take Daniel surrounded by three of Canada's best writers. When will he ever have this chance again?"

Margaret Laurence grabs Daniel and sits in a chair. Daniel nuzzles her breast. "No, no." she says gently, moving his head away. "It's too late for that." Betty and Adele stand on either side of her.

"Scrunch down," I say to them. They scrunch closer.

"Okay, say sex."

"Not cheese?" asks Margaret.

"No, sex is better than cheese."

They laugh and I press the shutter. My camera jams.

"Oh, damn." I grab Betty's camera.

"Sex," they all say.

I take the shot just as Margaret jumps up, holding Daniel in front of her. "Oh, God, he's peed on me," she announces. She holds him out, grinning conspiratorially at me, woman to woman, somehow saying, isn't life wonderful and funny and surprising and worth it all.

Oh, Margaret Laurence, I thought you would be here forever. I feel real grief that you are gone. There will be no new novels from you about women and survival, about growing and loving, about being true to oneself. How I will miss that. But I will continue to love and to grow and survive and try to be true to myself, partly because of you.

*Dorothy Beavington*
White Rock, British Columbia


My name is Dennis Kaye. I'm just over five-foot-ten, with brown hair and blue eyes. I like to think I'm an okay guy, but unfortunately, at thirty-four years old, I'm dying. Although I'm reasonably tolerant, I find this whole dying thing an imposition. The fact is, a terminal diagnosis can ruin your whole day.

The vast majority of people with my condition last three to five years, so you could say that, in my fourth year, I'm on the home stretch.

Does the name muscular dystrophy ring a bell? How about multiple sclerosis? Of course they do. These names and others, like cerebral palsy, cystic fibrosis, Alzheimer's, Parkinson's — the list could go on — all have something in common. The mere mention of any of these names usually conjures up a variety of clear images. I have ALS, and after four years of facing ignorance and indifference, I believe that both public awareness and the financial support that awareness brings are long overdue. When I mention ALS, there are no bells. If I say instead that I have Lou Gehrig's disease I often still draw a blank. To physicians ALS means amyotrophic lateral sclerosis, but to thousands of others it means slow death. I read recently that ALS is as common as MS. After careful study I have come to a conclusion: due to the high turnover of those afflicted, statistics only reflect the number of patients alive at any one time. Put more simply: they aren't counting the dead ones!

I find it hard to believe that people would not respond if they were made aware of the scope and effects of this disease. Four years ago I enjoyed good health and performed well at a physically demanding job, but now I need assistance at even the simplest of tasks. This disease attacks the motor centre at the base of the brain, and in turn slowly robs you of voluntary muscle control. The doctors say the end will come when the muscles controlling my lungs are affected. With a keen mind, a healthy heart, and my eyes open, I will suffocate.

Many people, like me, have grown tired of chasing magic cures and paying quacks; we have had a belly full of denial. I'd like to pass on the single most effective treatment I've turned up so far. It is, quite simply, a healthy sense of humour. I know it sounds corny but, like *Reader's Digest* says, laughter really is the best medicine.

The other night, while getting ready for bed, I was going through my usual contortionist throes of disrobing when the funniest thing happened. I was down to the second-to-last garment when suddenly, with one eye straining for the light at the end of the turtleneck and one arm almost free, my body stiffened. With a final desperate surge of strength I entered a horizontal spin, coming to rest in a panting heap of arms, legs, and shorts. Any other time I would have slipped into an all-consuming pit of manic self-pity and frustration, but instead I was seized by the sweet slapstick of the situation. Laughter came grudgingly at first but soon built to manic proportion. My wife, Ruth, who had by this time awakened, looked over the edge of our bed. She joined the chorus. Together we shrieked and howled. When Ruth finally regained enough composure to pull the sweater off and saw the look on my face, the whole foolery started anew. Laugh — I thought I'd die! I had discovered the true meaning of comic relief.

Had I expended that much energy on any other activity, I would have been sapped of all strength. Instead I felt rejuvenated. It may not be a cure, but it's better than anything the specialists have come up with.

I've indulged many times since that night, and the result is always the same — a genuine boost of energy. To promote my treatment I even considered a career in stand-up comedy, but it's getting too hard to stand up, and I'm sure the world is not ready for fall-down comedy. I'll remain a household humorist.

So my message is simple: lighten up. Humour is fail-safe and free, and you may already possess it. It can make a seemingly unbearable situation bearable, and in the process it will make life far more bearable for those around you. You still may not outlive your dog, but you'll have fun trying.

The coffee's always on.

*Dennis Kaye (The Incredible Shrinking Man)*
Quathiaski Cove, British Columbia

I've wanted to write to you for a long time but for many reasons I talked myself out of it. For one thing, I subscribe to Walt Kelly's principle that nothing is so urgent now that won't be urgenter tomorrow.

The last little while has been interesting for me. For one thing, my Hodgkin's disease recurred. After a few delays and a confirming biopsy, I finally started chemotherapy at the end of August. I wonder if I can even describe how nervous I was before I started the chemical warfare again. I talked to a kid who had this treatment for a whole year, and he told me a bit about what to expect. I thought I could survive anything, but I really dreaded the thought of losing all my hair, especially since I thought the wigs were *so* awful. And I resented having to do this again. I asked myself on more than one occasion whether I was really going to do it. I was convinced that I'd just get over this batch and have to do it all again and again and I'd end up dying from the disease (or the treatment) anyway. And this time I wasn't just going to miss getting old: I was also going to miss watching my son grow up — last time I didn't have him. (It's funny, but the longer I live, the more I feel I'm going to miss when I die. Just shows that if you've never been old, you really don't know what it's like!)

After the required self-pity, I got tough. One can only wallow so long and then it gets tedious. Besides, with six months of chemotherapy ahead of me, I didn't have the luxury of time. And there's nothing special about this whole thing — everyone alive gets their share. Mine happens to be cancer. Someone else's is paralysis; another's is a jerk for a spouse, and so on. If you're alive, you've got things to deal with, and it's only a result of being alive, nothing else. It's not fair or unfair. It just *is*.

I always felt like I had a choice: take the treatment, with all its problems, or don't take the treatment. By making an active and positive choice, I believe that some of the discomforts were easier to handle.

Well, thank heavens *those* six months are over! I really didn't think I was going to survive sometimes. I have never been so tired (there are six stairs from my kitchen to my son's room and I used to have to rest after climbing them), or so down. (Cesamet — synthetic dope — did help with the nausea and vomiting, but it made me so depressed and paranoid that I can barely stand to think of it even now.) I spent most of that six months feeling really good, though. The reality of chemotherapy is that your life doesn't stop while you get it — you just have to schedule things a little more carefully than other people do. The days you get the chemicals and the next few days are probably not good ones to plan to do anything, but after that you may have to go a little slower but you can still go. I had the good fortune (because of my wonderful husband) to get to play with my kid nearly every day of the week. Not only that, but because of the chemotherapy I am still alive to hear him count to ten for the first time, to hear him sing "Bawett's Pwivateews" (he loves Stan Wogers), and to watch him go down the slide *all by himself*. So you see, I was telling the truth when I said that the recurrence wasn't really a tragedy. It's a hell of a setback, but at least I've got a little while longer, and at the most I could even be cured. (I hate all this stuff. I hate the times I'm sick, I hate being unable to do some of the things I want to do, I hate losing my "immortality." I hate the thought that I probably won't be spending the next fifty years with my husband. But whoever gets any insurance in that department? We're all subject to the bus factor, aren't we?)

I have managed to stay busy these past few months. I am now vice-president of the local unit of the Cancer Society and I'm involved in a public-education study that is using some of the Steve Fonyo money to supply information to people about preventable types of cancer. It has always seemed more practical to me to try to prevent those diseases we can prevent than to concentrate on the sad results the general neglect of preventive medicine has engendered.

I also work for the SPCA as its secretary, and consequently I occasionally get involved in the controversies surrounding rodeos, cat control, and fur coats. I've discovered just how emotional people get when it comes to "their" animals versus "someone else's" animals. I find it quite amazing that some people are so preoccupied with the effect that cats and dogs have on *grass*! Oh, to have such an uneventful life that grass could be my major concern!

I've taken a couple of courses at the college here, and I've managed to keep up on some other things as well. But the most important thing of all is that I get to spend some great time with my kid. I had no idea that a little kid could be so much fun. (This is just the ignorance of inexperience, of course, but it has been quite a discovery for me.)

Speaking of Ben, he just woke up from his afternoon nap and is asking me to read *And to Think That I Saw It on Mulberry Street*. In fact, he's saying, "Mum read 'Marco keep your eyelids up.'" It is fascinating just how much little kids can remember. So I'd better go rescue him.

> *Krista Munroe*
> Medicine Hat, Alberta

My wife thought we should ask at the house. I said that there appeared to be no one home and anyway they wouldn't believe me. I had not told her what I was up to and she was a trifle impatient. We were not exactly skulking but we certainly were behaving in a suspicious manner as we walked around to the back of the property. This was the house in which I had lived as a boy some twenty years ago; it was not the building itself I was interested in but a certain spot in the back garden.

My boyhood friend and I, fired by stories in *Chums Annual* with lurid titles like "To Sweep the Spanish Main" and "Rogues of the Roaring Glory," acted out those seemingly romantic days in our vivid imagination with desperate sword fights on his garage roof. We repelled snarling pirates as they attempted to board our stout ship, cutlass between snaggled teeth, pistol in garish sash. Pirates had names like Red Castaban, Rat o' the Main, and the Barracuda. Alas, boys' stories don't have names like that any more.

One of the best parts was the lair. My chum had his bedroom in the attic. At one point, in his room where the sloping roof reached the floor, there was a small door hidden behind a bureau. It led under the eaves to a dark wondrous place where we had covered the rafters with some wood to provide a floor — a secret place that only we knew. Pictures had been hung up, and there were suitable artifacts of various kinds and a document embellished with our own crude illustrations, which we had copied from our favourite reading material, and which pledged our undying allegiance, properly signed in blood.

There was also a map depicting in graphic detail the spot where our treasure was buried. The treasure chest was a tin cashbox purchased from Woolworth's, that wonderful store where in those days one could buy almost anything one's heart desired for fifteen cents. In the chest were some foreign coins given to me by a wandering uncle, tarnished jewellery discarded by our parents (who, we admitted, did occasionally have their uses), and pounded-up bits of glass, as good as diamonds to our eyes. Of course we had endless arguments about where the treasure should be hidden — the merits of this place and the drawback of that one.

In the end, a site was chosen at my place at the bottom of the back yard, near the corner of the garage in the wall. An opening had been cut there to allow our dog access to his sleeping place on a pile of burlap bags. We dug the hole about a foot deep, put in the chest, covered it with earth, and then, to cunningly foil any intruders, we placed a large flat rock over the spot before filling in the rest of the hole. Afterwards, we would occasionally inspect this hiding place to make sure it had not been disturbed. Inevitably, over the course of time it became neglected. The pirate fights were replaced by other interests, a war intervened and we went our separate ways, got married. The buried treasure with its secret map became a childhood memory.

Many years later my wife and I found ourselves back in Toronto for a visit, and I decided it would be fun to see if anything remained of our cache. The neighbourhood had of course changed: the vacant lots across the street where we used to play football and baseball or knock out flies (kids don't seem to do that any more) was now a row of houses, and the trees were bigger. Curiously, the little grocery store had survived, the store where my mother used to send me occasionally to buy ten cents' worth of "round steak, minced," for supper. The house hadn't changed very much, though, and the back yard seemed much as I remembered it;

even the dog's hole in the garage was still there. I didn't need the map. My memory was clear and I went unerringly to the spot, but I must admit my heart was beating more heavily than usual. My wife was astonished and more than a little bewildered when I began to dig. First came the rock and then, miraculously, the box. It was badly rusted as befits a treasure chest, but still intact. Gleefully and with shaking hands I opened the box. There it was — treasure beyond one's wildest dreams! Forget about stout Cortez and his wild surmise; here was the *real* stuff of dreams. After letting memories flood over me for a few minutes, I carefully replaced the little chest in its hiding place and covered it again with the stone and dirt.

This happened over forty years ago, and I now live on the West Coast and have not been back. My boyhood friend and I, although we live at opposite ends of this big country of ours, still see each other at regular intervals, and the years roll back as if we had never been apart. We are as much a pair of romantics as ever.

Sometimes I wonder if the treasure is still there, but I don't really want to know. Instead, in my mind's eye I like to picture the scene as someone turns it up with a spade. Hopefully the discovery will be made by small boys who have the same imagination as we did so long ago.

*Reid Townsley*
Ganges, British Columbia

His name was Warren but we called him Bing. Oh, he didn't look like Bing Crosby; his face was too round and he was too tall, but we thought he could sing like Bing Crosby. He was always singing. And if he wasn't singing, he was whistling. Often as I lay in my bed at night, I could hear Warren whistling his way home down the darkened street of our little town.

He was always volunteering. At the school dances he was the one boy who always volunteered to dance with Miss Davidson. He was one of those kids who make a school live. The year he was our student-council president was a very happy one for all of us.

In 1942 Warren was eighteen and in grade twelve. The war was on and he volunteered for the air force and was accepted on condition that his teachers certify that he had earned the equivalent of a grade-twelve diploma.

Now, Warren was just an average student and he was failing Latin. Faced with Warren's enthusiastic desire to join the air force, the Latin teacher called him in and asked Warren to tell him all the Latin he knew. It didn't take long. The next day Warren wrote a Latin exam and found questions that were remarkably close to his small store of knowledge.

He passed his Latin exam, joined the air force and became an air gunner, first with 424 Squadron flying in Halifax and then, in May 1944, he and his crew transferred to 405 Squadron, flying Lancasters. By June 1944 he had safely completed more than twenty missions, including the disastrous raid on Nuremberg on March 30, 1944. On that one night more Allied airmen were lost than during the whole Battle of Britain. However, though attacked by a German night-fighter, Warren and his crew evaded the attack and returned to base safely.

On June 6 the Allies invaded Normandy. By the middle of June, Allied forces were facing stiff German resistance. It was crucial that German supply lines be cut at Lens, near Arras, in northern France. On June 16 Warren's crew successfully bombed the railway yards at Lens; but on the way back, his plane was hit by shells from a German night-fighter.

From the window of their farmhouse on the edge of the little French village of Carency, Monsieur Galvaire and his wife and young daughter watched the flaming aircraft struggle across the sky. On the opposite side of the village, Madame Corneille saw it explode, break into two pieces and crash in a farmer's field.

When she got to the burning plane, Madame Corneille saw that three airmen were still in the wreck. Warren and three others were thrown clear, with their parachutes unused. One of the crew was missing.

The next afternoon, as he was working in his field, Monsieur Galvaire discovered the pilot, unharmed except for a slight cut on his hand, hiding in a woods nearby. At great personal risk, Monsieur Galvaire hid the pilot in his house for three days until he could be safely escorted back to England.

Meanwhile, at the crash site, Madame Corneille had given all that she could of love and her nurse's training. But it was not enough.

On a beautiful June evening, in a field near a French village that he had never heard of, at the age of twenty, Warren died.

Today is Remembrance Day. In Carency, Madame Corneille lies peacefully in the village churchyard. Until her death in 1976 she prayed daily for "her Canadian boys." On the edge of the village, Monsieur Galvaire, now more than eighty, will think again of the young Canadian life he saved. From his kitchen window he can see the tower of the French war memorial of Notre Dame de Lorrette and, beyond it, the tips of the twin towers of the Canadian memorial on Vimy Ridge, each a reminder of the sacrifices of an earlier war.

Not far away, on the French coast near Calais, Warren lies with his five crew members and eight hundred other Canadians in a military cemetery. On a clear day from this place, one can see the sparkling waters of the English Channel and, beyond, the white cliffs of Dover.

Today is Remembrance Day. Across the nation people will gather and remember. Somewhere a middle-aged ex-bomber pilot will again remember June 16, 1944. In truth he will never be able to forget it. In Richmond Hill, a successful young businessman may pause to ask his father again about the young airman after whom he was named. In Toronto, an elderly retired Latin teacher will reflect again about that examination and his fateful decision in 1942.

Young people who gather at cenotaphs on November 11 will note that most of us who are there seem old. And perhaps they will conclude that we are remembering old events and old people who lived or died in them. But, in bittersweet intensity, we are remembering our youth. We are remembering friends like Warren. He was twenty and he sang like Bing Crosby.

*Enerson Lavender*
Burlington, Ontario

Grandma is ninety-eight this Christmas. In spite of declining health, she forges on with characteristic determination, hope, and wit. We thought we might lose her last October — how many more heart attacks can her frail body take? — but, true to form, Grandma rallied again. "I couldn't miss a Christmas party, now could I!" she quipped on the way home from the hospital.

"No, Grandma." I laughed. "It wouldn't be a party without you."

I remember my first Christmas party with Grandma. I was just a kid. I remember tearing across town on my bike to visit her on the day my big sister dropped the bomb: "There is no Santa Claus," she jeered. "Even dummies know that!"

My grandma is not the gushy kind, never was. I fled to her that day because I knew she would be straight with me. I knew Grandma always told the truth, and I knew that the truth always went down a whole lot easier when swallowed with one of her world-famous cinnamon buns.

Grandma was home, and the buns were still warm. Between bites, I told her everything. She was ready for me.

"No Santa Claus!" she snorted. "Ridiculous! Don't believe it. That rumour has been going around for years, and it makes me mad, plain mad. Now, put on your coat, and let's go."

"Go? Go where, Grandma?" I asked. I hadn't even finished my second cinnamon bun.

"Where" turned out to be Kerby's General Store, the one store in town that had a little bit of just about everything. As we walked through its doors, Grandma handed me ten dollars. That was a bundle in those days. "Take this money," she said, "and buy something for someone who needs it. I'll wait for you in the car." Then she turned and walked out of Kerby's.

I was only eight years old. I'd often gone shopping with my mother, but never had I shopped for anything all by myself.

The store seemed big and crowded, full of people scrambling to finish their Christmas shopping. For a few moments I just stood there, confused, clutching that ten-dollar bill, wondering what to buy, and who on earth to buy it for.

I thought of everybody I knew: my family, my friends, my neighbours, the kids at school, the people who went to my church. I was just about thought out, when I suddenly thought of Bobbie Decker. He was a kid with bad breath and messy hair, and he sat right behind me in Mrs. Pollock's grade-two class.

Bobbie Decker didn't have a coat. I knew that because he never went out for recess during the winter. His mother always wrote a note, telling the teacher that he had a cough, but all we kids knew that Bobbie Decker didn't have a cough, and he didn't have a coat. I fingered the ten-dollar bill with growing excitement. I would buy Bobbie Decker a coat.

I settled on a red corduroy one that had a hood to it. It looked real warm, and he would like that.

"Is this a Christmas present for someone?" the lady behind the counter asked kindly, as I laid my ten dollars down.

"Yes," I replied shyly. "It's . . . for Bobbie."

The nice lady smiled at me. I didn't get any change, but she put the coat in a bag and wished me a Merry Christmas.

That evening, Grandma helped me wrap the coat in Christmas paper and ribbons, and write, "To Bobbie, From Santa Claus" on it — Grandma said that Santa always insisted on secrecy. Then she drove me over to Bobbie Decker's house, explaining as we went that I was now and forever officially one of Santa's helpers.

Grandma parked down the street from Bobbie's house, and she and I crept noiselessly and hid in the bushes by his front walk. Then Grandma gave me a nudge. "All right, Santa Claus," she whispered, "get going."

I took a deep breath, dashed for his front door, threw the present down on his step, pounded his doorbell and flew back to the safety of the bushes and Grandma. Together we waited breathlessly in the darkness for the front door to open. Finally it did, and there stood Bobbie.

Forty years haven't dimmed the thrill of those moments spent shivering, beside my grandma, in Bobbie Decker's bushes. That night, I realized that those awful rumours about Santa Claus were just what Grandma said they were: ridiculous. Santa was alive and well, and we were on his team.

*Carol Laycock*
Lethbridge, Alberta


My kids don't write much. I gather it is culturally inappropriate to write in the East. But every so often — or every so seldom, as I see it — they call. Recently, Drew, the youngest, phoned from Quebec City. He had called to tell me about an incident on a bus. He had struck up a conversation with an elderly man (quite possibly someone over fifty-five) who had lived right next door to Drew's less-than-posh address in the late forties. It was still a family neighbourhood then, and directly across the street, where there is now an abandoned storefront, he had worked for years in a bicycle sales and repair shop.

Reminiscing, he told Drew that those had been very tough times in Quebec. Unemployment was high, there were few social services, and many families in the area were struggling with poverty. Even so, he said, people were somehow kinder, more gentle then. He remembered when a skinny, ragged little boy, maybe four or five, used to wander into the shop almost every afternoon.

The first time he appeared, he just walked around the shop staring wide-eyed at the shiny new bikes on display. Then he looked up at the guy at the counter and lisped, "You got bikes!"

"Right," he was told, "and you can look, but don't touch." And he never did. All through the summer and fall, right into a fierce winter, he would quietly come in, scout the new bikes and then stand silently watching the customers at the counter.

There were few calls for new bikes that hard winter. People would more usually come in to ask for a new bolt to be put here or there on their old bikes. And the little guy always watched with solemn interest.

One day, close to Christmas, the boy came in, poorly bundled — shivering — and stood watching until there were no customers at the counter. Then he came right up to the front: his eyes barely topped the counter. Reaching up a badly mittened hand, he showed the sales clerk a rusty old bolt and whispered, "Will you put a bike on my bolt, please?"

He was still too young to know that causal sequences don't often reverse — like you grow big, but you don't grow small. I remember my kids thinking that way.

The man told Drew that the boys in the shop had a great laugh at that, and they told the little guy that that just wasn't the way things worked. They felt pretty badly after he was gone, though. He had looked surprised and even a little frightened by their laughter. Then he had put his head down and walked quickly out of the shop leaving the rusty bolt on the counter.

It was some time before the boy returned, but two days before Christmas, he slipped in and began his routine inspection of the bikes. He kept his eyes down this time, and he didn't come anywhere near the counter. He just stopped at each bike, gave it his usual serious attention and moved on. After he had looked at the entire display, he turned and quietly started to leave. But, just as he reached the door, one of the men shouted from the back room, "Hey, kid, you forgot your bolt!"

And out of the back of the shop, they rolled out a shiny kid's bike. They had built it from spare parts on their own time and painted it a bright, sparkling Christmas red.

*Donna Moffatt*
Errington, British Columbia

In the winter of 1965 my father was chief helicopter pilot for the Canadian Coast Guard, stationed in Prince Rupert, British Columbia. One morning, close to Christmas, Dad got up early and headed to work.

He left instructions for Mom to be at the hangar at four o'clock with us (me, Doug, and Boo) and the rest of the pilots' families.

It seemed that Santa was making special trips to all the lighthouses in the area and Dad was flying him. At four o'clock we were waiting in the hangar, wondering why were we here, as we had seen Dad at work hundreds of times. Once the helicopter was in sight the ground crew opened the big doors and we watched the helicopter taxi in . . . after the blades stopped turning the doors opened and to our utter amazement there was Santa! We were absolutely stunned. Not only did Dad know him personally, but he had been to his house!

That night we all went to the local hall for a Christmas party with the guest of honour. After Santa gave out all his gifts he excused himself and headed down to the washroom. I followed him downstairs hoping to get a little one-on-one time to make some special requests. Santa disappeared into the washroom and I waited and waited and waited. About fifteen minutes later the door opened, but it wasn't Santa, just some man. "Can I help you?" he asked. "No, thanks, I'm just waiting for Santa to come out." "Well, he's not in the washroom," the man said. How could he have possibly come out with me standing right at the door? I peeked in, and sure enough he had disappeared! At that moment I had no problem believing that everything my parents had said about Santa was true.

*Bonnie MacLean*
Carleton Place, Ontario


When I was eight years old, my father, a union organizer in the forties and fifties, was blacklisted, accused of communist activities. It meant no work — with a vengeance. My mother, then in her forties, had twin boys that spring — premature, and in pre-medicare times you can imagine the devastating costs for their care. I was hungry that year, hungry when I got up, hungry when I went to school, hungry when I went to sleep. In November I was asked to leave school because I had only boys' clothes to wear — hand-me-downs from a neighbour. I could come back, they said, when I dressed like a young lady.

The week before Christmas, the power and gas were disconnected. We ate soup made from carrots, potatoes, cabbage, and grain meant to feed chickens, cooked on our wood garbage burner. Even as an eight-year-old, I knew the kind of hunger we had was nothing compared to people in

India and Africa. I don't think we could have died in our middle-class Vancouver suburb. But I do know that the pain of hunger is intensified and brutal when you live in the midst of plenty. As Christmas preparations increased, I felt more and more isolated, excluded, set apart. I felt a deep, abiding hunger for more than food. Christmas Eve day came, grey and full of the bleak sleety rain of a West Coast winter. Two women, strangers, struggled up our driveway, loaded down with bags. They left before my mother answered the door. The porch was full of groceries — milk, butter, bread, cheese, and Christmas oranges. We never knew who they were, and after that day, pride being what it was, we never spoke of them again. But I'm forty-five years old, and I remember them well.

Since then I've crafted a life of joy and independence, if not of financial security. Several years ago, living in Victoria, my son and I were walking up the street, once more in West Coast sleet and rain. It was just before Christmas and we were, as usual, counting our pennies to see if we'd have enough for all our festive treats, juggling these against the necessities. A young man stepped in front of me, very pale and carrying an old sleeping bag, and asked for spare change — not unusual in downtown Victoria. No, I said, and walked on. Something hit me like a physical blow about a block later. I left my son and walked back to find the young man. I gave him some of our Christmas luxury money — folded into a small square and tucked into his hand. It wasn't much, only ten dollars, but as I turned away, I saw the look of hopelessness turn into amazement and then joy. Well, said the rational part of my mind, Judith, you are a fool, you know he's just going up the street to the King's Hotel and spend it on drink or drugs. You've taken what belongs to your family and spent it on a frivolous romantic impulse. As I was lecturing myself on gullibility and sensible charity, I noticed the young man with the sleeping bag walking quickly up the opposite side of the street, heading straight for the King's. Well, let this be a lesson, said the rational Judith. To really rub it in, I decided to follow him. Just before the King's he turned into a corner grocery store. I watched through the window, through the poinsettias and the stand-up Santas. I watched him buy milk, butter, bread, cheese, and Christmas oranges.

Now, I have no idea how that young man arrived on the street in Victoria. Nor will I ever have any real grasp of the events that led my family to that dark and hungry December. But I do know that charity cannot be treated as an RRSP. There is no best-investment way to give, no way to insure value for our dollar. Like the Magi, these three, the two older women struggling up the driveway and the young man with the sleeping bag, gave me, and continue to give me, wonderful gifts — the reminder that love and charity come most truly and abundantly from an open and unjudgemental heart.

*Judith MacKenzie*
Nelson, British Columbia

I am writing this on a notebook computer, sitting in my wing-chair, listening to some piano jazz. Art Tatum, I think. You can tell from the extended runs. Almost a surfeit of notes, cascading over one another, nearly getting caught in the net of melody and rhythm, but emerging as a clear, evocative structure with, unbelievably, each phrase perfect and self-contained.

But I'm getting off track. I always use a computer now. I used to use a pen and paper. It was actually a special pen. My father gave it to me when I was twelve. He got it when he left his job at the newspaper. Sort of a going-away present, although he never said at the time why he had to go. He used to complain about the paper but I knew he really liked it. He would go on at dinner about how they didn't pay enough and, if it wasn't for Max, the city editor, he would have left long ago. Or they couldn't get along without him. Or — I liked this one the best — someone had to teach these college grads how to write. But we all knew that the paper was his life and he would never quit. I guess that made his leaving even more of a shock. Surprisingly, Mother didn't seem too upset. "I've seen it coming for years," she once said over breakfast. Dad didn't reply.

He introduced me to jazz. He had a collection of old 78s that he would listen to for hours. All by himself in the den, door closed, that scratchy old music all but obscured as it seeped out through the walls. You could still hear the rhythm, though, the bass line steady, rock hard, anchoring the rest of the band; the drums sharp and insistent, keeping the other musicians in line. One day I was standing outside the door when he opened it and said, "That's Count Basie. He plays piano. He's not a real count, of course, but they call him that because he's like royalty. He's so good that the other musicians look up to him like he was a king or a duke or a count."

He was leaning against the door and the music was loud now. The band was in full flight, all sections playing in unison, trumpets high above the rest, the sound surging through the doorway as if it would sweep away my father and everything else before it. Then it ended, suddenly, except for four short notes on the piano. Plink, plink, plink, plink. And it was over. I thought those four notes the most wonderful sounds I had ever heard. They just hung there, complete in themselves yet an inseparable part of the whole piece. The music was finished, but I could still hear those notes.

"Well, don't just stand there. Come on in," Dad said and backed out of the doorway, rather unsteadily. I entered the room while he removed a glass tumbler from the top of the desk, rummaged through his desk and brought forth a small cigar. "You don't mind if I smoke, do you?" he said. I grinned and nodded. He had never asked my permission for anything before. We sat in the acrid fumes for an hour and listened to the most wonderful music ever played: Duke Ellington, Benny Goodman, Tommy Dorsey, Glenn Miller. Most of all, I remember my father leaning back in his chair, eyes closed, fingers tapping out the simple rhythms on his knee or the top of the desk, stopping only to put on a new record. I don't think I said a word for a whole hour.

We had many sessions after that, and I came to appreciate what jazz meant to him, how it was a solace, a retreat where only he could go, a wall behind which he could shelter when the paper or Mother or something inside him made life too hard to face. We never talked about it but I knew.

About a week after he was fired, Dad called me into the den. He was sitting at his desk, turning something over and over in his hand. There was a bottle on the desk, half filled with amber-coloured liquor. A glass was lying on its side next to it. No music was playing. It was very quiet. His record collection, which was normally stacked neatly on shelves beside the window, was scattered on the floor. Two records lay broken but he didn't seem to notice. He stared straight ahead and hardly seemed to see me when I started to enter the room.

"This is it," he muttered. "This is what twenty years of hard work and devotion are worth. One more chance. That's all I wanted. One more lousy chance. I could've done it. How many times did it happen? It would have been the last time. The bastards."

I looked up quickly. I had never heard him swear before. Really swear.

Never in all those complaints and accusations had there ever been more than a "damn" or "hell."

He stopped talking and looked down at the object in his hand. I saw it was a pen, a shiny black fountain pen, with a gold clip. His head waved slightly from side to side while he examined it. He picked up the glass, poured some of the liquor into it and drank the contents in one gulp. I recognized the sweet, sharp odour. I had smelled it in the room before. "What good is a pen, if they don't let you write? Am I just supposed to write letters with it? Goddamn it, I'm a newspaper man, not a bloody poet."

He was almost shouting now and totally oblivious of me.

"I give them my life and they give me a . . . a pen." He stopped suddenly and finally acknowledged me in the doorway. I had never seen him look so completely vulnerable. His body seemed barely to occupy his thin shirt. His eyes looked through me, rather than at me, as if trying to locate me by reference to the objects in the room. His hands continued to play with the pen. He was drunk, of course, but I didn't know it.

"You take it. You take it. You can use it more than I can."

He leaned over the desk and pushed the pen towards me. I smelt the pungent odour again, only stronger. I didn't take the pen. I couldn't move.

"No, no. It's yours." I was almost crying now. "They gave it to you. I can't have it. It was meant for you."

He got up slowly and unsteadily. Grasping the edge of the desk with one hand, and holding the pen with the other, he made his way towards me. When he reached the end of the desk, he stopped, closed his eyes and pitched forward onto his knees. The pen dropped in front of him.

I ran forward to him. "Dad, Dad," I cried, "are you all right? I'll take the pen, if you want. I didn't mean it. Please, give it to me."

But he didn't. He opened his eyes, smiled and put both hands on my shoulders. The smell of the liquor was overpowering. His face, so close to mine, was pained yet comforting.

"Son," he said in a voice now soft and thick as syrup, "I'm sorry. I'm sorry. I'm sorry. I've had too much to drink and I'm feeling sorry for myself. It's a problem adults have when things get . . . get out of hand. I'd really like you to have the pen. It's important to me. When you write something, it might inspire you. You'll write something great and think of me. Okay? Promise?"

Still smiling, he took his hands from my shoulders, bent down, picked up the pen and handed it to me. It was a thick, shiny black cylinder, with a gold clasp like an arrow mounted on the cap. I unscrewed the cap and pushed it onto the other end of the pen. The nib was also gold. I took the pen in my right hand. It felt powerful in some strange way. I wouldn't use a pen like that for just anything. I hugged my father very tightly.

"Now go away and let your father drink in peace," he said with a smile on his face. As I turned to leave, he swayed, grinned at me again and passed out on the floor.

Dad was right. I did use the pen and it did seem to inspire me. Not for work, of course, but when I really wanted to say something. A love letter or a poem, for example. Then I would pick up the pen, get some sheets of really good bond paper, lock myself in the den and write. And, of course, put on some good jazz.

Dad died a year ago. I had moved to another city and we hadn't seen each other in a few years but we did write. I used my pen, of course. He didn't work steadily after the paper but managed to support Mother and himself with free-lance work. His last letter complained about rates for free-lancers and the fact that no one today can really write.

When Mother phoned me with the news of his death, I went into the den, put a Count Basie record on the machine, took the pen and sat down to write. I'm not sure what I wanted to do, an obituary perhaps, and maybe that was the problem. I couldn't find anything to say. The words just wouldn't come. I must have sat for an hour and the page was still totally blank. Finally, I got up, went to my desk, rolled the pen in a handkerchief and placed it in the bottom drawer at the back. I haven't used it since.

I guess there's no real difference between a pen and a computer. They're both just tools. In some way, though, it's like jazz. Some instruments, like some people, have more heart, and it's heart that makes music. Count Basie knew that. So did my father.

*Lion J. Sharzer*
Aylmer, Quebec

# AFTERWORD
## by Peter Gzowski

⌒

It is early in the morning — *very* early in the morning, even for me — of May 30, 1997, and I have wakened in the bedroom of a comfortably appointed suite (it has a bathroom in whose tub I could stage a synchronized swimming exhibition) of the Temple Gardens Mineral Spa in Moose Jaw, Saskatchewan.

I have been in the Temple Gardens before, except then it had a different name. Almost exactly forty years ago this week, I arrived in Saskatchewan as the supremely underqualified, twenty-two-year-old city editor of the daily Moose Jaw *Times-Herald*, and since the Harwood Hotel, as the spa was then called, is just a couple of short blocks along Fairford Street from the newspaper offices, I was quickly introduced to its beery charms. I spent quite a lot of time here, in fact. Especially on Saturdays, when we worked only half the day, we would walk over to the Harwood almost as soon as the paper went to press — real newspapermen, I learned, never said "was put to bed." We would fill a table with glasses of draft beer and, sometimes, tomato juice, and drink till our bellies, if not our wallets, were full. I learned a lot here.

I sometimes make too much of my time in Saskatchewan, I know. This week a bright young reporter from *Western People* magazine — there are reporters and television crews everywhere as *Morningside* reaches its finale — pointed out that I have never even experienced a real prairie winter. But Saskatchewan hit me hard. Yesterday the crew that's following me around for a CBC-TV *Life and Times* (that's embarrassing, eh, but I'm actually kind of enjoying it) packed me and my incomparable and effervescent young assistant Shelley Ambrose into a van to drive over from Regina. As the camera rolled — I think the cinematographer had his feet in the glove compartment and the sound guy was squatted behind the rear seat, holding his mike boom like Mahatma Gandhi with a fishing pole — they had Shelley prompt me to tell stories, some of which she must have heard a thousand times before. It worked, I think. The surrounding countryside took me back. As we cruised along the Trans-Canada, I remembered driving over the endless landscape myself, forty years ago, in my little green 1954 Austin convertible, whose ownership I shared with my friends at Household Finance. I told the story again of riding out on a train with an Englishman, bound for a new job himself, who sat with his chin in his hand from about Brandon until well across the invisible Saskatchewan border. When I asked him what he thought of it he said, "It's the biggest expanse of bugger-all I've ever seen in my life." And I remembered my own explorations teaching me how wrong he was, that the land was not monochromatic but an infinite variety of ever-changing browns and greens and yellows and purples, and how it began to teach me that all the land in this heartstoppingly beautiful country is like that. You just have to look at it. You just have to be on it for a while. I remembered the song of the meadowlark and the sloughs and the coulees, words unfamiliar to me from my youth, and the crashing power of prairie thunder, and W. O. Mitchell's *Jake and the Kid* on the radio, and how different it was to listen to here. Bill will be on *Morningside* this morning, in a chat we taped earlier as he sat in his home in Calgary. It's the last time we'll talk on the radio. I wonder if he knows how much he's meant to so many people.

I remembered the politics, too: Hazen Argue vs. Ross Thatcher in Assiniboia, former seat-mates, now bitter foes, Ross chewing his fat cigar and rumbling in answer to a heckler, "I changed my mind"; the Thatcher–Douglas debate in Mossbank, with people hanging from the rafters; the first successful campaign of John Diefenbaker, and how strongly the people of Saskatchewan felt about him. "Follow John," my own managing editor would say when he came to work. Politics seemed so much more important here than in Ontario, where I grew up. The hardship, I guessed. The Depression was only twenty years old when I lived here. All kinds of people could — and did — remember Bennett buggies and trains skidding on grasshoppers and fields blowing off towards the Lakehead, great black clouds in the relentless sky.

No, I never spent a whole winter here. But I'm sure that it was in Saskatchewan that my idea of one of Canada's defining characteristics — maybe its *essential* characteristic — began to grow. It explains a lot about us, I think, from Medicare to unemployment insurance (I *still* can't call it EI), from the railways or — dare I say it? — the CBC, to our inherent common decency and sense of *politesse*. We have a lot at stake here: we huddle together against the cold.

Conrad Black, who owns most of the newspapers in Saskatchewan now (as where doesn't he?) likes to pooh-pooh all this. You can't define a nation by its institutions, he says. I say maybe not. But you *can* define it by the attitudes and philosophies and values out of which those institutions grow.

I'm glad we're wrapping up *Morningside* from Moose Jaw.

It's five a.m. I'd better write some billboards.

One of the first things Nicole Bélanger did when she hired me to replace Don Harron in 1982 was to ask Alan Guettel, our music producer at the time, to commission a new theme. Alan gave the job to David Thompson, a musician-of-all-skills who lives and works in Toronto. David, in turn, hired only a percussionist and did the rest of the instrumentation himself, electronically. You probably know it: daddle-a-dah-dah, daddle-a-dah-dah, daaaah. (If you don't, it's on the CD that comes with this book.) Altogether, it was played on the program about twelve thousand times, if you count the top of every hour, not only by David on tape but live by all kinds of fiddlers and pianists and spoon players and Buddy Wassisname and the Other Fellers on a vacuum cleaner hose. Prairie Oyster sort of sang it. A string quartet played it for me at the Windsor Press Club, and the Barenaked Ladies played it at the El Mocambo in Toronto.

I never tired of it. Every day when I was on I'd do a little essay at the beginning of the program. I said, "Damn, I feel dirty," when Ben Johnson got caught (that quote made the *ABC News* in the U.S.), played a tape of a shortstop named Eddie Zoskie hitting one of his rare home runs (that home run didn't), and, after I'd messed up, apologized to my son the engineer for suggesting he couldn't do long division. I noted election results and stock market turns and the deaths of friends and, as my daughter the radio producer liked to point out, the weather, always the weather — though I was careful to keep it as far from *Toronto* weather as possible. I gave short recipes and read poems from the mail and once, to the annoyance of thousands of people who were still waiting to do it themselves, blurted out an answer from the *Globe and Mail* cryptic puzzle. I was also able, however, to correct the *Globe*'s "Morning Smile" for thinking they'd just come up with the phrase, "as Canadian as possible under the circumstances." In fact, it was written by a young woman from Sarnia, Ontario, named Heather A. Scott, and it won the first-ever contest on *This Country in the Morning*, in about 1972. Heather died a couple of years ago in White Rock, B.C., after a gallant battle with cancer. Her father came to tell me when I was signing some books. He had me write "Under the circumstances" beside my signature. He said winning the contest had meant a lot to her. I said — truthfully — it had meant a lot to me, too; a copy of her original submission, which he'd sent to me years ago, still hangs on my wall. I wish I'd met her, but having the billboards to salute her memory was a kind of consolation. I'll miss that outlet.

What an incredible, exhilarating, exhausting, exciting fifteen years it was. After the new theme, the changes kept coming. We added a business column (we tried several times to shape a balancing department of labour but never did work it out) and the first version of the panel that became Kierans, Camp, and Lewis. (The original participants were Dalton, Doris Anderson, and Roy Romanow, in case you've forgotten. ) We developed the two-person formula for regional reports — except for southern Ontario, which we felt was already adequately covered in the national media. Under Nicole and her successors we invented the radio "trial," the first example of which, of course, the case of Louis Riel, is in this book; the hour-long free-for-alls we did on such matters as the Montreal massacre, the technological revolution (a constant theme through the later years) and the Charter of Rights (ditto); and the national hootenannies that brought together singers and players from studios all over the country. Much later, after we'd lost KLC to the passage of time and the vagaries of careers, we worked out the Friday political forum with, first, five and, later, four participants whose *dramatis personae* varied each week but who were drawn from a bank of twenty or so occasional regulars, if you'll allow me an oxymoron.

Not everything worked, to be sure. We tried for a while to assemble a panel of women, whose discussions would not be limited to so-called women's issues but whose presence would help to balance our sometimes over-reliance on men. It didn't work; I found myself unable to explain on the air exactly what it was we were trying to do. We tried a number of times to hold a regular session on ethics, but couldn't find the right mixture. We were good on gay and lesbian issues, I think (too good in some people's view) and on the First Nations — certainly by the standards of most other national media — but bad about finding enough representatives of other visible minorities or people with accents. Far too many times when they were on *Morningside* it was only as spokespersons for their particular groups — they were there because they were Bengali or Sudanese or Vietnamese and not just because they were mechanics or dentists or people who grow delphiniums.

We played a lot of games, some we adapted from other sources, including one we called Lie Detector, which I personally stole from Quebec TV, but also our own version of *Front Page Challenge* after its cancellation. When Alex Trebek, who is — or was — Canadian, visited us, I tried to interview him in the style of *Jeopardy*, but he *couldn't* (or wouldn't) respond to my answers in the form of a question. When Boris Spassky was a guest, I challenged him to a game of mental chess. I opened P-K4. He replied P-K4. I offered a draw and Spassky, a good sport, accepted, giving me, I imagine, the best record ever held by a Canadian against a former Russian world champion. When Vladislav Tretiak, the Spassky of goaltending, was sitting across from me, I tried an experiment I'd learned from, I think, Jacques Plante, based on the theory that goalies have faster reflexes than normal human beings: I asked him to extend his hand towards me, fingers and thumb opposed. Over it, I held a dollar bill (remember those?), suspended from its end by my own finger and thumb. The game was for me to release the bill without warning and if he could catch it as it fell through his hand he could keep it. Tretiak was fast. But not fast enough for me — or, as I thought with remembered pleasure, for Paul Henderson. We held scavenger hunts and wine tastings, language contests when two new Canadian dictionaries (hurray!) came out and, regularly, hilarious debates on such matters as analogue clocks vs. digital or the case for or against pyjamas.

Did we play too much? Some people thought so — usually the same people who thought we carried too much Cape Breton fiddle music or made too much chili sauce. But I'd argue no. Yes, these were tough and stressful times we were living through: down-sizing, unemployment, constitutional crisis after constitutional crisis. But sometimes the reason we fooled around was precisely *because* of the gloom and the tension. On occasions such as the failure of Meech Lake or the hair's-breadth victory in the Quebec referendum we'd often go on the air with, for instance, one of our national hootenannies, with singers from all over the country just, for an hour or so, having a good time. And it was experiences like those, and the response of so many of our listeners, that helped convince us that our best answer to the Manitoba flooding crisis of the spring of 1997 was to hold what many people came to call *Morningside*'s finest hour — four hours, really, for we seconded some *Radio Noon* time across the country, so some of the best and most generous of Canada's singers and writers could keep on singing and telling stories and giving out a 1-888 number into which, before the phone stopped ringing, more than one and a half million dollars poured, and through which, we came to learn, the spirits of the flood victims were raised and reinforced.

The Red River Rally was actually the idea of CBC Radio's Bill Richardson, who grew up in Winnipeg, though he lives in Vancouver now.

But when he came up with it, he knew where to turn.

And what of me? Was I too . . . *nice* on the air, too soft with the bad guys and the politicians and the rich and the famous in general, too, as some people charged — and oh, how I hate this word — unctuous? Again, I'd defend myself.

I have to start with my grandmother, who, though she's long gone now, has quite a lot to do with how I conduct myself on the radio. She taught me — and insisted on — good manners. I was raised to chew with my mouth closed, to take my hat off indoors, to offer food to others before I helped myself, to say please and thank you and never to interrupt or to talk back to my betters, to stand when a lady entered the room and to hold the door open for her as she left. I called my grandfather "Sir," and the habit has stayed with me as I address my elders — even though they're fewer and fewer all the time. If a woman walks down a sidewalk with me, I still move to the street side, even though the reason for that custom, which apparently had something to do with slops being pitched from the windows of overhanging second storeys, no longer exists. Politeness — courtesy — is simply part of how I think I should behave (at least in public, someone is sure to say), and if it starts to slip I think of my grandmother, and tell myself she may be listening. It's also the reason, for what it's worth, that I'm as careful as I can be about not swearing on the air, though away from the microphones I sound like a stevedore — or, and since it's my fault, I'm a little sad to report this, like one of my kids.

But there's more than that, too. Part of my determination to be civil on the air is simply a decision of craft. I don't think you have to be rude or abrasive to be tough. I think you can say, as I have more than once, "Come off it, Minister," or say, "Speak from the heart, Jean," as I did to the current prime minister, without losing a quality of respect in your voice. And I think, in fact, that you get better information from, and a clearer sense of, your subject's person if you suggest by your manner that what you are after is his or her point of view or his or her reply to *other people's* charges, and not an opportunity to show your own righteousness.

And finally, I've learned from at least two different experiences, one with a Quebec labour leader and one with a Western separatist, that when I have lost my cool the listener's sympathy has switched from me to the person I've been trying to confront.

I do babble, though. But I can't do anything about that. It's just the way I talk. I think as I go, and sometimes I do change courses in the middle of a question. Sorry. I think at least I've learned to shut up when the other guy is talking — or when he isn't talking and the best follow-up question is a kind of incredulous silence.

Anyway, that's my response. And if you don't like it you can go and f— . . . no, no Peter, she may be reading, too.

Like the thought that became the Red River Rally, the idea of coming to Moose Jaw to wrap everything up was born in a head other than mine. Way back in the dead of winter, a nice guy named Barry Gray — I think he may work for the Chamber of Commerce — wrote to both me and the *Times-Herald* to make the suggestion. As soon as I saw his letter, I began to get excited. As soon as I passed it on to Gloria — that's Gloria Bishop, our excutive producer, in case you've forgotten — wheels began to turn. As soon as we got in touch with Sean Prpick, the pleasant and capable young man who is CBC Radio's network producer in Saskatchewan, arrangements began to be made.

It's been a very complex process. Under the direction of Willy Barth, we had to build the equivalent of two radio studios, one in a meeting room here in the Harw — oops, the Temple Gardens Mineral Spa — and one in the auditorium of the Albert E. Peacock Technical School, where, last night, we staged a little fund-raiser, featuring me and Stuart McLean talking and Connie Kaldor and Colin James, two former Saskatchewan people who have come back home to give us a hand, Connie from Montreal and Colin from Vancouver, making music. With a sold-out house, we raised some eight thousand dollars for the Prairie Festival of the Written Word, and by recording it, we'll get almost an hour of radio for this morning,

It feels very good here. The meeting room is jammed with people I know or think I do, who have driven through the prairie dawn to be part of the occasion, from Mary Grant, who came from Tisdale, and who shared with us and the *Morningside* audience the AIDS-related death, in Tisdale, of her son the opera singer (and yes, those are Mary's recipes in the cookbook in these pages), to Grant Devine, the former premier who climbed off his tractor a couple of hours ago, and Elly Danica, the heroine of the movement against sexual abuse whose story we recorded in — I still won't name the town. There are grandmothers in slippers and teenagers in T-shirts, and writers, and a choirmaster, and Eleanor Romanow, Roy's wife.

I'm sorry Connie Wilson isn't here. Connie, who lived in Morse and was a devoted CBC Radio fan (and occasional critic), was a vital part of Barry Gray's Bring-Gzowski-to-Moose-Jaw campaign. She died just a few weeks ago, of cancer, but one of the last things her husband was able to tell her was that the campaign was successful, and one of her last gestures was a thumbs-up. Her daughter's here, though. Her name is Deb Thorn, and she is the manager of the Temple Gardens Spa.

This is the heartland. This, I think, is what we've been about.

For much of the last few years I've had questions about whether I've been, this time for real, yesterday's man. I've wondered whether the values I've cherished and celebrated have been sustainable. I've wondered if the culture we've been building — one of the most rewarding aspects of *Morningside* has been its part in the incredible flowering of Canadian writing — can survive. Is the age of cutbacks and stinginess really upon us forever? Does Medicare have to crumble? Is the CBC itself, the great national meeting place, now weakly led and starved for funds, doomed? Is it everyone for himself now and will we no longer be able — or even want to — huddle together to make us what we've been? Does the

Americanization of our cities — and our critics say we do a poor job of reflecting urban life — mean that places like this and the ideas they represent either no longer matter or have been so weakened they're not worth fighting for? Maybe guys like me really should step out of the way.

And yet, and yet, as Mordecai Richler says. As I look around me now, and think of the guests who lie ahead even this morning, the singers, the poets, the novelists, the political thinkers, and think also of the thousands and thousands of people, many of them young, who are gathering even now in bookstores and on campuses, in parks and CBC lobbies, giving the lie to my theory that everyone listens alone . . . as I think of all that, I am moved by both gratitude and a surprising optimism. People do care about the soul of this country. We are different. We will survive.

"Good morning," I say as the theme rolls for the last time, "I'm Peter Gzowski and this is *Morningside*."

# A FOND FAREWELL

Bryce Duffy

## MORNINGSIDE, WITH PETER GZOWSKI
### September 5, 1982–May 30, 1997

On its best days, and there were many, *Morningside* seemed inevitable, as if it had to be precisely what it was. It carried an implicit message: today, these are the issues that demand your attention, this one author requires interviewing, this particular folkie must be given her world première. The assumption that Peter Gzowski and his daily CBC radio program were doing what had to be done was *Morningside*'s special genius, the source of its authority.

But that aura of inevitability was deceiving. Far from being foreordained, the contents of *Morningside* emerged from passionate internal wrangling that started well before Labour Day and didn't end till the last week in spring. Thirteen producers dreamed up ideas, thrashed them out in ego-punishing meetings, then researched them and clarified them like butter. *Morningside* was a highly professional, slowly changing institution, its atmosphere a mix of senior common room and newspaper office, its staffers required to satisfy not only the audience and the executive producer but also the host, a famous grump with an old magazine editor's disdain for overly familiar ideas.

The effort never showed, and if on a particular morning we heard something astonishing about archeology or brain surgery or autism, we took it for granted, because that's what *Morningside* did. And if Gzowski could get Alberta people interested in, say, the problems of New Brunswick, and vice versa — why, that was also taken for granted.

Fifteen hours of radio a week for fifteen years would have been remarkable if it had been merely interesting. That it also became a central component of Canadian life, intimately linked with national dreams and disappointments, made it astonishing. (Just to remind us how pan Canadian it has always been, *Morningside* elected to air its last show from Moose Jaw.)

Gzowski became host when Pierre Trudeau was halfway through his second mandate. The program died just as Jean Chrétien sought his second mandate. *Morningside* disappeared because Ottawa decided that CBC should get less money, because the CBC didn't believe radio deserved special budgetary treatment and because Gzowski was worn out by a brutal schedule. It had to end sometime, but it had burrowed so deeply into our lives that some of us imagined it would always be there.—*Robert Fulford*

This piece ran in *Toronto Life*'s "Obituary" section in June 1997.

# ACKNOWLEDGEMENTS

Like the radio program it celebrates, *The Morningside Years* is a collegial effort, and once again I find myself the beneficiary of the work of a lot of other people, who range in this case from the archivists of CBC Radio, who ploughed through thousands of hours of tapes to find what we were looking for (and then, to what must have been their dismay, decided we didn't want after all) to Edna Barker, who has been not only my editor but my friend for at least as long as I worked at *Morningside*, but who this time round took charge of the project we were collaborating on and made it her own. Without Edna, there would be no *Morningside Years*, and if it were possible to dedicate a book to the person whose labours and skill it represents, this one would be for her. Other heroes (and heroines) of the process include Kerry Cannon, now of *The Journal of Canadian Studies*, who mined the archives of Trent University for everything from early recipes to original letters (there are some twenty-seven boxes of my papers at Trent); Bonnie Stern, the cooking guru, whose sensibility and expertise we borrowed for the cookbook-within-a-book that appears as the second chapter; Judy Kingry of Bernardin, who read over all our canning recipes, and the staff of the test kitchen at *Canadian Living* magazine. Whatever confusions may still exist in our cookbook, though, are my fault and not that of anyone I've just named.

Larry St. Aubin and Donna Goodall transcribed the interviews — as well, again, as quite a few that didn't make it — and Rosemary Hillary did the inputting.

Long before there was anything to set in type, though, the process began with the producers of *Morningside*, and if there is, for instance, intelligence in my literary interviews, the credit should go to Robert Prowse, Hal Wake, Ian Pearson, Larry Scanlon, and Paul Wilson, who prepared them, or insights in the conversations with scientists to Richard Handler and Meredith Levine, among others. So many people produced food items — sometimes it seemed that you couldn't work at *Morningside* if you didn't like to cook — that I can't possibly name them all, but perhaps Talin Vartanian, Mary Lynk, and Sian Jones deserve special mention. "The Trial of Louis Riel" was very much a team effort, but if memory serves, Peter Puxley was the mainstay.

For the letters: thanks, Shelagh — for everything.

For the CD: Willy Barth (who also oversaw the production of *Mourning Dove*, along with many other dramas) is a genius.

And, finally, Shelley. "Letters Home," "Life with Jessie," "The Sixth Papers," "Fifteen Cherished Letters . . ." "Section Seventeen" are all chapters that Shelley Ambrose produced for the radio as well as for print. But there is not a word in this book or a facet of my life she hasn't had an impact on and made better, and I am grateful to her for it all.

Edna, Shelley, Shelagh — and dozens and dozens of the best radio producers and technicians in the world. Thanks, all, for the *Morningside* years.

PG